How to...

P9-EDL-422

Exchange Server 5.5

Jim McBee

NETWORK PRESS® SYBEX

San Francisco   Paris   Düsseldorf   Soest   London

Associate Publisher: Guy Hart-Davis
Contracts & Licensing Manager: Kristine O'Callaghan
Acquisitions & Developmental Editor: Maureen Adams
Editor: Emily K. Wolman
Technical Editor: Joshua Konkle
Book Designer: Bill Gibson
Graphic Illustrator: Tony Jonick
Electronic Publishing Specialist: Bill Gibson
Project Team Leaders: Catherine Morris and Lisa Reardon
Proofreaders: Blythe Woolston and Dann McDorman
Indexer: Ted Laux
Cover Designer: Ingalls + Associates
Cover Illustrator/Photographer: Ingalls + Associates

Library of Congress Card Number: 99-61307
ISBN: 0-7821-2505-0

Manufactured in the United States of America

10 9 8 7 6 5 4 3 2

This book is dedicated to my parents, Charles and Betty McBee, who taught me that no job is too big if you just break it up into smaller pieces.

Acknowledgments

Did you know that it takes a village to write a technical book? The hundreds and hundreds of hours that go into writing a technical book pale in comparison to the work that everyone else puts into it. My name goes on the cover, but the others involved in the production of this book remain silently anonymous. These are the people who deserve our profound gratitude.

Major kudos goes to Editor (and truly wonderful, patient person) Emily Wolman and Acquisitions and Development Editor Maureen Adams. I cannot begin to tell you how important these two people are to me and to the success of this book. Technical Editor Joshua Konkle (who knows more about Exchange Server than anyone else I know) skillfully and patiently read through the entire book, making suggestions and teaching me a thing or two about Exchange—and he never got tired of me ICQing him at 11:00 at night with Registry and raw mode questions. Thanks for always being there to give me a different perspective.

Big thanks also go to Lyle Bullock, Jr., for helping me with Chapter 8, and to Amy Padgett for helping with Chapter 16. Exchange gurus Clare O'Keeffe, Randal Pacheco, Ryan Tung, Dave Shaw, Greg Dart, and Ron Demery all reviewed the original outline for the book and provided me with great feedback and ideas.

During the development of this book, I talked to countless Exchange administrators. I picked their brains about common problems they experienced and things they wished they had known ahead of time. These patient people also reviewed my writing to make sure I had not left anything out. This group included Missy Koslosky, Al Mulnick, Kim Cameron, Benjamin Craig, Dave Milne, Annette Lewis-Capers, Gene Giannamore, Bob Hollinger, Barnaby DiAnni, Richard Dann, Maureen McFerrin, and Drew Nicholson. Thanks, everyone, for putting up with my last minute e-mail requests—and for answering them so quickly.

Sybex consists of the greatest people in the publishing industry. Thanks to Rodnay Zaks, Jordon Gold, Guy Hart-Davis, Neil Edde, Skye McKay, Adrienne Crew, and Senoria Bilbo-Brown for making me feel like I was part of the Sybex family. Thanks also to Sybexians who helped put this book together: Project Team Leaders Catherine Morris and Lisa Reardon, Proofreaders Blythe Woolston and Dann McDorman, Electronic Publishing Specialist Bill Gibson, Graphic Illustrator Tony Jonick, and Indexer Ted Laux.

To Jeff Bloom and all the folks at Computer Training Academy who put up with my surfer-like eccentricities, you guys "no ka oi!" And finally, thanks to Makoto Suzuki, who is always there with feedback, insight, suggestions, and support. Aloha!

Jim McBee

Honolulu, Hawaii

Contents at a Glance

Appendices   591

Table of Contents

Foreword

What a difference 10 years can make. When I started at Microsoft in 1989, working on the project which would eventually become Microsoft Exchange Server, e-mail and client/server applications were relatively young technologies. Collaboration was something you did in person. E-mail was almost exclusively the domain of mainframe systems, e-mail client interfaces were command-line–only, and an e-mail message, such as it was, consisted of 7-bit ASCII text, and that was about it—no rich text, attachments, documents, calendaring, multi-byte character sets, public folders, views, forms, rules, workflow, PKI, replication, laptops, and so on.

Still, even with this seeming simplicity of the past, connecting systems together was a major hassle. Just getting to the point where users in different departments—let alone different companies—could communicate electronically with one another in any meaningful way was a major accomplishment. Bonus points if that communication was reliable or served a core business need.

Ten years ago, the Internet was only for universities and the U.S. military. The Web did not exist. DOS was the predominant desktop operating system. The ability we take for granted today to send a message—be it a lunch invite or a critical business document to anyone, anytime, anywhere in the world with the confidence that it will get there reliably, intact, and in a timely fashion—was at that time a fantasy, existing only in the world of science fiction.

PC networks (and PC hardware, for that matter) were notoriously finicky and unreliable. Sharing a printer and maybe the occasional file was the dominant application. The real business was still done primarily on paper or on mainframe systems. Microprocessor-based PCs might be fine as personal productivity tools, but their utilization as reliable and scalable platforms in the data center for serious business applications was nonexistent.

Today, of course, the situation has changed. PC-class hardware and software have certainly come a long way in terms of scalability and reliability. Many vendors, both hardware and software, now regularly make claims of supporting tens of thousands of users on a single system and, unlike even a few years ago, these claims are becoming realistic from both a cost and manageability perspective.

But perhaps the most compelling change is not one of mere scale but of radical difference in how people communicate. Which communication system is most critical to you? Which can you least live without? Ten years ago, you might have said your phone or fax or Federal Express. Perhaps you still would. But for more and more of us, the answer is access to our messaging and collaboration system—access to the e-mail, calendars, task lists, contacts, and business applications that make up an ever-increasing and important part of how we do business, how we communicate and collaborate with people, and how we work with knowledge in our electronic environments. You need look no further for proof than the army of business travelers searching for a power outlet and a data port at the nearest airport to understand the increasing dominance and importance of e-mail as the preferred business communication mechanism.

The "digital dial tone" provided by client/server PC systems such as Microsoft Exchange Server has become the critical business system. Tomorrow's successful companies have come to realize that the way to become more efficient, more productive, and more competitive is to build, deploy, and leverage a communication and application system with e-mail and electronic collaboration at its center. It only makes sense to architect that system for maximum reliability and redundancy for 24-hours-a-day, 7-days-a-week operation.

True reliability does not happen by accident even with the best of systems—it takes work. Achieving 99.9 percent reliability allows for about eight hours of interrupted service per year. Achieving 99.999 percent reliability allows for about five minutes. Reboot once and you've blown it. Simply buying the right software and hardware isn't sufficient. Maximum reliability requires planning for and therefore avoiding failures at all levels, from power to network to server hardware and software. It requires redundancy at all levels and, perhaps most important, operational practices and procedures designed to minimize the likelihood that a problem will occur—and minimize service interruption when it does.

Achieving maximum reliability with Microsoft Exchange Server is what this book is all about.

Eric Lockard
General Manager
Exchange Server Business Unit
Microsoft Corporation

Introduction

I love Exchange Server, and I had a great time writing about it! Exchange is a phenomenal product, and I never stop learning new things about it. You may be standing in a bookstore right now trying to decide if this is the right book to purchase. You may be curious as to what's in this book and what approach I took to put it together. Well, you are reading the introduction, so you are off to a great start.

This Book and the Development Process

During the initial development of this book (and the entire 24seven series), an emphasis was placed on conveying what you, as an administrator, need to know to keep your Exchange server healthy, happy, and operational 24 hours a day, 7 days a week. I queried many experienced Exchange administrators and asked them a few questions:

- What do you do to keep your Exchange servers healthy and happy?
- What facts did you learn the hard way?
- What have you done wrong (and right)?
- What would you like to share with other Exchange administrators?

It is with this information that I assembled this book. I focused primarily on Exchange Server operations issues—due to the space and time constraints associated with this book, there were issues I had to avoid or only partially cover. I avoided client-related issues except when necessary; the Outlook family is the subject of its own book. I also avoided discussing public folders and public folder application topics except where they affect server operations.

I have also avoided the topic of Windows Server 2000 (Window NT 5) and Exchange Server 6 (a.k.a. Platinum) except when absolutely necessary. Though I hope the life expectancy of this book will survive until both of these products are released and stable, they are probably not relevant to you now. If there is one thing I hate, it is going to a conference (or buying a book) and spending 75 percent of the time hearing how great things will be in the future. I have problems to solve right *now*, and I am sure you do, too!

Throughout this book, you will find Exchange@Work and Case Study sidebars. The Exchange@Work sidebars contain specific situations and problems that I have encountered in the field while deploying Exchange. I felt it important to use some special mechanism to emphasize how other companies are approaching problems. The case studies at the end of each part of the book are often longer than the Exchange@Work sidebars and deal with more general problems and solutions that some companies have faced. (The actual names of the companies have been changed.) At the end of each chapter, there are references to additional resources that can give you even more detailed information.

Who Should Buy This Book?

If you are standing in your neighborhood bookstore asking yourself this question, then ask no further. Maybe you are just starting a pilot deployment of Exchange. Possibly you have just come back from a Microsoft Certified Technical Education Center class and you want to know more. Maybe you are currently running Exchange and you want to know what you can do better. Perhaps you are curious about some of the pitfalls and sticky situations that can happen with Exchange. If you are in any of these situations, this book is for you.

Maybe you need to know how to upgrade your servers or add new servers to your site. Are you wondering what the best management practices for Exchange Server are? What events indicate that the Exchange server is having problems? How often should you run backups? Have you given any consideration to what would happen if disaster strikes? How about what you can do to proactively prevent problems? Are you wondering what Microsoft recommends versus what works in the real world? If you answered yes to any of these questions, this book is for you.

Are you looking for ways to further customize your Exchange organization? Are you trying to figure out the best Exchange connectors to use? Or maybe you are trying to track down a problem with a connector? Do you know what to do if the Exchange server fails to restart or if you lose a disk drive? Maybe you are concerned about messaging security? If you are seeking answers to any of these questions, this book will steer you in the right direction.

Several of the Exchange Server books on the market today seem to be applicable only if you are supporting 10,000 mailboxes or more. I have endeavored to keep the topics in this book useful for you whether you are supporting 10 mailboxes or 100,000. For those of you with larger sites, you are already aware that any guidance I can provide in a 700-page book will have to be generic enough for you to customize to your own environment.

This book is not for beginners. Its readers should have networking experience in Exchange or some other messaging system, including knowledge of network operating systems, communications media, and related technologies. If you want to understand how to install Exchange, create mailboxes, create connectors, or perform other basic Exchange Server administration tasks, then this book is *not* right for you. For less advanced content, pick up a copy of *Mastering Exchange Server 5.5* by Barry Gerber (Sybex, 1998). It is an excellent introduction to the world of installing, configuring, and administering Exchange Server. After you learn the basics, I hope you will consider purchasing this book to take you up to the next level.

If you are studying for the MCSE exams, this book will be helpful, but should not be considered an exam study guide. If that is what you are seeking, purchase a copy of *MCSE: Exchange 5.5 Study Guide* by Richard Easlick and James Chellis (Sybex, 1998).

Assumptions

The book is centered around Exchange 5.5, but many of the things discussed here will work with all versions of Exchange. Some of the features described here require Exchange 5.5 SP1 or later; I have noted when Exchange 5.5 SP1 is required.

In the text, I often assume that the Windows NT directory is located on the C drive in the \WinNT directory. I am also assuming that the \exchsrvr\bin directory is on the C drive.

Anytime you see HKLM in a Registry path, it is a shortened version of \HKEY_LOCAL_ MACHINE. The same is true for HKCU (HKEY_CURRENT_USER).

I assumed throughout this book that you are an Intel processor user. I did this intentionally so that I did not have to provide two separate paths to software through the book. Are you a Compaq Alpha user? If so, as you are probably used to, substitute the \I386 path for a \ALPHA path, and you will generally find the software you are looking for. I am actually just jealous, because I work with almost exclusively with Intel hardware—I'm suffering from Alpha envy. <grin>

How This Book Is Organized

I have divided this book into six parts that consist of 18 chapters, plus four appendices. The topics and complexity of the book vary from chapter to chapter. Each chapter was intended to stand on its own, but Chapters 6 and 7 should be read together, and if you are interested in messaging security, you should read Chapters 13, 14, and 15. Though overall, you can read the chapters in just about any order you wish.

Part I—Preparing for Exchange

The first part of this book, Chapters 1 through 3, covers important facts that you need to know when preparing your Windows NT environment, planning Exchange, and performing a migration from a legacy mail system. I tried to emphasize things that have gone wrong with installations I've been exposed to, including common design mistakes with Windows NT and Exchange organizations, and suggestions for how to plan, deploy, and migrate to Exchange Server.

Part II—Operations

Part II covers the Exchange server operations. A particularly popular chapter with the reviewers is Chapter 4, which covers upgrading and modifying existing systems, including how to add a new server to and remove a server from a site. Chapter 5 consists of detailed facts on managing permissions, the directory, and mailboxes, including approaches for managing mailbox space restrictions. Chapters 6 and 7 cover maintenance, disaster prevention, and monitoring procedures. Chapter 8 is an overview of the collaborative capabilities of Exchange.

Part III—Connectivity

Chapter 9 covers connectivity within an Exchange organization. Chapter 10 covers connectivity between Exchange and other organizations, specifically using the X.400 connector and the Internet Mail Service. I included information on using the IMS securely over the Internet, because currently this is a popular topic.

Part IV—Automation

Part IV delves into things you can do as an administrator to make your job easier. Chapter 11 reviews tools you can use to automate client software deployment and configuration. Chapter 12 discusses some of the automated maintenance tasks that occur on the Exchange server, as well as the schedules that control those tasks.

Part V—Security

My goal with Part V was to unravel some of the mystery behind Exchange Server Advanced Security. Chapter 13 reviews some of the basics and principles of messaging security, and Chapter 14 introduces the use of the Exchange Server Key Management Server and the Microsoft Certificate Server. Chapter 15 wraps up this part with a discussion of things you can do to keep your Exchange servers more secure.

Part VI—Troubleshooting

With this book, I wanted to pass along as many troubleshooting tips as possible. Part VI is the receptacle for this invaluable information. Chapter 16 covers client-related troubleshooting, including the all-too-popular question, "Why does it take so long for the client to start?" Chapter 17 covers troubleshooting Exchange server–related problems, and Chapter 18 covers disaster recovery. Disaster recovery is a hot topic with Exchange and one that certainly deserves your attention—*before* a disaster actually occurs.

Appendices

With still more information to cram into the book, I organized the appendices with some additional information that just did not seem to fit anywhere else. Appendix A includes a list valuable technical books, Web sites, and other resources. Appendix B covers information about some of the standards used to develop Exchange and other messaging systems. Appendix C covers many Exchange Registry–related settings that I have found useful, and Appendix D has some recommendations for documentation that you should keep about your Exchange system.

More to Come

I could not fit everything I wanted to in this book. There is just too much information to share. I also had certain things that I wanted to include on a diskette or CD-ROM, but there was not enough material to justify including a CD-ROM with the book.

However, this book does have a Web site onto which I will periodically post additional information such as sample documentation sheets, a sample Service Level Agreement, and anything else that may be relevant to the topics covered in this book. This Web page can be found on the 24seven series Web site at www.24sevenbooks.com. Information on other Sybex books is available at www.sybex.com.

I hope the material in this book answers some of those nagging questions you have had about Exchange Server and that it helps you to prevent a few problems in the future. Most importantly, though, I hope it helps you get out of the office by 5:00 P.M.!

Part 1

Preparing for Exchange

Topics Covered:

- Why Microsoft Exchange?
- Preparing Windows NT to support Exchange Server
- Exchange Server 5.5 Enterprise Edition versus Standard Edition
- Exchange 5.5 licensing
- Reviewing your current messaging system
- Planning Exchange sites and organizations
- Choosing and sizing the right server hardware
- Creating test labs and system incident/change logs
- Considerations for a successful migration to Exchange
- Using Exchange as a messaging backbone during migration
- Generating user excitement about the Exchange deployment or migration

1

Making Way for Exchange

"What enables an intelligent leader to overcome others and achieve extraordinary accomplishments is foreknowledge. All matters require foreknowledge."
—Sun Tzu, *The Art of War*

If you are reading this chapter, I hope you are still in the planning or pilot stages of your Microsoft Exchange Server deployment or migration. You may have even read a few books on planning and deploying Exchange. Still yet, you may be in the process of consulting with an organization that is experienced in rolling out Exchange-based messaging and collaboration systems.

When arranging a new Exchange deployment or migration, there is no such thing as too much planning. Yet, there comes a time when you have planned a pilot and planned some more until there is no where to go but ahead with the deployment or migration. At the stage when you move from planning and piloting to production, you should know as much as possible about your current system and what to expect from a production Exchange deployment or migration. If you have done everything right, you will save yourself some sleepless nights and some gray hairs, and your kids will still recognize you when you come home from work.

Is This Your Job Description?

You have been chosen (or are self-appointed) to be your organization's Exchange administrator or architect. Unless you have previously administered an Exchange organization, you are going to be asked on a daily basis to do things you did not know how to do before. You will be asked to plan for contingencies you never knew would happen, solve problems you did not know could happen, and make Exchange perform the miracles of a messaging system yet to be.

Will a good plan help ease your administrative load once you are operational? You bet it will! Will understanding common problems when you start designing your Exchange organization save you some sleepless nights? Most certainly!

Why Microsoft Exchange Server?

I have worked with every major LAN-based messaging and groupware system on the market. Therefore, I can say with the utmost confidence that Exchange Server is superior to other messaging systems available today. I tell people that it is not only my favorite messaging product, but it is also my favorite Microsoft product (that is saying a lot, because I especially like Windows NT Server and SQL Server!).

Why should you choose Exchange Server over another messaging system? Well, if you bought this book, then you or someone else has already made that decision. So this question is a little late. Or is it? The very things that make Exchange Server a powerful messaging system will also affect your deployment plans, management, troubleshooting, and disaster recovery planning. Let's review a few of things that make Exchange a superior solution.

Messaging System Types

Mail systems can be broken up into two categories: *shared-file* messaging systems and *client/server* messaging systems. All the LAN-based packages available on the market today fall into one of these two categories.

NOTE   At some later release, Exchange Server will become an *n-tier* messaging system. This kind of system has the typical client component, but there may be multiple server components. The message database may reside on one server while the directory database resides on another.

Shared-File Messaging Systems

Traditional electronic mail systems such as Microsoft Mail and Lotus cc:Mail were considered shared-file–based messaging systems. These required a file and print server and a shared folder to give access to the folders and files that made up the messaging systems. The clients connected drive letters to these shared folders to retrieve and send messages, as illustrated in Figure 1.1. Connectivity to other systems (such as other SMTP systems) required dedicated PCs running separate processes, which were normally DOS-based programs.

Figure 1.1   A shared-file messaging system

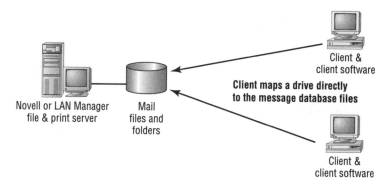

Though you could have many users connected to a single, low-end file and print server, shared-file messaging systems left a lot to be desired in terms of redundancy, reliability, stability, security, and growth (scalability) potential. Here are just a few of the reasons why I no longer deploy many shared-file messaging systems:

- Client software must have read, write, and often delete permissions to the entire messaging file system. Files can be compromised or deleted.

- If a client is sending a large message and a power failure or network outage occurs, the entire message database could become corrupted.

- Client software always has the mail data files open (in use), thus most tape backup software cannot make backup copies of the data without kicking all users off the server.

- Programs must be run manually on the server to maintain the integrity of the message database files.

- Adding additional servers locally or across WANs is often difficult and complicated.

Client/Server Messaging Systems

Exchange is a client/server messaging system. The Exchange server consists of many services, each with its own job responsibilities. The client software communicates with the services running on the server. Clients do not interact directly with the files and folders that encompass the messaging components. Though there are many ways to communicate with an Exchange server over the network, the Exchange designers chose to have the clients and the server communicate using an Interprocess Communication (IPC) mechanism called *Remote Procedure Calls (RPCs)*. Though writing programs to use RPCs is generally considered to be more difficult than for other IPC mechanisms (such as Named Pipes, NetBIOS, and Windows Sockets), RPCs provide high performance, more functionality, and excellent security.

One of the main advantages of client/server messaging systems is clients do not need to map drives to the Exchange server, nor do individual clients access message folders or files. Client/server messaging systems bring some other distinct advantages to the table:

- Users can only access the data that they have been given permission to see.
- The Exchange services, not the file server's file system, enforce security.
- All messages are stored in a single database that uses transaction logging. Transactions written to the database are ensured to be completed in the event of a catastrophe.
- Since only the Exchange services have the transaction logs and database files open, online backups of the data files can be performed.
- Clients using RPCs are much more efficient than clients accessing mail servers via the file system.

These advantages will affect how you plan your system's usage and other aspects of your system such as operations, security, backup, troubleshooting, and disaster recovery.

Using Internet and ITU Standards

Building a completely proprietary messaging system is easier than building one that conforms to certain standards and recommendations. When programming, I can always think of things that the person who wrote the original standard left out. The problem with creating your own "improved" version of a standard is that these improvements often break interoperability with other systems and thus defeat the purpose of having standards. Some of the standards that Exchange works with include:

- International Telecommunications Union (ITU) standards
  - X.400 recommendations for building a message transfer and message storage system

- X.500 recommendations for developing an internationally-distributed directory
- Internet Engineering Task Force standards
  - Simple Mail Transfer Protocol (SMTP) to send messages across the Internet
  - POP3 (Post Office Protocol v3) and IMAP4 (Internet Message Access Protocol v4) to access e-mail on servers
  - LDAP (Lightweight Directory Access Protocol) for access to the ITU X.5000 internationally-distributed directory
  - NNTP (Network News Transfer Protocol)
  - MIME and S/MIME (Multipurpose Internet Mail Extensions and Secure/MIME) for transferring message attachments, formatting, and digital signatures across the Internet
- MAPI (Messaging Application Programming Interface) used to access a client/server mail system using DCE RPCs
- Messaging connectors to support SMTP (the Internet), X.400, Microsoft Mail, Lotus cc:Mail, Lotus Notes, Novell GroupWise, and PROFS/SNADS (mainframe) messaging systems

---

NOTE The common Internet and ITU messaging standards are discussed further in Appendix B.

Windows NT Integration

Exchange is ultimately designed to be interoperable with Windows Server 2000 (the operating system formerly known as Windows NT 5), but it currently integrates well with Windows NT 4.

NOTE Be on the look out for the ITU X.500 recommendation to be implemented in the Windows 2000 directory. This will effectively replace the Exchange implementation of X.500 in the future.

As an Exchange administrator, you need to know that Exchange Server requires a Windows NT domain. Some of my friends running Novell NetWare and Exchange wish this were not true. Access to mailboxes, the directory database, and public folders requires a valid Windows NT account (unless you allow users to access the server anonymously).

Exchange Server also makes heavy use of the Windows NT Event Log service and the Windows NT Performance Monitor. In Chapters 6 and 7, I review events that you should watch for and how to use the Performance Monitor to analyze and optimize your Exchange server.

Scalability and Reliability

For many years, Microsoft used XENIX-based mail internally, rather than Microsoft Mail. The problem was quite simple: Microsoft Mail was not scalable enough for an organization of Microsoft's size. Reliability and scalability were major concerns during the design phase of Exchange Server, and they continue to be a factor in every subsequent Exchange version.

The Exchange X.500-based directory database (which contains the list of custom recipients, mailbox information, distribution lists, and public folders) is replicated to every Exchange server in the organization. This is not truly what the designers of the ITU X.500 specification had in mind when they wrote it, but this replicated directory ensures that all directory information is available on the user's local server. Moreover, replication allows the system to scale to hundreds of servers and hundreds of thousands of users.

Directory replication will prove to be a factor in large Exchange organization design. It will affect not only the size of the disk that the directory database must reside on, but it will affect network bandwidth. Moreover, directory information will be immediately available on remote, or "loosely consistent," directories. However, this does ensure the reliability of *white pages* types of information available to our users.

> **NOTE** The science of directory replication will be discussed a bit further in Chapter 9.

A key component in Exchange is the *database services*. The information users interact with, their personal mail and public folder data, is protected by the information database service. Each Exchange server maintains a separate database for private and public mail, and having more users just means adding another server. Scaling upwards is easy: When our user count grows, we add a new server to the directory.

Exchange Server also offers stable database services by saving transaction information. Specifically, the service uses transaction logs to record the events surrounding message delivery and retrieval. Imagine this process as a purchase: If halfway through the transaction something goes wrong and the cashier has your money, but you don't have your candy bar, you could be out some money. But thanks to transaction logging, when the cashier reboots, the knowledge of the purchase will be available in the transaction log, which is maintained by the video camera!

Another feature of Exchange that many administrators love (and hate!) is the public folder replication feature. Though you cannot natively support user mailbox data on multiple servers, it is possible to replicate the contents of a public folder so that it is stored on more than one Exchange server. This content is available to users regardless of whether the original server is online or unavailable. While this can increase the availability of your public folder data, replication also generates additional load on your network.

> **NOTE**   I review public folders and replication in Chapter 5 and give you some hints for making sure that public folder replication does not consume your available network bandwidth.

In comparison, mail systems such as Microsoft Mail and Lotus cc:Mail were quite easy to install and put virtually no additional load on the file server. However, they did not scale well beyond one server. Other scalability features such as dedicating servers to support public discussion folders were not possible using the legacy–shared-file systems. Further, directory database replication in these systems (including Microsoft Mail) often proved to be futile. I frequently told people that getting Microsoft Mail Directory Synchronization running required complete knowledge of Microsoft Mail—and you had to chant thrice and throw flowers into the volcano. Moving mailboxes between one legacy system post office server and another was seldom done. In response to this, Exchange Server was designed with excellent directory and database replication technology and great mailbox management features.

Exchange Server 5.5 Standard Edition and Enterprise Edition

Exchange Server is available in two distinct flavors: Exchange Server 5.5 Standard Edition and Exchange Server 5.5 Enterprise Edition. Both editions will run on regular Windows NT Server 4, but if you require the Microsoft Cluster Server (MSCS), you must be running Windows NT Server 4 Enterprise. The features available in the Standard Edition did change between versions 5 and 5.5, so review these comparisons carefully.

Exchange Server 5.5 Standard Edition

Exchange Server 5.5 Standard Edition includes:

- Microsoft Exchange Server 5.5
- Public and private information store size maximum of 16GB each

- Internet Mail Service (SMTP)
- Lotus cc:Mail connector
- Lotus Notes connector
- Microsoft Mail connector
- Exchange site connector and the Exchange Connector

NOTE These two connectors did not ship with Exchange 4 and 5 Standard Edition. They were used to connect Exchange servers within a single site or to connect Exchange sites together.

- Active server components (Outlook Web Access)
- Internet news service (NNTP)
- Visual InterDev Web application development system
- Outlook 97 v8.03 (Outlook 98 ships with Exchange 5.5 SP1)
- Migration Tools for respective connectors on the Web

NOTE Refer to Chapter 3 for additional information about migration tools. To download the latest migration tools from the Web, refer to backoffice .microsoft.com/downtrial.

Exchange Server 5.5 Enterprise Edition

Exchange Server 5.5 Enterprise Edition includes:

- All the features of Standard Edition
- Public and private information store size maximum of 16TB each
- Support for Microsoft Cluster Server when running Windows NT 4 Enterprise Edition
- X.400 connector
- IBM PROFS/OfficeVision and SNADS connectors

NOTE Windows NT 4 Enterprise Edition is *not* required to run Exchange Server 5.5 Enterprise Edition (yes, I am frequently asked this question!).

To switch a server from Exchange Server 5.5 Standard Edition to Enterprise Edition, simply run the Enterprise Edition installation program. The database does not need to be converted from 5.5 Standard to 5.5 Enterprise.

> **WARNING**   Once the first X.400 connector is installed on one Exchange server in your organization, all servers in that organization must be running Exchange Server 5.5 Enterprise Edition. Otherwise you must purchase the X.400 connector license for each server. This is a licensing restriction, not a technical restriction. See the next section for more information about licensing.

So which version should you purchase? Get Exchange Server 5.5 Enterprise Edition if your server's public or private information store will grow past 16GB, if you need the X.400 connector, or if you will be running Microsoft Cluster Server. If you are not sure about your information store sizes, consider that data usually takes up more space than you originally plan.

Exchange 5.5 Licensing

Exchange Server licensing is important to understand early in your planning process, because the licenses are going to affect your budget. These issues break down into two categories: server licensing and client licensing.

> **WARNING**   Take great care to make sure that your have your licensing squared away and correct. The penalties for violating your software licenses are phenomenally expensive. To learn more about software piracy and the penalties, visit the Software Publishing Association's Web page at www.spa.org.

Exchange 5.5 Server Licenses

Each Exchange server that you are going to install and run requires a separate server license. A server license grants you the right to run a copy of the Exchange Server software on a single machine, regardless of the number of processors the machine has. This does *not* grant you the right to run Windows NT Server; each Windows NT server and Windows NT Server Enterprise Edition server in use must be purchased separately.

You can mix and match Exchange Server 5.5 Standard Edition and Exchange Server 5.5 Enterprise Edition, but once you start using the X.400 connector on one server in your organization, each server must have its own X.400 connector license regardless of version. You can purchase the X.400 license separately or as part of the Exchange Server 5.5 Enterprise Edition. If you start using the PROFS or SNADS connectors, you must purchase the Enterprise Edition for all servers in your organization.

TIP   You may find it more cost effective to purchase Exchange Server Enterprise Edition rather than purchasing connectors separately. Do some price comparisons to make sure you don't spend more money than necessary.

You may purchase Exchange Server 5.5 server licenses as part of a package that includes client licenses through the Microsoft Open License Program (MOLP), the Microsoft Select program, educational purchasing, or the Government Services Administration (GSA) purchasing schedule. Microsoft has several programs that allow you to buy software at a discount if you are purchasing in large volumes. Microsoft also offers a number of competitive upgrade programs. These purchasing programs can save you a considerable amount of money. Contact your systems integrator or local Microsoft sales office for more information on these programs and how your organization can participate. Any way you can save money on your system is good, because you can spend that extra money on redundancy, fault tolerance, and server design.

Exchange Server is also available as part of the Microsoft BackOffice package. BackOffice is not a separate product, but actually a one-price bundle of Microsoft's Windows NT Server-based products, which includes Windows NT Server, Exchange Server, SQL Server, Systems Management Server, SNA Server, and Proxy Server. Though the exact figure will depend on which BackOffice products you are planning to use, you can save considerable money if you will be using three or more of these.

TIP   Consider the BackOffice Client Access License (CAL) for your enterprise licensing needs.

Exchange 5.5 Client Access Licenses

A popular misconception for Exchange server administrators is that since their users are already using Microsoft Office 97, they have already purchased a client license for Outlook users to use the Exchange server. Another misconception is that authenticated access to POP3, IMAP4, and Outlook Web Access (OWA) does not require Exchange client access licenses.

All Outlook, Exchange, POP3, IMAP4, or OWA clients that authenticate with the Exchange server require a Client Access License. This is separate from the Windows NT Client Access License. The rule of thumb I like to use is "any computer that hosts a user connecting to a mailbox on the server requires an Exchange Client Access License."

I know you are now saying to yourself, "Self, did he just say *any* computer?" Yes, I did. Exchange Server 5.5 supports only the Per Seat licensing options. This means that every computer that is going to access the Exchange Server *must* have a Client Access License purchased for it, including remote users. However, if you have 500 computers and three shifts of people (for a total of 1,500 mailboxes), you only need to purchase 500 CALs.

What about users who work from home as well as in the office? What if they have a Windows CE device that they use to retrieve mail part of the time? In response to these questions, Microsoft concocted the 20 percent rule (actually, the license agreement refers to it as the 80 percent rule). This rule states that "each machine for which you buy a Client Access License may also use that same Client Access License for one additional digital electronic device (computer, PDA, WinCE, web client, etc.) that is used for less than 20% of the total connection time." So if you have a user who uses her home computer 30 percent of the time and her desktop computer 70 percent of the time, you will have to purchase two CALs.

For further information about Exchange licensing, print (or read on-screen) the license agreement. You can see the Exchange license agreement during the Exchange Server installation process. I simply copied the text from the license document screen and pasted it into a Word document. If you are not completely sure that you are purchasing the correct number of server and client licenses, consult with your organization's lawyer, your systems integrator, or the local Microsoft sales office.

> **NOTE**   When you purchase Client Access Licenses, enter the purchase information into Windows NT using the Windows NT License Manager program.

Hints for Licensing

Keeping your software licensing squared away and legal is confusing. Here are a few hints to help manage your licenses:

- Use Windows NT Event Viewer and Windows NT License Manager to make sure that you are not exceeding the number of installations that is permitted by the number of licensed client seats you purchased.

- Keep all documents related to licensing in a secure place. Keep a copy of the invoice associated with each license purchase; you want to be able prove that you own every license that you are using.

- To save money, purchase licenses in as large a quantity as possible. Check to see if you qualify for some sort of discount, upgrade, or large purchasing agreement.

- Don't pirate software. Bad software karma will catch up with you. If you use it, purchase it!

Reviewing Your Situation

The better informed you can become regarding the current state of your network and the more support you have from your own power structure, the more likely your Exchange deployment will be a success. So before you start your deployment or even your Exchange organization design, there are some things you need to think about and review. This includes management buy-in on the project, documentation of your current network, an understanding of the current capabilities you are providing for your users, and a list of information you'll want to acquire beforehand.

Management Support

I have worked for a number of organizations in the United States and around the world that have both centralized and decentralized information systems. Many of these organizations have done some outstanding planning for their Exchange deployments—and planning is a good thing!

Before you start the first step of planning, however, you need to make sure that you have upper-management support. These upper layers should go as high as necessary to make sure that you can deploy a system consistently throughout your organization.

However, in the midst of a centralized IS group planning things such as naming conventions, server standards, and operational rules, inevitably "rogue" Exchange servers start appearing around the globe. The problem with this is that most of the time, these rogue sites do not conform to the standards that may be dictated to the organization.

> **NOTE** In Chapter 2, I discuss a number of things that you should consider when planning an Exchange organization.

I know of two separate companies that have deployed Exchange, only to find another location or group has deployed an almost completely incompatible Exchange organization. The central IS group's management support did not go quite high enough to override the other group's decision, so they are stuck with two separate Exchange architectures because neither group wants to change their standard.

Existing Mail Systems

This topic alone could consume an entire book. Before you start migrating away from your existing mail system, some information you should collect and questions you should have answers to include:

- How do your current mail post offices communicate? Over the WAN? Via modem? X.25?

- Does your current mail system provide directory synchronization?

- What type of migration are you planning? Will you migrate everyone at one time or opt for a coexistence/migration deployment?

- What external systems does your current mail system connect to? SMTP? PROFS/ OfficeVision (mainframe)? Wang Office? Banyan? MHS? Compaq All-in-1?

- What services does the current messaging system provide? E-mail? Calendar and group scheduling? Task management? GroupWare and collaboration? Knowledge management? Indexed collaboration folders?

- What additional services does your current messaging system provide? Faxing? Numeric pager gateway? Voicemail/PBX integration?

- What are your current messaging system's statistics? How much disk storage is used? How many messages are processed per day? What is the average user storage?

NOTE Chapter 3 covers migration, though I have tried to keep it generic and still give you as much specific information as possible, given time and space constraints on this book. In that chapter, I discuss the above items and others in much more detail.

Windows NT Domains

I stated earlier that all Exchange implementations require a Windows NT domain structure to be in place when Exchange is installed. A popular misconception is that Exchange Server must be on a PDC or a BDC. Exchange Server does *not* have to be installed on a domain controller (PDC or BDC). Exchange can be installed on a member server as long as that server is part of a domain. Installing Exchange on a member server is actually preferable for performance and recoverability reasons.

Windows NT domains are the security platform for other Microsoft BackOffice products; this is especially true for Exchange Server. Prior to deployment of your Exchange Server organization, your Windows NT domain model should be in place, tested, and finalized.

Exchange Server uses Windows NT domain controllers to validate user access and Exchange services (such as the site services account) access to the Exchange server. Here are some tips to consider when looking at your Windows NT domain model when considering Exchange:

- Changing your domain structure is a pain in the neck once it is implemented. Changing it once Exchange Server has been deployed adds an additional layer of complexity to this puzzle. Avoid redesigning your Windows NT domain model once you have deployed Exchange.

- Exchange servers should be located in close proximity (at least from the perspective of the network) to a domain controller so that the Exchange server can authenticate users or services quickly.

- All servers in an Exchange site must use the same site services account.

- In a domain larger than 500 users, avoid putting Exchange Server on the Primary Domain Controller. This can affect the performance of the Exchange server as well as the PDC.

- If an Exchange server holds mailboxes for users who have accounts in multiple domains, then the domain that the Exchange server is located in must have a trust relationship with account domains. This also holds true for users from other sites or other domains who want to access resources such as public folders.

Does Your Existing Network Infrastructure Need Improvement?

For many organizations, messaging is a core business process now, and changing or upgrading this system is a big decision. So now is the time to look at your existing network. Prior to rolling out a new messaging system, ask yourself if there are improvements that need to be made. Is it time to deploy those snazzy new 10/100 Ethernet switches? Should all servers be placed on a high-capacity backbone? Do the WAN links need to be upgraded?

These questions summarize portions of what we call a *GAP Analysis*. More generally, also ask yourself: What can I do today? What do I *need* to do today? The difference in the answers to these two questions defines the solution you should deploy.

Questions to Ask and Information to Have Available

What do you want to know prior to moving ahead with the planning stages of your Exchange organization? Not that I want to appear too demanding, but here is a list of items and information I always collect about any customer's network that is about to deploy Exchange:

- A detailed WAN diagram of my entire WAN topology. This diagram may be a hand-drawn 8½ × 11 sheet of paper, or it could be a wall-sized CAD drawing.

Firewall, proxy server, network address translator, and remote access server locations should also be included.

- A detailed document describing WAN IP addresses, link types, router brands (and router software versions), and locations. As a network manager, I keep all of this in a notebook along with circuit identification numbers, contact information, and circuit repair phone numbers. If someone else manages your WAN, this level of detail may not be necessary.

- Documentation that tells me my current links speeds and the *available* bandwidth between each location. If available, I like to know how the bandwidth fluctuates during the day. For example, a WAN connection may only have 38Kbps available during peak hours of the day but 256Kbps in the off hours of the day. Available bandwidth is *much* more important than actual link speeds. I show you where this information is critically important when I discuss Exchange organization/site/server design in Chapter 2.

WARNING   A very common mistake people make when deploying Exchange is that they rely on their wide area network's "potential" bandwidth, not the "available" bandwidth. Making this mistake can be prove quite detrimental to the health of your wide area network.

- A diagram of each LAN that will have Exchange servers or Exchange clients, including all routers, switches, bridges, and repeaters, and the number of nodes on each subnet as well as the subnet's IP address. This diagram should contain locations of major network nodes such as servers (Windows NT Server, Unix, mainframe, and so on). Further, the location of all the domain controllers (PDCs and BDCs) should be shown.

- A document describing the physical layout of each LAN location, including the number of users, the number of servers, the network topology, and the network equipment in use. Estimates of current bandwidth usage on each segment are also helpful.

- A diagram of the organization-wide Windows NT domain architecture, including master domains and currently established trust relationships.

Do you have this information available? Most network administrators I know don't. However, this information is going to be helpful, if not vital, when you start the design portion of your Exchange organization.

Exchange@Work: Making Fatal Mistakes

Company XYZ made a fatal mistake. While planning to deploy Exchange Server around the U.S., they looked at their network link speeds between each of their 12 offices. The WAN architecture was dual hub and spoke, with one East Coast hub and one West Coast hub. Each hub had a number of satellite offices connected via Frame Relay T1 lines. The hub offices were also connected to each other via Frame Relay T1 lines.

Since the company had high-speed connections between all of the offices, they decided to put all 18 Exchange servers in North America together into one large site. When Exchange Server was fully deployed, their server administrators noticed many times throughout the business day that the MTA queues were backing up with hundreds (even thousands) of messages waiting to be delivered. The event logs were also filling up with connectivity-related (directory service and message transfer agent) error messages. Messages were not being delivered in a timely fashion—sometimes hours passed.

What went wrong? They had plenty of network bandwidth, didn't they? Or did they? A T1 line seems like it has a lot of available bandwidth, but the line was a Frame Relay line. When you order a Frame Relay circuit, the phone company gives you a CIR (committed information rate); this is the rate that the phone company will guarantee you will get on your Frame Relay circuit. A T1 Frame Relay circuit is capable of (and may be) delivering 1.544Mbps, but company XYZ's CIR was only 772Kbps. During the busiest times of the day, the total bandwidth available was many times less than what it would be during the off hours.

Further, during the planning stage, no one asked, "What is the average available bandwidth available on these circuits?" This can easily be measured with SNMP software. There was file transfer, domain replication, intranet, and printing traffic on these circuits prior to installing Exchange. And to top it all off, the routers were configured to give priority to mainframe data. The WAN dude put it best: "The connection between our two regional offices was already overburdened. Why didn't anyone ask me about this?"

Exchange@Work: Making Fatal Mistakes *(continued)*

Close coordination with the people who manage the wide area network is essential to the health and well being of an Exchange system. In this case, company XYZ purchased additional bandwidth on some of the critically slow circuits (especially between the two hub offices), which helped alleviate some of the load. Another, less desirable option was to split the East Coast and the West Coast into two separate sites. This was deemed too time consuming and would have resulted in more downtime than XYZ was willing to tolerate; paying for a higher CIR on certain circuits was a more palatable option.

Reducing Your Total Cost of Ownership

Starting in the late 1980s, the race was on to replace minicomputers and mainframes with PC-based networks. An argument that I heard often was that the PC was so much cheaper to purchase. However, much to everyone's surprise, PC-based networks are not any less expensive to operate. The 1990s ushered in a new term that we hear all too often, *TCO* or *Total Cost of Ownership*. Depending on who you ask, Exchange Server can cut your messaging system ownership by 50 percent or more over other systems currently available.

> **NOTE**   Two reports comparing the TCO of Exchange Server and Lotus Notes by the Radicati Group and Creative Networks, Inc., are available on Microsoft's Web site at www.microsoft.com/exchange.

I often see reports discussing total costs of ownership, comparing per seat operating costs, reports detailing percentage of uptime, and total training costs. This is not something that we techies are usually too interested in. We are more interested in the answers to "How can I go home at 5 P.M.?" and "How do I avoid the midnight phone calls informing me the mail server is down?" However, the questions you *should* be asking (and that I am going to answer) include:

- How can I automate Exchange Server maintenance functions? Chapter 12 discusses some of the tasks that occur automatically on the Exchange server and other things you can do to make sure Exchange keeps right on ticking.

- What tools are available to automate client installation and configuration? Chapter 11 covers automated client installations as well as some tools you can use to help with automating client installation.

- Are there things I should do on a regular basis to keep my Exchange server healthy and happy? Chapter 6 discusses maintenance procedures you should perform on a daily, weekly, and monthly basis. Chapter 7 gives you tips for monitoring your Exchange system in order to catch problems before your users notice.

- Disaster strikes! How do I get my Exchange servers back online quickly? Chapter 18 reviews common disaster recovery scenarios and questions.

- Before I have a disaster, what can I do to prevent it from happening in the first place? That is why I am writing this book. The best one-sentence answer I can give you is planning and preparation. Chapter 2 covers planning your Exchange organization and picking the right kind of servers.

If you follow good operating procedures, learn some of the tasks that you can automate, and pick good server hardware, you will find Exchange Server to be significantly easier to manage and maintain that most legacy messaging systems.

For Further Information

Would you like to learn more about some of the items covered in this chapter? Here are some informative sources:

- For more about designing and implementing Exchange Server in Windows NT domains, refer to *Mastering Windows NT Server 4.0,* Sixth Edition, by Mark Minasi (Sybex, 1999).

- A great general reference for Exchange Server is *Mastering Exchange Server 5.5* by Barry Gerber (Sybex, 1998).

- Microsoft has a white paper called "Planning and Deployment" found in the Exchange Deployment & Support section on Microsoft's Web site at www.microsoft.com/exchange.

- For more information on licensing and license agreements, look on the Web at www.microsoft.com/licensing.

- Interested in RPCs? Get a copy of *Understanding DCE* by Ward Rosenberry, David Kenny, and Gerry Fisher (O'Reilly and Associates, 1992).

2

Exchange Organization Design

Perhaps one of the biggest mistakes organizations make when deploying Microsoft Exchange Server is that they don't adequately plan a proper foundation for Exchange; they don't consider the consequences of site and organization design, and they don't choose reliable hardware. Time and time again, I find myself assisting someone who has deployed Exchange in great haste, only to find that they need to upgrade their server platform, add hard disk space, or restructure their Exchange organizational design structure. I don't know about you, but I really hate to do something over again; I prefer to get it right the first time.

Why are some Exchange deployments less than a stellar success? What are some of the mistakes I see made time and time again?

- Organizations don't employ a consistent naming standard between sites (and this can get ugly!).

- Exchange site design is often left to chance. Care must be taken to ensure that Exchange servers are grouped according the organization's WAN or administrative model.

- Exchange server hardware is chosen that is either insufficient or unreliable.

- There is no testing of new software, service packs, or hot fixes. Further, practicing for disaster recovery, which requires equipment that can be dedicated at least part of the time to a test lab and/or cold standby equipment in the event of server failure, is neglected.

- Operational plans and assignment of responsibilities are afterthoughts.

- Little or no thought is given to system maintenance and disaster prevention.

In Chapter 1, I covered some of the pressing issues you should consider when preparing your network for Exchange and information that you should have in your arsenal before starting the Exchange Server design. Now it's time to plan your Exchange organization. Foreseeing many disasters is impossible, but there are things that you can do to minimize the impact of most catastrophes. When you are making design decisions, there are six simple things to consider: consistency, reliability, usability, maintainability, security, and performance.

NOTE   Please keep in mind that this chapter is not a complete guide to designing and implementing Exchange, but rather a guide to things that people often overlook. See Chapters 2 through 7 of *Mastering Exchange Server 5.5* by Barry Gerber (Sybex, 1998) for more detailed information.

Building a Solid Foundation

Before your first Exchange server is installed, you must have a solid foundation for Exchange. And believe it or not, much of this is going to be on paper. This foundation will include your standards and design document, a good server design, and recommendations for operations and administration.

Standardizing Your Naming Conventions

The Exchange Server global address list (GAL) is replicated to every single site in an organization. In order for this to occur (and for it to *not* look like a mish-mash of names), you must have a naming convention in place for the many different types of names that are used in the Exchange directory.

Exchange Organization/Site/Server Naming

Prior to deploying Exchange, your organization must have agreed upon a naming standard for the organization, sites, and server names.

Organization name must be *exactly* the same for all sites. This name can be up to 64 characters in length, though I recommend keeping it to 16 characters or fewer so that it will match the X.400 PRMD field, which is limited to 16 characters.

Site name must be unique for the entire organization and can be up to 64 characters in length. I recommend using something that is descriptive of the Exchange site. Spaces, dashes, and underscores are permitted, but avoid the space and underscore characters if you want the site name to match the DNS name.

Server name is, of course, the Windows NT server's NetBIOS name. This name is limited to a maximum of 15 characters and should be unique for your entire organization. I suggest using some sort of naming standard that identifies the server type and location as well as assigning it a unique number. Something like HNLEX001 identifies a server in Honolulu (HNL) that is an Exchange server (EX) and has a unique number of 001. (HNL is the airport code, which I like using, but not always useful in a city with several airports.) Avoid using the "_" (underscore) character, because many versions of DNS do not support that character. Though this has little bearing on Exchange, I also avoid using the "-" (hyphen), because SQL Server does not recognize that character in a SQL Server name.

TIP Are the organization and site names case sensitive? I have never found a situation where case sensitivity mattered with Exchange. However, Microsoft continues to insist that the names should be treated as though they are. Thus I consider it a good practice to use all uppercase letters in my organization and site names.

DNS or WINS Server

"Should I use a WINS server or should I use a DNS server?" If your clients are using DNS, then the Exchange server's NetBIOS name should be entered into your DNS zone. For example, if the server name is HNLEX0Ø1 and the domain name is Somorita.com, then clients should be able to do a DNS lookup (or just a simple PING to HNLEX001.Somorita.com).

Further, all clients and servers should have their TCP/IP DNS Domain Name fields entered as Somorita.com, as shown in Figure 2.1. For more information on this "feature" of Exchange, see Chapter 16.

Figure 2.1 TCP/IP DNS domain name properties

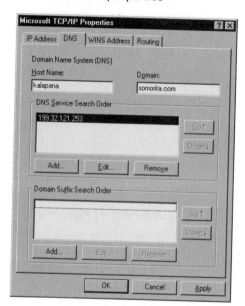

Exchange Server, Exchange Administrator, the Exchange client, and all versions of the Outlook client are *not* NetBIOS applications. Their preferred method of resolving a host name to an IP address is not the standard NetBIOS name resolution method.

Mailbox and Custom Recipient Names When creating an Exchange Server mailbox or custom recipient, there are a number of property fields that you have the option of filling out. Only a few of these are required. Figure 2.2 shows the fields that are available for an Exchange mailbox in a typical installation of Exchange. Of these fields, only Display Name, Alias, and Primary Windows NT Account are required. On the Advanced tab, the Directory Name field is required (and cannot be changed once the mailbox is created); if you do not provide data for the Directory Name field, it is copied from the Alias field.

Figure 2.2   Property fields available on the General tab of an Exchange mailbox

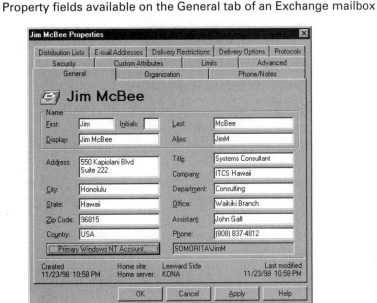

Many of the Exchange mailbox fields that you should consider standardizing are found on the mailbox's property page. They include:

Display Name is the field shown in the global address list and is displayed in the To field of the Outlook clients. It can be a maximum of 256 characters, though you should keep it shorter than that; I limit my display names to no more than 64 characters. Standardizing how this field is displayed is extremely important; if one administrator enters names one way and another does it differently, then the global address list does not appear cohesive. Following are some examples of how names are displayed:

McBee, Jim	Last Name, First Name—my favorite
McBee, Jim (Honolulu-Systems Admin)	Last Name, First Name, location and job information
N6503 – Mr. Jim McBee (Hawaii)	Job Code followed by salutation, name, and location, which is common in government and military installations

Alias is a short name identifying this mailbox. Many administrators like to limit this field to eight characters, though you can use up to 64 characters. Some legacy mail systems (such as PROFS and SNADS) don't allow e-mail addresses longer than eight characters. I personally like matching the e-mail alias to the Windows NT account name, but there is no requirement to do this.

Directory Name is found on the Advanced tab and can be up to 64 characters long. This name is used internally by the Exchange directory service and is part of the DN (Distinguished Name). The directory name is also sometimes called the RDN (Relative Distinguished Name). It defaults to the same as the alias when the mailbox is created, but it cannot be changed once it is created.

First Name is a 16-character field for the user's first name.

Last Name is a 40-character field for the user's last name.

Primary Windows NT Account is the field that contains the Windows NT user account that is allowed to access this mailbox. You can also assign Windows NT global and local groups to access a mailbox rather than individual accounts. Additional accounts and groups can be given access to a mailbox through the Permissions property page.

Mailbox Properties

Why should I fill in all the property fields for a mailbox? Well, if you are in an organization of 20 people, I am betting you don't need to. Suppose, though, that you are in an organization of a couple hundred (or a few thousand or even tens of thousands) people. Have you ever needed a phone number, fax number, or shipping address of someone in your own company? Install Exchange Server and voilà!— instant company-wide phone directory.

Is keeping the character case of mailbox directory entries important? People tell me that I am being picky when I do this, but yes, I think it certainly is important. You have gone to the trouble of setting standards for how names will appear in the global address list; take it just a bit further and make sure your administrators enter people in the correct case (upper or lower). The global address list will look a lot more professional and credible.

Distribution Lists

Exchange Server distribution lists are used for a couple of things. The obvious use is, of course, sending messages to many users at once. Distribution lists are also used for assigning permissions to public folders. Distribution lists are an organization-wide resource and will be seen throughout the organization in the global address list. Here are a few hints for making your life with distribution lists a little easier:

- Restrict the list membership size to less than 5,000 recipients. You can always nest large distribution lists if necessary.

- Create a distribution list for all mailboxes in each site. These site-level distribution lists can then be added to organization-wide distribution lists (this is called nesting). Site-wide distribution lists can also be used when assigning permissions to public folders that only the users in a specific site need access to.

- Assign an owner to the distribution list. The owner can assign and revoke membership in the list through Outlook. The Exchange Administrator program only allows you to assign one "official" owner, but using the Permissions tab, you can give others the User role, which will allow them to control membership just like the owner.

- For large distribution lists, set delivery restrictions so that only specific people can send to a distribution list. This does not stop a determined person, but it sure makes it harder to send to everyone in the entire company!

- I like to put an underscore (_) or ampersand (&) character in front of my distribution lists so they all sort to the top of the global address list. (Most any special character will work.) In larger organizations, I also like to put a blank distribution list at the top of the list. My global address list, including distribution lists, would look like Figure 2.3. For companies that want all their distribution lists to sort to the bottom of the global address list, put a *zz_* in front of the distribution list display name.

Figure 2.3   A global address list with a few distribution lists sorted to the top of the list

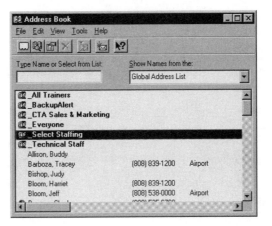

Restricting Access and Providing a Blank Distribution List

A company I know made heavy use of distribution lists. Unfortunately, anyone could send to any of these lists. One user displayed the address list to select her friend's name. She inadvertently also selected a distribution list. She sent a rather long message detailing her love-life woes to over 1,000 people. The MIS director, mail administrator, human resources manager, and several other people spent the better part of the morning in a panic attack trying to figure out how to remove the message.

The moral of the story: By restricting who can use large distribution lists and by putting a blank distribution list at the top of the directory, you can help prevent accidental distribution list usage.

Using Recipient Containers

A *recipient container* is quite simply a receptacle in which you can put recipients (mailboxes, custom recipients, public folders, and distribution lists). Recipient containers are created at the site level. Currently, once an object is created in one recipient container, it cannot be moved to another.

So if recipients cannot be moved from one container to another, then what's the use? If you plan containers correctly, you can still find a number of good uses for them. Here is a list of recipient containers I create and what each is used for:

Mailboxes is actually the original recipients container. I rename the Display Name property from Recipients to Mailboxes so that it more accurately describes what is in the container.

External Users is a container that holds all custom recipients such as users with SMTP addresses.

MS Mail Users and similarly named containers are used for recipients on other mail systems from which you are synchronizing directories.

Public Folders contains a list of public folders. Don't forget to change the default directory location of public folders in Configuration ➢ Information Store Site Configuration ➢ Public Folder Container. This ensures that any public folders created (hidden or not hidden) will be displayed in the Public Folders container.

Distribution Lists contains all distribution lists.

Resources contains a list of mailboxes that are actually resources such as conference rooms, projectors, and so on.

Other recipient containers might include containers for other organizations with which I manually replicate my directory.

> **NOTE**   Recipient containers are created and named per site, not for the entire Exchange organization. Each site should follow a similar naming convention.

Exchange@Work: I Love My Recipient Containers!

At one company, the Exchange administrator fell in love with recipient containers. He created one for every department in his company. Sure enough, problems started arising when people transferred from one department to another, which happened quite often. The administrator could not move a recipient from one container to another, so he had to delete the mailbox and re-create it. This required moving all the user's messages to a PST file, deleting the mailbox, re-creating the mailbox, deleting the user's Outlook profile, and re-creating the Outlook profile.

All of this extra work could have been avoided if the administrator had a better understanding of how to use recipient containers. If he had known that recipient containers were not as flexible, he would not have created departmental containers in the first place.

> **WARNING**   All objects have a Distinguished Name (DN) that is a combination of the organization, site, recipient container, and directory name of the object; Exchange refers internally to this name as the Obj-Dist-Name. Exchange uses the DN to route messages within a single Exchange organization. For example, user Reid Shigeoka's directory name is RShigeoka; he is in the Somorita Surfboards organization, the Hilo Region site, and the Recipients container. His DN will be / o=Somorita/ou=Hilo Office/cn=Recipients/cn=RShigeoka. You should plan your organizational naming standards so that this name does *not* exceed 256 characters.

Public Folders

Once the directory replication connector is set up between two sites, the names of public folders from all sites will be visible in the Exchange public folder hierarchy. This is not a very big deal for smaller organizations (fewer than 1,000 mailboxes) that may only have a few dozen public folders. However, for large organizations with hundreds of public folders, searching a huge list of meaningless public folders for one or two commonly used folders will be a waste from a user's perspective.

One of your administrative challenges will be to organize your public folder hierarchy in a manner that makes sense to all users in all sites. A few of my own approaches include creating root public folders for each site, each location, or each specific department. Another option is to make each location's public folder visible only to the users in that location.

Don't forget to create a public folder for organization-wide use. Figure 2.4 shows a public folder hierarchy based on a root folder being created for each site name. Each site can then create as many subfolders as desired. This makes navigating the public folder hierarchy much more user friendly.

Figure 2.4 This public folder hierarchy gives each site (or location) a root folder specifically for that site.

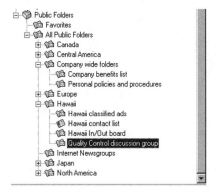

Address Book Views

Address book views solve an organization-level naming issue. They were introduced in Exchange 5 to help give a more hierarchical structure to the global address list. The address book view feature allows you to create "virtual" address books based on one of 18 recipient properties: city, company, country, department, home server, site, state, title, and any of the 10 custom attribute fields.

> **NOTE** I will talk a little more about creating address book views and supporting "virtual" organizations in Chapter 5. So why am I bringing this up in the context of a naming standard? Because address book views are an organization-wide resource; if you create one for your site, it is visible in all sites. Address book views need to be part of the deployment plan, and all administrators need to know that they can't start creating views without affecting what the other sites will see.

Organization Forms Libraries

Another organizational item, though not directly related to naming, is the Organization Forms Library. The Organization Forms Library gives you the ability to store forms for purposes of collaboration and workflow, and to help move toward the ultimate paperless office. <grin> These forms are stored in system-level public folders, and you can have one forms library folder for each language and each Exchange organization you are supporting.

By default, a Forms Library created in one site is not accessible from other sites. This kind of defeats the purpose of an "Organization" Forms Library, doesn't it? The Organization Forms Library should be created in one site and then made available to other sites through public folder replication or public folder affinity. Once replication or affinity is set up, users can use the forms, and individuals with the proper permissions can install forms into the library from any site.

Site-Level Details Templates

The site-level Details templates are quite useful when customizing the templates that your users see. Figure 2.5 shows the Find dialog box that is available from the Outlook client when a user needs to search for a mailbox in the global address list. The properties necessary to build and display the Find dialog box are stored in the Exchange directory.

Figure 2.5   A slightly customized Find dialog box includes fields for searching based on Job Code or Mail Stop.

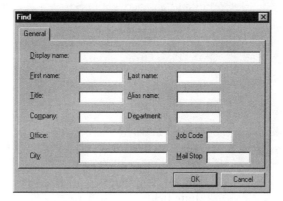

If you have seen this dialog screen before, then you may also notice that there are two additional search dialog boxes: Job Code and Mail Stop.

The issue that you need to keep in mind during the planning phase is that Details templates are modified on a per site basis. If you want all users in all sites to see the same custom Details templates, you must modify them in each site. The templates do not replicate between sites.

NOTE   For more on Details templates, see Chapter 5.

Custom Attributes

I just showed you a neat feature of Exchange—the ability to modify the Details templates to further customize your Exchange installation. In Figure 2.5, you may have noticed the Job Code and Mail Stop fields. These are not exactly built-in fields, but rather custom attribute fields. For example, I renamed the Custom Attribute 1 to Job Code. I then incorporated that field into my customized Find template, as you saw in Figure 2.5.

The data contained in the custom attribute fields are replicated to all sites by default. However, the custom attribute field names themselves are not replicated to other sites. For example, if another site decided to change the name of Custom Attribute 1 to Date Of Birth, whenever anyone looked at my Date Of Birth field in their site, they would see my Job Code *data* instead; my renamed field would not be replicated, but its data would.

This is another example of the necessity of careful coordination and planning when deploying Exchange. The custom attribute fields should be part of your design document as well.

TIP   If you don't want your custom attribute data to be replicated to other sites, this can be controlled from *Site Name* ➢ Configuration ➢ DS Site Configuration. On the Attributes tab, choose Inter-Site Replication in the Configure field and deselect any attributes that you don't want replicated out of your site. You cannot control this on a site-by-site basis; it affects all sites with which you are replicating directory data.

SMTP Address

If you are connecting to the Internet or an SMTP network, you must decide what your SMTP address will be for all users. This value is set for each site in the Site Addressing tab; go to *Site Name* ➢ Configuration ➢ Site Addressing. All sites can use the same SMTP address, or certain sites can use their own. The deciding factor is which sites are going to host inbound Internet Mail Services.

If several sites are going to host inbound Internet Mail Services and they want their mail delivered directly to their site from the Internet, then they must have a separate Internet domain name. A DNS server must set the appropriate MX and A record entries in the DNS zone database.

Developing a Standards and Design Document

By now you have been planning furiously, right? You've been to meetings, formed committees, talked to the bosses, and all of your colleagues in all branches of your company are in agreement! Now that you've also got your naming conventions down, you need a standards and design document that is going to detail everything that you and your fellow administrators have agreed upon. Everyone should have a copy of this document and agree to follow it to the letter when they deploy their piece of the Exchange puzzle. Everyone must sign off on this plan and follow it.

What should be in this document? Table 2.1 shows a sample of some of the more critical elements that I recommend you include.

Table 2.1   Somorita Surfboards Exchange Standards

Item	Value	Explanation
Organization name	SOMORITA	All sites will use this value when installing their Exchange servers.
Site name	HAWAII—for the Hawaiian Islands offices. NORTHAMERICA—for offices in the continental U.S. JAPAN—for the Tokyo and Osaka offices. EUROPE—for the Germany, France, Spain, and Italy offices.	Use the value for your particular region.
Server names	Use your nearest airport code, followed by EX, followed by three unique numbers. For example: HNLEX001, SFOEX001, LAXEX002.	Register your server's names and IP addresses with the Exchange Coordinator so that they can be entered into the DNS database.
Alias name	Use the Windows NT account name.	

Table 2.1   Somorita Surfboards Exchange Standards *(continued)*

Item	Value	Explanation
Display name	Last Name and First Name followed by "(Office Name, Job Title)". For example: Suzuki, Makoto (Tokyo, Sales); McBee, Jim (Honolulu, Trainer)	Follow these standards exactly. Case counts; don't use all uppercase or all lowercase.
Mailbox fields to be filled in	Fill in all address, phone, title, and departmental information.	This has to be followed carefully or you won't be able to replace your company phonebook application.
Recipient containers	External Recipients Distribution Lists Public Folders Resources	For your site, you are required to create these four containers. Put mailboxes only in the recipients container.
Address book views	By Department By City	The corporate MIS staff will create address book views. Do not create your own address book views.
Custom attributes	CA 1 → Date Of Birth CA 2 → Hire Date CA 3 → Hobbies	Rename your site's custom attributes as shown. When creating recipients, enter the appropriate information for each. Enter dates in the U.S. fashion (such as 03/28/1963).
SMTP address	@SOMORITA.COM	Set this in site addressing. All inbound mail will be delivered to the same domain name.

I cannot emphasize enough the importance of all system administrators agreeing to this standards document. Having someone of great importance within your company (the CEO, the director of IS—someone who can affect other people's paychecks) sign off on this document and declaring that all the organization's sites, offices, and locations will follow this document is also helpful.

Exchange@Work: Beware the Rogue Site!

Several organizations I have worked with have experienced rogue installations of Exchange. This happens when a particular office, department, or division decides they won't wait for the standards and pilot tests to be completed. They deploy Exchange and use their own standards.

In fact, I know of one very large company that had two competing divisions deploying Exchange; both divisions were racing to see who could get their division completely migrated first. Both believed that if they "won," someone up the food chain would eventually make a decision and name them to be the *de facto* standard.

Now they are stuck with two Exchange organizations whose directories are not very interoperable. Even the organization name is different, so they can't participate in Exchange directory replication. Users are now asking for address lists of people who are in the other division; they want to share public folders and to deploy a couple of standardized forms. Neither division's MIS department will bend, and the director of IS is afraid to make a decision because the situation has become so politically charged.

One suggestion is to use the Microsoft Exchange Move Server Wizard (also known as Pilgrim). I discuss the uses of Pilgrim in Chapter 4, but I will warn you now: Pilgrim is not a magic wand. You can't wave it and magically merge two distinctly separate organizations. There are a lot of issues to address.

Planning and standardization must be done before anything is deployed, even in a pilot project. All implementers must agree to adhere to the organization-wide standards. The standards and design document needs to be created, agreed upon, and followed.

Site Design

Many issues affect the decision to break organizations up into multiple sites. The following sections discuss two major factors: available network bandwidth between server locations and the administrative responsibility of the mailboxes and servers.

NOTE You may also consider connecting sites as part of your organizational design. A complete discussion of messaging connectors is outside of the scope of this book. I will discuss some basics of each of the messaging connectors and the directory replication connector in Chapter 9.

Bandwidth between Servers

Bandwidth between servers is the biggest issue to consider when deciding how many sites to have in your organization. All servers within a single Exchange site communicate with one another using Remote Procedure Calls (RPCs), a communication mechanism that expects full-time, high-speed connections; at least this is the official Microsoft rule. However, no one ever bothers to define exactly what "high-speed" connectivity is. Is it a T1 line? Is it a 28.8 modem? Is it a minimum of Ethernet speeds?

My own rule of thumb: "When separating two servers by a WAN that are in a single site, there should be a minimum of 64Kbps *available* bandwidth. For every additional server, add an additional 64Kbps." Is this a perfect rule? Not even close. (However, it is a good place to start.) Some network managers report that they are able to operate perfectly well with far less than 64Kbps available bandwidth. Some of my students have told me I should have the words "It depends" tattooed on my forehead because I say that so often.

How much bandwidth is required between Exchange servers greatly depends on the situation. Within a single site, things to ask to help figure out how much bandwidth is enough include:

- What types of and how much data is being transferred between servers?
- How often is the directory database being updated?
- How often are messages being sent from one server to another?
- Does the public folder hierarchy change often?
- Are you employing public folder content replication and if so, how often is the public folder data being replicated and changed?

Dial-on-Demand Routers and Exchange

Several people have asked me recently if they can put several servers in a single site but have them separated by dial-on-demand routers. This seems to be an especially popular idea with the ISDN aficionados. Unless you live in an area where you are not charged every time ISDN dials out and you are not charged per-minute surcharges, you will be unpleasantly surprised when you get your first ISDN bill.

Within a single site, there is a lot of chatter between Exchange servers. The MTA delivers messages as soon as they arrive in the MTA queues; the directory service sends any changes between servers every five minutes. There are also public folder replication (content and hierarchy) messages, link monitor messages, and knowledge consistency checks every three hours. With this amount of traffic between servers in a single site, dial-on-demand routers will stay "off the hook" quite often during the course of a regular business day. In most cases, you will find Frame Relay to be a cheaper option.

Site Services Accounts

All Exchange servers in a single site must share a common site services user account (the user account you assigned to the first server in the site during installation). It is used to validate all the services on an Exchange server upon startup and when one server's message transfer agent (or directory service) connects to another server using RPCs. This means that any domain with an Exchange server in it must have a trust relationship to the domain that contains the site services account.

Site Administration

The decision to break an organization up into several sites is not purely technical. Administrative requirements may also determine site boundaries. Administrative responsibility is assigned by site; an administrator of one site does not necessarily have permissions to another site. Organizations with centralized MIS will benefit from the ability to manage one large site, but organizations with very decentralized MIS will benefit from a site model based on their administrative model.

Server Design

One of the biggest problems that I experience in the field is improper or insufficient server hardware. Nearly 50 percent of the Exchange servers I have installed over the last year and a half have been upgraded to better (faster, stronger, higher capacity) servers since they were installed. The reasons given for upgrading or replacing servers include insufficient disk space, slow response time for clients, movement towards a standard server platform, and unreliable original server platform.

> **TIP** I have a tendency to overestimate the amount of server hardware and disk space I believe I am going to need. This approach gives me room to grow. I also operate under the philosophy that it is easier to ask for money for hardware up front than it is to come back six months later and ask for upgrade money.

Super Servers versus Off-the-Shelf Servers

It is always exciting to go shopping for the new breed of super servers. They have four, eight, or more processors, a few gigabytes of RAM, and cool-looking enclosures. These servers hold the promise of supporting thousands of mailboxes on a single machine. Table 2.2 lists some advantages and disadvantages of today's super servers.

Table 2.2 Advantages and Disadvantages of Super Servers

Advantages	Disadvantages
Centralized management	If the super server fails, then many users are unable to access their e-mail
Reduced cost for server software licenses for Windows NT and Exchange	Difficult to back up or restore quickly due to the size of the information stores
	Often proprietary
	Expensive
	More users on a single Exchange server means the MTA will be transmitting fewer messages between servers

But before you rush out and put your entire organization on a single machine, consider the advantages of using off-the-shelf equipment (servers that can easily be ordered through your friendly neighborhood systems integration company). Though the super servers are pretty cool, my personal preference is to use several less powerful, off-the-shelf servers rather than one or two super servers. Table 2.3 lists advantages and disadvantages of off-the-shelf servers that are widely available.

Table 2.3   Advantages and Disadvantages of Off-the-Shelf Servers

Advantages	Disadvantages
Distributed workload	More difficult to manage
Failure of a single server does not affect many users	More costly server software licenses, because you have to run more servers to support the same number of users
Information store backs up (and restores) more quickly since it is smaller	More servers to maintain

Exchange@Work: To Super Serve or Not to Super Serve

I recently spent several weeks with a client who was in the middle of Exchange design and planning. Before I came on board, they had decided to purchase a single super server to support 1,200 mailboxes and an identical super server to serve as a cold standby in the event of hardware failure. (Both servers were four-processor Pentium II 200MHz systems with 1GB of RAM.) They were also going to use this extra server for testing and doing practice disaster recovery restores. They had a very high-tech DLT tape loader system on a server on their backbone that could back up remote servers at a rate of about 2GB per hour. Furthermore, each user mailbox was going to be limited to 50MB.

Using the estimated size that the database would grow to over the first year, we calculated that a full private information store backup (or restore) would take 30 hours. Database repairs could take even longer. If there was a database corruption on this system, it would affect 1,200 users for many hours.

Was this acceptable? No, not even close. This company, like many others, found that messaging has become an integral business process.

Instead of one super server, we decided on five off-the-shelf servers (Pentium II 300Mhz systems, each with 256MB of RAM and its own DAT tape unit). Four of the servers were put into production supporting roughly 300 mailboxes per server, and the fifth machine is now a cold standby. We estimated that full backup (or restore) time could be reduced to around two hours.

Server Configuration and Hardware Decisions

How much storage space do you purchase? Should you get many different types of servers or try and standardize with one brand and model? How much RAM should you start with? How should the machine be configured? What processor type should you use? These are all questions that you need to have coherent answers for before entering the server design phase.

Disk Storage Space

How much disk space do you need to purchase? The age old question. My metric is to estimate about 50MB per user for the private information store. A lot of people's mouths fall open when I tell them this, but you will be surprised how quickly your power users will approach this amount. Some users will never reach 50MB, yet others will need to go way past the default limits I impose.

Estimating the amount of disk space required for the public information store is going to be much more difficult if you don't already have a good idea of what you are going to be storing there. If you don't know, then take the amount of disk space you are going to use for the private information store and double it to come up with an approximation of the total disk space you will need.

Table 2.4 shows a quick calculation for a server that will host both a public and private information store. There will be 450 mailboxes on the server.

Table 2.4 Estimated Database Storage Requirements for a Server Hosting 450 Mailboxes and Public Folders

Database Storage	Estimated Space
Private IS	$(50MB \times 450) = 22.5GB$
Public IS	22.5GB

Table 2.4 Estimated Database Storage Requirements for a Server Hosting 450 Mailboxes and Public Folders *(continued)*

Database Storage	Estimated Space
Extra space	25GB
Total database storage required	70GB

"Wow, 70GB of storage—just for e-mail?!" Have you heard that from your boss before? It is not just e-mail, though. The mailbox stores e-mail, calendar items, sent items, journal information, contact items, and any collaborative types of data that you may be routing using Exchange. Don't forget that you may also be integrating faxing or other systems that will keep data in the private information store.

What about that "extra space" of 25GB that I allocated? It is always a good practice to have an area of free space available on any server that is at least as large as the largest database you have. This allows you to perform offline database maintenance locally. There are other reasons why we need the extra space; I cover these in Chapters 6 and 17.

TIP Don't ever sell yourself short on disk space. Disk drives are cheap compared to the downtime costs associated with upgrading a server with new disk drives.

Exchange@Work: An External Disk Array

One of my friends operates four Exchange servers to support almost 1,500 mailboxes. Rather than purchase twice the amount of disk space that he actually needs (my recommendation), he purchased one external disk array with 20GB of usable storage. If he needs to perform database maintenance on any of his servers, he shuts the server down (make sure you do this!), plugs in the external drive array, and powers the system back up. Ta da! An instant extra 20GB of disk space to rebuild or defragment a database. Though he does have to contend with the minor hassle of moving the external storage from one machine to another, this approach works well for him and saves his company a pretty good chunk of money.

RAM Requirements

Another good question: How much RAM is required? The best answer: RAM is cheap, so don't skimp on it. I consider 128MB to be a good starting point. For servers that are going to support more than 150 users, I move the RAM requirements up to 256MB. For servers that are going to support more than 400 users, I increase the RAM to 512MB. (Keep in mind that any Pentium II–based server with 512MB of RAM or more should also have 1MB of Level II cache.) Additional memory will almost always improve performance of any Microsoft BackOffice product.

WARNING   Only use RAM recommended and provided by the server manufacturer. Using slower or substandard SIMMs can cause Windows NT to be unstable.

Hardware Standardization

Picking a server hardware vendor can be one of the most critical decisions you will make during the design phase, but you can save yourself a fair amount stress if you standardize on a particular hardware vendor. If at all possible, try to standardize on the same server family and model. Pick a vendor that not only has a good reputation for building quality hardware, but also is experienced in supporting Windows NT installations. I am still groggy from tracking down bizarre problems on a no-name brand late last night.

Disk Configuration

The disk subsystem on any system is always broken up into two major components: the disk controller and the disk drives themselves. Don't skimp on either. I highly recommend using hardware-based RAID 5 drive arrays to increase the level of disk fault tolerance. I further recommend using SCSI disk drives; the best drives widely available today are the fast ultra-wide SCSIs.

TIP   An emerging technology that is becoming more affordable is fiber channel disks and controllers. Fiber channel can significantly improve the throughput of your disk subsystem.

TIP   Use RAID 5 and SCSI disk drives that are recommended by the server manufacturer. Even better, use controllers that will allow "hot swapping." Provided there is redundancy built into the disk array, a failed disk can be replaced while the server is in production.

When I configure a server for any type of application, I use hardware-based RAID 5 drives in an enclosure that supports "hot swapping." If a drive fails, I don't have to schedule downtime in order to replace it; I simply make sure I have a recent backup and then replace the failed drive.

> **NOTE**   Should you use disk controllers with write caching enabled? Microsoft's official position on this is that you should leave write caching disabled. I have found performance to be enhanced considerably when write caching is used, but you should make sure that the controller has a battery backup system and that your data can be recovered off of the memory chips on the RAID controller. Inquire with your hardware manufacture about recovering data from memory chips on your RAID 5 controller.

Figure 2.6 shows a drive configuration for my ideal server, on which I would comfortably support more than 500 mailboxes. I am putting Windows NT software, Exchange software, and the page file on a 2GB, NTFS C drive, the log files on a 2GB FAT D drive, and the Exchange databases on a larger RAID 5 drive array formatted as an NTFS E drive.

Figure 2.6   Server drive configuration

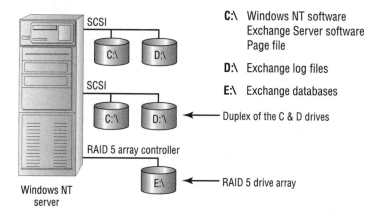

There are many different options for configuring disk drives. On a typical server supporting mailboxes, I would make sure that the log files are on a separate physical disk drive from the disk that has the database files on it. For a server operating as a messaging hub or bridgehead server, I would put the MTA working files on a separate disk.

Do the disks that contain log files and MTA working files need fault tolerance? Not in the strictest sense of the word, but I consider fault tolerance to be of paramount importance on any system. Which component in any PC-based system fails the most often? The disks. Regardless of which disk fails, you don't want it to affect the operation of the server. Disk fault tolerance, more than anything else, will help keep your server up and running.

Does the file system matter? You can give yourself another boost in performance by formatting the disk that holds log files with the FAT file system. FAT disks provide better performance for sequential writes. Formatting a server drive with the FAT file system does make some security specialists a little nervous, though there is no reason that any directory on a disk that holds the log files should be shared.

Processors

What speed processor should you use? The fastest processor you can purchase. There, that was simple, wasn't it? Any server you are buying today should have a minimum of a 300MHz Pentium II processor. If the server is expected to support more than 500 simultaneous clients, consider a dual-processor system. If the system is expected to support more than 1,000 clients, consider a four-processor system.

Other Server Options

When you are making out your shopping list for Exchange Server and server peripherals, here are some essential items:

- Uninterruptible power supply, monitoring software, and remote shutdown capabilities. You don't want a power failure to cause the sudden failure of your Exchange server and possibly corrupt one of the database files.

- A CD-ROM drive. Any Windows NT server you build should have one.

- A fast tape drive capable of backing up the entire system, preferably on one tape. I would prefer to use the exact same tape drive (and tape software) on all my Exchange servers so that my tapes are interoperable between servers.

TIP   Keep your servers simple! In my personal experience, the more software that is installed on a Windows NT platform, the more unstable the software and the operating system become. If you have the option, separate your Exchange Server software from other BackOffice server products. In addition, install Exchange Server onto member servers, not domain controllers.

Exchange@Work: Plug It in and Make Sure It Runs for the Next Three Years!

I have been working with a client for many years who is finally upgrading to Exchange Server; she has been operating a Microsoft Mail shop for years. I sat down with their Exchange project manager recently to develop a budget for server hardware. The system has to support 500 simultaneous users, be highly reliable, and provide some room for growth (no more than five percent per year). Further, my client told me that she is leasing the server equipment for three years and does not want to spend one additional penny on upgrades for leased hardware later on, so we should attempt to plan a server that will last for three years without upgrades. Her words were something like, "I want to turn on the power switch and have it run for three years without interruption." She and I both know this may not be possible, but it is a great goal to shoot for.

Though I urged her to split the load up across two servers, the company was intent on purchasing a single server. So we configured a Compaq Proliant 5500 server with two Pentium II 333MHz ZEON processors and 1MB of Level II cache. The server has a RAID 5 drive array with 75GB of usable storage and a 35/70 DLT tape unit installed in it. On a separate SCSI controller, there are two 4GB disks, one for the Windows NT operating system and one for the Exchange Server log files. There is an identical SCSI controller and drives that mirror the log files and the operating system. Though I would have preferred to see her go with two servers just to split the load up between two Exchange servers (for redundancy), this server configuration will be more than adequate for her new Exchange organization.

Server-Based Message Storage versus PST Storage

Where are messages stored? This is a decision you will be required to make. You have two primary options: Users can keep their messages on the server, or Outlook can automatically move messages from the server to a personal folder (PST). Naturally, if users are storing all their messages in a personal folder, you won't be needing any 70GB disk drives for the private information store.

NOTE   I cover methods of managing server-based message storage space in Chapter 5.

The important factor is who is responsible for backing up the data. If the user message data is moved off the server and to a personal folder that is on a local hard disk, then who is responsible for that? I know, we warn users repeatedly to back up their hard disks, but they don't. Still, they blame their friendly neighborhood administrator when their hard drive fails and they lose data.

To help you decide which option is better for you, Table 2.5 shows some of the characteristics of server-based message storage and PST-based message storage.

Table 2.5   Server-Based Message Storage versus PST-Based Message Storage

Server-Based Message Storage	PST-Based Message Storage
Messages are backed up when the server is backed up.	Messages are only backed up if someone backs up the PST file.
Can take advantage of deleted item recovery.	Cannot take advantage of deleted item recovery.
Difficult to restore a single mailbox.	If the PST file is backed up, mailbox restoration is simple.
Permits single instance message storage.	For each recipient, there is a copy of a mail message stored in a separate personal folder.
Message only stored once on the server.	Two copies of each message are stored in the PST file, an (RTF) version and a plain text version.
Only administrators and the user can access server-based messages.	Anyone who can access the file can access a personal store. If it is password encrypted, this password can be broken with tools from the Internet.
Outlook Web Access feature is available.	Since messages are removed from the server when they are transferred to a PST file, moved messages are not available to users using Outlook Web Access.

Grouping Your Users Together by Server

If you have more than one Exchange server, on which server should you place which mailboxes? The main factor in deciding where to place a mailbox is "Who does the user send messages to most often?" Though this can vary from organization to organization, usually the answer is users within the same department or group. You can further optimize Exchange by making sure that departments that often send messages to one another are grouped together on the same Exchange server. This will reduce the messaging load on your network and the message transfer agents (MTAs).

> ***TIP*** Don't put all the users with executive decision-making abilities on the same server (such as directors, vice presidents, CEOs, and so on) even though they might be grouped together logically because they frequently send messages to one another. You don't want all the people with the power to get upset because their e-mail is not available. <grin>

Exchange@Work: Preparing Your Windows NT System for Exchange

Windows NT Server is the basic platform for all Microsoft BackOffice products. This platform needs to be solid; otherwise, any BackOffice product you run on it will be subject to the whims of a flaky Windows NT installation. Here are some steps to follow when configuring Windows NT to support Exchange Server:

1. Start with a clean installation of Windows NT.

2. Install network-related services and protocols. Ensure that you have the latest device drivers for network adapters, disk drivers, video drivers, and so on.

3. Partition and format the remaining disk partitions. If possible, format the disk that will contain the log files using the FAT file system.

4. Set the correct DNS domain name in the TCP/IP properties. Test TCP/IP connectivity and host name resolution (using NSLOOKUP).

5. Increase the initial size of the system page file to 125MB plus the amount of RAM and increase the maximum size to 250MB plus RAM. If possible, make sure the page file does not occupy the same physical disk on which the log files are stored.

Exchange@Work: Preparing Your Windows NT System for Exchange *(continued)*

6. Apply the latest Windows NT service pack. I recommend using Windows NT 4 SP4, because it includes many security fixes only found in post-SP 3 hot fixes. If you are in the United States or Canada, contact Microsoft to get the North American edition of the SP4 CD (128-bit encryption). Order part number 236-01176 from (800) 370-8758. Check with Microsoft for recent releases of service packs and hot fixes that may affect Exchange.

7. Install Windows NT Option Pack services and Internet Explorer *only* if you plan to use them in the future. If you require products from the Option Pack CD, install Internet Explorer 4 and then install the Option Pack products. If you have installed SP4, you will get a message warning you that SP4 has not been tested with the Option Pack. This is okay.

8. Reapply the Windows NT 4 Service Pack 4.

Once you have the basic platform installed, you are then ready to progress to installation of Exchange Server. Once Windows NT is installed, there are a few simple rules you can follow to ensure that Windows NT remains stable:

- After any upgrades, blue screens, or new software installations, run the CHKDSK /F command.

- Keep an updated copy of your Emergency Repair Disk, especially after making system or disk configuration changes.

- Make sure you have a recent system backup.

- After installing software and Windows NT system services, reapply any service packs and hot fixes.

- Never install beta software on production servers.

- Do not use OpenGL screen savers on servers; they seriously impact performance.

- Reboot after any software updates or installing new service packs.

- Be careful of Windows 16-bit and DOS applications; poorly written applications can degrade performance.

> **WARNING**   Do not install unnecessary services; they take up memory and disk space. Unnecessary services can contribute to system instability and pose potential security risks.

> **WARNING**   Never use NTFS file compression to compress the Exchange databases, log files, or working directories. This could result in decreased response times and, if the database exceeds 4GB, possible database corruption.

Microsoft Cluster Services

With the release of the Windows NT Server 4 Enterprise Edition, Microsoft introduced the concept of clusters to the Windows NT family. This is by no means a new concept—Digital Equipment Corp brought clustering to the VAX/VMS family nearly 20 years ago.

In my own humble opinion, Windows NT clustering is still very much a 1.0 product. Not that it is going to stay that way, but it is a first-generation product from the perspective of Windows NT. Figure 2.7 illustrates a two-node cluster running Exchange services. Currently, Windows NT Server is only capable of supporting a two-node cluster.

Figure 2.7   A two-node Windows NT cluster

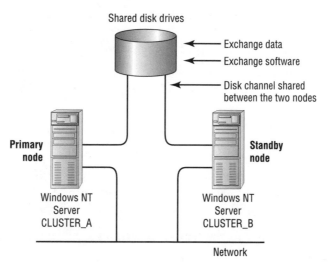

The cluster appears as a single Exchange server. Though there are two nodes in the cluster, Exchange services are only active on a single machine at a time. Both nodes in the cluster share a set of disks where the databases, working directories, and log files are located.

What Does Clustering Protect You From?

Clustering protects you from hardware failures. It does not protect against a database failure, because there is only one copy of the Exchange databases (on the shared disk). There is always the chance that the active node in the cluster will corrupt the database when it fails.

In a clustered environment, Exchange does not provide instantaneous failover. When failover from the active node to the secondary node in a cluster occurs, some services on the active node may have to be shut down. Database transactions may have to be rolled forward from the logs to the databases. The exact time that is required to transition between one node and the other will vary based on the server hardware and the software configuration, but I can assure you that if it occurs during a busy period of the day, your user community will take notice of the failure.

Installing Exchange on Microsoft Cluster Services

What is the best way to get started with Exchange in a clustered environment? Your starting point is to purchase the right hardware. Here are a couple of tips for getting started with Microsoft Clustering and Exchange:

- You will need to purchase the hardware recommended by the Microsoft Cluster Services hardware compatibility list at www.microsoft.com/hwtest/hcl. I would highly recommend purchasing all components from the same hardware vendor.
- The hardware configuration for the two servers in the cluster should be identical.
- You will need Windows NT 4 Enterprise Edition and Exchange Server 5.5 Enterprise Edition.
- Don't put a clustered server into production until you know exactly what to expect from it during operation.

You cannot upgrade an existing Exchange server into a cluster. Though there is a way to move the databases onto a newly installed cluster server, I recommend installing a new cluster server and moving all the mailboxes to the new machine.

Before you deploy clusters in your environment, you should have tested your new hardware thoroughly. The cluster-testing phase provides you with an excellent opportunity for you to play with the cluster, testing failover and learning more about what to expect once you put it into operation.

Exchange Services That Support Clustering   Microsoft Clustering is a new technology and is only supported for certain Exchange services. These services are:

- System Attendant
- Directory service
- Information store
- Message Transfer agent
- Internet Mail Service

Automatic failover for the Internet News Service, Microsoft Mail connector, Lotus cc:Mail connector, Lotus Notes connector, IBM PROFS connector, SNADS, and the Key Management Server services are not supported; in many cases, however, you can configure these services and manually restart them on the secondary cluster node.

> **NOTE**   Tony Redmond (from Compaq in Dublin, Ireland) is one of the best-known people in the Exchange community. He has a very good discussion of clustering in his book *Microsoft Exchange Server 5.5 Planning, Design, and Implementation* (Digital Press, 1998).

Build a Test Lab

I strongly recommend having an extra server standing by in case one of your production servers fails. This server's hardware should be identical to your production servers'. This way, bringing any failed server up can be as simple as moving the disks from a server that may have failed over to the standby server and powering the system back up.

Some of the most successful Exchange administrators I know have taken their extra server and built a test lab, often with a few additional servers and workstations. They use this test lab to test new service packs, handle mailbox restoration (in case of deletion), and practice disaster recovery.

An Overview of the LoadSim Utility

Microsoft offers a utility called LoadSim that you can download from `www.microsoft.com/exchange`. (Microsoft does not support this utility.) This utility simulates user load on an Exchange server by actually generating e-mail messages, calendar access, and public folder access. You control the number of users, the type of user (light, medium, or heavy), and the length of the test.

During the test, LoadSim records average response times. You then use a utility called LSLOG to report on the average response times for various types of activities. The combination of LoadSim and LSLOG lets you determine how a particular server platform will behave under various loads.

Though not the intended function of LoadSim, my favorite use of this utility is to generate large databases so that I can test activities such as backup, restore, and disaster recovery. In a few hours time, I can create a 2GB private information store.

I also use this utility to test upgrades and service packs on my test lab server prior to deploying the server into production. I will set up an Exchange server, run LoadSim to generate some activity, and then apply the service pack or hot fix. Then I will run LoadSim again for several hours (or days). This method is not guaranteed to find obscure bugs in service packs or hot fixes, but it certainly can help pinpoint any show-stopping bugs that might be specific to my environment.

NOTE From January to April of 1998, *Windows NT Magazine* published a series of articles on the LoadSim utility. These articles were all titled "Understanding and Using LoadSim" and are available on the *Windows NT Magazine* Web site at www.winntmag.com.

Planning Exchange Operations

As system administrators and engineers, our first responsibility is to keep our systems up and running. Therefore, a solid plan for operations should be in place and clearly defined expectations should be published. Some of the many items to consider include:

- Plan a maintenance window so that the user community will know exactly when they can expect the system to be unavailable.

- Publish a Service Level Agreement (SLA) to clearly outline the type of performance and response the user community can expect from both the messaging system and the support organization.

- As part of the SLA, end users should be required to sign an Acceptable Use Agreement that details what is considered acceptable use of the company's computers and what is not.

- Technical support and help desk responsibilities should be clearly outlined so that no one steps on another person's toes and to make sure that everyone understands who is responsible for what.

Publish a Maintenance Window

Even if you don't believe you are going to need it, publish a weekly or biweekly *maintenance window*. This is a time each week or month that your user community should expect to have limited networking services (or possibly no network services at all). This will provide you with an opportunity to perform any sort of scheduled maintenance.

Not everyone can publish a time that her system can be down. Many organizations expect the system to be available all the time. As you will see in Chapter 6, there are few operations tasks that truly require that the server be taken completely offline.

How long should your maintenance period be? I would ask for two separate types. Every night, say from 11:30 until midnight, I would ask for 30 minutes that I could use for a reboot or other quick maintenance. I would use this time interval only if necessary.

For the second period, I recommend a weekly maintenance window long enough to allow for an offline defragmentation of the private information store (or the public information store, whichever is larger). I don't do this every week, but I would like the option of having that much time.

Did your request for a maintenance window get turned down? If you can't get a nightly or weekly slot, then at the very least publish one six-hour window each month (such as the second Saturday night of each month) that will enable you to take your servers offline. I try to avoid the very first and last of any month due to deadlines and activities that tend to come at the end and beginning of each month, such as sales closures, accounting end-of-month processes, and so on.

NOTE Are you curious about what you may be required to do during these maintenance windows? Chapter 6 has recommendations for daily, weekly, and periodic maintenance activities.

Exchange@Work: Define Your Maintenance Windows Early in the Deployment

On a site I worked on a few years ago, we made a fatal mistake by not publishing a maintenance window as the LAN was being rolled out. The users were already conditioned to expect that the computer system would be unavailable; our three minicomputers were unavailable from 9:00 P.M. until 6:00 A.M. every day of the week.

> **Exchange@Work: Define Your Maintenance Windows Early in the Deployment** *(continued)*
>
> At first, the LAN did not need a maintenance schedule, so we never requested one. Yet over time, little tasks started popping up that needed to be done on a monthly or even weekly basis—minor software upgrades, database re-indexing and defragmentation, printer driver updates, and so on. However, our user community had gotten used to the LAN servers being available 24 hours a day, 7 days a week. Even at midnight, there would always be a few people working. We asked for a maintenance window during which we could perform these tasks, and the request had to go all the way to the CEO. Department managers raised a little holy heck when we tried to shut the system down. Eventually, we got our maintenance window; it was from midnight Saturday night until 6:00 A.M. on Sunday morning. We would start announcing the shutdown to our users at 11:30 P.M. on Saturday, and the help desk lines would inevitably light up with a couple of users who "had to keep working."
>
> In our case, the tail was wagging the dog. If we had merely defined a schedule when the system was deployed a year before, we probably could have gotten away with Saturday mornings from 8:00 A.M. until noon, or some other more reasonable schedule. But our users got used to working on the system whenever they wanted to, so we were reactive rather than proactive.

Publishing a Service Level Agreement (SLA)

Upper-level management wants to see better returns on their investments in Information Services. Driven by poor end-user support and frequent system failures, end-user communities are asking for (okay, demanding) guarantees that the system will be available when they need it. Information Services departments need a mechanism to set expectations. To that end, *Service Level Agreements (SLAs)* are becoming more and more important and common in today's corporate and government world.

An SLA is a document detailing a level of service that the end users can expect from their computer system. Further, SLAs demonstrate to management a strong commitment on the part of IS team to deliver quality service. Finally, the SLA gives the IS team certain levels of service to live up to.

What should your SLA contain? Here are a few suggestions:

- A statement of expected up time, system availability, and maintenance windows.

- Expected system response times and projected message delivery times within the site and throughout the organization.
- Help desk availability and expected responses to basic questions as well as problems that affect usage.
- Promise and availability of advanced training.
- Planned future functionality and expected deployment dates.
- Promise to provide a location for users and managers to review system statistics, such as a Web site or a public folder. These statistics could include average local and remote delivery times, volume of messages processed per month, average number of users supported each day, and storage utilized.

Naturally, if I were writing an SLA, I would put a few clauses in it to make sure that no one holds me to a certain level of service if the local volcano is erupting or an earthquake has destroyed the computer room. However, this document is an excellent and extremely important way to set reasonable expectations.

NOTE   Keep in mind that the SLA is an agreement of realistic goals between the IS support organization and the user community. Compromise will always be necessary.

Acceptable Use Policies

Running parallel with creating an SLA to set expectations of what the IS team will provide, organizations should also have a policy of acceptable use that outlines the limits of the e-mail system's usage. There are many boilerplate agreements available today, but I would make sure that anything my user community agrees to includes these elements:

- Users must understand that all messages are subject to monitoring and auditing by the proper authority. Management can request the content of any mailbox at any time. The rule of thumb I suggest to my users is, "Don't put it in an e-mail if you would mind your boss reading it."
- Detail policies regarding acceptable language usage in electronic communication of any kind. Users should be cautioned not to use profanity or anything that would suggest sexual harassment. Naughty graphics, jokes, and other material of a questionable nature should be considered unacceptable.
- Different companies have varying views on personal e-mail. My own view is that as long as the e-mail system is not abused, a few personal e-mail messages per day are acceptable.
- Passwords, private keys, or access devices should never be shared or written down.

- Computers and terminals must never be left unattended without first locking down the computer or logging out.

- Misuse of passwords, browsing directories or public folders, or other activity not related to a user's job is grounds for termination.

- Users must understand that any commercial activity other than that related to the operation of the company paying for the e-mail system is prohibited.

Users must understand that violation of any of these policies is grounds for termination. Prior to asking employees to sign or to agree to anything, the company lawyer and/or human resources specialist should review and approve the acceptable use policies.

TIP   Attorney Michael R. Overly has written a book called *E-Policy: How to Develop Computer, E-mail, and Internet Guidelines to Protect Your Company and Its Assets* (Amacom, 1998). This guide is a must for anyone developing an acceptable use policy for his or her messaging system.

Assigning Administrative and Technical Support Responsibilities

Who is responsible for what? Regardless of the size of your Exchange organization, responsibilities need to be clearly defined. Larger organizations can break up administrative levels into a couple of categories; smaller organizations may have one person who handles all of these tasks.

Front line support or help desk support handles Outlook user support, debugging connectivity, public folder issues, and profile problems. These people may also be given permission to update recipient attributes such as phone numbers, addresses, and so on.

Recipient administrator is responsible for creating new mailboxes, custom recipients, and distribution lists. This person may also be responsible for adding Windows NT accounts.

Server administrator is responsible for tape backups, ongoing maintenance, reviewing event and security logs, looking for stuck queues, checking performance data, and handling escalated tech support calls. This person should not be in direct contact with the user community but rather work with the help desk or recipient administrator.

Exchange security manager is responsible for managing permissions on objects (such as mailboxes) in the Exchange directory. In an environment where Exchange Advanced Security is in use, this manager would also be responsible for handing out public and private key pairs. Only a few people within the organization should have this level of access.

Exchange architect is responsible for the big picture of Exchange organization, including server design, connectivity, analyzing performance data, and handling technical support incidents that have been escalated from the server administrator. In some organizations, this person may actually work for the systems integrator or vendor.

Exchange@Work: Maintaining a Stable System

One of my big beefs with the microcomputer world is our relative nonchalance with our server hardware and software. I am not picking on anyone except myself, because I am as guilty of this as anyone else.

The original platform that I worked on (in the early 1980s) was the DEC VAX/VMS. (When I mention VMS, everyone has to get up, bow to the west, and chant thrice.) Back then, we would never dream of loading a new device driver during the business day. Operating system upgrades and patches were scheduled weeks in advance and only done with a DEC employee on site. Software upgrades were only done with the software vendor on site or, at the very least, on the phone. And we did not experiment with new software no matter how cool it sounded.

Yet I constantly find myself tempted to load unnecessary software onto production Windows NT servers. If you have the same urges, you should stifle them! Experimenting with a production system is a recipe for disaster.

Here are a few tips to help you make sure you run without unexpected incidents:

- Don't apply Windows NT or Exchange service packs and hot fixes unless you know for certain that they fix problems you are having or that they are going to add functionality that you need immediately.

- Nothing should occur on your production servers without first being scheduled and tested in a lab environment.

- Do not add new functionality to your servers without first testing it; this includes virus protection, message scanning, fax servers, and any other third-party solutions.

- Deciding on what functionality and interoperability levels to provide during and after migration
- Getting your users adequately trained to use Exchange and Outlook
- Using Exchange as a messaging hub to connect several different systems
- Addressing interoperability issues if you are going to be handling the migration in phases rather than all at once
- Using migration tools such as the Migration Wizard to convert user's messages from their old system to Exchange

---

NOTE In Chapter 1, I talked about collecting documentation relating to your legacy mail system. That documentation will be useful when we start talking about migration.

Migration—The Big Picture

Migrating a messaging system is at least as complicated as migrating your operating system. There are many issues to consider, including:

- Selling the system to the executive and operations folks
- Launching a pilot project and getting users involved
- Deciding what to migrate and what to leave in place
- Getting users adequately trained to use the new system

NOTE In this chapter as well as in others, I often refer to the system that you are migrating *from* as the *legacy system*. I am not insinuating that new versions of Novell GroupWise, Lotus cc:Mail, Lotus Notes, or other modern mail systems are legacy systems. I apologize ahead of time to my friends in those camps if they are offended. <grin>

Gaining User Support

Before starting the implementation phase of a new Exchange migration, you need the complete support of your management. In a larger organization, you should have full support from top-level management. Implementing a messaging system such as Exchange is a big enough decision that it warrants getting the CEO to understand and approve the project.

Just as important as getting management approval is generating a certain level of excitement within your user community. Prior to migrating the first mailbox, your users should understand what is about to happen and what the benefits of the migration actually are. I have worked on too many migrations where I encountered resistance from end users at every step of the project. Migrations do not have to generate animosity and resentment from the user community; this may come as a minor surprise to some IS veterans. Arriving at work to find a mob of angry end users burning you in effigy in the parking lot is not a great way to start a migration.

Exchange@Work: Using Good Marketing Techniques to Win User Support

Company LMN completed their Exchange design, validated their design in the test lab, set up solid operational procedures, agreed upon organization-wide standards, and had a solid migration plan in place. The only problem was that the user community was not enthusiastic about the migration.

To gain user support, LMN decided to market the next Exchange system just as if they were marketing a new product. They created a logo for the project and hired a technical writer (rather than a system administrator) to create a Web site about Outlook and Exchange. This site also included valuable project information such as:

- New benefits that the users would realize immediately upon moving to Exchange and Outlook. These included Internet mail capabilities, group scheduling, a company-wide phone/address directory, the ability to read their e-mail from home using a Web browser, and the ability to recover deleted messages; these were all hot buttons with this user community. This list was important to the user community—they needed to see distinct benefits!

- Future capabilities that IS was planning to introduce once everyone had migrated to Exchange and Outlook.

- Implementation and training schedules, including which departments were going to be migrated.

- Internal documentation on how to use Outlook and new features.

- Project contact and help desk information.

- Frequently asked questions and answers.

- Current project status information.

- A Service Level Agreement (SLA) detailing expected system availability.

Exchange@Work: Using Good Marketing Techniques to Win User Support *(continued)*

This project's Web site helped generate excitement and anticipation for the coming migration. No longer were the users going to "have to learn something new"; now they were getting new benefits. The SLA was important because it both set expectations of the user community and gave the system administrators a level of service to live up to.

Getting Users Involved in the Pilot Project

Regardless of how much you test in the lab, I promise that a pilot project is going to coax bugs and problems out of the woodwork that you never knew existed. Everyone has their own views on setting up a pilot system, as do I. Since company and environment is unique, I would say to take all my recommendations in this section with a grain of salt. There are, however, three important points to apply to *all* pilot systems:

- Listen carefully to the feedback from your pilot users—not only what went wrong, but also what went well and what they liked. This feedback should be a written, formatted critique with a place for pilot users to enter their own comments. Plan to sit down and talk with as many of these users as possible about their remarks.

- Don't be afraid to make major design changes if you find things that are wrong. It is a pilot system, not the final product.

- Review your pilot project findings with the rest of the IS team as well as with your supporters in the management food chain.

A critical part of any pilot project is getting key individuals involved. So who should be included as part of the pilot project? One of my clients suggested taking volunteers and then rejecting all of those who offer to help. Part of me really likes this idea based on volunteers I've worked with in the past. Pilot project volunteers generally have a strong interest in the new system and want their voices heard, and they can often overshadow critical feedback from other pilot users. Still, the enthusiasm generated by volunteers is harder to muster from drafted participants.

Deployment of the pilot system gives you an opportunity to verify your design and look for potential pitfalls. During the early stages of a pilot, you may discover that the entire design needs to be re-thought. Smaller numbers of people participating in a pilot system are much easier to steer in a new direction. This is why I like to include a few people from a cross section of the organization. I may even take an entire department, but I prefer to keep the number of participants down to 25 or 30.

In addition to a sample of users, the entire help desk team should be in on the pilot system once it is up and running. This is primarily because they are going to need as much experience as possible using and supporting Outlook and Exchange Server.

Functionality to Provide during Migration

What functionality does your current messaging system provide? Basic messaging? Internet mail? Personal calendars and group scheduling? Shared folders or bulletin boards? Desktop faxing integrated with your legacy e-mail system? Workflow? Forms routing?

During migration and immediately afterward, your goal should be to provide functionality only equivalent to your current system. Exchange has the capability to provide much more than basic messaging functionality, so there naturally is the temptation to unleash an avalanche of new features on your users the instant they have Outlook on their desktops. However, introducing users to many new features that they may not have had previously, such as public folders and workflow applications, in addition to the features they may have to learn just to do their jobs, will often result in very frustrated users. Therefore, features that your users do not currently have should be introduced over time once you have gotten your entire organization migrated off the legacy messaging system.

> **NOTE** If you are moving from a legacy messaging system that has limited functionality, you will probably not hear too many users whining, "But the old system did this!" However, if you are moving from a system such as Lotus Notes or Novell GroupWise, you have to make sure you are providing equivalent functionality. See "Adequate User Training" later in this chapter for more on helping your users through the transition.

While Exchange can provide interoperability for some basic functions, keep in mind that many advanced messaging functions will not be interoperable between Exchange and your legacy system. During the migration, you will either have to find alternatives or stop offering those services.

What Do You Want to Migrate?

One of the first things you need to decide is what you are going to migrate. Though it would be ideal to migrate nothing, most of the time you will not be given the luxury of doing so. For the majority of migrations I have worked on, the user community insists on migrating at least part of their old mail.

Some of the different types of items you may have to include in your migration include:

- Mail messages
- Calendar items
- Contact lists and personal address books
- Shared message data such as from bulletin boards or shared folders; any type of data that might have to be moved to a public folder

For example, suppose you are migrating from Microsoft Mail and Microsoft Schedule+ to Outlook 98. You have the option of migrating not only the existing e-mail, but also calendar and contact information. Further, the Migration Wizard, which is discussed later in this chapter, allows you to migrate mail from a specific date range.

Another option available for many administrators is to migrate only key mailboxes, such as those of managers and executives. If you are migrating all of the organization's mailboxes, stress the importance of migrating only essential information, and urge the users to clean their mailboxes.

TIP Exceptions will drive you crazy! If you can get away with it, migration should be an all-or-nothing circumstance.

Leaving the Legacy System in Place

You may be faced with the unpleasant task of leaving your legacy messaging system in place even after you have migrated all users to Exchange. This may become necessary in an environment where you choose not to migrate all the messages, or where the legacy system you are replacing permits message archives (such as cc:Mail or GroupWise). For instance, the folks in management decide that all users should be able to access their old mail, but they don't want to give you the disk space to migrate it over. Some of the factors that may make you avoid migrating existing data to Exchange include:

- The amount of time that it will take to migrate legacy data. In some organizations, users may have been using their legacy system for more than six or eight years! That is a lot of accumulated data.
- The programs necessary for migrating data may not be readily available or may be too costly.
- The new Exchange system may not have the disk space required to store years of converted legacy data.
- For various other reasons, the legacy system must remain in operation even after the messaging users have been moved off of it.

Avoid leaving the legacy system in place if you possibly can. If you do, you will have to maintain the old messaging system as well as Exchange or, at the very least, the old client software will have to be preserved so the users can retrieve mail from their archives.

TIP   If the legacy system must remain in place, look for a way to disable the user's ability to send messages with it. Otherwise, they may revert back to old habits, and messages may be delivered to a user's old mailbox and remain there, unread, for a long time.

WARNING   Care should be taken during the migration and coexistence phase to ensure that SMTP addresses do not change.

Address Books

Many users want to use their personal address books for entries that can also be found in the global address list. I saw this just recently in a large Microsoft Mail installation. Users were selecting addresses that they commonly used in the GAL and were copying them to their personal address books. Once the migration began, these personal address book entries were breaking because the addresses were Microsoft Mail addresses.

Users should be encouraged to use the global address list whenever possible and, for entries that they feel they need in a personal address book, to use the SMTP address of the user instead. Exchange can function quite effectively as a message routing hub.

24seven Usability: Migrating Nothing?!

I had a particular set of students through several MCSE courses, including all the Exchange training that Microsoft offers. We discussed migration strategies at great length during and after class. In the end, they decided that migrating nearly 4000 mailboxes was going to be too much of a strain on their small IS staff (nine people). They approached their boss with the pros and cons of migration and interoperability, along with the estimated costs to support it. The boss said "Fine, we won't migrate anything. We will leave the legacy system up for a while after migration so that users can read their old messages, but we will provide no migration of messages."

So they are migrating nothing and providing interoperability only via SMTP. I hope they realize that they are my new heroes. I admire their decision; migrating nothing was a very unpopular idea with their user community, but the migration went much more quickly and smoothly since there was no legacy data to convert to Exchange. This was a tough decision, but it was necessary in order for them to get their users moved over in a timely fashion with the resources they had been given.

Adequate User Training

An area that is often overlooked during deployment of a new system is user training. When you are a technical person managing the Exchange deployment, it is easy to rationalize that your end-user community can "figure things out." This is a bad assumption. My advice is to plan for two phases of training.

The first run of training should address equivalent functionality issues. Show the users how to use Outlook and Exchange to get the identical functionality that they had previously. Your user community is going to have enough worries adapting to a new software product; teach them just what they need to know to do exactly what they were doing with their old system. Many companies also provide "floor support" for their users immediately after training. This is a trainer or person who is already comfortable with the new system. Throughout the workday, the floor support person checks with the users who have just started using the new system to see if they have questions or need assistance.

Once your user community has become accustomed to the new system and to the basic features of Outlook, the next phase of training should introduce them to features they may not have had previously, such as group scheduling, rules, journaling, and task assignment. Additional phases of training can introduce new features such as using forms and public folders.

Exchange@Work: A Training Plan

What is one great way to reduce your help desk costs? Turn your end users into power users! Company GHI migrated a 2,400-node network from Lotus cc:Mail to Exchange. Prior to migration, the cc:Mail users had no features such as calendaring or group scheduling available to them.

The first phase of user training introduced the basic abilities of Outlook. The three-hour mandatory training session covered:

- The acceptable use policy for using the system, keeping mailboxes cleaned up, password and confidentiality issues, and help desk procedures. Also discussed were the introductory training materials, which included a short "How to..." guide and frequently asked questions section.

- Message formatting, attachments, and other features of an Outlook message such as delivery and notification receipts.

Exchange@Work: A Training Plan *(continued)*

- How to send, receive, reply to, and forward e-mail messages using Outlook; how to manage the Inbox and Sent Items folders; and how to create subfolders to better organize messages. Searching features and views were also introduced.

- Contact and Calendar folders (with the promise to users of future Calendar training).

- Exchange's public folders feature versus cc:Mail bulletin boards. Three public folders were discussed: a system announcements public folder, a Microsoft Office tips and questions public folder, and a classified ads public folder. (This last folder was specifically designed to stimulate people's interest in public folders.)

Once all users had been migrated and trained on basic functionality, GHI held another two-hour mandatory training session for all users that included:

- Calendaring and group scheduling

- Scheduling shared resources such as conference rooms, laptops, and so on

- Creating a personal folder (PST file) and archiving messages to it

- A vacation/time-off request form

- A new public folder application, departmental In/Out boards

After the system had been in production for nearly nine months and users had been given time to get very comfortable with the basic features of Outlook, weekly training sessions were offered. These "no nonsense" sessions covered one particular topic in detail. The sessions were offered five times during a week (at lunchtime), and the users were encouraged to bring their own lunch (they were called "Brown Bag" sessions). Though this got off to a slow start, the Brown Bag sessions became very popular and were often standing-room only. These one-hour meetings included topics such as:

- The Rules Wizard and the Inbox Assistant

- The Outlook Journal feature

- Accessing other user's mailboxes (calendars, contacts, and so on) or giving other users access to a user's mailbox

Exchange@Work: A Training Plan *(continued)*

- Outlook usage for remote or home users

- Outlook refresher courses

Well, you get the idea. GHI had implemented this particular strategy when converting from WordPerfect to Word with excellent results, and they continue to offer Brown Bag sessions for Word, Excel, and Outlook. This is a great example of a company doing whatever it takes to turn their user community into power users. This company realizes that in the long run, better-educated users will reduce the total amount of IS support they'll require.

Messaging Champions

In any department or workgroup, a few users inevitably arise from the migration ashes as champions of the new technology. Early on, these folks see the benefits of the Exchange and Outlook and become evangelists for your cause. You should identify these people and encourage them. Often, these users will end up being your "on-the-spot help desk."

Getting the Training Done

A lot of companies today have an in-house training staff. If this is the case with your organization, make sure that your in-house trainers are brought into the Exchange design process early. The trainers should have been using the server and client features long before they start training the individual user community.

If your in-house trainers are not ready to teach your users to use Outlook and Exchange, or if you simply don't have in-house trainers, don't ignore the critical issue of getting your users trained. Contact outside training companies that can provide you with the type of education that you require for your user community.

> *TIP*   If you decide to contract an outside organization, carefully select both the company and the trainer(s) who will be providing your client training. The trainers should understand the client (such as Outlook) as well as Exchange Server. If possible, look for a training company that has experience with your legacy system.

Once you have selected your training company, ask if you can work with the same trainers throughout your training process so you'll have an opportunity to familiarize them with your existing system and procedures. The more comfortable the third-party trainers are with your organization, the better training your users will receive.

Other Training Topics

What should be covered in training? Using the messaging system is the obvious answer, but what else? What can you do in end-user training that will help keep your Exchange system healthy? I am betting that there is a long hit list of things you wish your users knew, and many of those things are not technical. In addition to the obvious, some things that I would make sure to cover during training are:

- Showing users how to use distribution lists (or to use the appropriate public folder rather than a distribution list).

- Instructing users to double-check their To, Cc, and Bcc fields to make sure that the message is addressed to the proper recipient(s).

- Teaching users the difference between the Reply button and the Reply To All button. Discourage the use of Reply To All. Users should ask themselves "Does everyone who originally received this message need to see my reply?" Inevitably, a few times a year, a user will hit the Reply To All function by accident and send a message like: "I'd like to make it to the company picnic, but I've got a proctology exam." For the accidental recipients of this message, I think this is too much information.

- Discouraging large message signatures and signatures with graphics in them.

- Showing users how to send shortcuts or links to large files rather than attaching the files directly to the message.

- Storing files in personal folders, archiving messages and other Outlook data to these files, and retrieving data from personal folders.

- Reviewing the acceptable use policy.

- Educating users about chain letters and urban legends so they will not be so quick to forward "Good Times" virus warnings, free money ads, and warnings of kidney theft rings.

- Teaching users to delete messages once they have acted on them and to keep their Sent Items folders clean.

Documentation for End Users

Another integral part of the training process is providing your user community with detailed documentation. This guarantees that you don't leave your users out in the cold during and after the migration. Their first line of defense will be your help desk, but you want to give your users something they can use *prior* to calling the help desk. This may be a simple handout or a complete manual. This documentation should include:

- "How to…" guides for common tasks

- Frequently asked questions (and answers)

- Common problems and how to resolve them
- Special notes on what you learned during the pilot project

For example, one small company that I worked with assembled this material in a very professional, bound booklet. Each user was given a copy of this booklet a few days prior to attending training. I personally like hard copies of my reference material, but a Web site or an Exchange public folder is also an excellent location for posting this material.

24seven Usability: Can You Just Give Me a Hint?

A particularly resourceful network administrator created one-page handouts describing how to do certain tasks in Outlook, Word, Excel, and so on. These handouts focused on a single hint or task, included a graphic or picture, and were never more than a single page.

She posted these in the employee kitchens, photocopy rooms, above fax machines—anyplace people would stop for a few minutes and might have idle time. I suspect she even tried posting these in the elevators and restrooms.

At first, the user community did not know quite what to think. However, the network administrator's writing style and humor, along with the concise nature of each page and the usefulness of the information proved quite effective. She recently created an internal Web site of her "greatest hits"; unfortunately, it is not accessible outside of her company.

Single-Phase versus Multi-Phase Migration

You have two options for migration: *single-phase* (also called *complete*) migration and *multi-phase* migration (which requires *coexistence* between the two messaging systems). A single-phase migration moves all mailboxes, calendar items, shared folder items, and so on in a very short amount of time, possibly in as little as one weekend. A multi-phase migration breaks the migration down by department, group, or office and migrates messaging data more slowly, possibly over months (or even years!).

My personal metric for deciding if I can adequately migrate an entire system at one time is the number of users. If the system supports more than 500 mailboxes, then I definitely do not want to migrate it all at once. Of course, this figure is going to vary dramatically based on the number of people who are available to work on the migration and the level of automation I can achieve when deploying clients. I personally would not want to tackle a one-weekend, single-phase migration with fewer than eight people by my side.

Depending on the amount of data that has to be converted and whether you have to visit every single workstation, an even larger migration team may be necessary.

Here are some factors that may make single-phase migration a better choice:

- You have adequate support to migrate your entire user community in a short period of time (for example, one weekend). Your help desk can handle the volume of calls after migration and you can quickly distribute the client software and make changes to the client computers.

- The user community can be trained to use the new system in a short period of time.

- The data can be moved quickly from the old system (or there is very little data to move).

- You have the hardware in place and ready to move over to immediately rather than using some of the hardware that is currently supporting the legacy system.

You should consider a multi-phase migration if any of these factors apply to you or your user community:

- There is a large end-user community (more than a few hundred people). (Migrating many hundreds of users simultaneously requires more support and training resources.)

- Your help desk and support staff are not up to speed on supporting Outlook and Exchange Server. (This factor alone might make me delay the migration and do an extended pilot project.)

- End users cannot be adequately trained to use Outlook and Exchange features in a short period of time.

- Your Exchange design depends on some of the hardware that is currently deployed and in use by the legacy mail system.

- For business or political reasons, not all departments can migrate simultaneously.

Coexistence Issues

If you cannot migrate everyone over during a single-phase migration, then issues surrounding a multi-phase migration and coexistence between two messaging systems are introduced. Here are some things to keep in mind when considering coexistence:

- Adequate connector bandwidth will have to be configured between the two systems. Many systems will only need a single connector to adequately transfer messages between two mail systems, but large systems may require more than one connector.

- Directory synchronization should be established in order to enable legacy-system users to send messages easily to those who have migrated to Exchange, and vice versa.

- Different messaging system clients offer differing levels of features and functions. Features such as read receipts, delivery receipts, rich text formatting, embedded URLs, shortcuts, and attachments may differ between systems, and thus you may lose some functionality between the two systems.

- Forms between the two systems will probably not be compatible. If forms are necessary, you should consider moving forms to the Web or discontinuing their use during migration.

- Groups of users who often send messages to one another should be migrated at the same time.

- The maximum size of a message that can cross between the two systems should be restricted, and be sure to select fast computers to run the gateway programs.

- Other messaging systems have functionality similar to public folders, but this functionality will be lost during migration, because the connectors do not support replicating data between Exchange public folders and other messaging systems.

TIP When you set up directory synchronization between the legacy mail system and Exchange, consider creating a recipient container to hold the replicated custom recipients. This will help keep the container that holds mailbox recipients a little cleaner and more orderly. See Chapter 2 for more information.

Distribution Lists

If your company makes heavy use of distribution lists, then you are up for some challenges when you start the migration to Exchange Server. During the migration phase, the location of users is going to be changing often. One week, a group of users may still be located on Microsoft Mail, and the next week they may be located on Exchange Server. Therefore, the distribution lists will have to be updated to reflect these changes. Just keeping two separate systems' distribution lists synchronized can become a pretty major challenge, but there are several ways to help you tackle the distribution list dilemma:

- Create new distribution lists on Exchange and continue to maintain the legacy distribution lists. Users will need to select both distribution lists when addressing messages to users on Exchange and on the legacy system.

- Similar to maintaining separate distribution lists, you can set up a forwarding scheme whereby a distribution list on one system contains (as a member) the corresponding distribution list on the other system. This simply prevents users from having to select both distribution lists to send to both systems.

- Create distribution lists on Exchange Server and delete the legacy system distribution lists. Manage the distribution lists from Exchange Administrator; the distribution list will contain both mailboxes and custom recipients. This will require that every time you migrate a new set of mailboxes, you make sure the new mailboxes are members of the appropriate distribution lists. This strategy also depends on whether or not the directory synchronization process will coordinate Exchange distribution lists with the legacy system.

- Stop using distribution lists until the migration is complete. If your user community is not in love with distribution lists and the migration time is short, then this might be acceptable. It is certainly the easiest option for the administrators.

- Replace distribution lists with public folders. This is really a long-term solution, but migration might be the time to implement it. Create public folders to suit your various distribution list needs, and give the appropriate groups permissions to these folders. Legacy system users can either browse these lists through Outlook Web Access, or you can set up a rule to forward messages posted to these public folders to the legacy system distribution lists.

Using Exchange as a Smart Relay or Forwarding Host

During (or even after) a migration, you may need to use Exchange Server as a messaging hub to relay mail messages from one system to another. In the SMTP world, a *smart relay host* accepts messages from other systems. It then forwards those messages on to the appropriate system based on a knowledge of where a mailbox is really located. In Unix-based SMTP systems, this is normally handled by alias and/or forward files.

The Exchange message transfer agent (MTA) and connectors were designed with this functionality (and more) in mind. Exchange can act as a smart relay host for any mail system for which there is an Exchange connector. The secret of this is the proxy addresses found in a mailbox or on the custom recipient's E-Mail Addresses tab.

When messages are delivered via an Exchange connector, the connector checks with the directory service to see what address the message should be delivered to. In Figure 3.1, you see the E-Mail Addresses tab for custom recipient Gerald Nakata. A quick check on the General tab will tell you that the recipient's e-mail address is a Microsoft Mail address (SOMORITA/MSPO1/GNakata).

Preparing for Exchange

PART 1

Migration Wizard Source Extractors *(continued)*

Additional migration tools are available from Microsoft on the Exchange Server CD-ROM, the BackOffice Resource Kit, Exchange Service Pack 2, and the Microsoft Web site (http://www.microsoft.com/exchange). These include tools for migrating from Verimation Memo MVS, Digital ALL-IN-1, IBM Professional Office System (PROFS)/OfficeVision, AT&T Mail, Unix Mail, GroupWise 5.*x*, and Microsoft Mail for AppleTalk Networks.

Still more tools are available for migrating Lotus cc:Mail distribution lists, Lotus Notes mail database files, and cc:Mail archive files. These are available from Microsoft's Web site or as part of Exchange Server 5.5 Service Pack 2.

The Migration Wizard Files

When you run the Migration Wizard, you are prompted to choose whether the wizard should perform a one-step or a two-step migration (see Figure 3.2). The one-step migration performs all the migrations during a single pass. The two-step migration extracts the data to files where it can be imported into Exchange Server by the Migration Wizard at a later time. If you select the two-step migration, editable migration files are created.

Figure 3.2   This screen allows you to select a one-step or a two-step migration. The two-step process creates migration files.

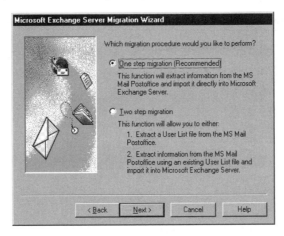

When the Migration Wizard runs its source extractors, it moves data out of the legacy system. The data are then put into text files, which can be manipulated to control the amount and appearance of data that is imported into Exchange. Three types of files are created:

Packing list file contains the code page information as well as a list of the primary and secondary filenames used during this particular session of the Migration Wizard. The code page suggested values are 850 or 1252 but can vary based on your system and the languages you are supporting. This file has an extension of .PKL.

Primary intermediate file is a comma-separated value file broken up into one or more sections. These sections outline the changes that will be made to the directory (mailbox information), mail message headers, and personal address book information; they include directory data, personal address book data, mail message data, public folder data, and schedule data. You would edit this file to make changes in the appearance of data that are imported into Exchange. The primary intermediate file also has pointers to secondary intermediate files. These primary intermediate files have an extension of .PRI.

Secondary intermediate file contains the actual message bodies and attachments. Though these files are text files, you should not edit them because you can easily break the import process. The secondary intermediate files have an extension of .SEC.

NOTE All three of these text files are in the same format, regardless of the source e-mail system.

Microsoft Mail and the Migration Wizard

The Migration Wizard creates only one file when extracting data from a Microsoft Mail post office. This file is a user list file that contains information about mailboxes found on Microsoft Mail. Once the file is created, a second pass by the wizard migrates the data from the Microsoft Mail post office to Exchange. The packing list, primary intermediate, and secondary intermediate migration files are created but are not accessible for editing.

TIP During the first pass by the wizard, you can edit the user list file and add additional fields to suit your needs during the migration to Exchange. Since Microsoft Mail did not include a lot of user information, this might include adding the Given-Name, Surname, and Assoc-NT-Account (if the Windows NT account name is different than the mailbox name) fields.

Exchange Migration

Organization MNO's Asia regional office is part of a larger, worldwide organization. But for years, MNO had no consistent international e-mail platform; each region had complete autonomy to choose and support its own e-mail and network operating system. Connectivity between the regional offices was accomplished via SMTP gateways and the Internet.

In mid 1998, the Asia region migrated to GroupWise 5.1 from WordPerfect Office Mail. Shortly afterward, the edict came down from above: The entire organization will upgrade to Exchange Server by July of 1999. There were a number of reasons behind this decision:

- The lack of a consistent and global e-mail and phone directory.

- The need for year 2000 compliance for all messaging systems.

- Incorporation of a new global messaging application that required much higher security than their current and diverse messaging systems could provide.

Existing System

MNO supported nearly 3,900 GroupWise users across 27 separate GroupWise post offices located on five NetWare 4.11 servers. Each of the GroupWise post office servers hosted approximately 800 user mailboxes and contained five to six departments that made up a major division within the region. In addition, they operated a NetWare 4.11 server that hosted their GroupWise primary domain and a NetWare 4.11 server that hosted both the GroupWise SMTP and

Async gateways. The individual post offices ranged from as few as 50 mailboxes to as many as 500, but the average number of mailboxes was around 200. Of the 3,900 users, over 500 were on a dial-in connection to the GroupWise Async gateway to send and retrieve mail.

Processes were put in place so that anything older than 30 days (or seven days if the item was in the Trash folder) was deleted. Most users were given GroupWise archive files so that they could archive older messages. Users could not transmit messages larger than 2MB.

Existing Management Architecture

The Information Systems group at MNO Asia was particularly proud of their management structure. The regional office had a small group of system administrators (SAs) who were responsible for all servers, connectivity, and the NDS tree. Each of the company's five divisions had a small group of administrators who worked within and for that division; these were the group system administrators (GSAs). Each department also had one or two people designated as administrators for the particular department; these were the department system administrators (DSAs).

Each department's NetWare NDS (Novell Directory Services) tree was structured so that the GSAs and the DSAs only had responsibility for the user accounts and GroupWise mailboxes within their designated area. The DSAs also had responsibility for tasks within their department such as management of computer hardware and software support. Experience had shown MNO Asia that this design provided the greatest flexibility and highest level of customer service.

Problems Presented during the Migration Planning

Several large problems presented themselves when the migration planning process began.

- The MNO corporate office provided little to no guidance early on in the project. All regioncs experienced some false starts, a few re-installations, and a profound lack of standardization.

- One decision made early on was that each region would become a single Exchange site. The Asia regional office had an elegant user/mailbox management structure that was based on NetWare NDS. The prospect of losing their administrative structure did not please the regional IS people. Since Windows NT 4 and Exchange 5.5 do not lend themselves well to compartmentalizing management of departments, MNO Asia was going to have to give up their management structure.

- Due to corporate standards, mailbox SMTP addresses were going to have to change. MNO Asia's old e-mail address was MNOAsia.com, and the new e-mail address for the entire organization was simply MNO.com. The headquarters office maintained the inbound SMTP gateways, and each region that was directly connected to the Internet maintained an outgoing SMTP gateway.

- The transition plan must prevent any loss of messages during the migration. Management wanted to make sure that messages were directed to the correct mailbox whether the user had been migrated yet or not.

- Because the administration of users and mailboxes had become so decentralized, the IS department did not have the manpower to easily convert and support all 3,900 users.

- Due to the very tight timeframe for the migration, many users were going to have to be migrated in a short period of time.

- For business reasons, the department managers required the ability to control user account activation. This feature was easily provided by NetWare NDS and the fact that each department had a local administrator.

- Users were going to want to keep the data they had stored in their GroupWise archives.

- Both Novell and Microsoft have Exchange-to-GroupWise connectors, and both were found to be unreliable with regard to directory replication. Rather than pursuing a fix for the problem, the company made a decision to move forward and synchronize the directories manually.

Operating System Administration Changes

The MNO headquarters office placed no restrictions on the network operating system, but they did insinuate that they

24seven **CASE STUDY**

would like everyone to migrate to Windows NT in the future. The prospect of moving entirely to Windows NT domains was a daunting task. It would require a much more centralized management model and much retraining. This would also mean that many of their GSAs and DSAs would probably not be given administrator or account operator permissions in their respective domains. The department managers found the prospect of losing their departmental administrators unacceptable. Further, the main IS group at MNO Asia did not have the resources to centrally manage the entire region without hiring several new administrators.

Since the MNO Asia office was already tied to Novell NetWare, they researched a product from Novell called NDS for NT that would allow all administration of the Windows NT domain to occur through the already familiar NetWare administrator (NWADMIN) program. The NDS for NT product also included an additional feature that allowed Exchange mailboxes to be created through NWADMIN rather than using Exchange Administrator.

Since administration was quite distributed throughout fairly autonomous departments, the MNO Asia regional IS group dreaded the prospect of training nearly 65 GSAs and DSAs to manage not only Windows NT but also Exchange mailboxes. NDS for Windows NT allowed the GSAs and DSAs to continue using the familiar NWADMIN management interface; they only had to be trained on the component

that created and managed Exchange mailboxes. The GSAs and DSAs did not need the Exchange Administrator program.

Two Windows NT servers were installed as domain controllers; one was the Primary Domain Controller and the other was the Backup Domain Controller. Exchange Server was installed on Windows NT member servers.

MNO Asia Exchange Site Design

MNO Asia made plans for six Exchange servers. The first five were to hold the same mailboxes that their original NetWare counterparts were storing. The sixth server was designated as the site's bridgehead server; it had the IMS and the directory replication connector installed on it.

Connectivity to the MNO headquarters office was still accomplished via the Internet, but it used the IMS as a messaging connector. The connection to the headquarters office was made using Windows NT challenge/response and encryption (a feature of the IMS) so that all intra-company traffic would be encrypted.

The IMS on the bridgehead server would also host inbound mail for the original MNOAsia.com Internet domain and send outgoing mail directly to the Internet. Servers at the headquarters would accept all incoming mail for the new MNO.com domain. All mailboxes in the MNO Asia site would need a secondary proxy address added to them so that they could accept messages for both the user's SMTP addresses, such as BenjaminC@MNOAsia.com and BenjaminC@MNO.com. (This is important so that the user will not miss any messages once the MNOAsia.com Internet domain is redirected to MNO Asia's Exchange IMS.)

Because the GroupWise remote users were accessing the system remotely through the GroupWise Async gateway, a new remote access system had to be put in place. A NetWare server running Novell's remote access software was installed; this server could support a maximum of 48 users simultaneously.

First Steps

The first step in the migration process was installing the Windows NT servers and the Exchange bridgehead server, and IMS connectivity with the headquarters was established.

The next step was to turn Exchange into an SMTP messaging hub for GroupWise users. GroupWise users' data was exported to a text file and imported as custom recipients into a special GroupWise Users container. Each of these GroupWise users was listed with a modified SMTP mail address: GW5.MNOAsia.com. In addition, each of these custom recipients had two additional SMTP proxy addresses for MNOAsia.com and MNO.com.

Next, testing was done to ensure that all messages sent to any custom recipient at either MNOAsia.com or MNO.com would be redirected to the GW5.MNOAsia.com domain. When the testing was complete, the DNS MX record that directed all mail to MNOAsia.com was pointed to the Exchange server with the IMS running; Exchange began routing all mail onto GroupWise.

Once the rerouting functions were complete, the directory replication connector to the headquarters was created.

MNO Asia had one extra server that eventually was to be used as their cold standby server. The servers that were to become Exchange servers were running NetWare 4.11, so not all Exchange servers could be installed simultaneously. This meant that each division was to be migrated together; once the entire division was migrated, their NetWare server could be taken offline and reinstalled as an Exchange server.

Migration Administrative Process

The GSAs and DSAs were trained to use the Exchange administration snap-ins for the NWADMIN tool that ships with NDS for NT. This was the only additional training they needed other than being briefed on migration procedures for their respective groups. On average, migrations were handled about once a week (sometimes two smaller departments would migrate on the same weekend). Here are the procedures in their administrative process:

1. On Wednesday, the week prior to the migration, a notice was e-mailed to all users within the department asking them to move to their mailboxes any mail they wished to keep from their GroupWise archive. Similar reminder notices were then sent out again to users on Monday prior to the migration and on Friday. Users were also told that at Friday, 8:00 P.M., their GroupWise mailboxes would be disabled, and the next time they used e-mail it would be through Outlook.

24*seven* CASE STUDY

2. At 8:00 P.M. on Friday, the GroupWise post office containing the users was disabled so that it would no longer accept new mail messages.

3. The Exchange custom recipients for the users that were about to be migrated were deleted using the Exchange Administrator's import command-line option.

4. The Exchange Migration Wizard was run; Windows NT account creation was not necessary since the accounts were synchronized with NetWare NDS using NDS for NT. All mail in the mailboxes was migrated.

5. Select mailboxes were confirmed to ensure that the migration occurred properly.

6. A complete backup of the migrated GroupWise post office was performed.

7. Migrated mailboxes were deleted from the GroupWise post office.

8. External e-mail addresses were created for the migrated users in a GroupWise foreign domain.

9. Before the end of the weekend, one of the Exchange administrators exported the directory and confirmed that all users had a secondary proxy address for both MNOAsia.com and MNO.com.

End-User and Desktop Migration Processes

IS stopped the GroupWise process that deletes all user mail and told users that only the messages stored in the Group-Wise post office would be converted to Exchange. Users were told that if they had any "important" messages, they could move them out of the GroupWise archives and back into their mailboxes.

The largest group of users was the 500 who accessed the system remotely; this group was located primarily in one location. (Yes, 500 remote users all in a single location—just no LAN/WAN connectivity.) The IS group decided to migrate this group first. The DSAs and GSAs from other groups worked on this migration as well as the regional IS group. Since this was the first migration, the view was that the migration would provide all DSAs and GSAs with invaluable experience. All DSAs and GSAs participated in this particular phase of the migration.

Each computer had to be visited individually to configure the Windows 95/98 and Windows NT Dialup Networking client to call the RAS server, but the Outlook 98 Deployment Kit was used to create an installation package to deploy Outlook 98. The package was burned to CD and taken to each computer individually.

Due to problems with the GroupWise client interoperating in an unpredictable manner with the Outlook 98 client, the GroupWise client was removed, and the messaging profile that GroupWise used was deleted prior to creation of the Exchange profile.

Unexpected Problems during Migration

One of the biggest problems that occurred initially was the MNO headquarters office provided no guidance for standardization. This was corrected only after one regional location had to use the Move Server Wizard to correct their organization and site name and another region had to edit every display name in their site order to provide a more consistent address book. Eventually, several of the IS staff members throughout the MNO offices and a few staff members in the headquarters developed a standards and design document to which everyone could agree. This document was distributed to all regional offices and became their planning bible.

Another problem occurred because MNO Asia was using the TCP/IP connectivity option to connect to their GroupWise post offices rather than mapping drive letters to the GroupWise servers. The NetWare 4.11 servers only had five user licenses installed on them, limiting the number of people who could have a drive letter mapped to a GroupWise post office. Further, the Exchange Migration Wizard requires the GroupWise client and a file and print services connection to the post office server.

To complicate matters, the first several batches of users who were migrated were given a booklet about the migration which included frequently asked questions, what to do when things when wrong, and common procedures. Unfortunately, this booklet was developed based on what the administrators *thought* would go wrong. The help desk and the GSAs were overwhelmed with support calls and problems that they had not thought to address in their user migration handbook. They then revised the manual to include additional tips and FAQs based on the initial migration process. Many of the issues that arose, including remote access procedures, archiving old messages, importing old address books from GroupWise and accessing GroupWise archives, were also incorporated into the training that the users were receiving. This helped cut down on support issues in subsequent migrations.

Another difficulty MNO experienced during their Exchange migration had to do with the users' mail not reaching their new mailboxes. Users were assured that they would be able to keep the same SMTP address, yet when a new batch of mailboxes was created, the secondary proxy addresses often were not created for several days (or weeks). Midway through the migration, the procedures and responsibilities for creating the SMTP secondary proxy addresses were solidified.

Finally, many of the users had large (250MB+) GroupWise archives; a decision was made and later rescinded to allow these users to keep a copy of the GroupWise client on their computers. This was due to problems with the messaging profiles. On a case-by-case basis, these users were helped with the process of copying everything up to their GroupWise mailboxes, and they were helped later with moving things to a local PST.

4

Upgrading and Modifying Existing Servers

The only thing that seems to be constant with an Exchange Server messaging system is change—users moving from one department to another, server hardware upgrades, and server software upgrades. The changes never seem to end; they probably won't. As Exchange administrators, our best hope is to be prepared for the changes we will have to make and to make them in a timely fashion. This chapter dives into the pains of upgrading. The topics covered include:

- Determining what is the driving force behind an upgrade—if there is not a solid reason to upgrade, maybe you shouldn't
- Preparing for the upgrade
- Upgrading to Exchange 5.5 from previous versions of Exchange
- Putting new servers into production
- Reinstalling Exchange Server on new hardware
- Moving mailboxes
- Removing an Exchange server from a site
- Using the Move Server Wizard

Why Upgrade?

Our industry is very upgrade driven. Every time we think we have our systems stabilized, a vendor releases a new version or service pack. Who is responsible for the fast pace our industry has taken? To a great degree, we are; we are the ones demanding and consuming the products. I send at least one message a week to Microsoft's wish list (MSWish@Microsoft.com) asking for new features and product enhancements. I often talk to Microsoft Consulting, Product Support Services, and salespeople, each time mentioning features and enhancements that my clients and I would like to see implemented. Then, when new service packs or versions are released, I upgrade systems as soon as it is practical. I am sure that you have similar experiences.

But, I digress. The topic is "Why upgrade?" Two major reasons come to mind: new features and bug fixes. With each subsequent service pack of Exchange Server, Microsoft has introduced fixes for many annoying bugs. Not only have bugs been fixed, but service packs often introduce new functionality, as well. For example, Exchange Server 5.5 Service Pack 1 introduced enough new features to nearly have justified calling it Exchange Server 5.6 instead. Service Pack 2 introduced a number of additional bug fixes and incorporated some additional functions that previously existed (such as the Move Server tool, additional client migration tools, and making Exchange server Y2K-ready).

As a techie, I always want the latest and greatest version of whatever product I am running. New features, improvements in scalability, new capabilities—these are reasons for me to go to the boss and ask for money for upgrades. Also, security-related issues occasionally drive the decision to perform an upgrade or apply a service pack.

Should You Upgrade?

Users inevitably ask me during each upgrade, "Do we really need to upgrade?" The boss usually asks that too, but I can dazzle her with an impressive array of new features and bug fixes. Impressive features aside, the question of whether an upgrade is necessary is a valid one.

Before you plan your next service pack installation or major upgrade, ask yourself these questions:

- Is the current system unstable and/or are we experiencing bugs that the upgrade or service pack will fix?
- Are we running out of capacity and/or does the upgrade provide system-level features we currently need?
- Are the end user's capabilities going to be significantly enhanced by this upgrade? (Be honest with yourself!)

- Does our current system version pose any security-related threats that the upgrade or service pack will address?

If the answer is "yes" to *any* of these questions, then take a hard look at the benefits and schedule the upgrade. If you answered "no" to *all* of these questions, then chances are good that you don't need to apply the upgrade, service pack, or hot fix.

> **NOTE** Microsoft's position on Exchange service packs used to be, "Apply this service pack if it addresses a problem you are experiencing." Their current position seems to be more to the tune of, "Apply this service pack as soon as practical." My definition of "as soon as practical" includes an acceptable wait time after the service pack has been released (at least a month). Monitor the newsgroups and mailing lists during this time to see if the service pack has caused any major problems for others. Also, deploy the service pack in your test lab to make absolutely sure that it does not conflict with your existing hardware and software.

Exchange Upgrade Preparation

So the upgrade bug has bitten you! New features, improved scalability, and bug fixes await you just around the next corner. But before you get started, a little planning and a few simple checks will make sure that your migration from an older version of Exchange to Exchange 5.5 is a smooth one. This section on upgrade preparation reviews:

- Things to consider when upgrading from older versions of Exchange
- Version coexistence issues
- Upgrade preparation tips

> **TIP** If you have more than one Exchange server in a single site, you should also make sure that you are prepared for the coexistence issues that will pop up until you have all the servers migrated.

Considerations for Older Exchange Versions

Prior to upgrading the Exchange Server software, you should make sure that Windows NT is up to date. Exchange Server 4 should be running a minimum of SP2. Exchange Server 5 SP2 is not necessary, but it is a good idea.

Operations

PART 2

The Windows NT server should be running a minimum of Windows NT 4 SP3 and the Post-SP3 ROLLUP hot fix. (A ROLLUP hot fix is the result of Microsoft's incorporating all the critical hot fixes released after a service pack into a single hot fix. This is much better than applying many separate hot fixes, which is how it used to be done.) If Internet Information Server (IIS) is to be used, the ASPFIX hot fix should also be installed. I recommend installing Windows NT 4 SP4 since it has all the necessary hot fixes released since SP3. You should also consider applying the ROLLUP fix for Windows NT 4 SP4 found in the Post-SP4 directory on Microsoft's FTP server.

If you are planning to use Outlook Web Access (OWA) and install Internet Information Server 4, you should install IIS 4 prior to upgrading to Exchange 5.5.

Exchange Version Coexistence Issues

If you are going to be operating both Exchange 4 and Exchange 5.5 servers in the same site, you should upgrade all Exchange 4 servers to Exchange 4 SP2 at a minimum. The current service pack (as of this writing) is SP5, so that is the version that I would use on all my Exchange 4 servers.

For Exchange 5, there are some issues surrounding RTF to HTML and the Imail conversion engine component; these issues are fixed by applying Exchange 5 SP2. These issues can affect users who are using more recent versions of the OWA components and pre-Exchange 5 SP2 servers. For example, you may have trouble if you have already upgraded the servers that support OWA but have not yet upgraded the Exchange 5 servers that have mailboxes stored on them.

Once an Exchange 5.5 server is installed in a site, the schema for that site is upgraded on all servers. You should not plan to install older servers in a site that now has a 5.5 server installed. If you must do this, consult the Exchange Server 5.5 readme file for a procedure that will allow you to install new Exchange 4 servers.

NOTE The Exchange schema is a set of rules, attributes, and permission controls that governs the objects in the Exchange server directory.

Preparing for the Upgrade

If you have a single-server site, then you don't have many choices with regards to which server to upgrade first. <grin> If you have multiple servers in your site, then you need to pick a logical order in which to perform the upgrade. In a larger Exchange site, generally there are four types of Exchange servers: private information store, public information store, connector/bridgehead, and general-purpose (which do a little of everything). Here is my recommended order for upgrading these servers:

1. Upgrade your connector and bridgehead servers. These servers generally don't have large information stores and will upgrade quickly.

2. Upgrade any dedicated public-folder servers.

3. Upgrade the private-folder servers and general-use servers.

WARNING For Exchange servers that are running third-party connectors and products such as host, fax, voicemail, and pager connectors: Make sure that the third-party connector, virus, and other enhancement software you are running will be compatible with Exchange Server 5.5 and the service pack level you are planning to install.

Prior to running the upgrade, a number of things can be done to reduce the time the upgrade takes, minimize the possibility of conflicts, and make sure that the process goes smoothly. These include:

- Urge your users to clean unnecessary items out of their mail folders and Sent Items folders. Make sure that they empty their deleted items folders. Some administrators also run the Exchange Administrator's clean mailbox utility on the server prior to the upgrade.

NOTE See Chapter 5 to learn more about keeping mailbox storage under control.

- Make complete backups of the system: databases, Exchange software, Windows NT operating system, and the Windows NT Registry.

- Run the EDBUTIL consistency check on the public information store, the private information store, and the directory database. To do this, stop the information store and directory services. From the `C:\exchsrvr\bin` directory, run these three commands: `EDBUTIL /C /ISPRIV`, `EDBUTIL /C /ISPUB`, and `EDBUTIL /C /DS`.

- Document all connector configuration settings as well as general Exchange documentation such as the location of the log files.

NOTE See Appendix D for more information on what documentation should be kept for your Exchange and Windows NT servers.

TIP Where are my OWA and event service components? Since Exchange Server 4 did not have these options, they will not be installed during an upgrade. If you require these options, run the Setup program again and choose the Add/ Remove option. If you have already applied Exchange 5.5 SP1 or SP2, you should reapply the service pack immediately after adding additional components.

Exchange@Work: Estimating an Exchange Server 4 to 5.5 Upgrade

Prior to shutting down the current Exchange system, you must notify your user community of how long you expect the system will be unavailable. I like to build some fluff into my upgrade time estimates in case I have minor problems. Here is a sample scenario:

- Dual Pentium Pro Compaq Proliant 5000 with 256MB of RAM

- 2.5GB public information store

- 11.3GB private information store

- 25MB directory services

The total size of databases to be converted was nearly 14GB. I estimated (conservatively) that the upgrade process would take about 10 hours. I scheduled the system to be unavailable for an entire Sunday and started the upgrade on that morning with a full backup. The upgrade process started at 10:30 A.M. and was completed at about 5:15 P.M. (Much quicker than I had expected!) We applied the service packs, then tested a few of the mailboxes and connectors. The system was available again by Sunday evening at 7:00 P.M.

Upgrading Exchange 5 to 5.5

The Exchange 5 to 5.5 upgrade will go a little more rapidly since the database only has to be converted a single time. Further, you are given two options during the upgrade process. You can choose a standard upgrade or a fault-tolerant upgrade. The fault-tolerant upgrade is somewhat faster, but it builds new copies of the databases from the old databases. Since the Exchange 5.5 software upgrade and Registry changes don't take place until the databases have been successfully converted, you can rollback to version 5 easily if the upgrade fails.

> **TIP** Even though the fault-tolerant upgrade takes more disk space to complete, I recommended it because if problems occur, it's easy to rollback to a previous version of Exchange Server.

Upgrade time can vary greatly, but I have seen database upgrades that took about 1.5GB per hour and faster. Once the upgrade is complete, run the Exchange Performance Optimizer. Finally, apply the current service packs and hot fixes, then test a few mailboxes and the connectors.

If you require the Exchange Server event service, you must run the Setup program, choose Add/Remove, and install the event service after the installation is complete. The event service was not part of Exchange 5, therefore it is not installed during an upgrade.

> **NOTE** If you are already running Exchange Server 5.5 Standard Edition and you need to upgrade to Enterprise Edition, the upgrade is quite simple. Run the Exchange Server 5.5 Enterprise Edition Setup program, and, when prompted, choose Reinstall. Once the files are copied, make sure you reinstall the service pack and hot fixes you had installed previously.

Sometimes, Things Go Wrong

You may have a charmed life, and things don't go wrong during your upgrades. I wish I could say the same. Mr. Murphy is always present when I upgrade. Just thinking about introducing updated code and upgrading databases always gives me a slight chill down my spine. Testing every possible permutation of hardware and software is impossible for Microsoft to do anytime they release a new version or service pack, so problems are nearly inevitable.

Applying service packs or system upgrades may introduce problems that you were not prepared for. If possible, test all service packs on your standby server hardware. This can help with the show-stopping bugs. Watch your systems carefully after any service pack installation or upgrade.

Some common problems that may occur during upgrades include:

- Running out of disk space for the temporary files required to upgrade the database
- Interference from software such as virus-scanning applications
- Incompatibilities with third-party software packages that are installed

TIP If possible, apply service packs or upgrades to only one of your production systems and monitor it carefully. Only after a week or two of stable operation, consider applying the service pack to additional servers.

Exchange@Work: Avoid Upgrade Hell

It is 9:30 P.M. on Saturday night. I am in the process of laying out this chapter to start writing it (and yes, I have no social life). I am also carrying on an e-mail conversation with one of my friends, who is reporting to me her latest upgrade adventures. She has just completed a scheduled, daylong upgrade of one of her Exchange servers from version 5 to 5.5. (She needed some of the 5.5 features, specifically larger database storage capabilities.) Of all the people I know, it seems like she supervises more upgrades than anyone else.

In the midst of the upgrade, she discovered an obscure bug affecting the upgrade. The bug occurs if the Exchange 5 Server has the Internet Mail Service installed and the Windows NT system has Internet Explorer 4.01 Service Pack 1 and Outlook Express. This bug cost her several hours during the upgrade. I am not certain, but I might have given up and called Microsoft PSS.

Not one to be set back easily, my friend consulted the Microsoft Knowledge Base and found the solution to her problem. The KB article (Q194820) directed her to copy some files from the Exchange Server CD-ROM onto the Windows NT server to correct the problem.

What did my friend do right during this upgrade?

- She scheduled the system to be down for the entire day; she did not try to perform the upgrade during her regular maintenance period. She would not have had it back up in time if she had used her regular maintenance period.

- She made judicious use of the Microsoft Knowledge Base and found the solution to her problem in a very reasonable amount of time.

- She did not allow bizarre incompatibilities and obscure bugs throw her for a loop.

> **Exchange@Work: Avoid Upgrade Hell** *(continued)*
>
> My friend will also tell you that hindsight is 20/20. She possibly could have saved herself some time if she had searched the Knowledge Base ahead of time to see if there were any specific issues regarding her configuration and the tasks she was about to undertake. Searching the KB prior to upgrading will not guarantee that you will avoid problems, but it can help eliminate many problems.

Reinstalling Exchange Server

There may come a time when you have to reinstall Exchange server on your existing hardware or on new hardware. For whatever reason, you may not be able to install a second server in the site and move all the mailboxes and public folders to the new server. You may want to keep the existing server name, or you may simply need to reinstall Exchange on larger disks.

There are a couple of approaches to doing this, but I have found a particular set of procedures that I call the "forklift move" or "the forklift procedures." These procedures are somewhat time consuming, but I have found them to be reliable; I have rebuilt a number of servers in this fashion and had excellent results each time. The forklift move is a simple offline backup, rebuild, and restoration.

1. Make sure that your Windows NT documentation and your Exchange documentation is up to date for the server configuration as well as for Exchange-specific configuration items, such as connector configuration.

2. Ask all users to get exit their client software.

3. Edit the Registry and insert a "Logon Only As" key to restrict who can access the information store.

NOTE See the section in Chapter 5 titled "Disabling Mailbox Logins" or KB article Q146764 for more information on this Registry key.

---

4. Stop and restart the Exchange services to make sure that all users have been disconnected.

5. Run a normal (full) online backup. Review the backup logs and the Windows NT event log for any errors. Do not proceed if the backup generated errors.

Replacing Server Hardware

New hardware often drives an upgrade decision. Too often, organizations discover that their server hardware is not capable of handling the load that they require of it. Getting new hardware is one of my favorite times of the year because it feels like Christmas.

It is possible to back up all the data on an Exchange server, remove it from service, install a new piece of hardware, and restore the data to it. However, this is not the route I recommend. Instead, install the server as a new server in the site and then move mailboxes to that server. This will help you to avoid any of the pitfalls associated with backups and restores.

By far, the simplest method for upgrading to new hardware is to install Exchange on the new server and move mailboxes to it. This works unless you absolutely have to keep the original server name. Here is my checklist for installing a new server:

1. Install Windows NT 4 with SP4 and any relevant hot fixes. Install IIS 4 if required.

2. Install Exchange Server 5.5 and join the existing site as a new server. Apply the Exchange Server 5.5 SP2 and any relevant hot fixes.

3. Install relevant backup software and test the backup procedures for the new server.

4. Let the server burn in for a few days.

5. Migrate the connectors to the new server and let them run for a few days to ensure that they are delivering new mail correctly. One possible approach is to install new connectors, set the old connectors to a higher cost, and then monitor the new connectors. Once you are sure the new connectors are working properly, remove the old connectors.

6. If you are moving a directory replication bridgehead server, remember that you will have to perform a full replication.

7. Use the "Moving Mailboxes" procedures outlined later in this chapter to move the mailboxes to the new server.

8. Leave the old server online for a few weeks so that all the Outlook clients will have time to contact the old server and be redirected to the new server.

9. When it comes time to remove the old server, see the section later in this chapter titled "Removing a Server."

Moving Mailboxes

In a multi-server site and even in a multi-site organization, you are going to find yourself moving mailboxes from one server to another. This may be because people are transferring within the organization or because you are retiring an older server and want to move everyone off of it.

Moving mailboxes falls into two separate categories: moving mailboxes to another server within a site and moving mailboxes to a new site. First we will consider moving mailboxes within the same site.

Moving Mailboxes within a Site

The Exchange Administrator program has an excellent tool for moving mailboxes between two servers in the same site. This tool, called Move Mailbox, can be used to move a single mailbox or multiple mailboxes simultaneously and is found on the Tools menu of Exchange Administrator. If you have recently brought a new server online or are consolidating mailboxes from several servers to one server, this tool will be a lifesaver.

Here are some hints and information about using the Move Mailbox tool:

- Users should not be connected to the server while their mailboxes are being moved, nor can mailboxes accept mail while they are being moved.

- Select small groups of mailboxes (15 to 30) to move rather than selecting all the mailboxes to be moved simultaneously. This allows mailboxes to be available again more quickly. You can even spread out the groups that you move over a few days or weeks.

NOTE Though your actual mileage may vary, my experience is that the Move Mailbox tool can move about 500MB of mailbox data per hour. Be patient.

- If you have circular logging disabled, watch your transaction log files and the disk space on the log file disk! Since there will be a lot of additional messages being moved to the new server, the log files will fill up the log file disk very quickly. You might want to run a normal or incremental backup every few hours so that the log files are removed. Another option is to turn circular logging on during the time that you are moving many mailboxes.

NOTE Circular logging is discussed in Chapter 7.

- Move users who work together at the same time. This reduces the messages sent between servers while you are getting all the mailboxes moved, if you choose to move mailboxes over a period of days or weeks.

- Turn off information store maintenance or don't run the Move Mailbox process during times that IS maintenance occurs. (Default is 1:00 A.M. until 6:00 A.M.).

- Exchange single-instance storage is preserved.

- Deleted items (those in the Deleted Items store) are not moved. If your users believe they may need their deleted items, they can recover them before the move and then delete them once their mailboxes are moved.

- Perform the Move Mailbox operations from the server that the mailboxes are being moved to. This will improve transfer times and reduce network traffic. Try to avoid running large numbers of mailbox moves from an administrator workstation.

- Run the Move Mailbox tool from only one place at a time. I have had administrators tell me they have run up to nine separate instances of Move Mailbox, but the thought of doing this makes me uncomfortable.

- If you get a stranded mailbox (a mailbox that appears to be located on both the new and old information stores), run the Move Mailbox procedure again for that mailbox.

- Don't take an old server off the network immediately. See the "Removing a Server" section later in this chapter when you are ready to remove it.

Outlook and Moved Mailboxes

Even if all the mailboxes from a server have been moved, I highly recommend leaving the original server online for a week or two. All of the Outlook clients should be given time to contact the old server before removing it from production.

The Exchange server name is stored in a user's messaging profile, which you can edit and view by choosing Mail (or Mail And Fax) from the Control Panel, highlighting the Microsoft Exchange Server information service, and clicking Properties. Even if you do not manually update the Microsoft Exchange Server field in the messaging profile, when Outlook contacts the server that the mailbox used to be located on, the directory service on that Exchange server will point Outlook to the new server. Then Outlook will automatically update the Microsoft Exchange Server field to reflect the new server. From this point forward, the Outlook client will contact the correct Exchange server. However, this feature will not work if you remove the old Exchange server from the network immediately after moving the mailboxes.

NOTE The automatic update feature works only for the Exchange clients and the Outlook clients. POP3 and IMAP4 clients must be updated manually.

Moving Mailboxes to Another Site

Moving mailboxes from one server to another in the same site is easy. However, moving mailboxes to a server in another site presents more of a challenge, because the Exchange Administrator program does not do this. It is not impossible to move a mailbox to another site, but it does require a little more work.

> **TIP** If you are going to be moving an entire server to another site (or another organization), use the Move Server tool that ships with Exchange Server 5.5 SP2.

There are two options available to you when moving a single mailbox or group of mailboxes from one site to another. The first and simplest solution is to move all the mail out to a personal folder (PST file) and then move it back in on the new server. The second option is to use a BackOffice Resource Kit utility called Mailbox Migration that automatically moves the messages and creates the directory entries.

Moving a Mailbox Using a Personal Folder

The simplest way to move a small number (fewer than 15) of mailboxes to another site is to export all the data out of the server-based mailbox to a PST file. You can take advantage of a few of Outlook's features to make this even easier.

To export the entire mailbox:

1. From Outlook, choose File Import And Export Export To A File and click Next.
2. Choose Personal Folder File (.pst) and click Next.
3. In the Export Personal Folders dialog box, highlight the entire mailbox or select the folder(s) you want exported. Click Include Subfolders if you want all subfolders exported, and then click Next.

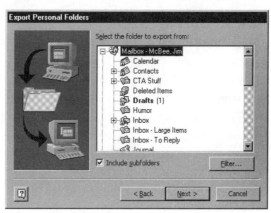

4. Enter the name of the PST file you are creating and click Finish.

To export the data from the entire mailbox, someone with the User role permissions needs to be connected to the mailbox either by logging in as that user or by opening the mailbox using the Open These Additional Mailboxes feature of Outlook; go to Tools ➤ Services, choose Microsoft Exchange Server properties, and select the Advanced tab. You can also use the Exchange service messaging profile to open additional mailboxes.

This process will export all messages, folders, calendar entries, contact items, and more that are found in the server-based mailbox. This can take some time, but the export process will tell you what it is working on. (One of my mailboxes has 39MB of data in it and took nearly 15 minutes to export.) Though you can easily copy the folders individually to a PST file and back to the mailbox, I find the procedure of exporting the entire mailbox much quicker and more efficient.

Now that you have the data in a PST file, you simply reverse this procedure and import the data from the PST file into the user's new mailbox.

1. Select File ➤ Import And Export ➤ Import From Another Program Or File. Then click Next.

2. Choose Personal Folder File (.pst) and click Next.

3. Browse the directory structure and select the PST file that contains the exported messages and folders. Then click Next.

4. Select the entire PST file and check the Include Subfolders check box. Make sure the Import Items Into The Same Folder In button is selected and that the server-based mailbox is selected in the drop-down list box. Then click Finish.

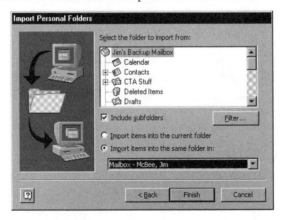

Moving Mailbox Rules and Folder Views   If the mailbox you are moving has rules, views, permissions, or a description that you want to copy, Outlook 98 provides an easy way to do this:

1. Open the PST file that you previously created (or any PST file for that matter) as a folder in your folder list.

2. Select the Inbox in the PST file.

3. From the Outlook menu, select File ➤ Folder ➤ Copy Folder Design. The following dialog box will open:

4. Select the server-based Inbox and click the check boxes for the desired items you want to copy (Rules, Permissions, Description, Forms & Views). Click OK.

5. Click Yes to acknowledge that the design on the folder will be replaced if there are any conflicts in the design.

Once the rules, permissions, description, and forms and views are exported, you simply need to reverse this process and get them into the new mailbox. Simply highlight the Inbox on your new server-based mailbox, select Copy Folder Design, and copy the folder design items from the PST file.

NOTE   See Microsoft KB article Q152852 for more information.

The Mailbox Migration Tool

The BackOffice Resource Kit Mailbox Migration tool was developed to move users from one site to another (for example, moving users from a pilot server to a production server in another site). It can move a single mailbox or many mailboxes at once. It does this by

it provides are no longer necessary due to consolidation. Though this is not a difficult operation to perform, you should double-check a few simple items to make sure the removal won't impact your existing servers. These things include:

- Making sure that the server is no longer supporting public folder content and that no public folders are homed on this server
- Removing any supporting services such as routing table recalculation and offline address book storage
- Moving any messaging or directory replication connectors that this server supports to another server
- Making sure that the server is not supporting distribution list expansion or OWA

The removal procedures are slightly different if you are removing the first server that was installed into the site originally, but the "first server" procedures are good to follow for removing any server from a site.

Server Removal Checklist

Here is a brief summary of things you should consider and address regarding your current Exchange server prior to removing it:

- Are there any messaging or directory-replication connectors on this server? If so, they need to be moved to one of the remaining servers.
- Are there any mailboxes remaining on this server? These will need to be moved prior to taking the server offline, or they will be lost.
- Make sure that all public folders have been replicated to another server and remove them from this server.
- Are any other servers using this server as a designated public folder server? Check the information store properties of the remaining servers.
- Move the offline address book server if this server has been designated as the site's OAB server.
- Select a new server to be the site's routing table recalculation server if this server was designated as such.
- Are any Outlook Web Access servers pointing to this server? They will have to be reassigned to a new server.
- After moving all mailboxes from this server, have you left it online long enough for all Outlook clients to be redirected to their new server?

TIP I recommend leaving the removed server online for at least a week. Outlook will automatically be directed to the new server (the server to which a mailbox was moved) the next time the Outlook client tries to connect to the old server, provided the old server is still there. Once redirected to the new server, Outlook does not contact the old server again.

Connectors Located on This Server

Are there any connectors, including directory replication connectors, still operating on this server? To make sure, check the list of connectors in the Connections container. These are found in *Site Name* ➢ Configuration ➢ Connections. If there are any site connectors installed, make sure that they are not using this server as a bridgehead server. You should also make sure that the site connector on the other side is not using the server that is about to be removed.

Don't forget to check the Directory Replication container for any directory replication connectors that may be using this server as a bridgehead server. These are found in *Site Name* ➢ Configuration ➢ Directory Replication. Be sure to check the directory replication connectors in the other site.

Exchange@Work: Removing a Server with Messaging and Directory Replication Connectors

One branch of Company JKL had to remove the original server that was installed into their site. Though they moved all the mailboxes and folders off the server correctly, they overlooked the fact that the server was functioning as a bridgehead server for an X.400 connector and a directory replication connector.

When the server was removed from production, no one immediately realized that messages were not arriving from other sites. As a matter of fact, it was nearly 30 hours before anyone noticed.

Though this was not a big deal to fix, the issue was that messages and directory replication had not occurred with remote sites in 30 hours. An X.400 messaging connector had to be re-created in the branch office and reconfigured in the main office. Then the directory replication connector had to be re-created, and the directory had to be completely re-replicated.

Check for Mailboxes on This Server

You want to make sure that there are *no* remaining mailboxes on this server. The quickest and easiest way to determine this is to use Exchange Administrator and navigate through the Exchange hierarchy to the list of recipients that is found on this particular server. This list is found in *Site Name* ≻ Configuration ≻ Servers ≻ *Server Name* Recipients.

This recipient container should be empty except for the possibility of the Schedule+ Free/Busy Agent, which cannot be moved. You will have to create a new Free/Busy Agent on one of your remaining servers. This is done through the Exchange Setup program.

Replacing the Schedule+ Free/Busy Connector

The Schedule+ Free/Busy connector is used to exchange free and busy times between Exchange and Microsoft Mail clients. If you accidentally delete the Schedule+ Free/Busy connector, this information cannot be exchanged. It can be replaced, but you have to delete and recreate the Microsoft Mail connector.

To recreate the Schedule+ Free/Busy connector, follow these steps.

WARNING No users can be logged in while this procedure is being done. Exercise extreme caution when performing these steps, because you can accidentally remove your entire server!

1. Make sure have the Microsoft Mail connector completely documented, including any PC MTA configuration information.
2. Run the Exchange Server Setup program and click the Add/Remove button.
3. Highlight the Microsoft Exchange Server component and click the Change Option button.
4. Clear the check box on the MS Mail Connector and click OK.
5. Continue with the installation process, and the connector is removed.
6. Run the Exchange Server Setup program again and click Add/Remove.
7. Highlight the Microsoft Exchange Server component and click Change Option.
8. Check the MS Mail Connector check box and click OK.
9. Continue with the installation process, and the MS Mail connector (and the Schedule+ Free/Busy connector) will be reinstalled.
10. Reapply the service pack and any hot fixes you were previously using.
11. Reconfigure the Microsoft Mail connector, PC MTAs, and Schedule+ Free/Busy connector.

Remove All Public Folder Replicas

Public folder replicas should be completely removed from this server. To confirm that there are no remaining public folders on this server, use Exchange Administrator to see a list of public folders stored on this server. The list is found in *Site Name* ➤ Configuration ➤ Servers ➤ *Server Name* Public Information Store. Then, from the File menu, choose Properties and view the Instances tab in the Public Information Store Properties dialog box (see Figure 4.1).

Figure 4.1 shows the instances of my public folders that are stored on server KONA; these are listed under the Folders On This Information Store column. Prior to removing this server from production, you will need to put replicas of these folders on other servers in the site.

Once the public folders have been successfully replicated to other servers, you can remove the instances from the server that is about to be removed. You can confirm that the folders are synchronized by clicking the Folder Replication Status tab of the Public Information Store Properties dialog box.

To remove instances of public folders from the server that is about to be removed, use the dialog box shown in Figure 4.1. Highlight the public folders and click Remove. If you try to remove a public folder that does not have an instance elsewhere in the site, you will receive a message stating "You cannot remove the folder *folder name* because it is the only instance in this site."

TIP   Make sure that you put a replica of the Schedule+ Free/Busy Information and Organization Forms (there may be several of these depending on the number of languages you are supporting) folders onto another server. Losing the Schedule+ Free/Busy information may not be too big of a deal, but if you forget the Organization Forms, you may lose all of the forms stored in the Organization Forms Library. However, you do not need to worry about the Offline Address Book, OAB Version 2 folders, and EventConfig folders.

Operations

PART 2

2. Choose File ➤ Import And Export.

3. Select Export To A Personal Folder (.pst) from the Choose An Action To Perform list and click Next.

4. Select the folder you want to export in the folder list and click Next.

5. Enter the name of the PST file that you want to export the data to and click Finish.

You can now safely delete the public folder using the Outlook client.

This PST file can be imported by a user whose home public folder server is the new destination server in the other site. To do so:

1. Log in to Outlook as a user who has at least Author permission (or Publishing Editor if the user needs to create a new folder).

2. Create the folder you want to import the data into and highlight it.

3. Choose File ➤ Import And Export.

4. Select Import From A Personal Folder (.pst) in the Choose An Action To Perform list and click Next.

5. Select the PST file to import from and click Next.

6. Make sure that the Import Items Into The Current Folder button is selected, and then click Finish.

New features with Exchange 5.5 allow public-folder administrative access to administrators only from that public folder's home site. Exchange 5.5 also allows you to specify a different server as that folder's home server.

To set the home server of a public folder to another site and then remove the last replica of that folder from the old site, follow these steps:

1. Put a replica of the public folder on the server that will be the folder's home server and wait until it is fully synchronized.

2. Locate the public folder in the Exchange hierarchy under Folders ➤ Public Folders and display the folder's properties.

3. On the General tab, make sure the Limit Administrative Access To Home Site button is cleared.

4. On the Advanced tab, in the Home Server drop-down list box, select the new home server for this public folder.

You will need to wait until these changes have been propagated and the contents have been replicated before removing the replica from the original home server.

> **TIP** If you have many folders in a tree to change these settings on, you can select a parent folder and choose the Propagate These Properties To All Sub-folders check box.

Offline Address Book Server

By default, the first server that is installed into a site is responsible for generating and storing the Offline Address Book for that site. Switching this server is easy:

1. Using Exchange Administrator, choose *Site Name* ➤ Configuration ➤ DS Site Configuration (found in the right pane). Select the Offline Address Book tab. You will see a dialog box similar to this:

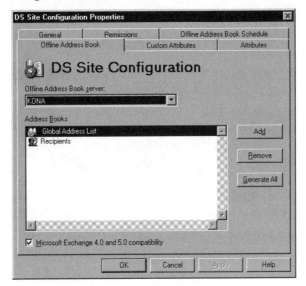

2. In the Offline Address Book Server drop-down list box, select the server that will generate and store the offline address book.

3. Click the Apply button, then click the Generate All button to regenerate a new copy of the offline address book.

Routing Recalculation Server

The site's routing table, also known as the Gateway Address Routing Table (or GWART), is rebuilt nightly (2:00 A.M. local time, by default). The first server installed into the site is responsible for regenerating the routing table. This is simple to change:

1. Using Exchange Administrator, choose *Site Name* ➤ Configuration ➤ Site Addressing (found in the right pane). The following dialog box opens:

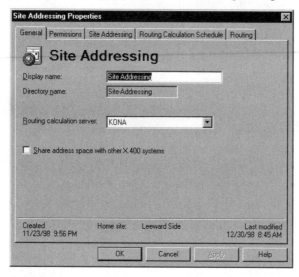

2. On the General tab, select the server that should be responsible for recalculating the routing table in the Routing Calculation Server drop-down list box. Click Apply.

3. Select the Routing tab of the Site Addressing Properties dialog box and click the Recalculate Routing button.

Designated Public Folder Server

Has the server that you are about to remove been configured as a designated public folder server for any other servers in the site? As soon as you decide that you are going to remove a server from production, check all the other servers to make sure that they have not been configured to use the server that is about to be removed as their designated public folder server. If they have, this must be changed to a server that will remain in operation. This is changed for each private information store in the private information store properties (see Figure 4.3). To find these properties, in Exchange Administrator, choose *Site Name* ➤ Configuration ➤ Servers ➤ *Server Name* ➤ Private Information Store, then choose Properties from the File menu.

Figure 4.3 Server KONA's private information store properties

To change the designated public folder server that all mailboxes on this server will use, select the correct server in the Public Folder Server drop-down list box.

Distribution List Expansion

Distribution list expansion occurs when a server MTA takes the distribution list and figures out which mailboxes and recipients to send a message to. You can assign a distribution list a specific server that will be responsible for its expansion. As shown in Figure 4.4, you can select a specific server or Any Server In The Site as your expansion server.

Administrators often pick a single server within their site to handle distribution list expansion. In environments with many users (more than 20,000 or 30,000) and heavy distribution list usage, a dedicated server may be designated as the distribution list expansion server.

Another common use of this feature might be when all the people in the Engineering department are on the same Exchange server. When the distribution list is created, that server can be selected as the expansion server. There is no simple way to see if a specific server has been specified as the expansion server for a distribution list, short of checking the distribution list properties one at a time and checking the Expansion server field.

Figure 4.4 Choosing an expansion server

Outlook Web Access

If the OWA server is on a separate server from Exchange, then the OWA server has to have the name of a server to connect to initially to find the location of mailboxes. If the OWA server is pointing to the server that you are removing, then your OWA users will receive a message telling them that the Exchange server is down.

There is a Registry setting that will allow IIS to point to a new Exchange server. This Registry setting is configured on the IIS/OWA server, not the Exchange server.

```
\HKLM\System\CurrentControlSet\Services\MSExchangeWeb\Parameters
```

There are three values that you should check in the list of values on the right pane of the Registry Editor:

Enterprise should match the Exchange organization name.

Site should match the Exchange site name that contains the Exchange server that you want the OWA server to contact.

Server must match the Exchange server that you want the OWA server to contact. Confirm that this value points to an existing server.

Finally Removing the Server from the Site

Once you are certain that the Exchange server is ready to be removed, I recommend running the Exchange Server Setup program and selecting the Remove All option.

Once the server software has been removed from the old server, connect to another site using Exchange Administrator. Navigate to the server's container by choosing *Site Name* ➤ Configuration ➤ Servers. Select the server that should be deleted, and from the Edit menu, choose Delete. The removal may take a few minutes, and you will be asked to confirm that this is really what you want to do. If it is, choose Yes.

Exchange@Work: Accidental Removal of the First Server in the Site

Did you accidentally remove the first server in the site without completely moving all the components to another server?

You will need to recreate the site folders and create a new globally-unique identifier (GUID). To do this, you use the GUIDGEN.EXE (GUID generate) utility, which is available from Microsoft PSS or the Microsoft Developers Network. The GUIDGEN utility randomly generates a new GUID. Creating a new site GUID for the site folder requires Admin permission.

1. Run GUIDGEN, select Registry format, and choose New GUID.

2. The utility creates a 32-digit hexadecimal number in the result box. Write down the GUID or cut it out and paste it into a Notepad document.

3. Run Exchange Administrator in raw mode (ADMIN /R).

4. Go to *Site Name* ➤ Configuration container ➤ Information Store Site Configuration, and display the raw properties of the Information Store Site Configuration object by selecting File ➤ Properties.

5. Scroll down through the Object attributes list, locate the Site Folder GUID attribute, and select it. Then click the Editor.

6. Paste the 32-digit hexadecimal number you created in steps 1 and 2 into the value field. Make sure that the Hex button is checked.

7. Click OK, and then click the Set button. The Edit value and the Attribute value should be the same. Click OK to exit the Information Store Site Configuration Properties dialog box.

8. Stop and restart the information store service.

Other First-Server Site Folders

Other folders in the site that may need to be recreated include the offline address book, the Schedule+ Free/Busy folder and the Organizational Forms Library. The Schedule+ Free/Busy information will be unavailable until the first users connect to their server; their Free/Busy information will be regenerated. To reconfigure the offline address book:

1. Browse the Exchange hierarchy using Exchange Administrator: *Site Name* ➢ Configuration ➢ DS Site Configuration, then select File ➢ Properties.

2. Select the offline address book property page and click the Generate Offline Address Book button.

If you are using the Organizational Forms Library and you deleted the server that held that folder, you will have to recreate the folder. You will lose all the forms that were stored on that server unless you had a backup of the forms stored in a PST file. You can recover these forms by reinstalling the deleted Exchange server and copying them to a PST file.

Don't forget, if the server supported more than one Forms Library (there is one library for each language supported), you will have to recreate all the libraries.

1. Run the Exchange Administrator program.

2. From the Tools menu, select Forms Administrator.

3. Click New and enter the name of the Organization Forms Library; the default is Organization Forms English (USA).

4. Don't forget to assign at least the Author role for anyone who needs to create forms.

To avoid these problems and others associated with removing a server, make sure you follow the procedures in this chapter so that you remove a server correctly.

The Move Server Wizard

"Can I move an entire server to another site or organization?" Until recently, the answer was no, not without a complete reinstallation. In the fall of 1998, however, Microsoft released the Move Server Wizard (code-named "Pilgrim"). I downloaded this tool on the second day it was available, built myself a test lab, and did some basic testing. What follows in this section is a result of my initial work with the Move Server Wizard and helping one of my clients plan a little "clean-up" operation.

> **NOTE** The Move Server Wizard is available on the Exchange Server 5.5 Service Pack 2 CD or at backoffice.microsoft.com/downtrial.

Exchange Server administrators and designers have been asking for this tool since the release of Exchange 4. The Move Server Wizard was designed to provide several types of services:

- Split a large site into smaller sites by moving servers to a new site.
- Merge several smaller sites into fewer large sites.
- Move an Exchange server into a new organization.

Those of you who have major changes you want to perform are probably jumping up and down in the aisles right about now. Many sites I have worked on over the past three years will seriously benefit from this tool. However, your fairy godmother has not handed you a magic wand to wave over your Exchange organization and make it all better. This tool is powerful, but it requires careful planning, and it does come with some caveats.

Read the following sections to learn about what the wizard can and cannot do. Then judge for yourself if this tool will fix your problems. Regardless of your situation, though, this tool is not a point-and-click solution.

The Move Server Wizard: What Does It Do?

First, let's take a look at the bells and whistles of the Move Server Wizard. What is it capable of doing for the slightly broken Microsoft Exchange organization?

- The Move Server Wizard moves the entire server to a new or existing site (or organization). The wizard examines the entire directory database and the private information store database; it then replaces all instances of a site and organization name in all distinguished names (DNs) with the new site and organization name. Sound time consuming? It can be!
- The wizard will check for duplicate directory entries, which may occur as a result of moving a server, and suggest a course of action.
- The wizard will move distribution lists and custom recipients.
- The wizard creates new primary proxy addresses based on the new site's addressing information, and it keeps any secondary proxy addresses the user had from the old site.

Next I was asked how to treat custom recipients and distribution lists during the move, and then to determine how I want to handle the primary Windows NT accounts for each mailbox. If the domain structure will not change, I could keep the existing Windows NT accounts; however, I had the choice of specifying a different domain that accounts would be created in.

The wizard then examined the directory of the destination site for duplicate addresses and presented me with alternatives. Notice in Figure 4.6 that I had two duplicates: a distribution list called _Everyone and a user called MakotoSa. If the object was a distribution list, I could have chosen to merge the distribution lists. Notice also that the wizard suggested an alternative name (MakotoSa) for the duplicate mailbox that was about to be merged into this site.

Figure 4.6   Move Server Wizard suggesting a course of action for a duplicate mailbox and distribution list

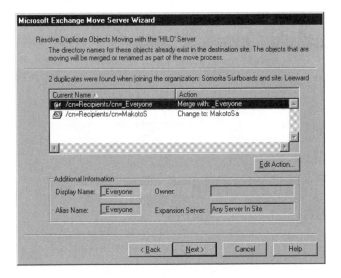

Prior to starting the actual move, I was presented with a dialog box summarizing the actions that were about to take place and any warnings such as public folders existing on the server to be moved. Once I confirmed that I understood the actions and warnings, the move commenced.

Figure 4.7 shows the Move Server Wizard progress screen, which is actually quite nice. Rather than just displaying an hourglass, it actually shows which portion of the move the wizard is working on as well as a progress bar indicating how complete the current portion is. By far, the longest part of the move is updating the messages in the private information store.

Figure 4.7   The Move Server Wizard progress screen

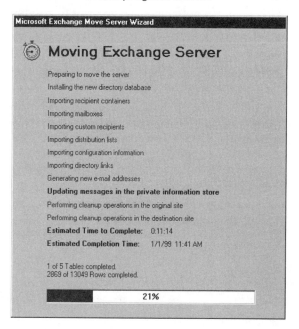

As usual, Microsoft's estimate was nowhere near the actual time it took to run the migration process. Figure 4.7 indicates an estimated time of 11 minutes and 14 seconds, but the actual time was just over 32 minutes. (The private information store database was 950MB.) My own estimate is in the range of about 2–4 GB per hour, so I was pretty close, though your actual mileage may vary depending on the number of messages and the speed of your hardware. I did this move operation on a single-processor machine with IDE disk drives, so a server-class machine will be able to do a move much more quickly than my test system did.

Hints for Using the Move Server Wizard

Here is some useful information that I have discovered about using the Move Server Wizard:

- Most of us like to take a new program and run it for the first time without ever reading the documentation. The Move Server Wizard is *not* a utility you can easily do this with. You will be doing yourself a big favor if you read the documentation found in either the MVEXSRVR.HLP or MVEXSRVR.RTF files in C:\exchsrvr\bin\ movesrvr directory.

- Make sure the server you are about to move is running at least Exchange 5.5 SP1.

- The wizard makes many changes to the directory and private information store. Make sure that you have a complete backup prior to starting.

- Remove any messaging connectors and directory replication connectors prior to starting the wizard. This includes the site connector, the Internet Mail Service, and any third-party connectors or gateways. Don't forget to check other sites for connectors that point to the server to be moved.

- Prior to moving the last server in the site, make sure that all public folders have been moved to another site and that the replicas have been removed from the last server to be moved.

- Make sure that the server you are moving is not the site's routing recalculation server or offline address book server.

- Prior to moving a server, users should decrypt any encrypted mail using Exchange Advanced Security. These users will be issued new keys when their server is moved.

- Remove any Windows NT and Exchange Server virus protection programs prior to starting the wizard.

- Run Exchange Setup and remove the event service prior to starting the wizard.

- Move any public folders to another server or site (as discussed earlier in this chapter) prior to starting the wizard.

- Do not try to migrate two servers simultaneously.

- Run `ESEUTIL /G /ISPRIV` and `ISINTEG -TEST ALLTESTS` prior to the move to make sure that the private information store does not have any problems.

- The server you are moving should have at least 500MB of free disk space available to hold the temporary files that the wizard will create.

- Though the move may occur much faster than this, estimate about 2GB per hour.

Exchange@Work: Breaking Up a Large Site

Organization DEF started using Exchange Server 4 shortly after it was released. During their design phase, a decision was made to put all the servers into a single site that would span the entire country. An assumption was made that there was sufficient bandwidth on the company's WAN to support this. Fourteen servers were placed in two locations that were to support users spread throughout eight locations. The predominant client was the Windows 16 and Windows 32 Exchange clients, though they were quickly moving to Outlook 97.

Exchange@Work: Breaking Up a Large Site *(continued)*

The Exchange organization grew dramatically over the first year of its life and currently supports just over 11,000 users. Users in the remote sites often complained that they could not connect to their server or that response times were unacceptable. Bandwidth between the two primary locations that hosted Exchange Server was also critically low. (It was so bad, in fact, that often FTP file transfers would timeout.)

The company has several options for dealing with this situation, but purchasing additional bandwidth was not one of them. The IS group took several steps to clear up the bandwidth problems with their WAN, one of which was to separate the single site into three smaller sites and to locate the servers nearer to the users they serviced.

The IS group decided to wait until the Move Server Wizard tool was available to start this process. They would then separate the users into three groups based on geographic distribution. The largest group of users was to remain in the existing site, and the two smaller groups were to become part of two new sites.

The first step in this process was to build an appropriate infrastructure. All servers had to be upgraded to Exchange Server 5.5 with SP1. Next, two new servers were installed to create the two new sites. Messaging connectors (X.400) and directory replication connectors were established to these two new sites from a server in the original site that had been designated as the bridgehead server.

Prior to the first server being moved:

- All public folders that were homed on a server to be moved were replicated to another server and re-homed to a server that would not be moved, and the replica was removed from the affected server.

- Scripts were developed using the NEWPROF and PROFGEN utilities (see Chapter 11) to automate the process of creating new profiles for the users whose servers were moving.

- An informational e-mail was distributed to all users describing the move process, the benefits that the users would realize as result of the move, a schedule for each group of users that were to move, and what to do if the client did not work the day after the move.

- One server had an Internet Mail Service that had to be moved to the bridgehead server in the original site.

Exchange Permissions

Getting the Exchange administrative and user permissions right is important. One of the mainstays in the computer security world is the principal of *least permissions*. A user or administrator should *never* be assigned any more permissions or rights than they need to do their job. To effectively set up your Exchange organization, you must understand the concepts of Exchange Server permissions.

Viewing Rights and Roles

Every object in Exchange Server has permissions associated with it. These permissions are visible on each object's Permissions page. This page is not automatically visible for all objects. Use Exchange Administrator to enable this tab to be visible for all objects:

1. Select Tools ➢ Options to open the Options dialog box (see Figure 5.1).

2. Click the Permissions tab.

3. Check the Show Permissions Page For All Objects and click OK.

Figure 5.1   The Permissions tab of the Options dialog box

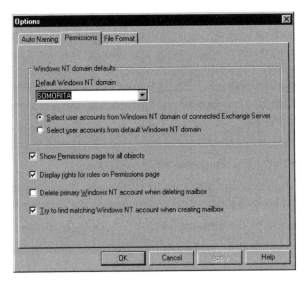

Though it is not necessary in most situations, I like to click the Display Rights For Roles On Permissions Page check box. This lets me see which rights are granted to each role and often helps when I'm troubleshooting permissions.

> **NOTE** The Permissions page only needs to be enabled for administrators who will be working with Exchange permissions. An administrator who does not have the Permissions Admin–level permissions will not need the Options dialog box. Its settings are stored in the current user portion of the Registry, so this does not enable the display of the Permissions page for all administrators.

Figure 5.2 shows the Permissions page for a mailbox. The top part of the Permissions page shows the Windows NT accounts and groups that have inherited permissions to this mailbox. The lower portion of the Permissions page lists the Windows NT accounts that have been explicitly granted permissions to access this mailbox. Notice that user SOMORITA\JohnT has been given the User role to this mailbox. This is because he is the primary Windows NT account assigned to this mailbox.

Figure 5.2   Windows NT accounts that have permissions to a mailbox

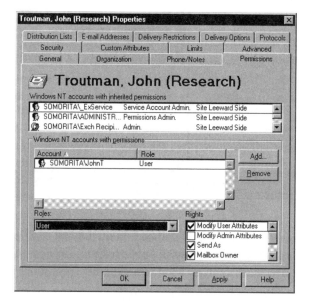

Assigning Rights and Roles

The permissions assigned to users are usually a combination of several rights called a *role*. A role makes it easier to grant common rights to an object. Generally, administrative permissions are granted at three levels: the organization, the site, and the configuration container. The objects under one of three levels will inherit permissions from their respective parent container.

Granting Administrator Permissions

For any medium to large Exchange organization, you are probably going to have a few different types of Exchange administrators. I would break my administrators into three categories: security administrators, system administrators, and recipient administrators. I would further assign these administrators to one of three global groups to make it easier to control the permissions, as most of your Exchange servers will be member servers:

Group **Exch_Security_Admin** would be capable of all levels of administration, including managing permissions, servers, connectors, queues, and public folders as well as mailboxes, distribution lists, and custom recipients. I would assign this group the Permissions Admin role at the organization, site, and site-level configuration container. Membership in this group should be limited to a select few people. Administrators who are assigned this role can give themselves permission to another user's mailbox.

Group **Exch_Systems_Admin** would be capable of managing servers, public folders, queues, and connectors as well as mailboxes, distribution lists, and custom recipients. This group is assigned the Admin permission at the organization, site, site-level configuration container, and Permissions Admin on specific public folder hierarchy.

Group **Exch_Recipients_Admin** would be capable of managing distribution lists, custom recipients, and mailboxes. These administrators, however, would not manage queues, public folders, or connectors. This group is assigned the Admin permission at the site and organization only. I recommend that you assign this group permission at the configuration container and remove all rights for the specific group, rendering it with the View-Only Admin custom role. If this group will be responsible for creating Windows NT accounts, the users should also be members of the domain's Account Operators group.

WARNING   Using groups introduces a potential security hole, because anyone with membership in the Account Operator group has the ability to put themselves into the recipients or security admin groups. If this is a concern, you might consider assigning Exchange permissions directly to users rather than to groups. You can also make the Exchange administrator global groups members of the domain's operators groups (such as Account Operator, Server Operator, and so on). Only an administrator can modify the membership of operator groups.

TIP Membership in the Windows NT administrator group is not necessary in order to be an Exchange administrator. However, if the Exchange administrator is going to be responsible for managing the server hardware, I recommend making that Exchange administrator a member of the Windows NT Server Operators group (if the Exchange server is on a BDC) or the Windows NT Power Users group (if the Exchange server is on a member server).

Windows NT Group Quandary

You can assign users or groups from any domain to have permissions to Exchange Server, provided there is a trust relationship between the domain that the Exchange server is part of and the domain that contains the user or group.

Microsoft's official strategy for creating groups goes something like this: Create global groups to organize and categorize your users; create local groups that will be used to assign permissions and rights to resources; make the appropriate global groups members of the local groups that have the permissions. When I try to explain this to people for the first time, their eyes get crossed. If you are in an environment that has multiple domains, I recommend following this strategy. However, for a single-domain environment (and no plans for multiple domains), I find creating local groups to be an unnecessary step.

The Site Services Account

When you install the first Exchange server into a new site, you are required to select a site services account. If you do not select one, then the user you were logged in as when you installed Exchange will be used. This is normally the Administrator user. (You should not use the Administrator user account.) Here are some things that you may not realize about the site services account:

- This is the user account that the Exchange services will log on as when they start.
- All Exchange servers in the site share the same site services account, but different sites in the same organization do not need to use the same site services account.
- The site services account is also used when the Exchange message transfer agent and directory service communicate with another server in the same site using RPCs.
- The site services account is used when two sites are communicating with each Exchange site connector using RPCs, though this can be overridden.

- Membership in the Windows NT domain's Domain Admins group is not required unless the server is going to support Secure Sockets Layer (SSL) applications. The only Windows NT rights required by this account are the "Logon as a service," "Backup files and directories," and "Act as part of the operating system."

- The site services account has the permissions necessary to open all Exchange mailboxes in the site.

The site services account is given the Service Account Admin permission at the site and site-level configuration container during installation. At the organization level, the role says Custom, but the site services account is still assigned all the appropriate service-account rights needed at that level.

Protecting the Site Services Account

This account should be treated with the same sanctity and respect that you treat your administrator account. (You do treat your administrator account with respect, don't you? <grin>) Here are a few hints to keep in mind when working with the site services account:

- Exchange administrators who may be responsible for installing new Exchange servers, gateways, or connectors should be the only ones who know the account password.

- The account password should be strong: numbers, special characters, upper- and lowercase, with a minimum of 10 characters.

- Name the account something that will set it apart from your user accounts. I like to name mine something like _Exchange_Service or !ExService.

- Windows NT account operators should be familiar with this account and other service accounts (such as SQL service accounts) and know that it should *never* be deleted.

TIP The site services account does not have to be made a member of the Domain Admins group. The technical editor of this book, Joshua Konkle, suggests making the site services account a member of the Domain Admins group. This prevents someone with only Account Operator rights from changing (or even deleting) the site services account password. He also suggests the staff who know the site service account password should be more trusted than the account operators.

Creating a Backup Services Account

Do you need an additional account that has Service Account Admin permissions to your site? Most security experts will probably disagree with me on this issue, but I have had two instances where I have lost the site services account, and recovery is a major pain. For this reason, I always create a backup site services account. To do so, follow these steps with the Exchange server up and running:

1. Create a Windows NT user to be used as a backup site services account. This should not be a user you log in as on a daily basis.

2. Using Exchange Administrator, assign the backup account permission at the organization, site, and site-level configuration containers.

3. Permissions must be assigned to the Schema object. Run Exchange Administrator in raw mode by running C:\exchsrvr\bin\admin /R.

4. From the View menu, select Raw Directory.

5. Highlight the Schema object and from the File menu, select Raw Properties.

6. From the Object Attributes Column, select NT-Security-Descriptor and choose the Editor button.

7. Select NT Security Descriptor and click OK.

8. Browse the domain and add the Windows NT account that is going to be your backup site services account.

9. Give this account the Service Account Admin role and click OK.

10. Click the Set button and click OK.

I assign the backup site services account the necessary Windows NT User rights and treat it with the same care that I treat the regular site services account.

If it is ever necessary, I can reassign the site services account using Control Panel ➤ Services. To do this, I have to select each of the Exchange services listed and change its Log On As account name and password. This must be done for each server in the site.

Changing the Site Services Account Password

If someone leaves a company and knew the site services account password, *change the password*. The Exchange Administrator makes this task quite easy:

1. Using Exchange Administrator, highlight the configuration container for the site whose service account password you are changing and choose File ➤ Properties.

2. Select the Service Account Password tab.

3. Enter a new password in the Password and Confirm Password fields. Click OK. This procedure may take a few moments, because it has to contact all the Exchange servers in the site. This will change the startup password for all the services on all the servers in the site.

Operations

PART 2

Address Book Views

Exchange 5 introduced a new feature called *address book view (ABV)* which allows you to organize your recipients (mailboxes and custom recipients) into logical containers. For example, you can create an ABV grouped by department; mailboxes, custom recipients, and sometimes distribution lists will be organized by their department attribute independent of which site or container they are actually found in.

Address book views are created for the entire organization, so any address book views you create will appear in all Exchange sites in your organization. For this reason, they should be planned and created by a single person or group in the organization.

> **WARNING**   Address book views are created based on the recipient attribute or attributes you choose when you create the view. If you create one mailbox and enter the department as Engineering and you create a second mailbox and enter the department as Engineers, you will have two separate ABV containers: Engineering and Engineers. Great care must be taken when creating your mailboxes and custom recipients so that you follow a predefined set of standards.

Creating an Address Book View

Exchange ABVs are created in the Exchange Administrator program, and anyone with the Admin role in a site can create one. From the Exchange Administrator menu, choose File ➤ New Other ➤ Address Book View. Choose a display name and a directory name; I choose something like "By Department" that is indicative of the logical grouping I am trying to achieve, and the users will see By Department in the address book view.

Next, click the Group By page to see the Group By attributes (see Figure 5.4). Select the Group items by attribute to create a grouping category; you can make up to three subgroupings. The Group Items By drop-down list box allows you to group ABVs by the following recipient attributes: city, company, country, department, home server, site, state, title and any of the 10 custom attribute fields.

> **NOTE**   Any recipients that have blank values for the Group By attribute will not appear in the ABV.

Figure 5.4   Creating an address book view to logically group recipients by their Department attribute

The Advanced tab (shown in Figure 5.5) of the ABV properties gives you a few additional options. The Promote Entries To Parent Containers check box is used when you have sub-categories of Group By options. For example, if you are grouping first by state, then by city, this check box allows you to control whether or not everyone from all cities in a particular state will appear in the state portion of the view, or only under the city.

You can further determine whether or not this particular ABV will appear in the client's address book. To clear up any ABV containers that no longer have entries in them, click the Remove Empty Containers button.

TIP   When preparing a new message or viewing the address book, Outlook clients can change their default address list so that their preferred view appears when they click the new message's To, Cc, and Bcc buttons. This is done in the Exchange service properties. Choose Tools ➢ Services, then click the Addressing tab. Select the preferred ABV in the Show This Address List First drop-down list box.

Figure 5.5   The Advanced tab of the By Department ABV

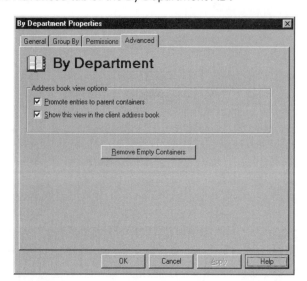

Refreshing and Replicating Address Book Views

Suppose you have several recipients you want to add to an address book view, but you don't want to edit each recipient object separately. Well, you don't have to. Using Exchange Administrator, highlight all the recipient objects simultaneously, then, from the Tools menu, choose Add To Address Book View. You are presented with a list of ABV containers (and you can even create a new one). When you choose a container and click OK, the recipient objects you had selected will have their attributes set with the appropriate values. For example, if I highlight a list of mailboxes and add them to the ABV By Department container Design, those mailboxes will have their Department attribute value changed to Design. This is a quick way to add many people to an ABV or to change attributes using ABVs.

When you add a new mailbox or custom recipient to the directory, the object will not automatically appear in the ABV. A directory services thread called the View Consistency Checker (VCC) runs every five minutes. The VCC scans the global address list looking for recipient objects that meet the criteria of any ABVs that have been created. If you change a recipient attribute that is used to group recipients in ABVs, the VCC will automatically move the recipient to the correct container.

Adjusting ABV Intersite Replication   ABVs replicate to other sites independent of the rest of the Exchange directory. The default schedule is every four hours, but this can be adjusted if you take great care. To adjust the schedule:

1. Run Exchange Administrator in raw mode (C:\exchsrvr\bin\admin /R).

2. Select the ABV's container and choose File ➤ Raw Properties.

3. In the Object attributes list, highlight Period-Rep-Sync-Times and click the Editor button.

4. Highlight Schedule and click OK.

After you have edited the times and clicked OK, don't forget to click the Set button before exiting the raw properties dialog box. This saves the changes you have made.

Though the default replication schedule is every four hours, I personally feel that once every 12 hours is more than sufficient. In an environment where bandwidth is a consideration, I would replicate only once every 24 hours. I would also pick times when the bandwidth is not at a premium. Also, switching the view to a 15-minute view rather than a 1-hour view will allow you to more precisely tune when replication occurs.

Exchange@Work: Virtual Organization Support

There are organizations that for one reason or another do not want their users to see the entire global address list. One example of this would be where two companies are hosted on the same Exchange server. Another would be when most users should be restricted from seeing anyone outside of their own department.

In this situation, ABVs come to the rescue. Windows NT groups can have the Search right assigned to specific ABV containers, thereby limiting who can view the recipients in these containers.

Let's take my favorite fictitious company, Somorita Surfboards, as an example. The CEO has decided that users should only be able to send e-mail between people in their own respective departments and that management should be able to see all addresses for everyone in the company. There are five departments at Somorita: Design, Research, Engineering, Consulting, and Management. How do we go about restricting the address lists?

The first step is to create five Windows NT groups. In this example, I am going to create global groups; however, in a multi-domain environment, you should consider assigning permissions to local groups and grouping the Windows NT users together in global groups. If the Exchange server is installed on a member server, the local groups must be created on the member server.

Exchange@Work: Virtual Organization Support *(continued)*

Now I must make sure that a Windows NT account has been assigned anonymous access for the DS Site Configuration object. This must be done before I can assign the Search right. I can use the IUSR account created by the Internet Information Server if I like, but for security tracking purposes, I prefer to use a designated Exchange account such as EX_ANON or something similar. The anonymous account is assigned on the General tab of the DS Site Configuration object's property page.

Next, I need to create an address book view grouped by the Department attribute. Once I have created the ABV and it has been populated, I need to highlight each ABV container, display the container's properties, and select the Permissions tab, as shown in the following dialog box. Notice that I have added the Windows NT group Management to this container and assigned it the Search role. This will prevent any-one except those in the Management group from viewing this container.

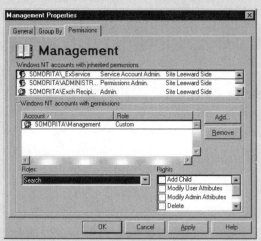

Exchange@Work: Virtual Organization Support *(continued)*

If you have tried restricting permissions to an ABV on your own system (hopefully on a test system first), you may have noticed that you can still see all the mailboxes listed in the GAL. This is because all users still have permission to search the GAL.

The final step toward restricting a user's view of the address list to only specific ABV containers is to restrict who has permissions to search the GAL. To do this, using Exchange Administrator, highlight the organization object (not the GAL object), display its properties, and select the Permissions tab. Highlight the site services account and in the Roles field, click the Search check box to enable the search right. This will hide the GAL from everyone (except the site services account).

In this example, I would give the Windows NT Management group the Search role at the organization level so that anyone in this group could see the GAL.

TIP   Anyone who is restricted from seeing the GAL should change their default Outlook address list in Tools ➤ Services ➤ Addressing so they do not get an error message each time they bring up the address book.

NOTE   Restricting access to an ABV or the GAL prevents users from seeing the names in their address list. However, it does not prevent them from sending messages to those "hidden" addresses if they know the mailbox's X.400 or SMTP address.

Exchange Administrator and Raw Mode

The Exchange Administrator program has a special command switch that allows you to start it in raw mode (the /R switch). What does raw mode give you access to? Well, you can think of it as sort of a Registry Editor for the Exchange directory. You can display and edit the raw attributes of an object rather than messing with that friendly, easy-to-use user interface! Figure 5.6 shows the raw attributes that make up a mailbox. The display name is currently highlighted.

NOTE   To start the Exchange Administrator program in raw mode, type **C:\exchsrvr\bin\admin /R**.

Figure 5.6 The attributes that make up a mailbox object

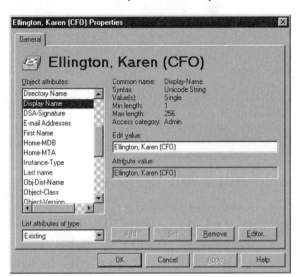

Is this not completely cool? Well, probably not *completely* cool, but it is neat. However (there is always a "however" with cool stuff), raw mode is also dangerous. The friendly user interface is there to keep us from making mistakes, preventing us from deleting objects we did not really want to delete or putting values on objects that should not be there.

WARNING Raw mode should be treated with the same care that you use with the Registry Editor. Careless changes can prematurely end the life of your Exchange server!

The Exchange Schema

The Exchange *schema* is a set of rules and attributes that govern objects in a distributed directory environment. The X.500 recommendations define a default schema; the Exchange schema has extended the basic X.500 recommendations, and developers can further extend or enhance it.

The schema also determines what type of access is granted to objects and attributes and which attributes are associated with which objects. The directory service enforces these rules and access to objects and attributes.

Opening the schema is easy, but it must be done when the Exchange Administrator program is in raw mode. Click View ➤ Raw Directory to see the schema container, which appears beneath the site object.

Figure 5.7 shows the Exchange Administrator with the raw directory displayed. The properties of the Assistant Phone Number attribute are displayed in the Assistant Phone Number Properties dialog box. These properties are used for any Exchange directory object that requires a phone number (including mailboxes and custom recipients).

Figure 5.7   Exchange Administrator showing the properties of the Assistant Phone Number attribute

The Assistant Phone Number is considered an attribute in the schema. There are other items that exist in the schema such as Mailbox that define a "class" of objects. Mailbox recipients are of the "mailbox" class and they have certain attributes, like Assistant Phone, associated with them. The schema is responsible for this association.

NOTE   The Exchange schema is site specific. Organization-wide changes must be configured for each site.

Distribution Lists

In a small environment, distribution lists are great! They enable you to send data to a selected group of people quickly and easily. However, if you are a system administrator for a large Exchange organization and you have large distribution lists, they may become the bane of your existence. Here are some tips and tricks that may make life with distribution lists a little easier.

Assign an Distribution List Owner

When a distribution list is created, you can assign a user as the distribution list owner. This owner is given the Modify User Attributes right to the distribution list object. From within the Outlook address book, the owner can add and remove users as necessary. This can reduce your administrative overhead by delegating membership management to someone else.

To assign an owner to a distribution list, highlight the distribution list, choose File ➤ Properties, click the Modify button and assign an owner.

You can indirectly assign more than one owner to a distribution list. Assign the primary owner through the Modify button on the General tab of the distribution list. Then, on the Permissions tab, assign the Modify User Attributes role to additional Windows NT users who need to modify membership in the distribution list. It is possible to add the additional users with the User role, but this allows them to send mail as the distribution list, which can be construed as a security risk.

Owners can modify membership in the distribution list through Outlook by selecting Tools ➤ Address Book. Then they select the distribution list from the GAL and choose File ➤ Properties. Finally, they need to click the Modify Members button to add or remove members.

> **TIP** The distribution list object has a Notes field, which you can use to enter detailed information about the distribution list such as who should be contacted if there are problems with the list. These notes are visible from the Outlook client's address book. Educate your users to read these notes so they can understand what the DL is for and who manages it.

Distribution List Expansion

The process of figuring out which recipients are members of a distribution list is called *expansion*. The Exchange message transfer agent (MTA) is responsible for expansion, even in a single-server organization. Even though the distribution list may have thousands of members, the MTA figures which servers the message has to go to and sends a single message to only those servers.

One optimization tip that may be useful if you have large distribution lists is to select a specific server to handle the expansion. Some sites with extremely large distribution lists (tens of thousands of members via nested distribution lists) set up dedicated distribution list expansion servers.

Distribution List Size

Microsoft recommends no more than about 3,000 to 5,000 members on any single distribution list. If you reach a distribution list size that looks like it is going to cross the 3,000-member mark, try breaking up the distribution lists into smaller lists and nest them. For example, instead of having one large list that has everyone in the organization, try having a list for "Everyone in Hilo," "Everyone in Kona," "Everyone in San Francisco," and so on. Then create a master distribution list called "Everyone" and make the smaller distribution lists members of this master list.

> **NOTE** In the event you have a large (10K+) distribution list, membership may not be replicated correctly. I recommend that you keep the size of the DL to a lower number by taking advantage of site DLs (DLs that consists of everyone in a specific site), which become part of the larger DL of users for the entire company. If you do have a rather large DL, you need to take some precautions. In Exchange Server 5.5 SP1 and SP2, custom changes need to be made to the Windows NT Registry. If you are supporting DLs with 10K+ members, you should review the service pack documentation and look for "Replicating Large Distribution Lists."

Restricting Distribution List Usage

When creating a distribution list that is going to have more than a few dozen users, you should always restrict who can send to the distribution list. This will help prevent abuses of the mail system when someone decides to send a message selling their used car. Restricting who can use a distribution list does not prevent them from selecting the entire GAL, but it does make it a little more difficult to send to a large number of mailboxes.

> **TIP** There is a Registry value you can set that will restrict the maximum number of recipients that a single mail message can be sent to. To do so, locate the \HKLM\System\CurrentControlSet\Services\MSExchangeIS\Parameters-System Registry key. Add a new value called MaxRecipientsOnSubmit with a data type of REG_DWORD. Enter in the data field that maximum number of recipients you wish to allow. See Knowledge Base article Q126497 for additional information.

Operations

PART 2

Microsoft Product Support Services (PSS) describes a problem that they refer to as "Bedlam." In this situation, someone sends a message (possibly a junk mail message) to a very large distribution list; inevitably, several people on the list select Reply To All with a message that says "I agree," "Leave me alone," or something similar. All these Reply To All messages also have to be processed by the Exchange MTA, which quickly becomes bogged down processing nothing but these messages.

TIP Users should be taught the difference between Reply and Reply To All!

To restrict usage on a distribution list, display the distribution list's properties and choose the Delivery Restrictions tab. Click the Accept Messages From List button and add users to the list using the Modify button.

Another good step to take with large distribution lists is to deselect the Report To Message Originator (default is on), Report To Distribution List Owner (default is off), and Allow Out Of Office Messages To Originator (default is off) check boxes found on the Advanced tab. Also found on the Advanced tab is the Message Size Limit box. Though your mileage may vary, I see no reason why anyone should send a message larger than about 100K to a large distribution list.

TIP The BackOffice Resource Kit provides a command-line tool called ONDL, which you can use to manage distribution list membership. This tool might also prove useful if you ever have to break up a large distribution list into several smaller ones.

Ambiguous Name Resolution

The Exchange and Outlook clients are capable of performing something called *Ambiguous Name Resolution (ANR)*; this is turned on by default. (Though I define ANR as Ambiguous Name Resolution, I have seen the "A" referred to as Ambiguous, Automatic, and Address.) You can type an ambiguous name into the message To, Cc, or Bcc fields, and Outlook will search the Exchange directory for mailboxes and custom recipients whose alias, office, e-mail addresses (such as SMTP addresses), last name, or the first word of the display name matches the ambiguous name. If more than one name is found, the Exchange and Outlook clients will display the results, allowing you to choose the correct display name.

Just entering a name will return all matches, including partial matches. You can also enter an equals sign (=) in front of the name you are looking for, and the client will return only exact matches.

If you want to include other fields in the search criteria for ANR, you can do this through Exchange Administrator in raw mode by modifying the schema. For example, let's say that I want to be able to enter a first name and have ANR resolve it. I need to run Exchange Administrator in raw mode, view the raw directory (as described earlier), display the raw properties of the First Name attribute under the Schema container, and select Search-flags under Object attributes. In the Edit Value field, I then need to change the value to 2 and click Set.

Exchange@Work: Using Automatic Name Resolution on Other Attributes

One of my customers is a large military installation. Users often use a person's job code rather than his or her name when exchanging correspondence. This is because people change positions frequently, but the job requirements for a specific job code is always the same. My client wanted to be able to type the person's job code into the To field and have Outlook automatically resolve to the correct display name.

To achieve this, we used a custom attribute field, renaming it to Job Code. We changed the Job Code attribute's Search-flags in the schema to a value of 2. This allowed ANR to automatically search using a person's job code.

Letting Users Manage Their Own Directory Attributes

I am a big proponent of using the mailbox fields when creating a mailbox. I will enter the address, city, state, phone number, fax number, title, and more. For a number of organizations I have worked for, the Exchange directory can now double as the organization-wide phone book. However, the biggest problem is that this information is quite dynamic in a larger organization, and someone has to keep it up to date.

The Microsoft BackOffice Resource Kit (Second Edition) introduced a new tool called the GAL Modify Tool which lets users modify their own personal information that is displayed in the global address list. With this tool, users can modify many of their mailbox attributes including the addressing information, title, company, office, assistant, and all the phone number fields. There is an additional component that, if installed, allows users to modify their custom attribute fields.

Installing the GAL Modify Tool

There are two simple programs that install the GAL Modify Tool: `GALMOD32.exe`, which modifies the standard items, and `GALMODCA.exe`, which includes the ability to modify the custom attributes. These programs are found on the BackOffice Resource Kit in the `\Exchange\Win95\Client\GALMOD` directory or the `\Exchange\WinNT\I386\Client\GALMOD` directory. There is also an Alpha version of the tool.

To install the tool, copy both programs to a location that the clients can access; copy only GALMOD32.exe if the users do *not* need to modify their custom attribute fields. The programs are actually quite simple and must be executed from a computer that has a messaging profile setup.

Figure 5.8 shows sample GAL properties. To change a field, simply change the value and click OK.

Figure 5.8 GAL Modify Tool showing the current mailbox properties

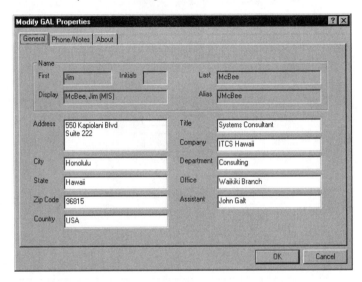

Can Users Really Change All Those Fields?

I know you are probably saying to yourself, "Self, what if I don't want my users to change their company name or department name?" This is not a problem. First, let's review the permissions a Windows NT user is assigned to his mailbox. When a mailbox is assigned a primary Windows NT account, on the Permissions page for that mailbox, that Windows NT account is assigned the User role to that mailbox. The User role includes the Modify User Attributes right; that Windows NT account can now change any attribute whose access category is considered User.

How do you know which attributes are User and which are Admin? A quick tour through the raw properties will tell you this. Figure 5.9 shows the raw properties for mailbox Lyle Bullock; the City attribute's access category is User.

Figure 5.9   Raw properties for mailbox Lyle Bullock; notice that the City attribute's access
category is User.

Which common mailbox attributes fall into the User access category and which fall into
the Admin level? Table 5.4 shows a list of the common attributes that fall into each category.

Table 5.4   The Default Access Categories of Common Mailbox Attributes

User Access	Admin Access
Address	Alias
All Phone Numbers	Company
Assistant	Department
City	Display Name
Country	First Name
Postal Code	Last Name
Notes	Office
	State
	Title

Table 5.5   Details Template Control Types *(continued)*

Control	Function
Page Break*	Defines a new property page.
Group Box	Defines a set of controls (fields) that are bound together by a box.
Check Box	Creates a check box control that can be either on or off.
List Box	Creates a box that has multiple choices available.
Multi-Valued List Box Control	Creates a multi-valued list box control.
Multi-Valued Drop Down	Creates a multi-valued drop-down control.

*The most common controls are the Label, Edit, and Page Break controls.

The next step in customizing the Details template is editing the existing labels for fields that you want to customize and those labels that you created from Custom Attribute fields. To customize the Mailbox template seen in Figure 5.12:

1. On the mailbox's Templates tab, locate and highlight each label field that you want to change, click the Edit button, and change the label buttons that need to be customized. In Figure 5.12, Title became Rank, Company became Branch, Department became Command, and so on.

> **NOTE**   Changing the values on the Mailbox template changes only the template seen by the clients; it does *not* change the Mailbox template seen in Exchange Administrator.

2. Next, take your printed screen capture and locate an area near the bottom of the template where you want to add the two new fields (Job Code and DSN Number). Jot down the coordinates of the fields near the bottom of the template; you'll need them to estimate the location of the of your new labels and edit fields. The Job Code and DSN Number fields were formerly Custom Attribute 1 and Custom Attribute 2, but I renamed them on the DS Site Configuration ➤ Attributes property page.

3. Perhaps through a little trial and error, postition the new Edit fields based on the coordinates, widths, and heights shown in Table 5.6. The Test button comes in handy when you are figuring out the exact coordinates and measurements.

4. Click OK to close the Details Templates box and to save your changes. Close and restart Outlook to make sure that the current template information is downloaded from the server. You can now test this template from an Outlook client.

NOTE If you place an ampersand (&) in front of a character, that character will be underlined on the template, making it the hot key. You can use the Alt key and the corresponding character to jump to that field.

Table 5.6   Coordinates, Widths, and Heights for the New Fields on the Mailbox Template

Control Type	Text/Field	X	Y	W	H
Label	&Job Code	12	140	35	8
Edit	Job Code	48	138	90	12
Label	&DSN Number	152	140	90	12
Edit	DSN Number	198	140	90	12

Does this all sound a little confusing? It is the first time you see it, but I guarantee if you give this a try, preferably on a test server, you will become an old hand at it in no time. Then you'll be able to easily customize Exchange to meet your organization's needs.

Directory Importing and Exporting

You have probably already discovered the import and export capabilities of the Exchange Administrator program. From the Tools menu, you have the choice of Directory Import and Directory Export. The Directory Export choice creates a comma-separated value (CSV) file with attributes associated with mailboxes, custom recipients, or distribution lists. Directory Import reads attributes from a CSV file and creates, modifies, or deletes mailboxes, custom recipients, and distribution lists.

You can either run the import and export functions from the Exchange Administrator program, or you can run the Administrator program from the command prompt. The import function can copy attribute values from an existing mailbox or custom recipient if the import file does not contain the values.

WARNING   Prior to importing anything to the Exchange directory, ensure that you have a complete backup.

Importing and Exporting Attributes

The key to importing and exporting all the attributes you want is the header (first line or field names) of the CSV file. If you export mailboxes from the Exchange directory and you do not specify a predefined CSV file, you will get the basic mailbox properties.

You can obtain a complete list of directory attributes for mailboxes, custom recipients, and distribution lists from the BackOffice Resource Kit Header tool. Alternatively, you can use your Administrator program in raw mode to figure out the name of each field.

Using the Header Utility   The BackOffice Resource Kit includes a utility called Header.exe that allows you to create headers for importing and exporting objects such as mailboxes, custom recipients, distribution, containers, mailbox agents, and other Exchange agents. You can also find this utility on the Exchange Server 5.5 CD-ROM in the Resource Kit \Server\Support\Autorun\Reskit\Header directory. Figure 5.14 shows the Header tool creating a header for exporting mailbox information.

Figure 5.14   The Header tool creating a header for an export file

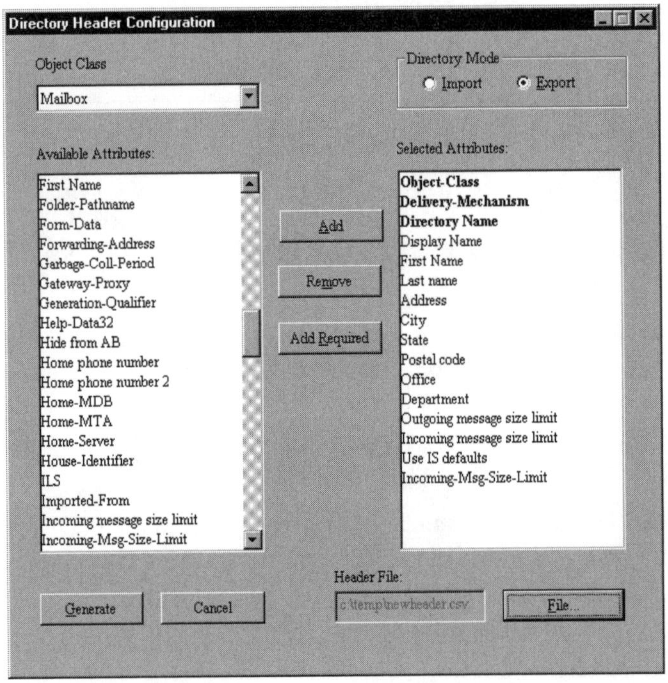

NOTE The Header.exe program must be run from the Exchange server, and the Exchange directory service must be running.

Exchange@Work: Using Administrator in Raw Mode to Access Header Field Names

The Exchange Administrator program can be run from any Windows NT workstation and therefore is more versatile for accessing attribute information for bulk imports. To do so, identify the attribute you want to change. If this attribute currently isn't populated, fill in a value resembling your end goal for all mailboxes. Now, retrieve the raw properties for this object and look for the attribute in the Attributes section of the Raw Properties dialog box. For example, if you are trying to change the incoming message size limit, then the value would be something like "Incoming Message Size Limit." Easy huh?

If you cannot find the attribute you want to change, just go to the top of the list and click each attribute until you find the one with the value you set previously. The values appear to the right. After identifying the value you entered, verify the attribute name and use this information to help build your header file for the next section, which describes importing and exporting processes.

Using Exchange Import/Export to Change Properties for Many Mailboxes

Suppose you want to want to set all (or many) of the mailboxes in a particular site to a maximum incoming and outgoing message size. You could work your way through the directory, editing one mailbox at a time, or you could export the directory to a CSV file, edit the CSV file, and import it once again.

The header file that I created in Figure 5.14 includes the incoming message size limit and outgoing message size limit properties. To do this yourself, first create the CSV file using the Header.exe tool. Then, using the Directory Export feature of Exchange Administrator, select the CSV file you created with the Header.exe tool and export the directory to that CSV file. Edit the file using Excel or some other tool that will edit a CSV file. I have even used Notepad to edit these files, but it is more difficult to keep track of which column is which in Notepad.

If there are currently no limits for the mailboxes, the fields will be blank. Simply enter the value for the maximum incoming and outgoing message size (in kilobytes) and save the file. Then, using Exchange Administrator's Directory Import feature, import the file back into the directory. The default import mode is Update, which modifies the object if it exists or creates the object if it does not.

Managing Mailboxes

When I first started working with Exchange, one of the things I was the most impressed with was its mailbox management capabilities. As a Lotus cc:Mail and Microsoft Mail administrator, I was constantly reminding users to clean up their mailboxes. Many users decided that it was okay to store messages with large file attachments in their e-mail folders. With older mail systems, which tended to be inefficient when it came to managing message storage, I had no control over the amount of data that users could store in their mailboxes nor the size of messages they could send.

Exchange addresses many of the mailbox and disk space management issues that caused me a lot of grief in older messaging systems. Here are a few things to keep in mind when you are managing Exchange mailboxes:

- Anything that you can do as an administrator to keep the total size of your information store database small will help reduce the amount of time it takes to perform backups, restores, and system maintenance.

- Restricting the maximum message size that users can send or receive will help to keep the message transfer agents and the WAN from becoming bogged down with large messages.

- Balancing the two previous restrictions against the overall level of usability that your user community expects will prove to be a challenge.

Reducing Mailbox Size

As an administrator, I am sure you experience many of the same problems that I do when keeping my Exchange servers running. One of these problems relates to the amount of storage that the information store databases require. Just keeping the database size in check and not exceeding the amount of hard disk space available is a challenge. I am also concerned about keeping the information store sizes from growing past a point where they can easily be backed up based on my backup schedule.

This section includes some tips for maintaining an Exchange server and keeping mailbox sizes in check. I have also included information about single-instance storage, which will help you understand how the information store saves messages.

How Much Space Is Each Mailbox Using?

If you want to check how much space is being used by each mailbox, you can report on this information for each server. Navigate the Exchange hierarchy: *Site Name* ➤ Configuration ➤ Servers ➤ *Server Name* ➤ Private Information Store ➤ Mailbox Resources. The right pane of the Mailbox resources dialog box will resemble the one in Figure 5.15.

Figure 5.15   Mailbox resources for the HILO server

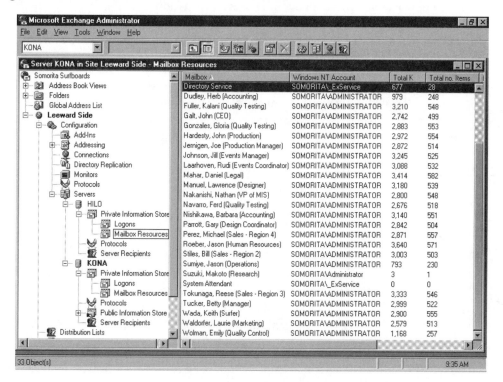

> **NOTE**   You can save the information seen in Figure 5.15 to a CSV text file, which you can then open in Excel and create graphs of the data. Highlight one of the mailbox entries in the right pane, choose File ➤ Save Window Contents, and enter a filename. This CSV file will contain the mailbox display name, the last Windows NT account name that accessed the mailbox, the total size of the messages, the total number of messages, the last login time, and the last logout time.

Single-Instance Storage

An Exchange server manages messages by storing a message only once, regardless of the number of users to which the message is being sent, and each recipient is given a "pointer" to this message. This is called *single-instance storage* (or *SIS*). However, a copy of the message is written to each server that contains a recipient's mailbox.

If I send a 5MB message to 100 mailboxes on a single server, the private information store size will only increase by about 5MB. However, each individual mailbox will report an additional 5MB of space used. If I total all the mailboxes listed in the Mailbox Resources screen (shown in Figure 5.15), the amount of space reported will be greater than the actual file size.

> **NOTE**   If a mailbox is moved from one server to another within a site, and there are already instances of messages being moved on the new destination server, the mailbox is merely given a pointer to the existing message. SIS is preserved.

Message Deletion   In order for a message to be completely deleted from the information store, all mailboxes that had a pointer to that message must have deleted the message. This includes the "copy" of the message that is located in the sender's Sent Items folder.

Recovering Deleted Items

A new feature introduced in Exchange Server 5.5 is the Deleted Item Retention feature (a.k.a. the dumpster). When an item is deleted, it is moved to the Deleted Items folder. Once the Deleted Items folder is emptied, the item can be moved to the *Deleted Items cache*. A user can highlight the Deleted Items folder and select Tools ➤ Recover Deleted Items to see the Recover Deleted Items dialog box, provided you have it enabled.

This feature alone is worth the cost of the upgrade to Exchange 5.5; several times, deleted item recovery has saved me from having to restore an entire server because an important user deleted important mail items.

Deleted item recovery is turned off by default. You must turn it on for each private information and public information store, and you must specify a certain number of days that the server will retain deleted items. Figure 5.16 shows the General tab for server HILO's private information store.

Figure 5.16   The HILO server's private information store General tab

Server HILO's deleted item retention time is set to 15 days. After a message is removed from the Deleted Items folder, it will still be recoverable for another 15 days using the Outlook 97 or 98 Recover Deleted Items toolbar option. At the end of the 15 days, if the deleted item is not in use by any other mailboxes, the space the item is using in the Deleted Items cache will be reused by the information store. The Don't Permanently Delete Items Until The Store Has Been Backed Up option instructs the information store to only permanently delete the item after a normal backup, not an incremental or differential backup.

NOTE   You must be using Outlook 8.03 or later to recover deleted items; this menu choice was not available prior to 8.03. If you are not using Outlook 98 or Outlook 2000 yet, you should upgrade to Outlook 97 8.03; it is available with the CDs that come with Exchange Server 5.5.

Can you recover deleted items using a POP3 or IMAP4 client? No. When POP3 or IMAP clients delete items, they are essentially doing a "hard" or "in-place" delete. The items are not moved to the Deleted Items folder. You can also perform an in-place delete from within Outlook; highlight the message item you want to delete and press Shift+Delete. The message is permanently deleted.

By default, Outlook will not allow you to recover an in-place–deleted message, because the Recover Deleted Items menu choice is not available unless you currently have the Deleted Items folder highlighted. There is a Registry setting that allows you to enable this menu choice for all folders. Add the value `DumpsterAlwaysOn` (data type is REG_ DWORD) to the `\HKLM\Software\Microsoft\Exchange\Client\Options` Registry key. Enter a data value of **1** to turn the Recover Deleted Items menu choice on for all folders, or enter **0** to turn it off.

NOTE Deleted item recovery can only recover items that have been deleted from a mailbox. If the entire mailbox is deleted, it must be restored from backup.

How Large Is Each Mailbox's Deleted Items Cache?   Figure 5.15 showed a quick and easy way to see how much disk space each mailbox is using. However, there is not an option there to see how much space is in that mailbox's Deleted Items cache. You can add support for this information through the Exchange Administrator program. Display the properties of the server's Private Information Store object, choose the Mailbox Resources page, and click the Columns button. This will allow you to choose to see the total size of deleted messages, the mailbox DN, and whether that mailbox has exceeded its storage limits.

TIP You can see how much space the entire Deleted Items cache is taking up for either the public or private information store using the Windows NT Performance Monitor. The MSExchangeIS Public and MSExchangeIS Private objects both have Total Size Of Recoverable Items counters. The value shown is in kilobytes.

Exchange@Work: Public Folder Deleted Item Recovery

You can enable deleted item recovery for public folders. You can even recover an entire deleted public folder. This is done for each public folder server just like enabling it for the private information store. To enable the public information store's Deleted Items cache, choose the properties of a server's public information store and on the General tab, enter a number of days other than zero in the Deleted Item Retention Time [Days] box.

To recover a deleted item from a public folder, select the public folder that the item was deleted from and choose Recover Deleted Items from the Tools menu. You must have read, write, and delete permissions to that folder.

Exchange@Work: Public Folder Deleted Item Recovery *(continued)*

Refer to KB article Q180117 for more information on recovering deleted items from the public information store.

How Large Is Each Public Folder's Deleted Items Cache?

Checking the size of delete items for a public folder works similarly to the mailbox. Select the Public Information Store object and choose the Public Folder Resources tab. Click the Columns button to include the total size of deleted messages (Deleted Items K) for the public folders in the list.

Exchange@Work: How Long Should I Retain Deleted Items?

Microsoft's Information Technology Group reports that nearly 90 percent of the messages sent in their internal Exchange system are read, acted upon, and *deleted* within a day of receipt. When I heard this, all I could think to say was, "Wow!" I feel like many of the user communities I have supported handled their messages in exactly the opposite approach—keeping 90 percent of all the messages they receive for years. This is a matter of user education, though. Users should be encouraged to keep their Inboxes, Sent Items folders, and other folders clean.

Though some people will argue with me on this point, I set my deleted item retention time to 15 days; other administrators use a number in the three- to seven-day range. Still others set the deleted item retention time up nearly 30 days. I find that if I delete something and then need it back, I usually realize it within about three days. I have never had to recover, nor have I been asked to recover, something that was deleted more than seven days earlier.

The longer you keep old items, the larger your database size will be. I have seen Deleted Items caches take up anywhere between three and thirty percent of the total information store size. A common problem is that users will delete items from their mailboxes, but they will not empty their Deleted Items folders. You can set up a policy to empty the Deleted Items folder each time a user exits Outlook. I think this is a good policy if you have the Deleted Item cache enabled. See Chapter 11 for more information on creating system policies.

Limiting Message Space Usage

Should you set up mailbox storage limits? Absolutely and without a doubt, yes! Back in Figure 5.16, you saw the private information store properties for server HILO. There are three storage limit settings on this property page that set the defaults for all mailboxes on this particular server. Here are my recommendations for each setting:

> **Issue warning** at 50MB (50,000KB). Each evening at 8:00 P.M., users will receive a message telling them how much over the limit they actually are. I recommend setting this value to 50MB by default. Special-case users can be individually increased or decreased on the Limits property page of their individual mailboxes.

> **Prohibit send** at 55MB. Once a mailbox reaches 55MB, the user will no longer be able to reply or send new messages. A pop-up dialog box will tell the user to clean up her mailbox.

> **Prohibit send and receive** at 65MB. If a user has ignored the warning messages (or his mailbox has filled up unexpectedly), the information store will reject messages after it reaches 65MB. The sender will receive a message saying that the recipient's mailbox is full.

These settings can be overridden per mailbox using the Limits tab of a mailbox's properties, which is discussed in the next section.

Restricting Maximum Message Size   What about limiting the maximum message size? In many environments, this may be an excellent idea, but in others, the user community may need to send very large messages on occasion. But if you can restrict the maximum message size your users can send, it will help reduce the congestion on the WAN links and prevent the MTAs from becoming backlogged delivering large messages. Plus, preventing users from sending large messages will reduce the likelihood that they will be tempted to use their mailboxes to store large files, thus increasing the size of the private information store.

It is possible to restrict the maximum size of a message in one of two ways. The first is to set the maximum message size on each of your connector properties including each server's MTA, the X.400 connector, the Internet Mail Service, and other connectors; this limits the message size that the connector can send or receive.

Though restricting the connectors is the easiest way to limit the maximum size of each message, another way is to limit the maximum incoming and outgoing message size for particular mailboxes. Figure 5.17 shows a mailbox's Limits tab; both incoming and outgoing message size can be restricted here.

> **NOTE** To restrict many mailboxes at once, export the directory to a CSV file using Exchange Administrator, change the value in the text file, and import it back into the directory. This procedure was described earlier in this chapter.

Figure 5.17 You can set both outgoing and incoming message size limits, as well as deleted item retention time and information store limits, on a mailbox's Limits tab.

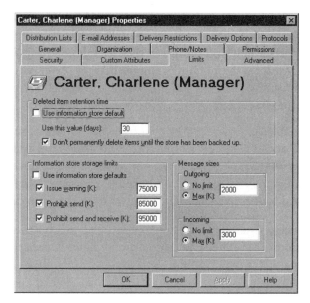

Encourage Your Users to Self-Manage Their Mailbox Space

Limiting mailbox space is the best way to control exactly how much disk space a mailbox user can take up. During their initial training, however, users should be taught to self-manage their own mailboxes. I have had too many experiences as a Lotus cc:Mail administrator where I stood over users' shoulders while they deleted messages. (There are reasons why they called me the Network Dictator. <grin>)

Outlook 98 and Outlook 2000 both have a feature that allows users to check how much space they are actually taking up. They simply highlight their mailbox or any single folder, right-click, and choose Properties. On the General tab, there is a Folder Size button that displays the total size of messages in the current folder and all subfolders.

Using Personal Folders I am a big proponent of Exchange-based storage for all current electronic mail. The biggest reason is, of course, that I am making sure that the messaging

Table 5.7 Standard Outlook Folders and Their Default AutoArchive Actions

Folder Name	AutoArchive Enabled	Default Action
Calendar	Y	Moves items older than six months to archive file
Contacts*	N	
Deleted Items	Y	Deletes items older than two months
Drafts	N	
Inbox	N	
Journal	Y	Moves items older than six months to archive file
Notes	N	
Outbox	N	
Sent Items	Y	Moves items older than two months to archive file
Tasks	Y	Moves items older than six months to archive file

*Contacts folders do not have the archive option.

NOTE Message items that are moved to an archive file are recoverable from the Deleted Item cache if you have enabled the `DumpsterAlwaysOn` Registry key.

Exchange@Work: That Pesky Deleted Items Folder!

I recently monitored a customer's Deleted Items cache size using the Windows NT Performance Monitor. Their deleted item retention time was set to 30 days. I was quite surprised that a server supporting nearly 100 mailboxes would have a deleted items cache size of only about 50MB. The `priv.edb` (private information store database file) was nearly 3GB in size.

Operations

PART 2

Exchange@Work: That Pesky Deleted Items Folder! *(continued)*

On a hunch, I sent an e-mail message asking that everyone choose Empty "Deleted Items" Folder from their Tools menu in Outlook. Within a few hours, the Deleted Items cache size had grown to nearly 400MB! Why did this happen? Users were diligent about keeping their mailboxes clean, but they were not emptying their Deleted Items folders.

The Deleted Items folder can be manually (from the Tools menu) or automatically emptied each time a user exits Outlook. To automatically empty the Deleted Items folder, from Outlook 98, choose Tools ➤ Options ➤ Other and click the Empty The Deleted Items Folder Upon Exiting button. This feature can also be turned on centrally through a system policy.

Cleaning Mailboxes

Are your user's mailboxes filling up? Do they absolutely refuse to delete their older and larger items? In many environments, deleting users' messages for them would be completely unacceptable; however, this is an acceptable practice in some businesses. I agree with it as long as the users have adequate notice and understand that once messages reach a certain date, they will be removed from the system.

The Clean Mailbox Option   Exchange Administrator allows you to highlight one or more mailboxes and choose the Clean Mailbox option from the Tools menu. The following dialog box will open:

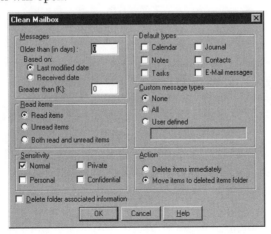

The Clean Mailbox tool allows you to clean up messages based on date, message size, read, unread, both read and unread, message sensitivity, message size, and message type. You can choose to delete the items immediately or to move them to the Deleted Items folder. I know of a company that warns users that they cannot keep messages larger than 100KB in their mailbox. Twice a month they run the Clean Mailbox utility to clean out any messages larger than 100KB.

Mailbox Cleanup Agent

The BackOffice Resource Kit (Second Edition) has a tool called the Mailbox Cleanup Agent that allows you to automate cleanup of mailboxes. The tool must be installed on one server in the site and can be installed from the \Exchange\WinNT\I386\Admin\ MBClean directory on the BackOffice Resource Kit CD-ROM. If you plan to use this tool, make sure you have a recent version of it; version 1.9 is the most recent version as of this writing.

The Mailbox Cleanup Agent configuration screen (shown in Figure 5.20) allows you to configure mailbox cleanup parameters for each recipient container, though I typically recommend putting user mailboxes only in the default Recipients container.

Figure 5.20   Mailbox Cleanup Agent properties for the Recipients container

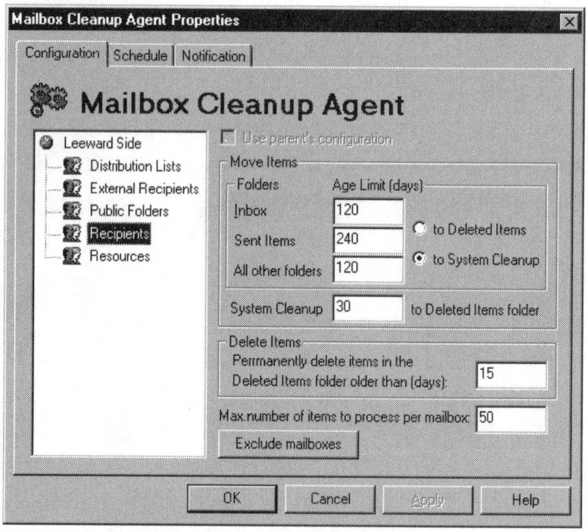

As you can see, I have configured all Inbox items older than 120 days, sent items older than 240 days, and all other items in other folders older than 120 days to be moved to a folder called System Cleanup, which the Mailbox Cleanup Agent will create. Any items

that have been in the System Cleanup folder for more than 30 days will be moved to the Deleted Items folder. Any items that have been in the Deleted Items folder for more than 15 days will be deleted permanently.

Some people may think that the period of time I am allowing users to keep items in their mailboxes is too short, while others may believe it is too long. If you choose to use the Mailbox Cleanup Agent, you need to decide for yourself what the right amount of time will be.

Exchange@Work: Should Messages Be Kept?

In a past life, I used to install messaging systems for law firms. During the installation of one particularly large system, the managing partner of the firm requested my presence in his office. He then asked me about the system backup strategy that we were using to back up the e-mail system. Figuring that he was concerned that he would lose data, I began extolling the virtues of the backup software, hardware, and plan.

He then requested that no backups of the e-mail database ever be made. Further, I was to put a procedure in place whereby the e-mail administrators were to purge from the system all messages older than 15 days. This was easy enough to do, but it left me puzzled. He then explained that any e-mail conversations about a client could be considered admissible as evidence in court and could be used against their clients and the firm.

So we did not do backups of the messaging system. However, I did make backups of the directory database so that we could at least restore the directory information if there were ever a catastrophic system failure.

Deleting Mailboxes

Earlier I mentioned that if a mailbox is deleted, it cannot be undeleted using the Deleted Items Recovery tool. For this reason, as an administrator, when I am notified of users who have left my organization, I do not delete their mailboxes or Windows NT accounts right away. A number of times in the past, I have deleted a mailbox or account only to find that the information I had been given was incorrect. A few times someone has needed something that was sent to a mailbox that had already been deleted.

So now, instead of deleting a mailbox (and corresponding Windows NT account), I just disable the Windows NT account. I then add that mailbox and Windows NT account to a list of mailboxes and accounts that need to be deleted. Periodically, I delete old, unused mailboxes and accounts as part of my regular maintenance schedule.

The Party You Are Calling Is Unavailable... Quite often, when a person leaves a company, he or she will continue to receive messages from both inside and outside the company—messages that the person who is replacing him or her would need to see, perhaps. For example, a sales representative leaves her company, but many of her customers are unaware of this and continue to send her messages.

I have two solutions to this type of dilemma. The first is to either automatically forward all mail to the new sales representative's mailbox using the Alternate Recipient feature on the mailbox's Delivery Options property page.

The second solution is to give myself permissions to the mailbox, log in to that mailbox using Outlook, and create a rule that automatically replies to the sender. (Don't forget that Internet automatic replies are disabled by default at the Internet Mail Service.) This would automatically reply to the sender with a text message and also forward the message to the person's new e-mail address (if it is a person whom I liked and I wanted to be nice). The auto-reply message might read something like this:

```
Thanks for contacting Somorita Surfboards. Gloria Gonzales is no
longer with our company. Your e-mail message has been automatically
forwarded to Ryan Tung; Ryan has taken over her projects. You can
reach Ryan directly at RyanT@Somorita.com. If you wish to contact
Gloria, she can be e-mailed at SurfBabe@VeryHotMail.com. Thank you
for your time.
```

Over time, I would also run the Exchange Administrator Clean Mailbox tool on any mailbox that was no longer used, but the rules remain in place to forward and reply to new messages. I could also put another rule in place that would forward all mail to Gloria's new address, but that might or might not be a prudent business decision.

You Can't Take It with You

Well, maybe you *can* take your mail with you. When someone leaves an organization, they often want all their mail forwarded to their new e-mail address. This is actually pretty simple to do; however, in a very large organization, I would not want to set a precedent for doing it every time someone left.

Let's take my previous example; user Gloria Gonzales has left the company. I am going to automatically forward all of Gloria's mail to her new address. First, I have to delete her mailbox. Then, I need to create a custom recipient for her new Internet address. On the custom recipient's E-Mail Addresses property page, I will create a new Internet address for her original address. I might also hide this custom recipient if it did not need to appear in the global address list.

The IMS will accept messages for Gloria's old address but will automatically forward them to her new address. The Unix community does this with either an alias file or a .forward (dot forward) file.

> **NOTE**   There are naturally going to be situations where you would not do this for your departing users—especially if Gloria were leaving to go to work for a competitor!

Restricting Access to the Exchange Server

Restricting access to the information store is a pretty obscure feature, but I recently had an opportunity to use it for the first time, and I think it is pretty cool. I restricted all users from accessing the Exchange server while I made a complete online backup. I did this prior to rebuilding the server's hard disks and reinstalling Exchange Server. Microsoft Knowledge Base article Q146764 describes a Registry setting that allows you to restrict which users can access the Exchange server.

> **WARNING**   Make absolutely sure you have a complete, up-to-the-minute backup prior to reformatting the server hard disks.

To restrict access to the Exchange server, follow these steps:

1. Run the Windows NT Registry Editor (REGEDT32, *not* REGEDIT).
2. Locate the HKLM\System\CurrentControlSet\Services\MExchangeIS\ ParametersSystem Registry key.
3. Select Edit ➤ Add Value, type **Logon Only As**, and select REG_MULTI_SZ in the Data Type box.
4. In the Data box that appears, enter a list of Distinguished Names (DNs) of mailboxes that are allowed to access the server. If you leave this box empty, *no one* will be able to access the server. The DNs should be in the following format:

   /O=Somorita/OU=Honolulu/CN=Recipients/CN=NancyM

5. Stop and restart the information store service for the change to take effect.

> **WARNING**   When you are finished backing up the server or performing whatever maintenance required you to restrict access, make sure that you delete the entire Logon Only As value.

Operations

PART 2

Preventing Other Sites from Managing Your Public Folders

A new feature of Exchange 5.5 is the ability to restrict management of a public folder to the public folder's home site. The default is to only allow administrators from a public folder's home site to manage the folder's properties.

This default setting can be changed by displaying the General tab of the public folder's properties and removing the check from the Limit Administrative Access To Home Site check box.

Message Journaling

The United States Securities Exchange Commission requires stock brokers and dealers to keep all records related to transactions between three and five years, depending on the type of transactions; this includes electronic mail. Many local and federal governments have enacted "sunshine laws" that require that government agencies make available to the public their written and electronic correspondence.

To help customers who need this type of message retention, Microsoft incorporated a feature called *message journaling* into Exchange 5.5 SP1 and later. This feature is not for everyone. Here some facts regarding message journaling as well as some of my own thoughts:

- Every message that is sent through an entire site or organization has a copy sent to a mailbox. Over time, the storage requirements of these messages will become a burden. Backups of the system that houses the target mailbox will begin to take longer and longer. A dedicated server for message journaling might prove useful in some situations—low powered, but lots of disk space. You may want to establish a procedure of archiving these messages to a long-term storage media such as CD-ROM or DVD.

- Any administrator with the Permissions Admin role can give herself permissions to this mailbox and see messages that anyone has sent.

- Message encryption is retained. To access an encrypted message, the administrator needs the user's security keys either with the user's assistance or by recovering the user's keys through Exchange Administrator.

- The MTA on each server must now handle all messages, even those being delivered locally. This may have an adverse affect on performance. By some estimates, a busy server could see a 10 to 20 percent performance drop due to message journaling.

- Message journaling must be enabled for an entire site or the entire organization, not just a specific server. Further, you cannot enable it just for a few users.

- Message journaling is enabled through the Registry on various values. After deploying Exchange 5.5 SP1 or SP2, ensure only users with correct permissions have access to these keys. Otherwise, any Exchange administrator can enable message journaling and monitor all the mail.

Enabling Message Journaling

Prior to enabling message journaling, make sure that all servers in the site have Exchange 5.5 SP1 or later installed on them. Each server will need to have its Registry edited, and you will need the DN of the mailbox you want to use as the target for journaled messages. To view the DN of the mailbox you are using, display the raw properties of the mailbox and locate the Obj-Dist-Name attribute. It will be in a form that will look similar to /O=Somorita/OU=Knoxville/CN=Recipients/CN=MsgJournal.

MsgJournal is the name of the mailbox that will be use to accept all journaled messages. Once you have the DN for the mailbox you are going to use, you have some Registry editing to do. Locate the \HKLM\System\CurrentControlSet\Services\MSExchangeIS\ParametersSystem key. Create a new value in this key called NoLocalDelivery and a data type of DWORD. Set the data on this value to 1 (a value of 1 disables local delivery; a value of 0 turns it on).

Next, if this server hosts an Internet Mail Service, locate the \HKLM\System\CurrentControlSet\Services\MSExchangeIMC key. Then create a new value called "RerouteViaStore" with a data type of DWORD. Set the data on this value to 1; this causes all messages to be routed via the information store.

Finally, the MTA settings must be set. Locate the \HKLM\System\CurrentControlSet\Services\MSExchangeMTA\Parameters key. Create a new value called JournalRecipientName with a data type of REG_SZ. Enter the DN of the mailbox that will receive the journaled messages in the data field of this value.

Next, create a new value called Per-SiteJournalRequired with a data type of DWORD. Set the data on this value to 1 if the journal is specific to the site or a value of 0 if the journal is organization-wide.

Finally, stop and start the MTA, information store, and Internet Mail Service.

Operations

PART 2

Synchronizing Server Clocks

Though this is not a common recommendation from Microsoft, I like to keep my server's time synchronized with a chosen time source. I have seen personal computers whose time drifted as much as 10 minutes per week, so I think time synchronization is important.

Every server object is stamped with a time/date stamp (date created and date last modified), but Exchange does not use this value as the primary indicator of whether the data is up-to-date or not. Instead, the Exchange directory replication uses *update sequence numbers (USN)*; Exchange public folder replication uses something called a *predecessor change list*.

> **NOTE**   If you look at the raw properties of an object, the time and date stamp is in Universal Coordinated Time (UCT). UCT is also sometimes called Greenwich Mean Time (GMT) or Zulu time (Z). If I look at a mailbox object's raw properties, I will see that the When-Created attribute has a value of 990309221546Z, or March 9, 1999, at 10:15:46 P.M. Zulu time (which is 2:15 in the afternoon here in Hawaii). I see 2:15 if I display the normal Mailbox Properties dialog box, because Exchange Administrator knows which time zone I am in based on my Windows NT configuration.

Synchronizing Time Manually

There are a number of ways to synchronize a server's time, the least desirable of which is manually. If you must do time synchronization manually, pick a specific server within your organization and keep that server's time and date correct. From all other servers, login as a server operator or administrator (someone who has the User right to set the time). Type the command **net time ***server name* **/set /y** (substitute *server name* for the server on your network that has the correct time). This is primitive, but it will work.

Synchronizing Time Automatically

The Windows NT Server 4 Resource Kit has a tool called the Time Synchronization Service. As the name suggestions, this tool runs as a service. At certain intervals, it goes out to a time source that you have defined and gets the current time from that time source. The time service tool can use a TCP/IP network or a modem to contact a time source.

There are two types of time sources. A *primary time source* is usually an external and highly accurate time source located somewhere like the Naval Observatory or the National Institute of Standards and Technology (NIST). A *secondary time source* is set from a primary time source.

When I use the Time Synchronization Service, I pick a server on my network that has a connection to the Internet to designate as my primary server. I then install the time server software and edit the `timeserv.ini` file to set the time source type to INTERNET and set the default period to 12. This points my server to the U.S. Naval Observatory to get time updates every 12 hours. I then start the time service; an optional parameter in the `timeserv.ini` file tells the time service to log events to the Application event log.

On all other servers on the network, I install the time server software and edit the `timeserv.ini` file to designate those servers as SECONDARY. I designate the primary server that I have just installed as the PrimarySource and set the period to 12 hours in the `timeserv.ini`. Every 12 hours, these servers will contact the primary server and get the updated time.

NOTE For more detailed information on installing the Time Synchronization Service, see the Windows NT Server Resource Kit.

TIP If you are running an Exchange server monitor, the server monitor has the option of setting an Exchange server's clocks based on the computer that is running the monitor. See Chapter 7 for more information.

For Further Information...

For more information about some of the topics discussed in this chapter, here are some resources:

- To learn more about address book views and virtual organization support within Exchange and troubleshooting ABVs, consult Knowledge Base articles Q180141 and Q182902.

- To learn more about the Exchange schema, search for the phrase "schema properties" in the Microsoft Exchange Books Online and Knowledge Base article Q182511. Microsoft has a TechNet article called "Active Directory Services Interface in the MS Exchange 5.5 Environment" that also explains more about the Exchange schema.

- To learn more about Ambiguous Name Resolution, see Knowledge Base articles Q146024, Q147400, Q151198, and Q155715.

For Further Information... *(continued)*

- If you are looking for more examples on how to modify the Search details template, read Knowledge Base articles Q151198 and Q152732.

- See the BackOffice Resource Kit for more information about the Mailbox Cleanup Agent.

- Public folders are a topic unto themselves. For more information on setting up and using public folders, see *Mastering Exchange Server 5.5* by Barry Gerber (Sybex, 1998). To see more about how to change a public folder's home server or home site, see Chapter 4 of this book.

6

Maintenance Procedures

I have a theory on system operations: The more prepared you are for a disaster, the less likely it will be that the disaster will occur. A very important part of your battle to prevent disasters is ongoing maintenance.

This chapter introduces you to the database technology that Exchange Server uses and the tools you will need to test and repair your Exchange public information store, private information store, and directory service databases. It then discusses the types of backups that are available. I make a series of recommendations on the types of daily, weekly, and periodic maintenance that you should perform. At the close of the chapter, I discuss some tips and ideas for helping to prevent disasters on your Exchange servers.

Exchange Requires Less Database Maintenance!

As I have mentioned earlier, I was a Lotus cc:Mail administrator for several years. While I loved cc:Mail, the maintenance drove me nuts. The post offices had to be shut down in order to be backed up, there was often no indication of problems until there was serious data corruption, and database diagnostics and disk space reclamation had to be ran often. Though there are maintenance tasks that you should perform with Exchange Server 5.5, I have found them to be minimal compared to cc:Mail and other legacy systems.

Transaction Logs

In the D:\exchsrvr\MDBdata and D:\exchsrvr\DSAdata directories, you will find the data transaction logs. All transaction log files are 5,120KB in size; any other size for a log file may indicate corruption or that the file is not an Exchange log file. The public and private information store databases share a common set of log files.

The active log file in both of these directories is the edb.log. When this file fills up, it is renamed to edb00001.log, and a new edb.log is created. When the newly created log file fills up, it is renamed to edb00002.log, and another new edb.log is created. If you view either of these directories, you will see a collection of these old log files.

If circular logging is enabled (default), generally only four previous log files are stored in the directory. On a server that has circular logging turned on, the previous logs might look like edb00009.log, edb00010.log, edb0001a.log, and edb0001b.log. Once a new log file is created, the oldest log file is automatically deleted, and the new log file list would be edb00010.log, edb0001a.log, edb0001b.log, and edb0001c.log.

> **NOTE**   If the server is heavily loaded, it is normal to have more than four log files in this directory.

If circular logging is disabled, the log files in the directory will continue to collect. It is not uncommon to see dozens of log files in this directory. Yet when a normal or incremental online backup is performed, Exchange purges these old log files.

> **WARNING**   *Never* delete log files manually. The Exchange server should manage these files itself. If the number of log files continues to grow, make sure that you are performing a normal online backup periodically.

The log file directories also have two reserved log files, res1.log and res2.log. Reserved logs are used in case Exchange runs out of disk space when it tries to create a new edb.log file. If this occurs, the reserved files are used instead; any transactions in memory are flushed to the reserved log files, and Exchange will shut down the affected services. You must correct the disk space problems before you can restart Exchange.

Checkpoint Files

In both the C:\exchsrvr\DSAdata and C:\exchsrvr\MDBdata directories (this is the location of the information store working path and the directory working path), you will find a file called the checkpoint file, edb.chk. This file is always 8KB in size.

A checkpoint is a place marker; it points a location in the log files. All transactions before the checkpoint have been committed to the database; all transactions after the checkpoint have not been committed to the database. The checkpoint is stored in the edb.chk file.

Other Files

There are a few other files that you may see periodically in the Exchange data and log directories. On the disk that hosts the information store and directory working paths, you may see a tmb.edb file. This file is used to store transactions that may not be able to be written to the disk immediately when online maintenance is occurring.

> **WARNING** Do not delete this tmb.edb file! Exchange Server will manage its creation and usage.

An additional log file may appear from time to time, depending when you look at the log file directory; it is called edbtmp.log. It is a temporary file used when creating a new log file. The process of converting edb.log to an edbxxxxx.log file requires a new edb.log file, hence edbtmp.log is created while the edb.log is renamed to edbxxxxx.log.

During an online backup, you will see patch files created. Each database that is being backed up has its own PAT file: priv.pat, pub.pat, and dir.pat. During an online backup, transactions can still be committed to the database files. However, if the transaction is committed to a part of the database that has already been backed up, the transaction is also written to the corresponding PAT file. When the database is completely backed up, the PAT file is backed up and then deleted.

> **NOTE** If you see a PAT file in either the \DSAdata or the \MBDdata directory, that indicates that the server is currently undergoing an online backup. If this file grows extremely large (more than a few hundred megabytes), make sure that there is not a backup running that has hung up or is waiting for an additional tape.

Database Tools

Microsoft provides two tools for checking, repairing, and defragmenting Exchange databases. These tools are isinteg.exe and eseutil.exe (this tool was named edbutil.exe in Exchange 4 and 5).

WARNING Do not attempt to run an edbutil.exe on a newer Exchange database, and do not run eseutil.exe on an older Exchange database. Each tool is specific to its version of the Exchange database and cannot be used for other versions.

WARNING Prior to running *any* database utilities, you should perform a full, complete (normal) backup of all Exchange databases. If you cannot perform an online backup, run an offline backup. Microsoft recommends running these utilities only when advised by Microsoft Product Support Services.

The ESEUTIL Program

The eseutil.exe program is located in the C:\WinNT\System32 directory. This tool is a database repair utility; it understands the structure of the Exchange databases and repairs, checks, and compacts Exchange 5.5 database files. It also understands the underlying structure of the database, tables, indexes, and records, but it does not understand the Exchange data that is placed in those tables and records. In short, it is a database tool for database errors.

ESEUTIL is a command-line tool. The information store and/or directory services must be stopped in order to run this utility. Table 6.2 has some of the common command-line options for the ESEUTIL program.

Table 6.2 Common Command-Line Options for the ESEUTIL Program

Option	Operation
/?	Displays ESEUTIL options.
/DS	Selects the directory database.
/ispriv	Selects the private information store.
/ispub	Selects the public information store.
/D	Performs offline defragmentation/compaction on the selected database.
/G	Performs integrity check on the selected database.
/P	Performs repair operations on the selected database. Used for a damaged database file. Data may be lost.

Table 6.2 Common Command-Line Options for the ESEUTIL Program *(continued)*

Option	Operation
/R	Performs a recovery bringing selected database into a consistent state.
/U	Upgrades the selected database (not normally used by an administrator).

> **WARNING** Command-line switch order is important. You should always put the switch that is setting up the type operation first, i.e. /R, /D, /G, and /P. (Example: ESEUTIL /D /DS.)

Database Defragmentation/Compaction ESEUTIL can perform an offline defragmentation/compaction of the public information store, private information store, and directory databases. Defragmentation takes the existing database file and builds a new temporary database file (`tempdfrg.edb` by default) from it by copying the records from the old file to the new one. This process cleans up any "white space" (unused storage) in the database, makes the storage contiguous, and reduces the overall size of the database file. When the temporary database is successfully created, the original database is deleted, and the temporary database is renamed to the original database name. If ESEUTIL discovers an error while copying records from the original database to the new temporary database, it will stop and display the error.

There are a few optional command-line switches that you should be aware of when running the ESEUTIL command with the defragment option.

Option	Operation
/T <*path\dbname*>	Redirects the temporary database to another location other than the default (the current drive). This can prove very useful, and you can direct the temporary database across the network, which can slow the process considerably. Consider installing an extra disk or disk array and redirecting to a local disk instead of to the network.
/L <*path*>	Specifies the location for the log files.
/B <*path\dbname*>	Makes a backup copy of the database before starting the defragmentation procedure.
/P	Defragments/compacts the database to a new temporary database, but does not delete the original database when complete. They call this the "don't instate" option.

To Repair or Not to Repair? *(continued)*

This method has worked for me in the past. If you are the slightest bit uncomfortable with these procedures, you should probably skip to the big finish and get Microsoft on the phone as soon as possible. Experimenting with these utilities can lead to worse problems than you are currently experiencing!

The ISINTEG Program

In contrast to ESEUTIL, which understands generic database files, the information store integrity checker (ISINTEG) knows all about Exchange messages, attachments, access control lists, folders, rules, deleted items, and so on. ISINTEG understands the data in the database file.

ISINTEG fixes problems where users cannot access messages or folders. It should also be run if you have had to repair a database using ESEUTIL. It can be used to "patch" the information store after an offline restore.

> **NOTE** The directory service must be running to use ISINTEG.

The isinteg.exe utility generates a small temporary database when it is analyzing the selected database. (I have never seen this database grow to more than 10 percent of the total size of the database being fixed.) This utility can take a few minutes or many hours to run, depending on the number of tests that you select. If I have to run the entire battery of tests on a database, I plan for about 1 to 3 hours per GB.

Table 6.3 lists ISINTEG command-line options that you should be aware of.

Table 6.3 Command-Line Options Available for ISINTEG

Option	Operation
–?	Displays online help.
–pri	Selects the private information store.
–pub	Selects the public information store.
–fix	Fixes problems if they are found. The default is to only check for problems and report them. Microsoft recommends running the –fix option only upon the advice of Microsoft PSS.

Table 6.3   Command-Line Options Available for ISINTEG *(continued)*

Option	Operation
-detailed	Performs additional tests beyond the tests covered by the default testing mode.
-verbose	Output in verbose mode.
-test	Specifies test name(s). Refer to the document isinteg.rtf file on the Exchange Server CD for specific test names and test definitions.
-L <*log filename*>	Specifies an alternative log filename and location. The log files are text files, and their default names are isinteg.pub and isinteg.pri.
-T <*temp database location*>	Specifies the location of the temporary database that ISINTEG uses when it checks the public or private information store database. The database it creates is called refer.mdb. Specifying another disk drive can improve performance, but specifying a network drive will hinder performance.
-patch	Patches the GUIDs (discussed below) found in the information store, directory service, and Registry after an offline restoration.

The ISINTEG "Patch" Option   Every object in the public and private information store has a unique, 64-bit hexadecimal string assigned to it. This string is called the *globally-unique identifier (GUID)* and is used to uniquely identify items in the information store databases. Information about the current GUIDs is stored in the Registry and in the directory service. After an offline restore of the public or private information store, the different locations that contain GUIDs will no longer agree with each other, and the information store will not know which GUIDs have been assigned already. (This is automatically corrected during an online restore.)

> **NOTE**   If the GUIDs are not correct, the information store service will not start. If the information store service does not start, scan the application event log for event ID 1087, 1089, 2083, and 7202.

If you have performed an offline restore of the public or private information store, from the \exchsrvr\bin directory, run ISINTEG -patch. This operation should only take a few seconds, but no more than a minute or two. The System Attendant and the directory service must be running in order for the -patch option to work.

TIP If your Exchange server is in a Microsoft cluster, you need to set an environmental variable prior to running ISINTEG. If the cluster server's network name is BOSEX001, at the command prompt, type **SET_CLUSTER_NETWORK_ NAME=BOSEX001**, and then run ISINTEG. It is a good idea to set this variable in the Control Panel; choose System, open the Environment property page, and select the System Variables list. This way, the environmental variable is always set regardless of who is logged in at the server.

Information Store Integrity Checker Examples

Here are a couple of examples of using the ISINTEG program.

To run an integrity check (but not to fix anything) on the private information store, report all details of the test, create a log file called pri-log.txt, and run all tests, type **ISINTEG –pri –verbose –lpri-log.txt –test alltests**.

To run ISINTEG to check and fix errors in the public information store for folder and message tables only, type **ISINTEG –pub –fix –verbose –test folder,message**.

To redirect the temporary database file to another disk while fixing messages in the private information store, type **ISINTEG –pri –fix –TG:\temp –test message**.

Should You Perform Database Maintenance?

Should you perform any sort of periodic database maintenance? To quote one of the more active contributors of the Exchange administrator's mailing list: "Just leave Exchange alone."

This is somewhat alien advice for me, but I have taken it to heart. In the late 1980s, I ran a large Lotus cc:Mail installation, and weekly and monthly maintenance were just part of our operations. This was also true to a great degree on some larger installations of Exchange 4; with monthly defragmentation, I found Exchange 4 to be much more stable (no errors or corruption).

Exchange 5.5, on the other hand, requires very little database maintenance. Many Exchange administrators have told me that "we just keep an eye on Exchange and let it do its thing." They perform very little in the way of database maintenance tasks and "Exchange hums along just fine." Over the life of Exchange 5.5, I have come to adopt this strategy as well. If it ain't broke, don't fix it.

All versions of Exchange Server performed information and directory database cleanup and management while online. Exchange Server 4 and 5 were not as efficient at this as Exchange Server 5.5 is. Exchange Server 5.5 is able to defragment and reuse 99 percent of the white space in the database.

Is There Ever a Time for Offline Defragmentation?

I used to feel that offline defragmentation was important to do at least every two or three months. This is, of course, the remnants of the cc:Mail administrator in me talking. For most Exchange installations in the world, there is never a reason to perform an offline defragmentation.

However, there are situations in which you might want to perform an offline defragmentation. One instance is if you have just deleted many mailboxes and you want to compact the size of the private information store database back down. Another possibility is if a large number of messages have been deleted recently, and now that space is freed up. In this case, offline defragmentation/compaction will reduce the overall size of the database files.

Event ID 1221 is generated each time online defragmentation occurs on the public or private information store. This event will tell you how much space can be recovered. Figure 6.2 shows an example of event ID 1221. Notice that the database has 147MB of free space available.

The total size of this particular database is about 890MB (though you cannot see that in Figure 6.2). This means that about 17 percent of the database's total size is unused. However, when new messages are stored, this space will be used.

Some paranoid Exchange administrators still run an Exchange offline defragmentation once every four to six months. Though I don't believe this is necessary, if you have good backups and the time to bring your server down to do this, go for it.

TIP Always perform a full backup before and after an offline defragmentation/ compaction!

continuous schedule. Using the Windows NT Performance Monitor, I noticed that the percentage of disk utilization and the total percentage of processor utilization was quite high and stayed that way for the next 24 hours.

- Once you are confident that the disk defragmentation software will be stable in your environment, I recommend defragmenting the disk the old fashioned way prior to installing the new software; the old fashioned way involves backing up, reformatting, and restoring. This is so that the disk is already defragmented when you install the new software. The software will only have to work at keeping the disk defragmented and will not have to work extra hard for several hours (or days) to initially defragment the disk.

WARNING Technical Editor Joshua Konkle noted that if each of the databases is on a dedicated disk drive, database fragmentation will not be a problem. However, the log file disks can still become badly fragmented because log files are continually being created and deleted.

Backing Up and Exchange

The most important daily task you are going to perform is making sure that you have good backup copies of your Exchange databases. Neither RAID 5 drive arrays, clustered servers, nor mirrored disks are fault-tolerant enough to get you out of performing daily Exchange backups. There are too many things that can go wrong with both your hardware and software.

Backup Hardware and Software

The first step in a successful backup plan is to get quality backup media and software. I am approaching this from the traditional *tape* backup perspective, though there are many in the Exchange community who feel other forms of backup (such as optical) are coming of age.

Purchase a tape drive system that is easily and quickly capable of backing up your entire messaging system. My own preference is to locate the tape drive hardware on the same machine that hosts the Exchange server. The costs are generally a little more, but the backups run quickly. When purchasing tape backup hardware, I also purchase the same tape drive type for all servers. This allows my tapes and my tape hardware to be more easily interchangeable.

When you install Exchange Server, a special version of the Windows NT Backup program is installed. This version is capable of backing up the Exchange server online. The Windows NT Backup program does have its limitations, but it's free. I prefer one of the third-party backup programs available, such as Seagate's Backup Exec, BEI International's UltraBac, or Cheyenne's ArcServe. These utilities have job scheduling, tape management, and better cataloging.

TIP When purchasing tape backup software, make sure that you also purchase the Exchange Agent; this option is not usually included in the base price of most third-party utilities. The Exchange Agent is required for backing up Exchange while it is online. On a side note, the third-party tools are faster.

I Feel the Need for Speed

A determining factor in how many users and how much data you can fit onto a single Exchange server is how long it takes to back up that data. I have seen vendors talking about backup rates of 25GB per hour. I can assure you that a typical production system backup utility cannot accomplish such a speed; this rate is only achievable with very specialized backup hardware (RAID 5 tape arrays and special tape array controllers).

Recent backup and restore rates that I have been able to achieve range from 2.5GB per hour (with an HP SureStore 5000 DAT tape drive) to 10GB per hour (with a Compaq 7000 DLT tape drive). Both of these were on Pentium systems with no active users, PCI SCSI adapters, ample memory, and Seagate Backup Exec.

Online Backups versus Offline Backups

Should you use the Exchange Server online backup feature? Yes, absolutely, certainly, for sure! Though many of us feel comfortable with the old, tried and true file-level backup, online backups are much better for Exchange for several reasons:

- The online backup allows you to back up the database even if it is in use.
- Online backups back up the database files "page by page." As the page is transferred to tape, Exchange Server does a cyclic redundancy check (CRC) on the data to make sure that it is valid. If there are problems with the page of data, the backup stops and an event is logged to the Windows NT Event Viewer application log. If you were performing offline backups, you would not be aware of this.
- Online backups permit the use of incremental and differential backups (backing up only the log files) which occur much more quickly than normal backups.
- Online backups are easier to schedule, because the information store and directory service does not have to be shut down.

Exchange Backup Options

Software that is capable of backing up Exchange can perform three backups: normal, incremental, and differential. You need to fully understand what each of these options are doing so that you can select the right backup type for your organization.

A *normal* backup will back up the entire information store or directory database. The normal backup then backs up the transaction logs and the .PAT files. When the log files and the .PAT files are backed up all log files that have been committed to the database are purged from the disk.

An *incremental* backup selects and backs up only the Exchange server transaction logs. Once the logs are backed up, the log files are purged. A tape that had incremental backups put on it will have only the log files since the last full or incremental backup.

A *differential* backup selects and backs up only the Exchange server transaction log files. The log files are not purged after the backup, meaning they will continue to accumulate until an incremental or normal backup is performed.

> **NOTE**   In order for an incremental or differential backup rotation strategy to work properly, circular logging must be disabled. This ensures there are log files to back up and recover.

Circular Logging, Transaction Log Files, and Backups

If you have disabled circular logging, the transaction logs will accumulate until either an online normal backup or an online incremental backup occurs. Online differential and offline backups do not purge transaction logs. Here is what happens during a normal backup:

- The backup program selects and starts backing up the specified database. During this process, any transactions that are written to parts of the database that have already been backed up are also written to a patch file.

- After the database has been backed up, the patch file is backed up.

- The patch file is purged from the system.

- The checkpoint file is consulted, and any log files that were completely committed to the database and/or patch file are purged. These files are not necessary, since the transactions in these files have already been committed to the database.

> **Circular Logging, Transaction Log Files, and Backups** *(continued)*
>
> During an incremental backup, only the log files are backed up. Based on information in the checkpoint file, transaction log files completely committed to the database and/or patch file are purged.

Performing a Server Backup

For me, a nightly backup consists of the information store and directory service databases. In addition, I want to make sure that there is a good backup of the Windows NT Registry, the Exchange software, and the domain database that contains my users (especially the site services account).

For me to feel warm and fuzzy about the procedure, I set the backup to perform a verification pass when it is finished; this usually doubles the amount of time required. Further, I check the backup log files each day. The ultimate in warm and fuzzy backup procedures is to periodically perform trial restores to a standby server. This not only guarantees that the tape really contains the data, but it also helps keep me familiar with my disaster recovery procedures.

The Exchange Server Key Management Server database and the Exchange Server Directory Synchronization (used for MS Mail, PROFS directory sharing) databases do not get backed up during an online backup. These files are in use by their respective services. In order to back these databases up, you need to shut down their respective services and back them up offline.

The Key Management Server data is stored in the \exchsrvr\KMSdata directory, and the Directory Synchronization database is stored in the \exchsrvr\DXAdata directory. When backing up the Key Management Server database, care must be taken. This database contains the escrowed private keys and should be stored in a secure location.

You may also want to include all the files in the \exchsrvr directories. This will include the MTA database, IMS archive, and log files as well as the Exchange Server and connector software.

Here are some other tips for implementing a successful Exchange server backup plan:

- Rotate your tapes; don't use the same tape every night, and don't use a tape for more time than the manufacturer recommends.

Operations

PART 2

- Protect your tapes. Store them in a location that cannot be accessed by just anyone. Always keep a copy of a recent backup stored in a location other than near your computer room. In the event of a disaster that destroys the primary tape storage location, you will have a copy of your data elsewhere.
- Examine your backup log files and application log daily to ensure that the backups are running and that there are no errors.
- Clean your tape drives according to the schedule recommended by the tape manufacturer.
- Perform a trial restore to your standby server periodically.

By default, each morning from 1:00 A.M. until 6:00 A.M., the information store service runs scheduled maintenance. This includes removing online defragmentation, cleaning up indexes, expiring old messages from public folders, and making sure that space formerly taken up by deleted messages is returned to the pool of available space. This should run at least once per day for both the public and private information stores.

WARNING   The online defragmentation process will not run if the tape backup is running. Make sure that the tape backup *does not completely* overlap the IS maintenance schedule. Each morning, sometime between 1:00 A.M. and 6:00 A.M., you should see an event ID 180 generated by ESE97; you should see one of these for both the private and public information stores.

Backing Up Other Messaging-Related Data

Even though you may be performing a normal backup of your Exchange server data, Registry, SAM file, and Exchange Server software, there may still be other messaging-related data that you should consider when making backup plans.

Does your user community have PAB files (personal address books), PST files (personal folders), SCD files (Schedule+ data), and other data that is related to the messaging system? Outlook offers a useful feature called AutoArchive that will automatically archive older message data to an `archive.pst` personal folder file. By default, this file is on the user's local hard disk. Be sure it is being backed up.

Sample Rotations

I prefer to back up everything every night. I have had too many incidents where I was unable to get something off of a tape for one reason or another. I have developed a mistrust of tape systems in general, though PC-based tape systems are generally much more reliable today than they were 10 years ago. However, I also recognize that many organizations don't have the luxury of performing a full (normal) backup every night. Here are examples of both daily and weekly backup rotations; choose which is suitable for your situation.

Daily Rotation

My daily rotation requires a normal backup each day. I put together a rotation of tapes that will enable me to have two weeks worth of backups, plus a month worth of Friday backups. I label my tapes as follows:

Tape Label	Used On
Monday – Even	Monday the 2nd, 16th, etc.
Monday – Odd	Monday the 9th, 23rd, etc.
Tuesday – Even	Tuesday the 10th, 24th, etc.
Tuesday – Odd	Tuesday the 3rd, 17th, etc.
Wednesday – Even	Wednesday the 4th, 18th, etc.
Wednesday – Odd	Wednesday the 11th, 25th, etc.
Thursday – Even	Thursday the 12th, 26th, etc.
Thursday – Odd	Thursday the 5th, 19th, etc.
Friday – First	First Friday of the month
Friday – Second	Second Friday of the month
Friday – Third	Third Friday of the month
Friday – Fourth	Fourth Friday of the month
Friday – Fifth	Fifth Friday of the month

This rotation strategy can be extended to include a Saturday and Sunday backup as well. You should consider performing weekend backups if you have staff working on the weekend or if you have a tape autoloader system. If you have many users who send and receive mail on the weekends, you should *definitely* perform weekend backups. In many situations, I also include a monthly or bimonthly tape backup that is archived for an entire year.

For each day of the week, I schedule a backup to start at some point in the evening after the majority of my users are gone. The backup type is normal, so the entire information store and directory service should be on each tape.

Exchange@Work: A Little Extra Backup Paranoia

I know several folks who are extra paranoid about their Exchange server backups. They perform a normal backup each night, and then every two hours during the day, they run a differential backup and append a backup of the transaction log files to the end of the normal tape.

Operations

PART 2

Exchange@Work: A Little Extra Backup Paranoia *(continued)*

Though their log files are on a separate physical disk from the database files, this still protects them from a catastrophic server failure. If the server experiences a catastrophe where all hard drives fail, the most data they will lose is two hours worth.

Weekly Rotation

Though I much prefer running a normal backup each night, I don't always have that option due to time constraints, database size, or capacity of the tape drive hardware. In such cases, I revert to differential backups. The schedule consists of a normal backup one day a week and differential backups on the remaining days. Here is a sample set of tapes for a weekly backup:

Tape Label	Used On
Normal – 1	First Friday of the month
Normal – 2	Second Friday of the month
Normal – 3	Third Friday of the month
Normal – 4	Fourth Friday of the month
Normal – 5	Fifth Friday of the month
Differential – Monday	Monday night
Differential – Tuesday	Tuesday night
Differential – Wednesday	Wednesday night
Differential – Thursday	Thursday night

I schedule a normal backup for Friday night and have a different Friday tape for each week. Since each Friday night tape will have a complete backup of the server, I don't see much need in having even/odd tapes for the weekly differentials; however, you may decide that you want to put those into your rotation.

When you need to restore a server, restore the most recent normal backup tape first, and then restore the most recent differential tape. The differential tape will contain all the log files created since the last normal backup.

WARNING The differential backup does not purge the log files. Watch the disk space on your transaction log drive to make sure that the log files do not accumulate and exhaust all available disk space.

Brick-Level Backup

Many Exchange 4 and 5 administrators have cried mournfully, "I hate restoring a single mailbox!" The principal reason a single mailbox has to be restored is that a user deleted some important messages or folder. Microsoft has responded to the "oops, I deleted a really important message" statement with the Deleted Item Recovery feature.

However, deleted item recovery will not help you if the entire mailbox gets deleted. If this is the case, you must restore the entire information store (usually to your standby server) and recover the contents of the mailbox to a PST file.

Third-party vendors such as Seagate (www.seagate.com) and Cheyenne (www.cheyenne.com) have addressed this with a feature called *brick-level backups* (a.k.a. single mailbox backup and restore). While normal backups back up the information store databases a page at a time, a brick-level backup opens each mailbox separately and backs up the folders and messages.

The advantage of this feature is that you can now restore a single mailbox or even a single folder within a mailbox. The *dis*advantage is the amount of time that the backup takes to run and the space required on the tape. By some estimates, the backup can take up to ten times longer than a standard backup.

Here is an example of a typical backup time using a standard, normal Exchange backup versus a brick-level backup. The hardware is a single processor P/60 clone system with 128MB of RAM, two SCSI hard disks, and an HP 5000 SureStore tape unit. Software includes Exchange Server 5.5 with SP2 and Seagate Backup Exec 7.2 with the Exchange Agent loaded. The private information store is 1.1GB, and there are 350 mailboxes on this server. A standard information store backup of the private information store (all mailboxes) only took 42 minutes. A brick-level backup of the private information store took 5 hours and 10 minutes.

Exchange@Work: Is a Brick-Level Backup Useful?

With Exchange 4 and 5, I primarily had to restore entire Exchange servers in order to recover a few items that a user accidentally deleted from his mailbox. (Normally, the person carried a certain amount of weight with the information services department.) Since the release of Exchange Server 5.5 and the advent of deleted item recovery, I have not had to restore a single Exchange server due to accidentally deleted messages.

Operations

PART 2

Exchange@Work: Is a Brick-Level Backup Useful? *(continued)*

The main use now for a brick-level backup would be to restore a mailbox that was accidentally deleted. Though I think this is a great feature, the brick-level backups I have tested take anywhere from four to ten times longer to perform than a regular Exchange backup and usually take up considerably more tape space. Here are some steps that some Exchange administrators have taken to eliminate the need to do a brick-level backup and restore:

- Implement deleted item recovery with enough time for people to recover any items they deleted. Recommendations range from 10 to 30 days. The longer you retain deleted items, the larger the information store must be, but most Exchange administrators believe the increase is worth it.

- Implement a policy of not deleting mailboxes right away. This may mean not deleting the mailbox for 60 or 90 days.

- Implement a mailbox deletion policy similar to the following procedure:

  1. Do not delete the mailbox right away.

  2. Disable the associated Windows NT account.

  3. Assign mailbox ownership permissions to the departed user's manager. This will let the manager access any messages in the user's mailbox.

  4. Rename the Display Name to something like "zz_McBee, Rebecca – Delete after 9/15/99".

  5. On the Advanced tab of the mailbox's property page, hide the mailbox from the global address list.

  6. Remove all e-mail proxy addresses except for the X.400 address from the mailbox's E-Mail Addresses list.

  7. In the Notes field, enter the date you made the changes and the reason the mailbox should be deleted.

  8. Scan the directory periodically for hidden mailboxes that are ready to be deleted. If you have renamed the Display Name to something like I have recommended, any mailboxes that need to be deleted will be sorted to the bottom of the list and stand out with the date you have entered in the Display Name, which indicates the date after which the mailbox can be deleted.

Daily Maintenance Tasks

What should you do on a daily basis to keep your Exchange server healthy and happy? What can you do so that you can sleep well each night? Here is a checklist of things that you should perform daily on your Exchange servers:

- Backing up your server is the most important activity. Make sure that the backups are running and completing. Review your backup log files. Make sure that tapes are rotated.

- Examine the application and system logs for error (red) and warning (yellow) events. See the list of events that should catch your eye in the "Event IDs to Watch Out For" section later in this chapter.

- Check all hard disks to make sure that ample disk space is available.

- Check the message queues, including the MTA queues and any connector queues. If there is an unusual number of messages backed up, find out why.

- Check the transaction log file directories to make sure that there are not a large number of transaction logs accumulating. If you are using a rotation that incorporates differential backups, it is not uncommon to see dozens of log files. Busier systems could see a couple of hundred log files if a normal backup has not been performed recently.

- If running server monitors and link monitors, review their respective log files or status screens.

Event IDs to Watch Out For

On your daily scan through the application and system event logs, there are some events that you should watch out for. In general, any error events (red) should catch your eye and should be investigated *immediately* to find the cause. Warning events (yellow) should also be looked into. Though yellow events are generally not as critical as red events, they may indicate a problem that will become critical later.

Table 6.4 lists some event IDs that you will want to be familiar with when looking at events generated by Exchange Server. This is by no means a complete list—when reviewing daily events, you will see dozens.

Table 6.4   Common Exchange Server Events Found in the Event Viewer Application Log

Event ID	Source	Meaning/Description
104	ESE97	The database engine has stopped indicating that a backup has completed. This is good.

Table 6.4 Common Exchange Server Events Found in the Event Viewer Application Log *(continued)*

Event ID	Source	Meaning/Description
9411	MSExchangeMTA	The MTA has terminated due to low disk space on the disk where the MTADATA directory is located.
179 and 180	ESE97	The online defragmentation process has completed a pass on the private or public information store. This is a good event, and you should see this at least once per night for both the public and private information stores.
1221	MSExchangeIS Private, MSExchangeIS Public	This message will include a description letting you know how much free space is available in the database file.
1112	MSExchangeIS	The Exchange database has reached its maximum size and the Exchange server is shutting down. Make an offline backup and perform an offline defragmentation (ESEUTIL /ispriv /D or ESEUTIL /ispub /D). Once the information store restarts, clean up as many mailboxes as possible.
105, 112, 116, 117, 118, 135, and 184	ESE97	Some type of database corruption has occurred. Make sure you have a good backup. If the corruption occurs during backup, you may have a serious problem. The event log may suggest restoring from the last good backup. You can ask users to copy all their messages to a PST file or perform an offline backup. At this point, I would check the Knowledge Base or call Microsoft and report the error.

Table 6.4 Common Exchange Server Events Found in the Event Viewer Application Log *(continued)*

Event ID	Source	Meaning/Description
1000 or 1001	MSExchangeSA, MSExchangeDS, MSExchangeIS Private, MSExchangeIS Public	Indicates that the respective service is starting. If you see this event, make sure it corresponds to a time when the server was officially restarted. If the server is starting at a time when you were not aware of it, there may be software problems, or unauthorized work may be being performed on the Exchange server.

Table 6.4 offers a small sample of the error codes that you may see in the description portion of an event. Others include –1018, –1022, and –510. If you see these numbers, there is a good chance that there is a disk hardware or device driver problem.

When you see an error or warning event in the application event log, you need to take immediate steps to find out what it means. The best starting point is the Knowledge Base. If you see any event that indicates database corruption of any kind, consider bringing Microsoft into the picture, especially if you are uncomfortable with troubleshooting database-related problems.

> *TIP* If you would like the entire list of Exchange event messages, locate the BackOffice Resource Kit (Second Edition) CD and search for the exmsgref.xls file. It contains a list of event IDs, sources, and messages.

Event Log Monitoring Tools

There are two utilities supplied with the Microsoft BackOffice Resource Kit that can assist you in gathering information from the event logs: evtscan.exe and elf.exe. These utilities are found on the BackOffice Resource Kit CD in the \Exchange\WinNT\I386\ Eventlog directory.

The ELF (Event Log Filter) tool allows you to collect certain types of entries from multiple servers. You can specify event IDs that you wish to scan for, and the ELF program will monitor for these on multiple servers.

The EVTSCAN (Event Scan) tool can be used to monitor event logs for specific events. If a specified event occurs, EVTSCAN can launch an application, send an e-mail message,

Operations

PART 2

send an alert message, or stop/restart a service. This tool is especially useful if you want to monitor for certain events that you suspect might occur. The EVTSCAN tool requires that a configuration file containing the events and event sources to monitor be created along with an action that needs to be performed if that event occurs. This configuration file should contain a single line for each type of event. The format for the file looks like this:

```
EventID;Source;Action;Alert list;Mail list;Command line; Comment
string
```

Each configuration entry may only have a few of these items. Here is a list of the configuration entries for this file and what each is used for:

Configuration Entry	Use
EventID	The Event Viewer's event ID.
Source	The source name for the event.
Action	Action to take if this event occurs. The options are Restart and Stop. You can leave this field blank.
Alert List	A list of computers or users to send a network pop-up message to if the event occurs. You can specify more than one computer by separating them with commas.
Command Line	Specifies a command to execute if the event ID occurs.
Comment String	Specifies a comment string that will appear in the network pop-up messages.

Here is a sample EVTSCAN configuration file. This file will monitor for three different event IDs. The first one, event ID 1221 from the source MSExchangeIS Private, will send a mail message to mailbox BenjaminC; the second event is 104 from the source ESE97 and will send a message to the computer WS-HELPDESK; the final event sends a mail message and alert message if event 9411, source MSExchangeMTA, appears.

```
1221;MSExchangeIS Private; ; ;BenjaminC; ;Report on available space
in the IS

104;ESE97; ;WS-HELPDESK; ; ; Tape backup has completed

9411;MSExchangeMTA; ;WS-HELPDESK;BenjaminC; ;MTA has shutdown!
```

Next, I save this file as `important.cfg`. Now I have to run the EVTSCAN program to use this file and send the appropriate notifications; in order to run EVTSCAN, I must be logged in. The EVTSCAN has several command-line options:

Option	Use
`-F <config file>`	Specifies the name of the configuration.
`-U <profile name>`	Specifies a messaging profile to be used if the event needs to send a mail message. Avoid spaces in the profile name.
`-P <password>`	The password used for the messaging profile.
`-T <delay>`	The interval (in seconds) between event log scans.

Launch EVTSCAN with a list of servers to monitor and any necessary command-line options required. A sample command would look like this: **EVTSCAN –F important.cfg –U notification_profile –P profile_password SFOEX001, LAXEX001, HNLEX001, HNLEX002**. This command will run EVTSCAN using the to use the configuration file I created (`important.cfg`) and scan the servers SFOEX001, LAXEX001, HNLEX001, and HNLEX002 every 120 seconds.

NOTE   If you want EVTSCAN to send mail messages, make sure that there is a messaging profile created. The configuration file should be in the same directory as the `evtscan.exe` program.

Exchange@Work: Is the Problem Hardware or Software?

Everyone has heard this joke: How many software engineers it takes to change a light bulb? None, that's a hardware problem! I often agree with this punch line, yet when a database becomes corrupt, I tend to blame the software—and not consider that the problem could be related to hardware.

One of my clients starting having error messages popping up in the application event log. "Event ID 23. Description: MSExchangeIS ((455)) Direct read found corrupted page error -1018 ((1:251563) (0-2295758), 251563 379225672 381322824). Please restore the database from a previous backup."

Not very pretty, eh?

Exchange@Work: Is the Problem Hardware or Software? *(continued)*

Twice within a three-month period of time, we had to restore the database from a previous backup. After the first time, we made sure we had the latest service pack and hot fixes. Only after the second time did we notice there had been SCSI errors in the system event log that closely corresponded to the database failures. We replaced the SCSI controller and the problem did not recur.

What is the moral of the story, kids? Don't be so quick to blame the software and check your system event logs daily!

NOTE −1018 and −1811 errors in the application event log (in the event description, not the Event ID) indicate some type of database corruption, yet the cause is almost always linked back to failing hardware or buggy device drivers. An exception to this would be where NTFS compression is enabled on the Exchange databases.

Weekly Maintenance Tasks

About once a week, I have an additional series of checks that I like to run on each of my Exchange servers:

- Check the Windows NT Performance Monitor to ensure that the server is not running out of memory or exceeding other resources such as the capacity of the disk system or processor.

- If message tracking is enabled, check the message tracking log directory (\exchsrvr\tracking.log) to make sure that the older log files are indeed being purged by the system attendant service.

- Confirm that directory replication is occurring between sites within your organization and to external mail systems such as Microsoft Mail and Lotus cc:Mail.

- Check the public folder replication properties to make sure that the public folders are being replicated and are up-to-date.

- View the public information store's public folder resources container and the private information store's mailbox resources container to make sure that user mailbox and public folder disk resources are in line with expectations.

- If necessary, archive the application event log. Though I don't keep copies of the old event logs, many administrators archive event logs (especially the security logs) for later review.

- If applicable, run mailbox cleanup routines.

- Clean your tape drives according to the manufacturer's recommendations (usually weekly).

Periodic Maintenance Tasks

In addition to daily and weekly procedures, there are several tasks that I perform on a periodic basis. Some of these might be performed as often as every month, while others are done less frequently (possible as little as every six months).

Operations

PART 2

NOTE Some of the tasks on the periodic maintenance list may not apply to your environment. For the most part, this is not a list of things to do to the server, but rather a list of things to watch out for so that the server continues to do its job.

- Perform a test restoration to validate that your tapes are good and that your disaster recovery plan is functional.

- Audit the Exchange permissions to make sure that the actual permissions granted are in line with expectations.

- Delete any mailboxes or other directory objects that are no longer in use and that exceed the "holding" period for your company.

- Archive and remove any organizational forms and public folders that are no longer in use.

- Apply service packs and hot fixes that you have ascertained that you need. Do this only after testing them on your standby system and reviewing the Knowledge Base for any potential problems that could affect your environment.

- Using the Windows NT Performance Monitor, create a log of critical counters during a typical operation period. This information can be compared to previous logs to project system growth.

- Test the UPS hardware that is connected to the server every few months. Don't forget that the batteries in a UPS are only good for about three years.

- Every six months, verify that the firmware and ROM revisions in your server equipment is up to the current revisions. Many hardware manufacturers provide tools to upgrade the firmware and ROM.

- Run the RDISK command monthly to make sure that you have a backup copy of the Registry on an Emergency Repair Disk (ERD). On the PDC, run the RDISK /S command to make sure that you have an updated copy of the Windows NT security database (the SAM file) on the ERD. This disk should be stored in a secure location.
- Every four to six months, perform an offline backup followed by a CHKDSK.

Though I have come to believe that the following tests are not necessary, some particularly cautious administrators run them in addition to those above:

- Perform a semi-annual offline backup.
- Run the ISINTEG -tests alltests option on both the public and private information stores.
- Run the EDBUTIL -G integrity check option on the information stores and the directory database.

TIP   If you feel you must run these tests but don't want to do it on a production system, perform a test restore to your standby server and run the tests on the standby server. Restoring the database to a standby server is also excellent disaster recovery practice.

Disaster Prevention Tips

Disaster prevention is one of my favorite subjects; I can spend hours discussing ways to make Exchange (and other BackOffice products) more stable and less susceptible to failure and downtime. Deep down, I believe that this has something to do with being inherently lazy; I hate being awakened in the middle of the night to come in and fix a down server or restore a database. Therefore, the more things I can do ahead of time to prevent disaster type situations from happening, the better off I am.

Preventing disasters and keeping Exchange Server up, running, and healthy are the primary reasons I am writing this book, and I'll bet they are the primary reasons you are reading it. One of the most useful activities I participate in is spending time with other administrators and system engineers, listening to them talk about their systems and the problems they have experienced and solved.

When I started working on this book, I talked to several dozen experienced Exchange administrators and asked them, "What tips can you pass on to other administrators to keep your Exchange servers running twenty-four hours a day, seven days a week? What types of things do you do to make your job easier?" Here is a list of tips from those who took an interest in sharing what they had learned (in no particular order of importance):

- Enable the Deleted Item Recovery feature for both the public and private information stores. This will decrease the likelihood that you will have to restore data from tape if a user deletes something important from their mailbox or a public folder.

- Use a separate physical disk for the database transaction logs; this will dramatically improve your chances for recovering data up-to-the-minute in case of a database failure.

- Perform regular online backups, check your tape logs, and perform periodic trial restores.

- Standardize the tape backup hardware, software, tapes, and tape rotations you are using.

- Install a UPS and UPS-monitoring software on your servers, hubs, and other network infrastructure devices such as switches and routers.

- Scan your event logs daily for critical errors.

- Never use NTFS file compression to compress Exchange databases and logs.

- Restrict mailbox disk space.

- Have a disaster recovery plan and a disaster recovery kit. The kit should contain a written copy of the plan, system documentation, and all software required to rebuild any server in your site or organization. Practice disaster recovery and database restoration a few times a year.

- Restrict usage of large distribution lists.

- Run a Windows NT CHKDSK periodically and after any system upgrades.

- Take Windows NT and Exchange Server training classes early on in your Exchange deployment. Learn as much as you can about both products.

- Install Exchange Server on a member server or backup domain controller (BDC).

- Don't delete mailboxes right away; wait 30 days or longer to delete mailboxes.

- Subscribe to Microsoft TechNet—and use it whenever something comes up that you don't understand!

- Run Exchange database maintenance utilities to repair the database only as a last resort.

- Keep your user community informed.

Operations

PART 2

You will find most of these tips explained in much more detail in this and other chapters of this book; this list is just the "sound bites" version of them.

Inevitably, disaster will strike when you least expect. Chapter 18 covers disaster recovery and what to do when that fateful moment arrives.

For Further Information...

To learn more about some of the topics presented in this chapter, here are some resources that may prove helpful:

- Microsoft Consulting Services has put together two excellent documents called MS Exchange Disaster Recovery Part 1 and Part 2. These documents can be found on the Microsoft Web site at www.microsoft.com/exchange. You should download these documents and read them—they provide excellent information relating to database technology, backups, restores, and of course, disaster recovery.

- On the Exchange Server CD-ROM, there is a document in the \server\ support\utils\ folder called isinteg.rtf that includes a list of all the ininteg.exe tests that you can specify with the –test options along with a description of the tests.

- Executive Software has a product called Diskeeper, which I have found to work well with Exchange Server. You can download a 30-day evaluation version of Diskeeper on the Web at www.execsoft.com.

- Consult the Microsoft BackOffice Resource Kit for more information on the ELF and EVTSCAN event log monitoring tools.

- Consider third-party monitoring tools for medium to large size businesses. I recommend NetIQ (www.netiq.com) for 90 percent of the installations I work on. They have two white papers on monitoring Exchange with their tools.

7

Monitoring and Optimizing Exchange

As an Exchange administrator, I have come to think of myself as being similar to an air traffic controller, with the Exchange server being the pilot and airplane. As long as I monitor the skies around the airplane and provide basic services, the airplane flies along without incident. All Exchange administrators have certain tasks they have to perform to make certain the skies stay clear around their Exchange servers.

In Chapter 6, I reviewed not only system backup procedures and a little theory on the database operation, but I also recommended some operational tasks. Here, in Chapter 7, I take a closer look at some tools that you can use to keep the skies clear. Microsoft provides some excellent tools through both Exchange Server and Windows NT, and numerous third parties provide tools for monitoring and reporting on Exchange Server activities.

Why Monitor Your Exchange Servers?

A clear understanding of what is happening in your Exchange (and Windows NT) environment is important. As an administrator or systems engineer, you have to be able to react to changing resource needs accordingly. A network manager once joked to me that he had the cheapest network management system available. He pointed to the telephone, indicating that when there were problems, he didn't find out about them until his users called.

Notice in Figure 7.2 that Performance Optimizer did the following:

- Inventoried the processors, memory, and logical disks drives.

- Checked to make sure that the Exchange databases were consistent.

- Ran random access and sequential performance tests on the logical disk drives.

- Moved the information store databases to the D drive and the information store and directory transaction logs to the E drive. Performance Monitor will always ask you whether it is okay to move the files and will show you its recommendations, which you can override.

- Set the directory store and information store buffers to 32559.

- Set the number of threads for various services and threads.

Where Are All Those Buffers Going?

You may have noticed that the total number of buffers for directory service and information store was set to 32559 for both. 32559 buffers × 4096 bytes per buffer = 133361664 bytes. This is also the total amount of physical memory in the server. This would have been a serious oops if this were Exchange 5. Older versions of the Exchange services immediately allocated all the memory that was available and did not release that memory.

Exchange Server 5.5, however, introduced a new memory management feature called Dynamic Buffer Allocation (DBA). DBA allows Exchange services to allocate memory as required and release unused memory if another service requires it. Thanks to DBA, Exchange is much friendlier with other services that are running on the same Exchange server.

The Performance Optimizer does give you the option of restricting the total amount of memory that Exchange will allocate (see the bottom of the screen shown in Figure 7.1). This is not necessary for servers that are dedicated exclusively to Exchange.

When to Run Performance Optimizer

The Exchange Performance Optimizer should be run any time there is a change in the server's hardware or role. Here are a couple of situations where you should run Exchange Performance Optimizer:

- If there is an increase or decrease in the Exchange server's physical memory.

- If new disk drives are installed and you want to move databases, working directories, or transaction logs to a new drive. Performance Optimizer is the best way to do this.

- If new or faster disk controllers or caching controllers are installed.

- If there is a change in the organization size (more items in the directory) or the Exchange server is supporting more mailboxes than originally configured.

- If there is a change in the server's role. For example, if it is now supporting public folders, connectors, or is part of a multi-server site.

Exchange@Work: Importing and Migration

One administrator reported to me how handy Performance Optimizer is during migration. For one weekend's worth of mailbox migrations, the server was set so that it did not support Connector/Directory Import because there were no connectors installed on it. The migration and import of nearly 250 Microsoft Mail users took almost 25 hours.

The next weekend, this administrator ran Performance Optimizer prior to beginning the migration process, and he chose the Connector/Directory Import option under Type Of Server (see Figure 7.1). He then ran another import of about 250 Microsoft Mail users; this time it took only about four hours. Quite an improvement!

Tweaking Exchange through Performance Optimizer

The Exchange Performance Optimizer actually can make over 125 separate changes to the Windows NT Registry as it is optimizing Exchange memory, disk, and thread parameters. You see almost none of the fine-tuning that goes on in the background when Performance Optimizer runs. However, if you run the Performance Optimizer with the –V parameter (verbose), Performance Optimizer will reveal nearly 50 additional settings. Figure 7.3 shows one of the seven additional screens you will see during a verbose session.

If the Exchange binaries are on the C drive, for example, type **C:\exchsrvr\bin\perfwiz –V** to run the Performance Optimizer in verbose mode. After the Exchange services stop and you see the standard system parameters screen (Figure 7.1), you will then see the seven additional parameter screens. In Figure 7.3, the Prev. Value column allows you to see the previous value of each parameter, and the New Value column allows you to see the value that Performance Optimizer is recommending. You can override the recommended value by entering your own value in the New Value column.

Table 7.1 Basic Counters for Monitoring Your Server's Performance *(continued)*

Object ➤ Counter	Explanation	Desired Value	How to Improve
Memory ➤ Available Bytes	Amount of memory available after all processes and caching memory have been allocated.	Should not ever drop below 4,000,000 bytes (4MB).	Add RAM.
Logical Disk ➤ % Disk Time	Percentage of time that a logical disk is used for both reads and writes.	Ideally, should be less than 60 percent on a sustained basis.	Add additional physical disks, faster disks, or faster disk controllers.
Logical Disk ➤ Avg Disk Queue Length	The average number of pending read and write requests for a specific disk.	Should be less than 2.	Add additional physical disks, faster disks, or faster disk controllers.
TCP ➤ Segments Retransmitted per second	The number of TCP segments retransmitted per second as a result of network problems.	In a perfect world, should be zero, but regardless, it should be less than 10 percent of the TCP ➤ Segments Sent/sec counter.	You have a network problem. Your network is too busy or there is an unreliable link.
Network Segment ➤ %Network utilization	The percentage of network bandwidth used on this segment.	The ideal value for this counter will vary from network type to network type, but should be below 30–40 percent on an Ethernet network. I have seen healthy, switched networks run much higher.	Break your network into small pieces or implement switching technology.

The counters found in Table 7.1 are only a few of the many that are available to any Windows NT installation, but they are the ones that I consider critical to locating system bottlenecks and determining if a single resource is overburdened. The desired values are my own; I have derived these from a combination of a dozen books and white papers I have read, as well as personal experiences. These counters and desired values can apply to any Windows NT system, including those running Exchange Server services.

When monitoring a system, you need to take a holistic approach; never perform system monitoring with blinders on. Look at the critical memory, processor, disk, and network counters. Performance monitoring is not an exact science; rather, it's an art form.

Exchange-Specific Performance Monitoring

Now that you have looked at your basic Windows NT system counters, you can enhance your knowledge of what your server is doing on the Exchange side by monitoring some of the Exchange-specific counters. Table 7.2 lists some of the more useful counters (not all of them—remember, there are over 350 of them!). These counters are useful when monitoring Exchange Server performance and response times.

Table 7.2   Exchange-Specific Counters for Monitoring Performance and Response Times

Object ➤ Counter	Explanation
MSExchangeMTA ➤ Messages	The number of messages that the MTA sends and receives each second. Lower values are desired, but higher values indicate a server that is transmitting and receiving a lot of messages.
MSExchangeMTA ➤ Work Queue Length	The number of messages queued for delivery to the local and other servers. Lower values are desired. Higher values indicate the system is getting backed up delivering messages. Compare this with Messages/Sec.
MSExchangeIS Private ➤ Average Time for Delivery	Average time (in milliseconds) that the last ten messages waited before being delivered to the MTA. (High values could indicate the MTA is operating too slowly.) I do not like to see this value climb above 1500 milliseconds.

Operations

PART 2

Table 7.2   Exchange-Specific Counters for Monitoring Performance and Response Times *(continued)*

Object ➤ Counter	Explanation
MSExchangeIS Private ➤ Average Local Delivery Time	Average time (in milliseconds) that the last ten messages waited before being delivered to recipients on the same server (local delivery). High values could indicate the Information Store service is very busy. I don't like to see this value climb above 1000 milliseconds.
MSExchangeIS Private ➤ Send Queue Size and MSExchangeIS Public ➤ Send Queue Size	The number of messages waiting to be delivered by the information store. During busy times this value may spike, but on average it should be very near zero. Non-zero values indicate the information store is not keeping up with the load that has been placed on it.
Database ➤ Cache % Hit (monitor both the information store and the directory instances)	This is the percentage of database file page requests that were serviced by the database cache rather than having to go to the disk. If this value is less than 95 percent, add memory and run the Performance Optimizer again.

Other Useful Performance Monitor Counters

Table 7.3 lists some other counters that provide useful and interesting insight into an Exchange server, particularly when watching trends. These are not directly related to performance optimization, but they are useful when correlating activity to other variables such as the number of users connected.

Table 7.3   Performance Monitor Counters

Object ➤ Counter	Explanation
MSExchangeIS ➤ User Count	The total number of connected client sessions.
MSExchangeIS ➤ Active User Count	The total number of users that have generated any activity within the previous ten minutes.
MSExchangeIS Private ➤ Messages Submitted/Min and MSExchangeIS Public ➤ Messages Submitted/Min	The number of messages that have been submitted to the private (or public) information store. This does not include the total number of recipients per message.

Table 7.3   Performance Monitor Counters *(continued)*

Object ➢ Counter	Explanation
MSExchangeIS Private ➢ Total Size of Recoverable Items and MSExchangeIS Public ➢ Total Size of Recoverable Items	The amount of space used by deleted items in the private (or public) information store database.
MSExchangeIS Private ➢ Total Count of Recoverable Items and MSExchangeIS Public ➢ Total Count of Recoverable Items	The number of messages used by deleted items in the private (or public) information store database.
MSExchangeIS Private ➢ Single Instance Ratio	The average ratio of mailbox "pointers" to each message in the information store. Many organizations consider themselves lucky if this value is above 1.8. This value will change over time as users delete "their" copy of a message (in the Sent Items folder) that was sent to many mailboxes. A very low value indicates a lot of the messages sent and received are coming from and going to points beyond the Exchange server.
MSExchangeIS Private ➢ Messages Submitted and MSExchangeIS Public ➢ Messages Submitted	The total number of messages submitted to the private (or public) information store database since the information store service was started.
MSExchangeMTA ➢ Message Bytes/sec	The number of message bytes being processed by the MTA every second. Divide this value by the Messages/sec counter to get the average message size.
MSExchangeMTA ➢ Outbound Messages Total	The total number of messages the MTA has delivered off the server since the MTA service was started.
MSExchangeMTA ➢ Inbound Messages Total	The total number of messages the MTA has received since the MTA service was started.

> **NOTE**   Refer to the BackOffice Resource Kit help file eperfmon.hlp for a complete listing of the Exchange-related Performance Monitor counters.

MTA Connection Counters   Each messaging connector that is established from a server is listed as a separate instance under the MSExchangeMTA Connections Performance Monitor object. In the list, you will see an instance for the Microsoft Private MDB and Microsoft Public MDB; in addition, you will see instances for any connector you have installed including X.400, Microsoft Mail, the Internet Mail Service, and the site connector. If you have the site connector configured to connect to any server in a remote site, you will see an instance for each server in the remote site.

The MSExchangeMTA Connections object and the instances of each connector provide you with the unique ability to monitor the amount of message traffic that is flowing through each of your messaging connectors. Table 7.4 lists some interesting counters that I like to watch.

Table 7.4   MSExchangeMTA Counters

Counter	Meaning
Associations	The number of associations between the two servers. A single connector can open multiple associations, but it will do so only if the first association is becoming backlogged based on "threshold" levels for creating a additional associations.
Inbound Bytes Total	The total volume of messages in kilobytes that has been received from this connection since the MTA was initialized.
Inbound Messages Total	The total number of messages that have been received through this connection. Inbound Bytes Total divided by Inbound Messages Total will give you the average message size received through this connector.
Oldest Message Queued	The amount of time in seconds that the oldest message has been queued up and waiting to be delivered. Naturally, you want this to be low (less than a few minutes, perhaps).
Outbound Bytes Total	The total volume of messages in kilobytes that has been sent from this connection since the MTA was initialized.

Table 7.4   MSExchangeMTA Counters

Counter	Meaning
Outbound Messages Total	The total number of messages that have been sent through this connection. Outbound Bytes Total divided by Outbound Messages Total will give you the average message size received through this connector.
Queue Length	The number of messages waiting to be transferred.
Queue Bytes	The total volume of message in bytes that are waiting to be transferred.
Received Bytes/sec	The rate in bytes at which messages are being received per second.
Received Messages/sec	The total number of messages that are being received per second.
Sent Byte/sec	The rate in bytes at which messages are being sent per second.
Sent Messages/sec	The total number of messages that are being received per second.
Total Recipients Inbound	The total number of recipients specified in all messages that have been received since the MTA was initialized. This is provided since each message received may be addressed to more than one recipient.
Total Recipients Outbound	The total number of recipients specified in all messages that have been sent since the MTA was initialized. This is provided since each message received may be addressed to more than one recipient.
Total Recipients Queued	The total number of recipients specified in all messages currently in the queue for this connection.

Operations

PART 2

- Process
- Processor
- Server
- System

Next, you need to set the log filename and the interval at which Performance Monitor will take a snapshot of the system. Choose Options ➤ Log to see the Log Options dialog box. Set the name and location of the log file. Unless you are going to be manually taking measurements, make sure that the Periodic Update button is selected and a reasonable value is entered in the Interval box.

What is a reasonable interval value? The default is 15 seconds, but this interval is far too often in my opinion. The counter values that are collected are actually an average between the last collection interval and the current collection interval. Do you really need to collect this data every 15 seconds?

As an example, if I were going to collect data for my system's activity from 8:00 A.M. until 11:00 A.M., I would choose a value about every 120 seconds. Over a three-hour period of time, that is still going to give me 90 separate measurements. The log file will grow to considerable size with only 90 measurements. Even with just the objects I recommended above (and none of the Exchange counters), a log file with 90 separate measurements in it will be over 1MB in size.

Viewing Logged Data   One of the great mysteries of Performance Monitor data logging is, "How do I see the data that I have logged?" When viewing data in chart view, you are normally viewing data in real-time (or Current Activity). From any Performance Monitor view, you can select to view data from a log file instead. Select Option ➤ Data From to see the Data From dialog box. Two radio button options here give you the option of viewing data from Current Activity or a Log File.

Simply select the Log File option and click the radix button (the button with the three periods in it) to browse the file system for the log file you want to look at. Once you have selected the log file and clicked on OK, create your chart or report as you would if you were viewing data from current activity. You can create a log from a log, called *relogging*, for purposes of creating new logs or reducing the size of existing log files.

Automatically Creating Performance Monitor Logs   Suppose you want to create a Performance Monitor log a few times per week. You estimate that the busiest time of the day for your servers is 9:00 A.M. and 11:00 A.M., so you want to log activity during these times. If you are like most system administrators, you probably don't have time every morning to start and stop Performance Monitor at the exact times required. The Windows NT Resource Kit includes two programs that can assist you in automatically creating the logs you wish to create. These two utilities are collectively referred to as the data logging service.

To set up the data logging service, make sure that the `datalog.exe` and `monitor.exe` programs that come with the Windows NT Resource Kit are copied to the `\WinNT\System32` directory. Then type **MONITOR SETUP** at the command prompt. This will install the Performance Monitor service (you will see a new service in Control Panel ➢ Services called Monitor Service) and configure the appropriate Registry values. The default startup type will be set to manual startup mode.

Next, you need to create a Performance Monitor workspace that specifies the objects you are going to collect in the log and the log file you are going to create. To do this:

1. Start Performance Monitor and switch to the log view.

2. Add the objects you wish to monitor. Remember when creating a log that you have to capture the entire object, not specific counters.

3. In the Log Options dialog box (Options ➢ Log), set the Periodic Update interval to a reasonable value (somewhere between 300 and 900 seconds). Also, enter a filename (e.g., `C:\dailylog.pmw`) that you want the data to be logged to, and click Save (not Start Log).

4. On the Performance Monitor main menu, choose File ➢ Save Workspace and create a workspace file in the `C:\WinNT\System32` directory (e.g., `dailylog.pmw`).

Next you need to specify the file and start the service. Since you want this to occur automatically, use the Windows NT Scheduler server and the Windows NT AT command to schedule two commands to run daily. The first command will run every morning at 9:00 A.M. and will start the monitor service; the second will run at 11:00 A.M. and stop the monitor service.

Create two batch files, one called `startlog.cmd` and one called `stoplog.cmd`. These batch files will be placed in the `C:\PERFDATA` directory. The `startlog.cmd` is easy—all it has to do is set the correct workspace for the monitoring service to use and then start the service. Here is a sample:

```
@ECHO OFF

REM STARTLOG.CMD file starts the logging service
```

Once the alert thresholds are set, you can specify the update time and whether to send a network message or generate an event in the application log using the Alert Options dialog box found at Options ➣ Alert.

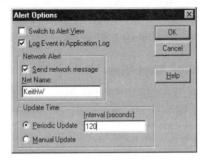

The resulting Performance Monitor view will look like Figure 7.7. The only alert that has been generated in Figure 7.7 is for the Work Queue Length counter. Notice that the values reported were 212, 216, 223, and 225.

Figure 7.7 Performance Monitor alert view

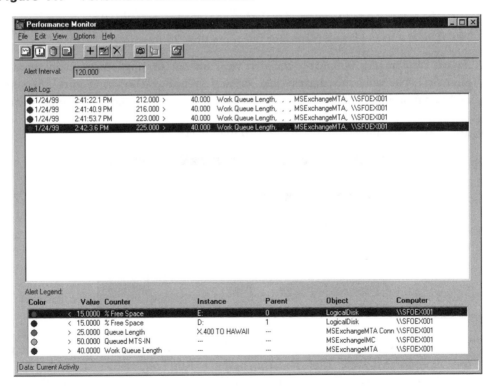

> **TIP** The alert view of Performance Monitor can be saved and run automatically as a service in the background using the Performance Monitor service found on the Windows NT Resource Kit. Follow the same procedures found in the section titled "Automatically Creating Performance Monitor Logs," but create settings for the alert view instead of the log view. Save the PMW file, specify that the monitor service will use that file, and start the monitor.

Saving Performance Monitor Settings to Use Later

So you have worked and slaved over Performance Monitor all day and have finally found the counters that you want to monitor. You have configured chart, logging, reporting, and alert options, and you *don't* want to do it again. To save the Performance Monitor setting from the Performance Monitor menu, choose File ➤ Save Chart (or Log, Report, Alert) settings. If you have not previously saved these settings, you will be asked to provide a name for them.

To save the settings found in all four Performance Monitor views, select Save ➤ Workspace and provide a name for your workspace if it has not been previously named. These settings can now be retrieved for later use or they can be used with the data logging service found on the Windows NT Resource Kit.

Built-In Performance Monitor Charts

During Exchange Server installation, the Setup program includes eight pre-built Performance Monitor charts. These charts are stored in PMW (Performance Monitor workspace) files in the C:\exchsrvr\bin directory. For convenience sake, these charts are also on the Microsoft Exchange menu (choose Start ➤ Programs ➤ Microsoft Exchange). These charts are designed to track critical activity on your Exchange server. They include:

- The Server Health chart, which tracks CPU usage for all the Exchange core services including the directory service, MTA, information store, and System Attendant. It also displays the total CPU usage and the Memory Pages/sec counter. Figure 7.8 shows the Server Health chart. This chart is updated once a second.

Operations

PART 2

Figure 7.8 Server Health chart showing the CPU usage for core services and pages per second

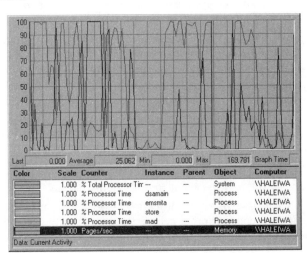

- The Server History chart tracks the total number of users that have connected to this server, the memory object's Pages/sec counter, and the message transfer agent's Work Queue. This chart is updated once every 60 seconds.

- The IMS Queues chart displays the messages waiting to be transferred to and from the Internet Mail Service (stored in the information store) and the messages queued up at the IMS, both inbound and outbound. This chart is updated once every second.

- IMS Statistics show the total messages sent out and received inbound via the Internet Mail Service. IMS statistics are updated once every 30 seconds.

- The IMS Traffic chart displays messages passing through the information store going to the Internet Mail Service (through the IMS mailbox MTS-IN and MTS-OUT queues) as well as the total number of connections. This chart is updated once every second.

- The Server Load chart is used to track the total load on the server by tracking statistics on the number of messages submitted and delivered per minute, the number of address book reads, and the number of RPCs (Remote Procedure Calls) per second. This chart also tracks activity generated by servers in the same site by tracking the Adjacent MTA Associations counter. This chart is updated once every 10 seconds.

- Server Queues display the number of messages that are stored in server queues and are waiting for processing. Naturally, you want these numbers to be low. The counters charted include the MTA's Work Queue Length and the Send and Receive queues for the public and private information stores. Server queues are updated once every 10 seconds.

- The Server Users chart shows the total number of users that have a connection to the server (the MSExchangeIS User Count counter). This chart is updated every 10 seconds.

TIP   If you work with any of these supplied counters, you will notice that these Performance Monitor charts have no pull-down menus and often no legend. You can resize these charts with your mouse and close it by pressing Alt-F4. And, if you absolutely have to see a menu, press the Enter key while the chart is the active window.

Server and Link Monitors

Microsoft provides two tools that function as part of the Exchange Administrator program. These tools are the Exchange server monitor and link monitor. Server monitors are used to monitor the status of services on one or more Exchange servers placed throughout your organization. Link monitors are used to send what I like to call a "ping" message to other mail servers; it then measures the amount of time it takes to get a response.

Both of these tools can be used to help maintain your organization and to make sure that you know that a server or link has failed before your user community has a chance to call you. This type of monitor is critical if you want to stay one step ahead of the ringing phone.

The server monitor and the link monitor allow you to specify different polling intervals and escalation notifications. The *polling interval* choices are normal and critical. You may want to poll sites that are operating normally (with no problems) less frequently than a site that has started experiencing problems (critical sites).

You can further specify an *escalation interval* that is different for sites that have experienced a minor delay (warning) versus sites that have been designated as critical. Critical sites are sites where the problem has not been resolved within a certain amount of time.

Operations

PART 2

Server Monitors

Any service on a Windows NT server that has Exchange Server running on it (not limited to the Exchange services) can by monitored by the Exchange server monitor. The server monitor is configured to monitor the service and notify the administrator if the service fails. The server monitor can also attempt to restart the service or the entire server, if so configured.

By default, only three services are monitored by a server monitor: the directory service, the information store, and the MTA. The services to be monitored are specified on the Services tab of each Exchange server's properties. In Figure 7.9, this server is configured so that the Backup Exec Job Engine, Exchange Directory, Exchange event service, Exchange information store, Exchange Internet Mail Service, and Exchange message transfer agent are monitored.

Figure 7.9   Services on server SFOEX001 configured to be monitored by a server monitor

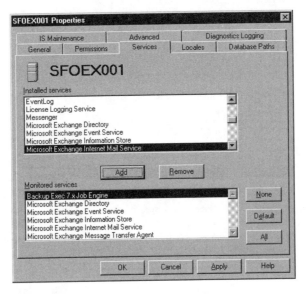

Creating a Server Monitor

Server monitors are created and run from within Exchange Administrator. To create a server monitor, choose File ➣ New Other ➣ Server Monitor. The server monitor has five tabs: General, Notification, Servers, Actions, and Clock.

General   On the General tab, you must provide a directory name and a display name for the monitor. You can also specify a log filename where status information and notifications are kept.

At the bottom of the General tab, you can specify a normal polling interval and critical sites polling interval. The *normal polling* interval (15 minutes) is used for servers whose services are all functioning and whose clock is not off by more than a specified interval (specified on the Clock page).

If a server does not meet the criteria for a normal polling interval, it will be polled at the *critical sites* interval instead. The default for critical servers is every 5 minutes. Polling intervals can be set as frequently as a few seconds or as infrequently as a few hours. The defaults work quite well in most environments; polling too frequently will generate excessive network traffic, whereas polling infrequently may mean you are not notified of service failures for a long period of time.

Notification   The Notification tab (shown in Figure 7.10) is used to specify how notifications should occur if a server or service enters either a warning state or an alert state. A server will enter a *warning state* if the server clock is off by more than the number of warning seconds you specify on the Clock tab. A server or service will enter an *alert state* if a service does not respond to the server monitor or if the server clock is off by more than the alert amount specified on the Clock tab.

You can set a server monitor to deliver notifications to administrators or computers via an e-mail message or a Windows NT alert. You can also configure the server monitor to launch an application if a warning or alert occurs.

To specify a type of notification, click the New button on the Notification tab; you will see the Escalation Editor dialog box. This dialog box is slightly different for different types of notifications. The mail message notification box is shown in Figure 7.10. When you specify a notification type, you may also specify a time delay; the default is 15 minutes. The Time Delay is the amount of time that server monitor waits after a warning or alert is generated before it sends out a notification.

TIP   When configuring notification types, e-mail is a great way to send notification messages. This is, of course, provided that the e-mail server that is causing problems is not yours. To make sure you receive critical server monitor messages, configure Windows NT alerts in addition to mail message alerts. The Windows NT alert option allows you to specify a computer or user to notify.

Figure 7.10 A server monitor's Notification tab, including the Escalation Editor dialog box

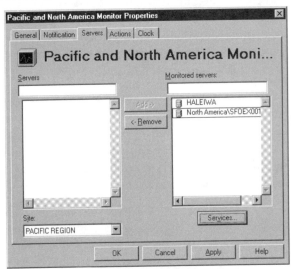

Servers The server monitor's Servers tab is where you specify which servers you want to monitor. A server monitor can monitor any server within the organization, as long as the monitor has RPC connectivity to the servers it is monitoring. Servers listed in the Monitored Servers column will be monitored by the server monitor.

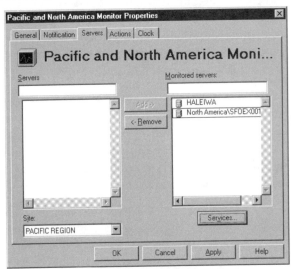

By highlighting a server in the Monitored Servers column and clicking the Services button, you are able to configure which services are monitored for that particular server. You can also configure the monitored services on the Services tab of the server's property page (shown in Figure 7.9).

Actions   The Actions tab allows you to specify what action the server monitor will take if an Exchange service is stopped or does not respond. You can specify a first attempt, second attempt, and subsequent attempts to take corrective action. The three options for corrective actions include Take No Action, Restart The Service, and Restart The Computer. If you specify the Restart The Computer option, you can specify a restart delay and a restart message.

NOTE   When configuring a server monitor to take corrective action, the Windows NT user who is running the server monitor must have server operator rights or greater on the destination servers.

Clock   The Clock tab allows you to set a warning and alert interval for monitored Exchange servers whose clocks differ by more than a specified interval. The computer that is running the Exchange server monitor is used as the baseline for correct time. The Synchronize check box option allows you to specify that you want the server's clock to be synchronized with the monitoring computer. Windows NT tracks time internally in UCT (Universal Coordinated Time); you see the local time displayed. If the monitored servers are in different time zones, the server monitor still sets their local time correctly.

Using Server Monitors

Exchange server monitors are operated as part of the Exchange Administrator program, which must be operating in order to start a server monitor. To start a monitor you have created, locate the monitor in the Monitors container (*Site Name* ➤ Configuration ➤ Monitors) and highlight it. From the Tools menu, choose Start Monitor. You are asked for a specific server to connect to; when you select the server and click OK, you will see the monitor window.

In Figure 7.11, you can see a server monitor called WorldWide Monitor that is monitoring 14 Exchange servers around the world. Notice that the ATLANTA (in the North America site) server's time is off by a little over five minutes, and the RIO (in the South America site) server's MTA service is not available. The VANCOUVER server (in the North America site) has an X next to it, meaning that it is currently undergoing maintenance. If you have configured the monitor to take corrective actions (such as restart a service or synchronize the clock), both of these issues will be addressed automatically.

Operations

PART 2

Automatically Starting Server Monitors   You can start Exchange server monitors from a command prompt or a batch file using Exchange Administrator's startup switches. The monitor startup switches for Exchange Administrator include the /M and /S switches. The /M switch allows you to specify a specific server monitor; the /S switch allows you to specify which server to connect to during startup.

To automatically start the WorldWide Monitor found in the Corp-HQ site, type **C:\exch-srvr\bin\admin /mCorp-HQ\WorldWide Monitor\London.**

Notice that you have to specify \London also; the server name is required for connecting to the server for reading monitor information and for any operations requiring a home server, such as sending e-mail messages. You can also specify multiple monitors to start in the same command line.

Exchange@Work: Automatically Starting Server and Link Monitors

If you want the server monitor to start automatically when the computer boots, there are two utilities provided with the Windows NT Resource Kit that may be of some assistance. The first, the Windows NT Auto Logon Setter (autolog.exe), configures a computer to automatically login. It asks you for the password of the currently logged on user and puts this information into the Registry. From this point forward, the computer will automatically login as the user you have specified. This is somewhat dangerous, because that password is now stored in the Registry and the computer automatically logs in. Make sure that this computer is physically secured if you do this.

The second utility is called Applications As Services (srvany.exe). This utility will configure any application to start as a service. If you configure a server or link monitor to run as a service, you will not be able to see the server monitor status screen, but notifications and corrective action events will still take place. This is a more secure option than the AUTOLOG option.

Putting a Server in Maintenance Mode   If you are going to take a server down for maintenance, ask yourself, "Is there a server monitor that is currently monitoring this server?" If you have implemented server monitoring, make sure that you put the server into maintenance mode prior to starting any maintenance, especially if the server monitor is performing notification or taking corrective actions.

I speak from experience. On more than one occasion I have stopped Exchange services to perform maintenance, only to find the services automatically restarting. In one instance,

I disabled a service so that it would not restart. Within a few minutes, the server monitor that was monitoring that server was rebooting the server. I had no way to stop it from rebooting.

To put the server in maintenance mode, use the Exchange Administrator command-line switch /T. You run this command at the server console of the server you are about to take down for maintenance. Here are a couple of examples of how to put a server into maintenance mode and the function that it provides.

Command	Function
Admin /T R	Suspends repair, but notification will still be generated.
Admin /T N	Suspends notifications, but repairs will still be performed if the monitor finds problems.
Admin /T NR	Suspends both notifications and repairs.
Admin /T	Resets the server to normal mode. Repairs and notification will resume normally.

If you use the switch /T feature, don't forget to use the /T command to put the server back in normal mode.

Link Monitors

Server monitors are used to verify the availability of Exchange servers and services. Link monitors are used to verify that messages are actually being transmitted between two Exchange servers or between an Exchange server and an external mail system. For Exchange to Exchange link monitor tests, the System Attendant service generates an e-mail message and sends it to the System Attendant on another server. The System Attendant on the other Exchange server replies as soon as it gets the message. When the message is returned to the originating server, the System Attendant determines how long it took for the round trip and if that time is within specified norms.

For Exchange to non-Exchange systems link monitor tests, the System Attendant sends a message to a custom recipient that represents a user on this non-Exchange system. The other system must be either able to recognize and automatically reply to the message or it must be able to send a non-delivery report.

Link monitors are excellent tools to use if you need to determine if your message delivery times are acceptable.

Creating a Link Monitor

Link monitors are created and displayed in the same Monitors container in which server monitors are held. To create a server monitor using Exchange Administrator, choose File ➤ New Other ➤ Link Monitor. The link monitor has five tabs: General, Notification, Servers, Recipients, and Bounce.

Operations

PART 2

General The General tab (shown in Figure 7.13) contains the link monitor's directory and display names. In addition, you can specify a log file (this file is in ASCII text) to which all link monitor activity is written. The Polling Interval box allows you to specify how often both normal operation and critical sites are polled.

Figure 7.13 Link monitor for the CORP-HQ site

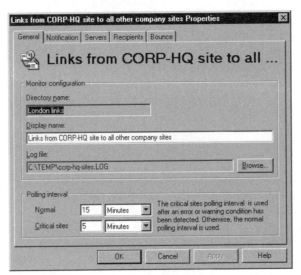

The default polling interval is every 15 minutes for a server that is operating normally and 5 minutes for sites that are considered critical. I would not set these values below this level, because doing so increases the number of messages that have to be transferred between servers. If the messaging system is very busy, frequent link monitor messages will interfere with the regular messaging traffic.

Notification The Notification tab behaves exactly like the Server Monitor tab described earlier in the chapter. From here you can set network pop-up messages and e-mail message notifications, as well as specify a program launching a process.

Servers The Servers tab allows you to specify which servers in *your own* Exchange organization you want to send link monitor messages to.

Recipients The Recipients tab gives you a place to put custom recipients for addresses that exist on external systems. When you create this custom recipient, you will most likely want to create a custom recipient that does not exist on the foreign system. If you specify a real recipient, you probably won't receive a reply right away unless that recipient has an automatic reply rule on its mailbox. After I create a recipient and set up the link monitor, I prefer to hide these recipients so they are not visible to the global address list.

When a non-delivery message is returned, the link monitor does not read the contents of the message, but rather the message subject. You have one of two columns you can use for custom recipients; these two columns represent the typical reply types. The left column (Message Subject Returned From) is the one you should most likely use. It is for systems that have an automatic reply feature and that put the original message subject text into the reply subject field.

The right column (Message Subject And Body Returned From) is used when you do not know how the foreign system will return the subject. Systems that return the message body are less efficient because they generate more overhead. If you do not know which one to choose, try choosing the Message Subject Returned From selection first and seeing if it works.

Bounce   The Bounce tab is where to specify the bounce duration. This means the longest acceptable round trip time for a message to travel between two systems. This duration is used for all servers and recipients configured for this link monitor. If you have different bounce times for different systems, you will need to configure multiple monitors.

You have two bounce duration-time options. Enter Warning State After determines how long to wait for a return message before entering a warning state. This time should indicate messages that are late. Enter Alert State After determines how long to wait for a return message before entering an alert state; the alert state is for messages that are considered very late.

To calculate how long to set these values for, you will need to take into consideration your message topology and typical times to send messages between servers and sites. I always consider the longest acceptable times during the busiest parts of the day; that way, I do not get a lot of false alarms just because the system is busy.

Using Link Monitors

Link monitors are started the exact same way that server monitors are started; this was described earlier in this chapter. The Exchange Administrator program's command-line switches can also be used to automatically start a link monitor.

Once you start the link monitor, you will see the link monitor status screen. This screen will be similar to the one shown in Figure 7.14, which shows the list of servers and custom recipients to which you have established link monitoring.

Figure 7.14   Link monitor status; notice that all three servers in the South America site are overdue.

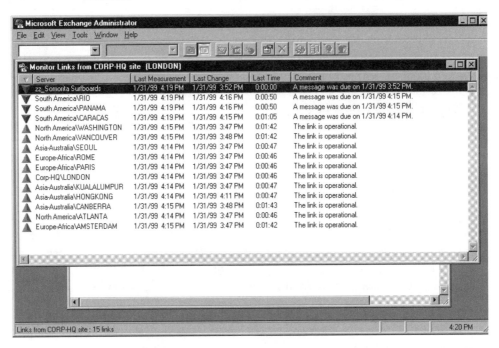

Notice the columns in Figure 7.14 that tell you the last time that a measurement was taken, the last time there was a change, and the total time it took for the last message to be returned. This link monitor is running in the London office; notice that it took one minute and 42 seconds for a message to travel to and from the WASHINGTON server in the North American site.

Also, notice that there are four servers from which this monitor expected a response but did not received one. The top one in the list is a custom recipient that was created for an SMTP user. Notice that the Last Time figure is 0:00:00; this means it has never received a reply.

Another fact we can disseminate from this status screen is that this link monitor is expecting a response from all three servers in the South America site. This may well be indicative of a failed WAN link.

If you highlight any of these servers or recipients in the list, you can display its properties. Figure 7.15 shows the details for the CARACAS server in the South America site.

Figure 7.15   Property page of the CARACAS server

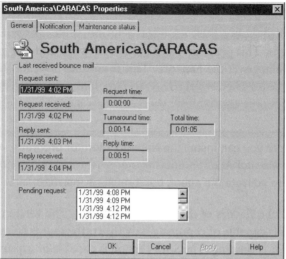

On the General tab, you can see the statistics for the request and reply messages. The Notification tab shows the notifications that have occurred, and the Maintenance Status tab shows whether the server is in maintenance mode or not.

Good Monitoring Practices

When you are planning your server monitors and link monitors, avoid the temptation to have multiple administrators all monitoring the same servers. While this is not detrimental, it can result in a situation where unnecessary monitoring traffic is being generated. You can, however, have problems if you have more than one monitor configured to take corrective actions.

Don't monitor too frequently, either. You need to find a good balance between getting up-to-date information and not saturating your network and servers with monitor requests. For me, that means starting with the default monitor settings and making small adjustments based on those defaults.

> **NOTE**   The Microsoft BackOffice Resource Kit provides a tool called Exchange Monitor Report Generator. This tool is used to scan server monitor and link monitor log files and create a report of problems and downtime. This tool can be found on the CD-ROM in the \Exchange\WinNNT\I386\Admin\EMRG directory.

Exchange@Work: Using the Network Monitor *(continued)*

I called the administrator back and told him that I would e-mail him the network monitor trace file (from another mail system). He still did not believe me, but I went ahead and e-mailed it to him. Magically, in about two days their domain started receiving messages properly. Though I never found out the exact reason, the rumor was that they had an Internet Mail Connector configuration problem.

Exchange Logging and Reporting

Exchange Server does a tremendous amount of logging and reporting. Some of this information is easily obtainable, while other information is a little more time consuming to retrieve. Monitoring this information can sometimes be tedious, but it is your first line of defense when solving problems or preventing small problems from becoming big problems.

The Windows NT Event Viewer

The Windows NT Event Viewer program should be one of the biggest tools in your toolbox. In Chapter 6, I recommended that you check the event logs daily. I also discussed a few of the events you should regularly watch for. As you learn more about Exchange, you will find many more events that are relevant to your installation.

Exchange@Work: Don't Be Afraid to Check the Event Logs!

A few years back, I was troubleshooting a message transfer agent problem. Every time I restarted the MTA, it automatically stopped within about five minutes. I ran the MTACHECK program, I restarted the server—you name it, and I was trying it. After nearly an hour of troubleshooting, I was at the end of my rope.

As a last resort, I checked the Event Viewer. There was an error (red) event generated by the MTA: Event ID 9411, Source MSExchangeMTA "The MTA is terminating because the disk where MTADATA is located has less than 10MB of space, or an error occurred while trying to check for free space on the disk." I still blush when I think about this, because I did not check the application event log first thing.

The moral of the story: At the first sign of trouble, *always* check the Windows NT Event Viewer.

Turning on Diagnostic Logging

There are a number of places that you can turn on diagnostics logging for the components in your Exchange server. All services and most connectors have a Diagnostics Logging tab; the connectors that do not have their own Diagnostics Logging tab can be logged through the MTA Diagnostics Logging tab. Services and connectors that have Diagnostics Logging tabs include:

- Message transfer agent
- Public information store
- Private information store
- Directory service
- Microsoft Mail connector
- Directory synchronization
- Lotus cc:Mail connector

One of the more central places to turn on diagnostics logging is on the Diagnostics Logging tab for each server. Figure 7.18 shows the Diagnostic Logging tab for an Exchange server called HALEIWA.

Figure 7.18   Diagnostics Logging tab for the HALEIWA server

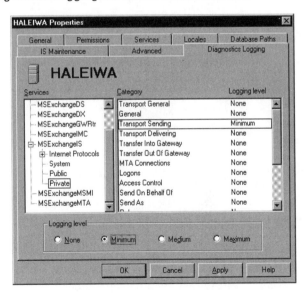

There are four levels of logging for each of the categories for which you can turn on logging. The first level, None, is pretty self-explanatory. Minimum provides only the bare necessities of information, basically just letting the administrator know that the event occurred. Medium provides a little more detail, and Maximum provides a great amount of detail. Unfortunately, there is no hard and fast rule for the logging levels that will let you know exactly what each level will provide. The services and categories are documented quite well in the Microsoft Exchange Books Online. Some good rules to follow when using diagnostics logging include:

- Follow the general rule of turning on only the categories you need.

- Start with the Minimum logging level to see if that provides you with the information that you require. Excessive logging will only serve to fill your event log up with extraneous and useless information.

- When you have diagnosed the problem or found the information you need, set the logging level back to None if you no longer require information from that category.

Tweaking the Windows NT Log Files

The default maximum size of a Windows NT event log file is 512KB. A log file of this size will become full quite quickly. Further, the default is to overwrite only events older than seven days. One of the first things I do when I install a new Exchange server is to change this default for all three logs (System, Security, and Application). This is done from the Windows NT Event Viewer by choosing Log ➤ Log Settings.

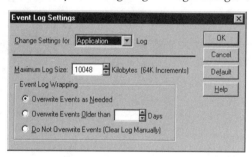

In the Maximum Log Size window, I change it to about 10MB (since the display is in kilobytes and is set in 64KB increments, I have to set it to 10048KB). Further, I change the Event Log Wrapping to Overwrite Events As Needed. In high security installations, this setting is often switched to Do Not Overwrite Events (Clear Log Manually); this is so the security officer has an opportunity to view each log. I change these settings for all three log types.

Archiving Logs

The Windows NT Event Viewer gives you the ability to archive the log you are currently viewing. You can archive the event log to an EVT file that can be later retrieved back into the Windows NT Event Viewer, to a comma-delimited text file, or to a simple ASCII text file.

To archive the current event log, choose File ➤ Save As and provide a filename and path. I usually save event logs as EVT files because they are easy to retrieve and read through Event Viewer. However, some administrators I know think it is important to keep this information in a database and thus require the comma-delimited text format.

Viewing Event Logs from Remote Computers

If you connect to an Exchange server from a remote computer, the remote computer will not have the Registry keys and files that are required by the Windows NT Event Viewer to display the correct descriptions for the Exchange-related errors. You may see the message:

```
The description for Event ID (104) in Source (ESE97) could not be
found.
```

If this is the case, you need to populate the local Registry with the appropriate Registry keys and copy the appropriate files to your local computer. The BackOffice Resource Kit has a tool called the Initialize Event Log tool that can do this for you.

Exchange Error Numbers

Exchange Server has several hundred error numbers that it may display in the application and system event logs. Sometimes the Event Viewer program will have an excellent description of the event; other times it will not.

On the Exchange Server CD-ROM there is a tool called `error.exe` that will look up an error message if you provide it with the error code. The tool is in the `\Server\Support\Utils\I386` directory of the CD-ROM. You supply the error number (including the dash, if the error code has one), and `error.exe` will give you the error message. For example, if you're seeing the error number –1018, you can type **ERROR –1018**, and it will reply with `Error –1018 (0xfffffc06) = JET_errReadVerifyFailure`.

Okay, it's not much, but at least it is one more piece of information you can use when searching the Knowledge Base or TechNet.

Logging MTA Events When Queues Reach a Specified Size

Starting with Exchange Server 5 SP2 and all versions of Exchange 5.5, there is a set of four new Registry values that allow you to set an alarm level to log MTA events when the outbound queue or the MTA work queue has more than a specified number of messages

Operations

PART 2

For Further Information...

For additional and more in-depth information about the topics covered in this chapter, check out these resources:

- Microsoft Windows NT Server Resource Kit and the Microsoft BackOffice Resource Kit (Second Edition).

- Microsoft Certified Technical Education Centers (CTEC) offer an excellent class called Windows NT 4.0 Enterprise Technologies, which covers the Network Monitor, Performance Monitor, Windows NT troubleshooting, and Windows NT domain design.

- You can learn more about Seagate Software's Crystal Reports on the Web at www.seagate.com.

- Get more information about NetIQ Corp.'s AppManager product at www.netiq.com.

8

Exchange 5.5 Collaboration

A *collaborative application* is a program or collection of programs that facilitates groups working together by helping to collect, organize, and track knowledge. Usually Exchange or Outlook is installed to provide users with the capability to correspond using e-mail. However, when used together, Exchange and Outlook can provide powerful collaborative capabilities.

A collaboration between users can be as simple as using a shared folder for message content to as complicated as developing an application using high-level programming languages (such as Visual Basic or C++) to access data in the information store and directory databases. As an Exchange administrator, how these applications interact with the system and the configuration issues that can arise should not be a major distraction to the administration of the mail system.

Discussing the interaction of these applications with Exchange is the primary purpose of this chapter; a complete discussion of collaborative applications and Exchange's capabilities could easily consume a thousand-page book. The topics covered in this chapter include:

- The basics of collaboration and features that Exchange and Outlook provide
- Forms libraries for storing collaboration forms
- Notes on using public folders, including moderated public folders
- Using the Exchange event service

NOTE This chapter focuses on the capabilities of Exchange Server and the use of the Outlook client, specifically Outlook 98. Some of the functionality described here is not available when using previous versions of the clients associated with Exchange, while some capabilities are enhanced further using Outlook 2000.

Basic Collaboration

As an administrator, in order for you to better manage a server that supports collaborative applications, you need to be aware of the basics of collaborative applications and some of the issues that will arise as a result of using them. It is also helpful to understand where the responsibilities for the various components will fall.

Developing Collaborative Applications

Outlook enables some basic collaborative functionality right out of the box, while other functionality must be developed. A basic collaborative application will include one or more of these components: forms, folders, views, fields, and external database connectivity. Responsibility for all these components will probably not fall into your arena unless you are a combination of system administrator and developer.

Collaborative applications can be developed for public folders as well as for building stand-alone (send or person-to-person) forms (applications) that users send to on another. The collaborative application developer is usually responsible for the development of the form, creating views, and possibly also setting public folder permissions.

Built-in Collaborative Applications

Outlook includes five "instant" collaborative applications: Calendar, Contacts, Journal, Tasks, and Notes. All users have these application folders in their own mailboxes. Public folders that host these types of applications can also be created. This practice is common when an entire department needs to share a calendar or the same contact list.

Here are some tips for using Outlook's built-in collaborative applications either in a personal mailbox or in a public folder:

- Users cannot share their personal Calendars, Contacts, Tasks, Notes, or Journal folders if they are stored in a PST file. They must be using Exchange-based message storage.

- Turn off the Journal feature (go to Tools ➤ Options, then click the Journal Options button) if the Journal is not required. The Journal feature records file creation for Microsoft Office products as well as events such as sending e-mail messages, booking meetings, and assigning tasks. This can consume a lot of space in users' mailboxes, and the user may not even realize it.

- Each Calendar, Contact, Journal, Note, and Task item counts as an item in a mailbox. Administrators are often confused when a new mailbox (not more than a day or two old) can have hundreds of items in it. This may be because the person used the Import Holidays function or imported an address book into their Contacts folder.

- When assigning forms to public folders, assign only those necessary for the collaboration activities in that folder, and be sure to specify that *only* the forms listed can be used with that folder. (This is done in the folder's Forms property page.) This prevents users from accidentally posting items with an incorrect form.

- When creating folders, make sure that the property item type is specified in the Folder Contains drop-down list box. Folders created using the Mail Items choice will not accept items such as Calendar, Contact, Journal, Note, or Task items.

- For public folders that need to be viewed a certain way, make sure that the custom views are created and the default view is set.

- Teach your users to put shortcuts to their commonly-used public folders in their Favorites folder or on the Outlook Bar. This will save them the hassle of often having to navigate the public folder hierarchy to find a folder they use all the time.

- When creating, designing, and testing public folders, do not give permissions to the users until you are ready for the folder to be used by the general public. And when granting permissions, grant only the permissions required.

Copying a Folder Design

When a folder is in the design process, it is often designed in a PST file and moved to a public or mailbox folder on the server after the design is finished. As the administrator, you may be asked to move a folder design into production.

To copy a folder design, first create the public folder you wish to use for the design you are about to copy. Then highlight the folder you want to copy the design to and, from the File menu, choose Folder ➤ Copy Folder Design. You will see the Copy Design From dialog box (see Figure 8.1).

From the Copy Design From dialog box, select the folder you want to copy the design from (the source folder) and which parts of the design to copy: Permissions, Rules, Description, and Forms & Views. Click OK, and the design of the source folder will be merged with the new folder that you have just created. If there are any conflicting properties on the destination folder, they will be replaced by properties from the source folder.

Operations

PART 2

Click the New button to add a new Organization Forms Library folder, the Modify button to change the forms library folder name, the Delete button to delete the folder, or the Permissions button to change the permissions granted to the folder.

WARNING If you delete a forms library folder, all the forms associated with that folder will be deleted.

Forms Library Permissions

Once the library is created, users have to be given permission to create forms in the Organization Forms Library. The default setting is for all users to have the role of Reviewer, which gives them the ability to read and use the forms. But for the forms to be placed in the library (*published* would be the more correct term), at least one user must be given the Owner role.

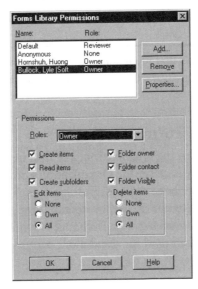

In this Forms Library Permissions window, notice that only users Lyle Bullock and Huong Hornshuh have the Owner role—and thus the permissions necessary to publish forms in the folder.

NOTE Though there are many possible permissions and roles that can be assigned, the only two that you need to worry about are the Reviewer role and the Owner role.

Publishing Forms

Once a form has been created and thoroughly tested, it can be published. Using Outlook, the form's creator opens the form and, by selecting Tools ➤ Forms ➤ Publish Form, selects where to publish the form.

If the form is published to the Organization Forms Library, it can be accessed from Outlook or used by programming languages such as Visual Basic or C++ from any other form or application. When it is published to the folder that it is to be used with (public folder, mailbox folder, or in a PST file), it is added to the bottom of the Outlook Action menu as *New Form Name*.

The Outlook Forms Manager

A published form does not have to be published to each and every folder for it to be available in those folders. Another method of pushing the form to a folder is the use of the Forms Manager within Outlook. To get to the Forms Manager, you must navigate several menus. In Outlook, go to Tools ➤ Options ➤ Other ➤ Advanced Options ➤ Custom Forms ➤ Manage Forms. The Forms Manager dialog box opens (see Figure 8.2).

Figure 8.2   The Outlook Forms Manager

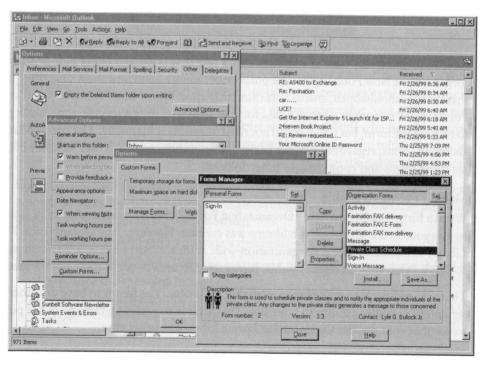

Event Services

Exchange Server 5.5 introduced the event services as one of the options that can be installed with the standard Exchange services. The event services watch public folders and folders in private mailboxes that have an agent associated with them and runs a script. Agents are triggered based on one of four types of events: when a new message is created, an item is changed in the folder, an item is deleted, or a scheduled event occurs.

> **NOTE**   Event services are not installed by default during upgrades of Exchange Server 4 or 5. If you do not see the Microsoft Exchange Event Service listed in the services list, then it is not installed. To install the event services, run the Exchange Setup program, choose Add/Remove, highlight the Microsoft Exchange Server option and click the Options button. Once installed, don't forget to re-install the Exchange Server service pack that you were using.

Enabling Event Agents and Permissions

Even though the event services are installed and started, they are not enabled within Exchange or accessible by the clients. Two different actions must be taken to make the services function as required. First, the event services must be enabled within the Exchange Administrator. Second, the Outlook client must be enabled to see the Agents tab.

To configure the event services, access the Exchange Administrator and at the organization level, open Folders. Within the System Folders directory, you'll find the Events Root folder. A separate folder is created under the Events root for each server within the organization (such as EventConfig_SFOEX001 or HNLEX002). It is here that the event services are enabled for the Exchange servers where you want events to happen.

> **NOTE**   Ensure that the event services are installed on the server where the scripting needs to be processed. The best place for the event scripting service is on the public folder server. In some cases, you may have an event scripting service on private folders to support collaborative solutions for resource booking or company calendars.

To enable management of event services, event managers must be granted permission to use the event services. Only those users with the Owner role to the EventConfig_*ServerName* folder will have the capability to install agent scripts on the folders. Once agent scripts are installed, those users who are granted Editor permissions within the EventConfig_*ServerName* folder can modify the scripts or the schedules installed. These permissions do not override the permissions that are granted to the users on the folders; they just define the users' roles for the generation of events.

The users will not see the Agents tab for the folders until they have installed the scripting agent add-in. To enable this capability, the user selects Tools ➤ Options ➤ Other tab ➤ Advanced Options ➤ Add-In Manager. The dialog box that opens lists the add-ins available to the client. Checking the Server Scripting selection enables and displays the Agents tab on all folder property displays.

> **NOTE** If Server Scripting is not a displayed option, click the Install button in the Add-In Manager dialog box and select the `scrptxtn.ecf` file to install it. This file is found in the `\Program Files\Microsoft Office\Office\Addins` directory.

Exchange@Work: Processing Forms Using the Event Service

Company FGH has sales people all over the world. They needed a method whereby their remote sales people could enter sales statistics and orders. Creating an intranet Web page seemed to be the ideal way to do this, but a pilot project indicated that this method did not work well as everyone thought it would because of the amount of time that it took to enter the data. This was compounded by the fact that many times throughout the remote sales person's day, they were not near a telephone line.

To solve the problem, a custom form was developed using Outlook 98 that allowed the remote sales people to enter their sales data directly into a mail message. This data could be saved and edited until the sales person was ready to transmit it at the end of the day.

The messages using the custom forms were all sent to a specific mailbox on the Exchange server. When the message arrived at the Exchange server, an event service script fired, opened the message, extracted the data, and imported it into an SQL database.

This solution worked great for Company FGH because the sales people could enter sales data periodically throughout the day, but remain offline. Further, the solution was not only easy to use, but it saved a substantial amount of money in long-distance phone charges.

For Further Information... *(continued)*

- Sue Mosher's Web site, Slipstick Systems (www.slipstick.com), has a lot of great hints and ideas on using Exchange and Outlook as a collaboration platform.

- There is an updated, improved version of the auto-accept script in Knowledge Base article 184271. See also KB article Q178351.

Learning to Operate Exchange Reliably

Company CRM supports nearly 3,200 Exchange users spread across five locations in the United States. These users are supported within a single site on eight servers dedicated to supporting mailboxes, on two dedicated public folder servers, and on a single Exchange server that operates the IMS, a third-party pager gateway, and a third-party fax gateway. The majority of the Exchange servers are located in their main office in San Francisco, but three of the servers are located in the Charlotte office. The rest of their user community uses the Exchange servers across their WAN.

Early in their Exchange deployment, CRM experienced a number of problems including several failed disk drives, a corrupted database, and incidents where the WAN connectivity failed and messages were not being delivered promptly. When Exchange 4 was deployed initially, the system was used as little more than an electronic mail platform.

To solve their problems, CRM deployed Exchange 5 and Outlook 97, and the user community's dependency on Exchange and Outlook began to increase. Now users were keeping not only their e-mail on the system, but also personal calendars and contract information. Further, the department managers were using the task management and group scheduling features. The potential uses of Exchange and Outlook were beginning to shine through.

The first public folder applications that appeared were simple bulletin boards for announcing company and department information. CRM had migrated from Lotus cc:Mail, and the users already expected such functionality. With the advent of Outlook 97, department public folders were created for uses such as contacts and calendars.

Once people began to see the joys of shared folders and Outlook applications, CRM's Information Services group deployed an electronic expense report form for a few departments in San Francisco. Within a month, the accounting department was asking that everyone in the company begin using this form. With some minor tweaks to satisfy the accounting and other departments, this form was deployed company-wide with great success.

It was not long before all of CRM's departments were rushing to see which processes they could automate using Outlook and Exchange. CRM hired a developer specifically to create forms and take CRM closer to the ultimate paperless office. Help desk requests, sales discussions, customer support tracking, time reporting, supply requests, and more public folder and stand-alone applications were created.

During this time, one of the Exchange servers experienced a hardware failure that left the Exchange server (and the 425 users that depended on it) without Exchange services for nearly three days. Also about this time, the lower-end servers that had initially been deployed were running out of steam, and the response time on these servers was suffering. Users were frequently complaining that the system was slow.

Though no one at CRM would have thought so at the time, this incident was a mixed blessing. The impressive features of Exchange Server and many of the company's newfound uses dazzled management, but they continued to treat it as "just the e-mail system" when it came time for spending money on hardware. The failure of a critical Exchange server and the user complaints forced management to realize how important Exchange and Outlook were becoming to their day-to-day business operations. The IS group was given additional money to upgrade the Exchange Server platform to improve performance and reliability. Further, two additional servers were purchased to be cold standby servers for both the San Francisco and Charlotte offices. Of course, management expected something in return. This something took the form of a Service Level Agreement that indicated expected performance and uptime.

Messaging had become a critical business process and had to be treated as such. CRM's IS team committed to 162 hours of operation per week (barring any unforeseen circumstances). This left only six hours per week to perform any system maintenance. This timeslot was midnight Saturday night until 6:00 A.M. on Sunday morning.

While running Exchange Server 5, the Exchange administrators had been defragmenting each Exchange server database once a month. Further, offline database backups were being performed. The information store databases on several servers were approaching 16GB. Larger database support, better online maintenance, and

the Deleted Item Recovery feature led to their decision to upgrade to Exchange Server 5.5 Enterprise Edition.

During this time, the backup procedures for all servers in both offices were standardized, as were the tape drive hardware and software. Each Exchange server had its own tape backup device. Only online backup procedures were to be run on these servers from this point forward. A normal backup was performed on each server every night of the week. Differential backups were made every two hours throughout the business day and were appended to the previous night's backup tape. The final differential backup of the day was performed at 7:00 P.M., and to protect against a tape failing and preventing restore of an entire day's worth of data, each server performed a differential backup on another server across the network. The Sunday night tapes were stored off-site and held for a month. There were two sets of weekly tapes, so that any server could be rebuilt in a previous state up to two weeks old.

Offline defragmentation/compaction procedures were discontinued due the increased efficiency of the Exchange 5.5 database engine.

In the San Francisco operations center, a computer running the Exchange link monitor and server monitor was up 24 hours a day. This computer was used to confirm connectivity and operation of all of CRM's Exchange servers. On the first hint of trouble, the server monitor or link monitor paged one of the Exchange administrators to begin troubleshooting. The server monitor also guaranteed that the time on all Exchange servers is synchronized with the administrator's workstation; the administrator's workstation used the Windows NT Resource Kit utility to synchronize its time daily with the U.S. Naval Observatory.

To guarantee that the servers were not overburdened, the primary Exchange administrator ran the Windows NT Performance Monitor on each server twice a month to ensure that both Windows NT and Exchange Server were performing as expected.

Once every two months, an Exchange server was picked and rebuilt on an isolated network using the standby hardware; the production server was never taken offline. This procedure guaranteed the integrity of the backups and databases. The server data was restored and tested to make sure that

messages were indeed restored and that the restore worked properly. Once the restore was confirmed, offline maintenance procedures were run on the database to make sure that there were no errors.

The upgrade to Exchange Server 5.5 was completed within two months of 5.5's release. Since that time, CRM has experienced no downtime outside of the occasional server reboots, service pack installations, and hot fix installations; these all occur during the normal maintenance intervals.

Though Exchange had a bit of a rocky start at CRM, the company continues to increase their dependency on it with the additional functionality it provides. The Administrators keep a close eye on Exchange and the event logs to make sure that nothing goes wrong and that they are aware of any potential problems that may pop up.

24seven CASE STUDY

Part 3

Connectivity

Topics Covered:

- Intrasite versus intersite connectivity
- The message transfer agent and routing
- Overview of the messaging connectors
- X.400 connectivity to foreign systems
- Directory replication
- Preventing unsolicited commercial e-mail (spam)
- Recipient e-mail addressing
- Using the Internet Mail Service without a full-time Internet connection
- Message interoperability with non-Exchange systems
- Securely using the Internet Mail Service
- Tips for using the Internet Mail Service

Intrasite Communication

Intrasite communication occurs automatically between all servers in a single site; no messaging connectors need to be defined. Within a single site, the two components that communicate directly between two servers are the directory service and the message transfer agent (MTA). Connectivity between servers is defined implicitly during server installation.

All communication between the servers in a site is accomplished using an Interprocess Communication (IPC) mechanism called Remote Procedure Calls (RPCs). Developers of DCE (Distributed Computing Environment) defined RPCs to be used in client/server computing because they are very fast, efficient, and are generally quite secure.

NOTE   The choice to use RPCs is the programmer's; there is not an instance where an administrator has to choose to use RPCs or not. However, you will see the acronym RPC often when working with Exchange, so don't be intimidated by it.

One of the biggest advantages of RPCs is that RPC data is encrypted when transferred between Windows NT servers. If the North American edition of Windows NT is used with the North American edition of the service pack, RPC data is encrypted with 128-bit RSA RC4 streaming encryption (this is provided by the schannel.dll file.) Outside of North America, a 40-bit version of the schannel.dll is used.

Between two Exchange servers in a single site, all communication is accomplished via secure RPCs. Figure 9.1 shows two servers communicating within a single site.

All other components running on an Exchange server, such as the System Attendant and the information store, use the MTA to communicate with another server's IS or SA. In Figure 9.1, if the information store on server SFOEX001 needs data (such as a mail message) delivered to server SFOEX002, the SFOEX001 information store sends that data to the MTA in the form of a message. The SFOEX001 MTA determines, by reviewing the recipient information, whether it needs to deliver it to SFOEX002. Using RPCs, the SFOEX001's MTA delivers the message to the SFOEX002's MTA; SFOEX002's MTA delivers it to the information store for processing.

Figure 9.1   Communication within a single site

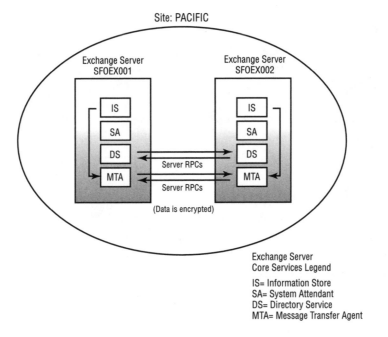

Within a site, the MTA is used as a delivery mechanism for:

- Mail messages
- Public folder hierarchy and content replication
- Link monitor messages

Within a single site, all server's directory services communicate directly with one another for the purpose of delivering directory updates; the directory service does not use the MTA. All directory updates are made via secure RPCs.

Site Security Context

So, Remote Procedure Calls are secure? Here is a quick overview of what happens when a "client" establishes a connection to the server.

Site Security Context *(continued)*

Let's say that the MTA on server SFOEX001 wants to deliver a message to the MTA on server SFOEX002. SFOEX001's MTA establishes a connection to SFOEX002. All connections to Windows NT require authentication, so SFOEX001 passes its current username to SFOEX002. What username do you think SFOEX001 uses? The MTA on both servers are logged in as the site services account because they are in the same site and thus must share the same security context. Therefore, Exchange-server-to-Exchange-server communication is authenticated using the site services account.

Intersite Communication

Even though two Exchange sites may share the exact same Exchange Organization name, they still have to be instructed to communicate with one another. This communication between sites (intersite) is handled through a messaging connector. Messaging connectors are discussed later in this chapter.

Intersite communication occurs using messaging connectivity as the delivery mechanism; even directory updates are just e-mail messages delivered to the directory service. However, updates to the directory database will not occur implicitly between two sites. A directory replication connector must installed between them. However, intersite directory replication relies on a messaging connector. Figure 9.2 shows two sites connected via a messaging connector and a directory replication connector.

Figure 9.2   Two sites with a messaging connector and a directory replication connector

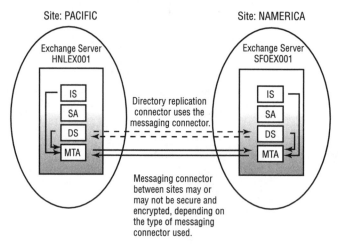

Note that *all* information must flow between the two sites as a mail message, thus using the MTA.

NOTE The security context does not have to be the same between two Exchange sites, nor do the sites even have to be connected via a full-time network connection. Hence, two different Exchange sites do *not* have to share the same site services account.

Message Transfer Agent

The message transfer agent is an amazing component. It is used in both intersite and intrasite communication and is a very important component in all aspects of Exchange. Rumor has it that at Microsoft, the MTA code is considered hallowed ground, because so few programmers and engineers there completely understand what the MTA does.

We do know, however, that all information leaving an Exchange server is processed by the MTA. Messages that are being transferred to other sites using the site connector or the X.400 connector are processed by the MTA and are visible in the MTA's queues. Messages that are being routed to an external X.400 system are also processed by the MTA; these messages are also visible in the MTA queues. Figure 9.3 shows the Queues property page of the message transfer agent.

Figure 9.3   A message waiting in an MTA queue

Connectivity

PART 3

The MTA also processes any messages that are leaving the server but are destined for a connector or third-party gateway. For example, the MTA is responsible for routing messages from other MTA's (or the information store) to the Internet Mail Service (IMS). The MTA places them in the IMS mailbox's MTS-OUT folder. The IMS is then notified to pick up the message from this folder.

On servers that support connectors such as the Internet Mail Service, you may have noticed that there some special mailboxes such as Internet Mail Service (*ServerName*) listed in the Mailbox Resources folder. These mailboxes are used as temporary holding places for messages awaiting delivery to an external connector. These mailboxes contain the MTS-OUT and MTS-IN folders for connectors developed using Exchange Development Kit (EDK). The gateway (i.e., IMS) places messages into the MTS-IN folder to be picked up by the MTA and delivered inbound to an Exchange recipient.

Managing Queued Messages

Figure 9.3 shows the Queues tab of the MTA property page. To view the messages waiting in an MTA queue, you must locate the server on which the messaging connector is installed. Choose *Site Name* ➤ Configuration ➤ Servers, view the message transfer agent property page, and click the Queues tab. The Queue Name drop-down list will show you a list of all the queues located on this particular server.

To manage a particular queue, select it in the Queue Name drop-down list box. Once a queue is highlighted, you can select a message and:

- Click the Details button to view the DN and the O/R address of the message originator. The Details button also lets you view the message transfer system identifier (MTSID), which is the message's unique identifier within the system. In addition, you can view the time the message was submitted, the message's priority, and the message size in KB.
- Click the Refresh button to refresh the list of messages waiting in this particular queue.
- Click the Priority button to change the message's priority. High-priority messages take precedence over all normal- and low-priority messages.
- Click the Delete button to remove the message from the MTA queue.

Often, when viewing the MTA queues, you will see "system" messages; system messages are easily identified by their originator. Messages from the *Directory Service* are messages generated by the directory service that contain directory replication information that is being sent to other sites. Messages from the *Public Information Store* are messages generated by the information store service that contain either public folder hierarchy or public folder content replication information. Messages from the *System Attendant* are link monitor status messages.

TIP The optimal approach to monitoring Exchange message queue size is to use the Windows NT Performance Monitor. See the section titled "Other Useful Performance Monitor Counters" in Chapter 7 for a list of helpful MTA queue-related counters under in the MSExchangeMTA Connections object.

Removing System-Generated Messages   You can remove messages originated by the directory service, system attendant, or the public information store. If you check a queue and find hundreds (or thousands) of messages queued up, these are system-generated messages that may have accumulated because of a failed WAN link or a server being offline for an extended period of time. These system messages can interfere with delivery of user-generated messages, because they will require delivery along with all of the other messages in the queue.

Once you have ascertained that messages are once again being delivered by confirming that the queue is getting smaller in size, you can remove these messages from the MTA queues using the MTACHECK command-line utility. This will help the MTA to catch up on message delivery more quickly. To do this:

1. Stop the message transfer agent.

2. Open a command prompt and change to the \exchsrvr\bin directory.

3. To remove directory replication-related messages, type **MTACHECK /RD**. To remove public folder replication-related messages, type **MTACHECK /RL**, and to remove link monitor-related messages (System Attendant), type **MTACHECK /RL**.

4. Restart the message transfer agent.

Monitoring MTA Events

Depending on the level of logging that is enabled, an MTA can generate a *lot* of events in the application event log. The None level generates a good many events, but the Maximum level logging generates too many events for day to day. Table 9.1 shows some of the common events that you may see in the application event log. The source for all these events is MSExchangeMTA. In order to see many of these events, the MSExchangeMTA Logging Category X.400 Service must be set to at least minimum.

NOTE How serious is an event that is related to the MTA? In the Description field for each MTA-related error message, the description ends with a number in parentheses. This number helps to determine the severity of the error; if the number is 8 or greater, the error number should be investigated right away.

Connectivity

PART 3

Table 9.1 Common Application Events Generated by MSExchangeMTA

Event ID	Explanation
320, 1288	An association has been initiated to another MTA. This will be followed by messages being transferred.
271, 272	Notification and confirmation that messages were delivered to another MTA.
1294	An association to another MTA has ended in an unexpected manner. This normally indicates a network problem or the failure of an MTA.
9215, 289	The MTA tried but could not establish a connection to another MTA. This can be network-related, or it could mean that the remote MTA is not available.
287	A message is being re-routed, probably due to the MTA failing to connect to another MTA using the preferred route. This may indicate a problem.
3049	System call failed. Stop and restart the MTA as a possible fix.
3048, 3050, 3051	All of these indicate a possible disk space issue. Free up some disk space and restart the MTA, or run the MTACHECK utility.
4301, 2248, 2221	A fatal error occurred reading a value from the directory. The directory service may not be running, or the Registry may be corrupted. Check the DSA Address entry on the MTA parameter key. A possible restoration from backup of the directory database may be necessary.
6613	A fatal internal MTA error occurred. The registration of the conversion routines has failed. You should stop and restart the MTA or run the MTACHECK utility.
9252	A fatal internal MTA error occurred. The isolation layer (IL) did not get properly registered with the base message store (BASE-MS). You should stop and restart the MTA or run the MTACHECK utility.
2098	A fatal error has occurred due to lack of disk space. Watching for this error allows you to fix a disk space issue.

Table 9.1   Common Application Events Generated by MSExchangeMTA *(continued)*

Event ID	Explanation
9212, 9216, 9228, 9254, 9268, 9402, 9403	A fatal error has occurred, and a fatal resource limit was reached while attempting to open an association. This normally means you need a larger paging file or more memory. Close applications, add memory, or increase the page file size.
310	A message transfer timeout has occurred. The message will be rerouted, but this means that a connection is probably failing.
9411	The MTA is shutting down. The disk that holds the MTA data directory is low on space.

Using MTA logging, you can also create interoperability and Application Protocol Data Unit (ADPU) text logs that can help with troubleshooting. These log files are stored in the \exchsrvr\MTAdata directory and can grow quite large if left unattended. The interoperability text logs contain the content of the actual messages that the MTA processes. The ADPU text logs contain the content of the message as well as the message envelope that the MTAs use to exchange the messages; the X.400 folks call this the P1 ADPU.

The current interoperability log is called AP0.LOG; previous logs are named APx.LOG, where *x* is a decimal number. To create interoperability logs, on the MTA Diagnostics Logging property page, set the Interface and Interoperability categories to Medium or Maximum. You do not need to restart the MTA after changing diagnostics logging levels.

The current ADPU log is called BF0.LOG; previous logs are named BFx.LOG, where *x* is a decimal number. To create ADPU logs, on the MTA Diagnostics Logging property page, set the ADPU category to either Medium or Maximum.

> **NOTE**   Chapters 6 and 7 describe some tools that you should use to proactively monitor your MTAs and message flow. These include the Windows NT Performance Monitor, Exchange link monitors, and server monitors.

> **WARNING**   If you turn on interoperability or ADPU logging to do troubleshooting, make sure that you turn it off when you are finished and clean up the log files it created when you no longer need them.

Connectivity

Exchange@Work: Solving MTA-Related Problems with the Knowledge Base

The MTA is a very dynamic and sophisticated program. As more and more diverse organizations are implementing Exchange, the MTA is moving into more, often uncharted territory. Inevitably, small problems (i.e. bugs) will appear.

Are you seeing a bizarre or unexplained message in your application event log? Scan the Knowledge Base using the event ID and error codes that the event log message provides. If everything else seems to be working fine, don't be surprised if the problem is software-related.

I have fixed numerous Exchange MTA-related problems by checking the KB and finding that the problem is a known bug and can be fixed by applying the latest service pack.

MTA Route and Connector Selection

How does the MTA make a decision about which connection to use if there are multiple paths? If you have been working with messaging connectors, you probably already understand the concept of costs. The cheapest cost always wins, right? If you have dug a little further, you will find that the cheapest cost does *not* always win, especially if a messaging link is currently experiencing problems.

Look at the Exchange sites illustrated in Figure 9.4. Notice that there are multiple paths from which an MTA must choose.

A server in the PACIFIC site could send a message destined for NAMERICA directly to NAMERICA, but it could also route the message through SAMERICA and have SAMERICA route the message to NAMERICA. The Exchange MTA will also learn about other possible routes (through the directory replication process).

So how does a poor MTA decide which way to go? The MTA goes through two processes to successfully route a message to the proper destination: route selection and connector selection. *Route selection* (or just *routing*) is the process of scanning the list of available routes (or connectors). *Connector selection* (or just *selection*) is the process of determining the best connector to use.

Figure 9.4   Look at all the connections between sites. What's a poor MTA to do?

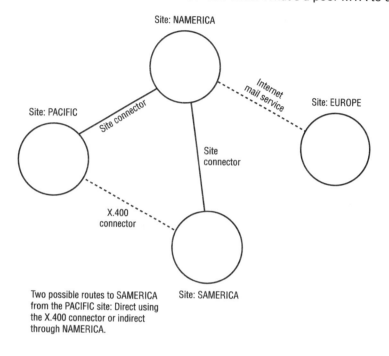

Site: NAMERICA

Site: PACIFIC

Site connector

Internet mail service

Site: EUROPE

Site connector

X.400 connector

Two possible routes to SAMERICA from the PACIFIC site: Direct using the X.400 connector or indirect through NAMERICA.

Site: SAMERICA

Route Selection   When selecting a route to take, the MTA looks at what's available; these routes are stored in the server's routing table, also called the Gateway Address Routing Table (GWART). The GWART is stored in the directory and is replicated to all sites. The routing table can be viewed at the site level Site Addressing object; choose *Site Name* ➤ Configuration, open the Site Addressing object properties, and view the Routing tab.

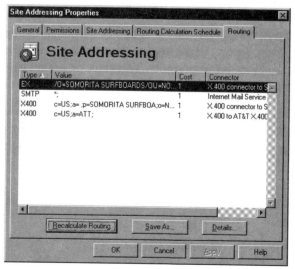

MTA object's General property page. Choose *Site Name* ➢ Configuration ➢ Servers ➢ *Server Name*, open the MTA properties, and view the General tab:

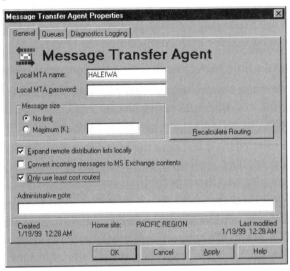

If Only Use Least Cost Routes is enabled, the MTA will only use the least-cost route and will not re-route messages through higher-cost routes in favor of schedules, Max Open Retry counters, and Open Interval settings. If the connector is unable to deliver a message based on the least-cost routes Max Retry and Open Interval, it will return an NDR to the sender. This occurs even if a higher-cost route is available. The higher cost routes cannot be selected, because the MTA skips the checks that would cause the higher cost to be used for lowest-cost route.

NOTE   To be effective, every server's MTA in the site must be configured to use only the least-cost route. See the "Connector Cost" section later in this chapter for more on cost value.

Bridgehead Servers

Depending on the number of servers in a site or the number of messages you are processing, you may have a server in your site that has been designated as the site's *bridgehead server*. The function of the bridgehead server is to handle all messages routed to it that are addressed to leave the site and/or the Exchange messaging system. This server may operate Exchange messaging connectors, the Internet Mail Service, connectors to other mail systems, and other third-party gateways.

Figure 9.5 illustrates a site with several servers designated as either mailbox servers or public information store servers. An additional server, SFOEX002, was installed in this site to function as the bridgehead server and all connectors.

Figure 9.5   A bridgehead server in action

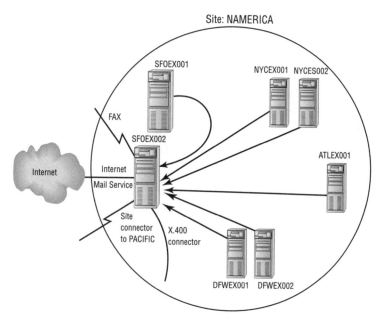

> **NOTE**   If you are an administrator of a smaller organization, you will not benefit from bridgehead servers, because you may only have one or two servers in your site. If these servers adequately keep up with your messaging load, then you probably don't need a bridgehead server.

Exchange@Work: Maximizing a Bridgehead Server's Effectiveness

The more products you install on your Exchange servers, the slower they will become. They may even become unstable as a result of additional components such as messaging connectors and fax gateways. Often the maintenance that must be performed on an Exchange server has little to do with the information store data, but rather the connectors and gateways.

Connectivity

PART 3

Exchange@Work: Maximizing a Bridgehead Server's Effectiveness *(continued)*

Many Exchange systems have incorporated an additional server into their sites and designated the additional server as the bridgehead server. Connectors to the intersite messaging connectors, connections to the outside world, and directory replication are installed and configured on this server.

When configuring a bridgehead server, keep in mind that the bridgehead server does not have to be as powerful or provide as much disk space as a server that hosts an information store. Nonetheless, provide fast hard disks and a fast processor. Other steps to take when setting up a bridgehead server include:

- If possible, split up the directory service database and the MTA working directory onto separate physical disks. Also keep in mind disk fault tolerance; though disk fault tolerance is not an essential requirement for a bridgehead server, I still consider it important.

- Delete the public information store from this server so that it does not have to participate in public folder hierarchy replication.

Make sure that the Performance Optimizer is run and that the server's role is defined correctly; this will correctly allocate memory for the bridgehead server.

When maintenance needs to occur, this server can more easily be taken offline since no mailboxes are located on it. Most mail systems will queue messages for your Exchange system or mail gateways for at least 24 hours.

Choosing the Right Messaging Connector

During the design phase of your Exchange organization, one of the most important decisions you will have to face is how to connect your sites. Sites are connected with messaging connectors (to transfer X.400 IPMs), and they share site knowledge using directory replication connectors. These are used to replicate entries in each site's container, which includes addresses, to other sites.

This chapter does not cover how to install each of these connectors, but rather the important factors you should consider when choosing an Exchange messaging connector, including the advantages and disadvantages of each connector type.

TIP   Prior to installing any messaging connector, make sure that the network infrastructure required to support that connector is installed and tested. This includes hardware and software to support connectors, i.e. X.400 over an X.25 network or the Dynamic RAS connector.

Overview of the Messaging Connectors

There are a couple of basic things you should understand about any messaging connector that you are going to install. The first is the concept of an address space and controlling address space visibility. Once you've got that handled, you need to consider the cost value associated with connectors.

Address Space

An address space defines what types of addresses can be reached through a connector; this information is used to build the routing table (or GWART). At the lowest-level, address spaces are the "where" aspects of recipient addresses. They're like zip codes defining the destination post office. Each connector that you install must have an address space associated with it. Otherwise, the MTA will not know what types of messages it can send through the connector.

NOTE   The only connector that has an address space by default is the Exchange site connector (it implicitly connects "Exchange" sites). This connector automatically has an X.400 address and an Exchange DN associated with it.

A connector can have more than one address space associated with it. Unless otherwise restricted, all connectors' address spaces are shared within the site. Once directory replication is configured between sites, the address space information is shared with other sites unless restricted.

Restricting Connector Availability Using a Scope   On the property page of each address space that is created for a connector, there is a Restrictions tab that allows you to specify the scope of that address space. A scope restriction allows you to control which

is connected to NAMERICA via a T1 that has an average available bandwidth of 512Kbps. NAMERICA has a T1 to PACIFIC with an average of 786Kbps bandwidth available during the business day.

The first issue the administrator of this organization has to consider is which link she wants messages flowing across. The X.25 link (with 36Kbps available bandwidth) is the least desirable link and should be used only in a "worst case" situation. The administrator decided she wants all messages from the PACIFIC site to be routed to the NAMERICA server first. She only wants the X.25 connector to be used to send messages to SAMERICA if the T1 is not available.

To control message flow, she sets the costs of the various connectors to control the preferred route. She sets the PACIFIC – SAMERICA X.400 connector to a cost of 3 and the PACIFIC – NAMERICA X.400 connector to a cost of 1. Due to the fact that the connectors and cost values are shared by directory replication, the MTA in PACIFIC will learn there is a route to SAMERICA through NAMERICA. The costs are cumulative.

The MTA in PACIFIC has two choices for sending a message to SAMERICA. For a cost of 3, it can send the message directly to SAMERICA (over the slow line). For a cost of 2, it can send the message to SAMERICA by sending to the NAMERICA site first. Unless the connection from PACIFIC to NAMERICA fails, the MTA will always choose the indirect route, because it is the cheapest.

Exchange@Work: Confusing the WAN Dudes

Every time I explain the concept of Exchange connectors and costs to a WAN manager, they get a dazed look on their face and exclaim, "But the routers take care of routing packets across the optimal link!" "This is quite true," I explain, "but routers work on the lower layers of the OSI model. The Exchange MTA is on the top of the heap at the Application layer." No router dude (or dude-ette) has ever bought this one.

In a perfect world, connector costs would not be terribly necessary, but the Exchange server may have more than a LAN adapter. As shown in Figure 9.6, the server in Honolulu may have another type of network connection, such as a X.25 network adapter. So the Exchange server must choose between using the LAN and using the (more expensive) X.25 network. Giving Exchange the ability to route messages over multiple network types (LANs, X.25, or Dynamic RAS) gives the administrator added flexibility if the WAN has failed, but the messages still need to go through.

I used X.25 as an alternative to a T1 or a Frame Relay connection, but it could just as easily be Dynamic RAS.

Site Connector

The site connector is quite possibly my all time favorite messaging connector (though it is losing favor to the Internet Mail Service). Here are some advantages and disadvantages to the site connector:

Advantages	Disadvantages
Easy to set up with few property pages to configure.	Proprietary to Microsoft Exchange.
All communication between sites is via RPCs, which means that everything is encrypted with either 40-bit or 128-bit encryption.	Since RPCs are used, the connection between the two sites must be a higher speed connection. A good rule of thumb is that a WAN link that supports RPCs should have at least 64Kbps of available bandwidth.
The site connector is up to 20 percent faster than other connectors because messages are transported across the connector in Microsoft Database Encapsulated Format (MDBEF), which is the internal database format. No message conversion is necessary, and compression is maintained.	Due to the fact that this connector assumes high speed connection, it can easily saturate a slow link if there is a large volume of messages.
Uses TCP/IP, IPX, or NetBEUI protocols.	No control over who sends messages across this connector, when it is used, or the maximum message size that can be sent. All messaging defaults for Max Open Retry and Open Interval are maintained on the Messaging Defaults property page of the MTA Site Configuration object.

NOTE Messages that are routed through the site connector can be managed at the server level on the MTA object's Queues tab. Remote servers are listed as queues by their server name.

X.400 Connector

I have a soft spot in my heart for the X.400 connector. It is difficult to set up and intimidates even the most experienced messaging system administrator, but it has some admirable qualities. The X.400 connector is versatile, is based on an ITU (International Telecommunications Union) and is thus an international recommendation (X.400 is not really a standard, per se).

MTA Transport Stacks

The first thing that throws people about creating an X.400 connector is that before you can create the connector, you have to create an *MTA transport stack*. An MTA transport stack is the software that determines which type of network the X.400 connector can use to communicate. Exchange Server includes three transport stacks for use with the X.400 connector:

- TCP/IP MTA transport stack is the transport stack that the X.400 MTA uses to communicate with another X.400 MTA over a TCP/IP network. This is the most common MTA transport stack used today.

- TP4 MTA transport stack is the transport stack that the X.400 MTA uses when communicating over a TP4 network. Though the TP4 network protocol is not very common in the U.S., it is prevalent in Europe.

- X.25 MTA transport stack is used for X.400 over X.25 packet-switched networks. X.25 networks are becoming less and less common in the U.S., but are common throughout Asia and Europe.

When you create the MTA transport stack, the first screen you see after choosing File ➤ New Other ➤ MTA Transport Stack is the New MTA Transport Stack dialog box. Select the type of transport stack and the server that you want it to be installed on and click OK. The next screen allows you to specify a Display Name and Server Name for the MTA transport stack as well as the OSI address information.

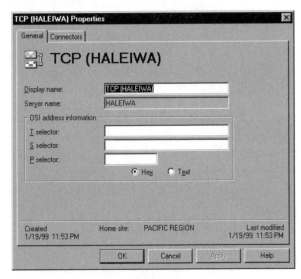

Unless the person configuring the other side tells me otherwise, I leave the OSI address information boxes blank. The T selector (or Transport Service Access Point) is the Transport selector, the S selector is the Session selector (or Session Service Access Point), and the P selector is the Presentation selector (or Presentation Service Access Point).

NOTE   The NSAP is the server name and is only configurable via the TP4 protocol.

You will need to provide values for these fields if any other application on the server is using the same transport stack or if the MTA transport stack on the other side of the X.400 connector has these fields filled out. The fields will need to match the configuration of the other X.400 connector.

Overview of the X.400 Connector

The X.400 connector has some great features that are often overshadowed by the fact that it is more difficult to configure. Here are some of the X.400 connector's strengths and weaknesses:

Advantages	Disadvantages
Provides control over who can send messages across the connector, when the connector is active, and the maximum message size.	No encryption between one server and another. Data transferred using X.400 is easily intercepted by someone using a network analyzer.
Connector can communicate with any X.400 MTA that conforms to the ITU 1984 and 1988 X.400 recommendations.	Slower than the site connector if messages are converted from MDBEF.
Uses TCP/IP, X.25, or TP4 networks.	Does not work over NetBEUI or IPX/SPX.

Managing the X.400 Connector

Configuring the X.400 connector is certainly a little harder that configuring the site connector. To make things a bit easier, there are some things that you should keep in mind when planning and configuring your X.400 connectors. First, the X.400 connector is a "peer-to-peer" connector; both sides must be configured correctly in order for messages to be transported across it. Further, both connectors must have critical values set the same. These values include the MTA conformance, which specifies with which X.400 recommendation the system will work: 1984 mode, 1988 X.410 mode, or 1988 normal mode. Most modern X.400 messaging systems support 1988 normal mode, but if the remote system you are connecting to is not an Exchange system, you should always ask.

Another critical set of values is the Remote MTA name and the Remote MTA password that is set on the remote system. For an Exchange system, the Remote MTA name is the NetBIOS name of the remote Windows NT system, and the password is blank. These values do not provide secure sessions, but only another level of MTA verification.

If the system you are connecting to on the remote side is not an Exchange server, there are two parameters you that must change so that the remote recipients do not receive unwanted attachments or garbled messages. The first of these is found on the X.400 General tab; this is the Remote Clients Support MAPI check box. If the remote clients do not support MAPI and rich text formatting, they will receive an additional attachment in the message called `winmail.dat`.

The second parameter is found on the Advanced tab; this is the Allow MS Exchange Contents check box. If this option is enabled, the MTA will not convert the message to an X.400 standard message format (known as P2 for 1984 systems or P22 if the system follows the 1988 X.400 recommendations). When the Advanced tab is set to Use Exchange Contents, it provides better performance by alleviating a conversion to X.400 message bodies. The data remains in the MDBEF format.

On the Stack property page is a field where you can provide either the remote host name or the IP address of the remote host. You may enter a Fully Qualified Domain Name (FQDN) or an IP address. If you enter an IP address, make sure that the IP Address radio button is selected. Conversely, if you enter a FQDN, make sure that the radio button has Remote Host Name selected. Name resolution often breaks the X.400 connector. Once configured, open an NT command prompt and ping the FQDN that you entered for the X.400 connector and confirm that the IP address of the remote system is resolved and is responding.

TIP Avoid typing just the "host name." The NT system will append the local domain name to the host name. This may work, but in many cases, it breaks down. Use the Fully Qualified Domain Name (FQDN).

If the remote system is an Exchange site that is part of your Exchange organization and you are planning to connect the two sites together using directory replication, ensure that the Connected Sites property page has the remote site listed. If the remote site is not listed, you will not be able to set up directory replication.

> **NOTE** Messages that are routed through the X.400 connector can be managed at the server level via the MTA object's Queues tab. X.400 connectors are listed according to the display name assigned to them on the General tab of the X.400 properties.

Exchange@Work: More Standardization

Do yourself a big favor when you start creating connectors: Standardize on the naming scheme that you use when you name the connectors. After a site has several connectors listed in the Connections container, you will want to be able to glance at the connector and easily identify the function of each. I recommend using a name that contains X.400, the source site, and the destination site. An example of this would be `X.400 Connector - North America\SFOEX001 to Pacific Region HNLEX002` as the display name and `X.400 Connector - North America - Pacific Region` as the directory name. The directory name can never be changed.

X.400 Connectivity to Foreign Mail Systems

In the 1980s and early 1990s, X.400 appeared to be the merging standard in messaging backbones. X.400 was designed to connect many dissimilar messaging systems together. Not only can the Exchange X.400 connector be used to connect Exchange sites together, but it can also be used to connect Exchange to foreign X.400 messaging backbones. Connectivity between Exchange Server and foreign X.400 e-mail systems is not difficult, but there are a few things you should know prior to attempting it for the first time.

Configuring the X.400 connector for the first time is not for the faint of heart; I recommend having someone around who has done it before (or at the very least, have them available by phone). When connecting to a foreign X.400 system (I am assuming that you will be using X.400 over TCP/IP), you need to be prepared to ask the person on the other side of the connection a few questions. These questions include:

- What is the remote MTA name? The name cannot exceed 32 characters.
- Does the remote MTA have a password? The password cannot exceed 64 characters.
- What is the remote MTA's host name or IP address? If they give you a host name, confirm that you can ping the host name and properly resolve the host's IP address.

Connectivity

PART 3

- Is custom OSI address information for the Transport, Session, and Presentation selectors (service access points)? The selector fields are quite often left at their defaults (blank). However, if the remote host has these fields set, you must have them set.

- Do the clients know the network you are connecting to support MAPI? Unless they are using a Microsoft messaging system, probably not.

- Can messages be transferred any time of the day or night, or do they have to occur on a scheduled basis?

- Is word wrapping necessary, or do the remote clients insert carriage returns and line feeds automatically? If so, into what column should the carriage returns be inserted? Most modern message systems take care of this automatically.

- Which X.400 recommendation does the remote MTA comply with—1984 or 1988? Most modern X.400 systems comply with the 1988 recommendations.

- Does the remote system support X.400 BP-15 (Body Part - 15) in addition to X.400 BP-14?

- Is there a maximum message size limit?

- What is the X.400 administrative management domain name (ADMD)? Depending on who you're connecting to, you may also require their organization name and their private management domain (PRMD).

- Does the GDI site addressing information need to be customized?

Chances are good that the person on the other side of the connection will have some questions for you. While I cannot give you answers to things such as messages size limits or times when you will send and receive, here are some basic X.400 answers relating to Exchange Server:

- The Exchange server's MTA name defaults to the Exchange server NetBIOS name; this can be overridden on the Override property page.

- There is not normally an MTA password, but it can be set for this connection on the Override property page.

- The Exchange server does not require message wrap to be turned on.

- Exchange clients support MAPI (at least Outlook, Exchange client, and Outlook Express do).

- The Exchange server fully conforms to the X.400 1988 recommendations, and it supports BP-15 as well as BP-14.

- By default, your private management domain (PRMD) is the same as the first 16 characters of your Exchange organization name.

Message Interoperability   When an X.400 connector is created, there are a couple of defaults that need to be changed if you are connecting to a foreign X.400 system. These will affect whether the message will actually get delivered and whether the message content will be converted properly. On the Advanced tab of the X.400 connector property page (see Figure 9.7), there are several important options that must be set properly for the MTA to transfer data to the foreign X.400 system.

The most critical of these settings is the X.400 Link option called Allow MS Exchange Contents. When this check box is enabled (checked), the X.400 connector transfers the message in MDBEF format. This check box should *always* be cleared when connecting to a foreign X.400 system. This instructs the MTA to convert the message to either an X.400 P2 format (if 1984 conformance is selected) or X.400 P22 format (if 1988 conformance is selected).

Figure 9.7   The Advanced tab of an X.400 connector's property page

Other options that should be confirmed include:

- MTA conformance must be set properly; the majority of the modern MTA software should support the 1988 normal mode.
- The X.400 Link option Allow BP-15 (In Addition To BP-14) should be set based on the capabilities of the receiving system. If you don't know if the foreign system can receive BP-15 body parts, clear the check box until you have the connection working. Once the connection is working, send a message to the other side with an embedded file.

Finally, you need to configure the Connected Sites property page of each IMS so that it knows to route messages meant for the other site through the other site's IMS. To do this, choose the Connected Sites property page and choose New. Then enter the name of the remote site in the Site box. Finally, click the Routing Addresses tab and enter the Internet domain name of the remote site.

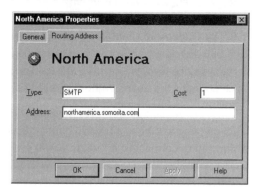

Securely Communicating between Two Sites via IMS

Are you concerned about the security of the data that is exchanged between two sites using the Internet Mail Service? I sure would be, especially if that data is being moved through a public network such as the Internet! There is more on securely using the IMS in Chapter 10; however, if you want to set up a secure channel between your Internet Mail Services, you can do so quickly and easily.

To start, create a Windows NT user; if the two sites are separate domains and no Windows NT trust relationship exists, create the user in both domains. Make sure that this user has a strong password (upper- and lowercase letters, numbers, and a special character or two). No other special rights or permissions are required.

Next, on the Internet Mail Service's Security tab, click the Add button. You are presented with the Edit E-Mail Domain Security Information dialog box (see Figure 9.8). Specify the Internet domain name of the remote domain and select the Windows NT Challenge/ Response Authentication And Encryption radio button. Click the Change button and provide the Windows NT user account, domain name, and password that was created for you in the remote Windows NT domain.

Figure 9.8   Securely exchanging messages with another domain using the IMS

The security features shown in Figure 9.8 does not have to be limited to other sites within your Exchange organization. You can use this feature to securely exchange messages with any Exchange-based messaging system; all the other side has to do is create a Windows NT user account for you.

TIP   Get to know usage of the IMS for connecting sites. SMTP is going to become increasingly important for Windows NT and Exchange in the future.

Directory Replication

One of the most sophisticated features of Exchange Server is the Exchange directory, specifically the directory replication feature. Microsoft was faced with the awesome task of developing a directory service that was not only distributed, but also multi-master. This means that there is a complete copy of the Exchange directory database on each server, and each copy of the directory can be updated. Since each copy of the directory may not be completely in synchronization with the other copies, the directories to be loosely consistent due to the multi-master model.

There are five separate naming contexts that make up the Exchange directory: organization, site, schema, configuration, and address book views. Modifications to the directory always take place within one of these five contexts, and changes to any of these contexts result in a separate directory replication message generated that requests changes to that specific context.

Directory Replication 101

The huge task of keeping all the directories synchronized and distributed falls upon the directory service. Some distributed directory service databases use a timestamp to indicate if one copy of an object is more recent than another copy. Microsoft chose to use a unique identifier called a USN (Update Sequence Number) to function as a timestamp.

The Exchange directory uses USNs in conjunction with a 32-digit hexadecimal number that uniquely identifies a server; this 32-bit string is the server's *Invocation-ID*.

NOTE Invocation-IDs are attributes of the directory service and can be seen viewing raw mode attributes of the DS.

The server where the change is made stamps the object with that server's Invocation-ID and the next available USN. You can see the USN values and the server's Invocation-ID in Exchange Administrator raw mode. Figure 9.9 shows a mailbox's raw properties and its USN attributes. The Invocation-ID (not shown in Figure 9.8) is listed in raw mode on objects as the DSA-Signature attribute.

Figure 9.9 Raw properties of a mailbox showing the Update Sequence Number

There are three separate USN values for each object:

- *USN-Changed* is the USN number that was assigned to this object after it was last changed.
- *USN-Created* is the USN number that was assigned to the object when it was created.
- *USN-Source* is the USN number that was assigned to the object on the server where it was changed last.

NOTE   Most of us will never need to see the USN numbers. However, it is interesting to know a little more about how the Exchange directory service keeps things synchronized and replicated.

Directory Replication within a Site

Within a single site, all directory services on all servers communicate with one another using RPCs. If there have been changes to the directory, the directory service where the change occurred notifies the other Exchange servers in the site of this. The directory service batches changes occur within a five-minute interval. The five-minute countdown starts after the last modification occurs. When replicating, the directory service does not notify all servers at once but rather waits 30 seconds between each notification. This prevents it from becoming overwhelmed with requests for updates. You can control these times through the Registry; Appendix C has information regarding the keys you need to change.

Here is a simple example of what might happen during intrasite directory replication. Let's say that there are two servers in the site. Server HNLEX001's most recent USN is 1001. Server HNLEX001's directory service notifies the directory service on server HNLEX002 that there have been changes made to the directory on HNLEX001. Server HNLEX002 (the server that needs the updates) checks its list, called REPS-FROM, to see what is the last USN that it received from HNLEX001. HNLEX002 discovers that the last USN that it received from HNLEX001 is USN 945. HNLEX002 will request all changes since USN 945 from HNLEX001.

TIP   Since changes must be replicated from one server to another, it is a good idea to make large numbers of changes (such as creating or deleting many new directory mailboxes, joining a new site, or importing many new custom recipients) during hours when network traffic and server usage are at their lowest.

Figure 9.10   The Sites tab of the directory replication connector's property page lists inbound and outbound sites.

> **NOTE**   Each time the directory service is restarted on a directory replication bridgehead server, the directory service forces a complete replication for all directory replication connectors. Though I cannot imagine why you would need to take your servers offline often, if you do this, you should consider disabling this feature in the Registry. (See Appendix C for an abbreviated list of Registry keys.) If this feature remains enabled and you operate a large number of sites, take your directory replication bridgehead servers down only during slow hours.

Restricting the Information Transmitted via Intersite Directory Replication

The directory service enables you to restrict the attributes that are replicated to other sites. By default, almost all object attributes are replicated to other sites. You can turn off specific attributes, however turning any attribute off is an all-or-nothing restriction. The attribute will either be replicated to all sites or to no sites; you cannot specify particular sites to which an attribute will replicate.

> **NOTE**   Restricting some attributes will not improve your intersite replication all that much; the only reason I can think of to do this is if I did not want certain attributes leaving the site, such as phone numbers or site-specific custom attributes.

To restrict an attribute, choose the DS Site Configuration object's properties; choose *Site Name* ➤ Configuration, open the DS Site Configuration properties, and view the Attributes tab. Then choose Inter-Site Replication in the Configure box. In the Show Attributes For list, deselect any attributes you do not want replicated to another site.

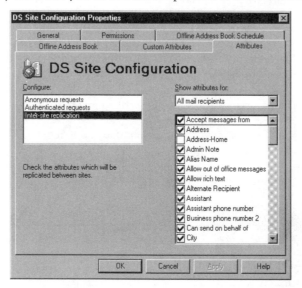

The DS Site Configuration object's Attributes tab is also where you specify which attributes are visible to anonymous and validated LDAP users.

> **NOTE**   The Protocols container and sub-objects are not replicated to other sites. During development it was determined that the Protocols container served no useful purpose in remote sites.

Monitoring Directory Service Events

The directory service can generate quite a bit of traffic and data in the application event log. Table 9.2 shows some of the common events that you may see in the application event logs generated by the directory service. The source for all these events is MSExchangeDS (or MSExchangeAdmin if you have manually forced replication). In order to see many of these events, the MSExchangeDS logging category Directory Replication must be set to at least Minimum.

Table 9.2   Common Application Events Generated by MSExchangeDS

Event ID	Explanation
13	A directory service could not be contacted due to a communications error.
1058	A replication request was successful.
1068	The directory service has requested changes from another server. This event should be followed by a 1058 event ID, which indicates success.
1070	The directory service has had changes requested by another server.
1071	The directory service has responded to a request for changes. This should follow a 1070 event ID.
1099	The directory service has received an update request from another site.
1100	This event details the update (which naming context is being requested).
1101	The directory service has sent changes to another site.
2021	This event's source is actually MSExchangeAdmin, and it occurs when the administrator requests directory replication with another site. You normally see three of these grouped together, each requesting a separate naming context: *Site Name*, Configuration, and ABViews_.

The Knowledge Consistency Checker

The Exchange directory is constantly undergoing changes; some are major and some are minor. Major changes include adding new servers or new sites to an organization. Minor changes include adding mailboxes and changing object attributes. No matter how good intersite and intrasite replication is, some changes are going to be missed from time to time. If the changes missed are server or site additions (major), the directory service can become badly out of synchronization over time.

To address possible directory database holes, directory services processes spawn sub-processes every three hours called the Knowledge Consistency Checker (KCC). The KCC ensures that the local server's directory database knows about all the other servers and sites who are directory replication partners.

The KCC Process

The Knowledge Consistency Checker process is a simple yet crucial part of directory replication. The KCC works at two different levels. First, it is used to verify replication links and lists of known servers for intrasite replication. Second, it is used to ensure that directory replication occurs between non-adjacent sites that this site learned about through directory replication with adjacent sites.

Intrasite KCC Replica Verification   In order for intrasite replication to occur correctly and completely, each server in the site must be aware of the existence of all the other servers in the site. It is entirely possible that a new server could be added to a site and one of the servers might not be aware of this (perhaps because it was offline).

Part of the KCC's job is to make sure that each server is aware of all the other servers in the site. To do this, the KCC process has to determine the current replication partners; this is done by examining the REPS-TO attribute on the site object (viewable in raw mode).

Once the KCC has a list of all the currently known replication partners, it contacts each of the servers in the REPS-TO list to ensure that their replication partners are the same as its own list. If the other servers have a server in their REPS-TO list that this server does not have, it will add that server to its own REPS-TO list. The KCC then makes sure that replicas are created for each naming context that the new server supports. From this point forward, this server will now replicate with the newly added server.

Intersite KCC Replica Verification   When a new directory replication connector is installed, the naming contexts for the new remote site are included in the local copy of the directory replication. As replication information from the other site starts to populate the local directory, the local directory may learn about other sites that are not adjacent to this site.

The KCC also checks to make sure that directory replication connectors are maintained for each replica naming context. To do this, the KCC checks all the directory replication connectors maintained in each Directory Replication container for replica naming contexts or REPS-FROM data. If a new site is discovered, the KCC adds all the naming contexts supported in the remote site to the local directory.

Once the remote naming contexts are identified, directory replication messages from those contexts can be processed. When a directory replication connector is installed to a new site, directory replication can be sped up from the remote sites by first forcing the KCC to run on the bridgehead server, and then forcing a manual directory update to the remote site. Repeat this process until all the sites appear in the local directory. This process will occur much more quickly if the directory replication architecture is a distributed star (hub and spoke) topology.

Connectivity

PART 3

Forcing the Knowledge Consistency Check

If a server or site has been installed and you do not yet see it in the directory, you can force the KCC to run. This is often useful immediately after installing a new site. Replication cannot occur until naming contexts for the new site exist in the directory. This will occur automatically in several hours, but if you're like me and have no patience, run the KCC yourself.

The KCC can be run on any Exchange server, but in this case, it should be run on the directory replication bridgehead server. The KCC is run from the server level; choose *Site Name* ➤ Configuration ➤ Servers ➤ *Server Name*, open the directory service properties, and view the General tab. Click the Check Now button. If the resulting dialog box contains a red circle with an X in it, then discrepancies were found and corrected.

Optimizing Exchange Connectivity

Even in a small Exchange environment, a dozen Exchange servers spread across six or eight Exchange sites can generate a fair amount of "chatter." What I mean by chatter is system messages that are passed back and forth between servers and sites in order to make sure that everything stays consistent. In a large organization with several dozen servers and 20 or more sites, this chatter turns into a dull roar.

What types of data are transmitted between servers, and at what intervals? You would be surprised:

- Every 24 hours, the information store service on any server that has a public information store sends out a public holder hierarchy status messages to all servers that have a public information store.

- Every three hours, the directory service sends a request to its directory replication bridgehead server for each site it knows about.

- Address book views do not follow intrasite or intersite replication schedules. Each server sends an address book view replication request to each server in the organization.

Tips for Optimizing Connectivity

What can you do to optimize your connectivity between sites? Messaging traffic between sites is not only affected by the total load a user puts on the system, but also the total load that the system places on the messaging infrastructure.

User-Generated Messaging Activity   Here are some tips to reduce the overall load that your users place on the messaging infrastructure:

- Restrict the maximum message size that the MTAs will transport. As an alternative to restricting the maximum message size that the MTA can transmit, restrict message size at the mailbox level. This will still allow you to control maximum message size for your users, but make the occasional exception for the user who must send large messages.

- If you are using the X.400 connector, create two X.400 connectors to the same site. Enable one to be usable 24 hours per day and set the maximum message size to a reasonable amount (maybe even under 100KB). Enable the second X.400 connector to only operate during hours that the network bandwidth is not heavily utilized, and set the maximum message size to a larger amount. This will let users send messages with large attachments, but they will not be transferred out of the site until off-hours.

- Review the Replication Schedule property page of public folders that replicate between sites. The default is that public folders can replicate changes every 15 minutes. For public folders that contain data that changes very infrequently (like company policies and procedures), replicate only once or twice a week.

- Avoid using the site connector in limited bandwidth environments. If you have less than 64Kbps *available* bandwidth between sites, the site connector is not the right connector.

- When using an X.400 connector to link Exchange sites, ensure the Allow MS Exchange Contents check box is selected on the Advanced tab. Also verify the Remote Clients Support MAPI option on the General tab is checked.

- As we saw before, limiting access to large DLs limits potential improper use of those DLs.

- Concentrating servers can help cut down on traffic generated. This means a fewer high capacity servers versus many smaller, distributed servers.

System-Generated Messaging Activity   Exchange generates a variety of message traffic merely to keep the Exchange directory and public folders consistent. Exchange Server's default values for many of the intervals used for replication are excessive for large, distributed organizations. In fact, for an organization with many sites and many servers, the organization's MTA may spend a large majority of its time and bandwidth delivering system-generated messages. Here are some hints that may help when tuning replication and system message generation for a large number of sites.

- Reduce the number of times per day that directory replication occurs between sites. For most organizations, twice per day is sufficient. Stagger the times that the

Connectivity

PART 3

hub sites request updates from the remote sites so that the hub sites will have all updates when the remote sites request changes.

- Stagger the times that the information store service sends public folder hierarchy status messages using the Registry. (See Appendix C.)

- Increase each server's Public Information Store Replicate Always interval to 20 or 30 minutes rather than 15. (Choose *Site Name* ➢ Configuration ➢ *Server Name* ➢ Public Information Store object, then view the Advanced tab.)

- Disable the directory service's intersite replication at startup Registry setting. (See Appendix C.)

- Consider adjusting the intrasite and intersite directory replication backup intervals. This interval is every six hours by default. In smaller sites of five servers, this would be of little use. However, in larger sites (20 or more servers), this value becomes important. (See Appendix C.)

- Disable the public information store's replication at startup Registry setting. (See Appendix C.)

WARNING If you are making changes to the Registry, make sure that you understand the implications of the change, especially when dealing with directory replication and public folder replication. Microsoft set the default values so that they will work for most of us.

For Further Information...

If you are deploying an Exchange organization with more than 15 or 20 sites, or if you have extremely limited bandwidth between sites, here are some resources that you should consult:

- Microsoft Consulting Services has a book called *Deploying Microsoft Exchange Server 5.5 (Notes from the Field)* (Microsoft Press, 1998). Chapter 8 is indispensable for large Exchange organization managers.

- Microsoft has a technical paper available on TechNet called "Microsoft Exchange Server 5.5 Advanced Backbone Design and Optimization."

- The routing table (GWART or Gateway Address Routing Table) is explained in detail in Microsoft KB article Q149121.

For Further Information... *(continued)*

- There is a Windows NT Registry entry that allows the Exchange administrator to limit the maximum number of recipients in a message. This Registry entry is discussed in KB article Q126497.

- X.400 connectivity is not a simple subject. I highly recommend the book *Microsoft Exchange Connectivity Guide* by Rodney Bliss and Rebecca Wynne (Microsoft Press, 1997).

- To learn more about the U.S. military DMS project (it is not classified), check out the Lockheed Martin DMS site at www.1mdms.com. This site includes some interesting links to many of the branches of the military, but some of them are only accessible from a .mil address.

Figure 10.3   A sample UCE message and the message's Internet headers

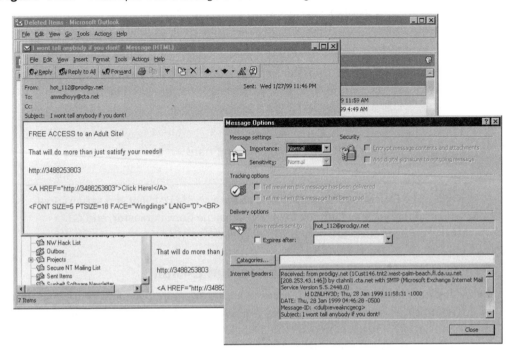

How Did This Happen to Me? I'm Really a Nice Guy!

Typical spam messages advertise stock deals, pager service, get rich quick schemes, miracle weight loss programs, cures to baldness, cheap vacations, adult Web sites, and more. The fact that I did not ask for any of this garbage makes it unsolicited. It makes me wonder, "How did they get my e-mail address? What have I done to deserve this?"

Well, for starters, I quite frequently post on the Usenet newsgroups. I used to use my real e-mail address; now I use something like JMcBee@Somorita.Com.NoSpam (newsgroup-savvy users will realize what my real address is if they want to send me a message directly). The folks who collect these addresses scan newsgroups looking for addresses; they call this "harvesting." My e-mail address is also posted on several Web sites, and spam companies will often scan Web pages looking for the <a ref="mailto:jmcbee@somorita.com "> HTML tag.

Stopping Spam

What can you do to prevent spammers from getting your e-mail address? What can you do to prevent advertisers from wanting to use spam as a method of advertising? Here are some answers to these frequently asked questions:

- Don't configure your newsgroup reader software with your real e-mail address; put your e-mail address in your message signature instead. (Good newsgroup etiquette dictates you should always identify yourself when you post.)

- Don't put your e-mail address on Web pages. If you do, disguise it so that it is easy for a human to see, but hard for an automated process to decipher. I like to use something like this: "My e-mail name is JMcBee and my domain is Somorita.Com."

- Avoid filling out surveys and "register to win" Web pages if you don't know the company whose Web site you currently viewing. Or set yourself up a Hotmail account for online registration forms, just in case you win that big prize they are giving away.

- Don't be tempted to reply to the message; it will either go nowhere, or the reply will be automatically accepted, confirming that your address is good and can be used again. Many spam messages tell you that they will remove you from their list if you reply with the word "Remove" in the subject or body. I have seen my volume of spam increase dramatically when I have tried this. Remember that these people have no Internet etiquette.

- Complain to the advertisers, not the spammers. If the message contains an 800 number, call it and complain. I know a few people who have used demon dialers to call those 800 numbers hundreds or thousands of times. I don't recommend this approach, but it does seem like poetic justice.

Understanding SMTP Headers

The SMTP header is the part of a mail message that defines not only who the message is sent to and from, but also information such as the subject, sending message system type, date sent, and MIME information. The Received field identifies the hosts that the message crossed during its journey through the Internet. Quite often, you will only see a single Received entry. However, some messages can have several Received fields. A sample of an SMTP header looks like this:

```
Received: from emh.Misawa.AF.MIL ([132.20.128.128]) by
ctahnll.cta.net with SMTP (Microsoft Exchange Internet Mail Service
Version 5.5.2448.0)

id FAO3OTY4; Wed, 17 Feb 1999 17:14:46 -1000

Received: from gw5.misawa.af.mil (gw5.Misawa.AF.MIL [132.20.123.35])
```

Connectivity

PART 3

Using the IMS without a Full-Time Internet Connection

Many smaller companies cannot afford a full-time connection to the Internet. Unfortunately, SMTP was originally designed under the assumption that all SMTP servers will be online all the time (or at least most of the time). Later, a new command for SMTP was developed called TURN, but it was implemented only with limited success, partially due to security concerns.

RFC 1985 now defines the SMTP command ETRN (Enhanced TURN), which allows an SMTP client to connect to an SMTP server that has been queuing mail for the client and issue the ETRN command. The SMTP server will then deliver any queued messages to the SMTP client.

Sound good? Sure, ETRN works great, but there are some things to keep in mind as you configure it. On the Exchange side, you must be running Exchange 5 SP1 or later. If the host that is queuing mail for you is Unix-based, it must support sendmail 8.8.*x* or later.

Configuring ETRN

There are a number of steps involved in getting ETRN working; you will have to work closely with your Internet Service Provider (ISP) or whomever is going to be queuing your mail until you connect. To show an example of how to configure ETRN, I am going to use my favorite pseudo-organization, Somorita Surfboards. Somorita wants to get connected for Internet mail, and they have an Exchange server with the IMS configured on it.

Let's begin our journey by exploring the steps the ISP must take in the configuration process.

Configuring ETRN at the ISP   The ISP must first allocate a static IP address on a dial-in modem or ISDN port. Usually, this means that the ISP has given (well, rented) a dedicated telephone line to Somorita that will be theirs and theirs alone. Let's say they assign Somorita 204.175.131.45; this is an IP address on one of their 56K modems. They take the telephone number for that modem and give it exclusively to Somorita.

Next, the ISP has to make some entries in the DNS server that contains the Somorita.com data files. (I am assuming the same ISP manages Somorita's DNS server; if not whoever manages the DNS server will have to make these entries.) The entries will look something like this:

```
Exchange.Somorita.com.   A      204.175.131.45
Somorita.com             MX     10                    Exchange.Somorita.com
Somorita.com             MX     20                    mailrelay.ispname.com
```

The first entry identifies the IP address (A) record of the Exchange server. The second line is a message exchange (MX) record and says that all mail that is sent to the domain Somorita.com should be directed to the host Exchange.Somorita.com. The number 10 is a preference or weighting; the preference controls which host the sender will try first. The third line indicates that if the host Exchange.Somorita.com is not available (which it usually will not be since it is a dial-up), deliver the mail to the host mailrelay.ispname.com, which in this case is the ISP's mail relay server.

The ISP may also have to configure its Unix system to store mail for your domain. Exchange Server 5 SP1 and later can be configured to queue messages for ETRN clients; if the ISP is using Exchange Server and the IMS, they can configure the IMS to queue mail for your domain. This is done on the IMS Connections property page; click the E-Mail Domain, then click Add. Enter the domain name, and then click the Queue Messages For ETRN check box.

Configuring ETRN on the Exchange Server   Once your ISP has configured its side, you must first configure the Dial-Up Networking software on the Exchange server that's running the IMS. If you have not previously installed the Dial-Up Networking software, don't forget to reinstall the Windows NT service pack. Once you have the Dial-Up Networking software installed, create a dialing entry for your ISP using the telephone number they provided for you. Test this entry and make sure you can connect to the Internet while dialed in; my litmus test is whether or not I can browse the Internet using Internet Explorer (and Fully Qualified Domain Names, not just IP addresses).

Next, the IMS needs to be configured to reflect that it is going to have to relay all outgoing mail to a mail relay host and pick up mail queued for it.

On the IMS Connections property page, the Message Delivery section has a radio button called Forward All Messages To Host. In the case of the Somorita Surfboards example, I would click this radio button and enter **mailrelay.ispname.com** (if I knew the IP address,

I could use that as well) in the box directly below the check box. This will cause the IMS to deliver *all* outgoing mail to the mail relay server at the ISP.

Then, on the IMS Dial-Up Connections property page, I need to configure the dial-up connection properties. Figure 10.6 shows the Dial-Up Connections property page on the left and the Mail Retrieval dialog box on the left. The Mail Retrieval dialog box is opened by clicking the Mail Retrieval button on the Dial-Up Connections property page. The Mail Retrieval button specifies how the SMTP client will retrieve mail from the SMTP server.

Figure 10.6 The IMS Dial-Up Connections tab and Mail Retrieval dialog box

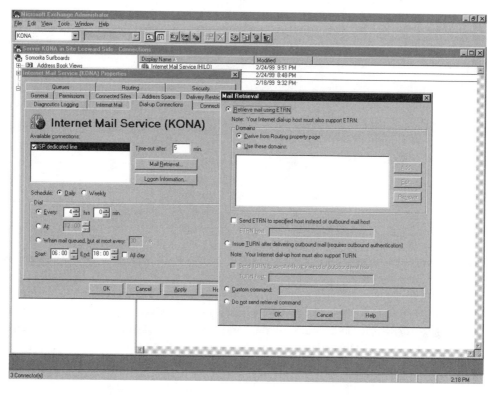

The Dial-Up Connections property page has quite a few options:

The **Available connections** list allows you to select the Dial-Up Networking connection for your ISP. This must have been created and tested prior to configuring the IMS.

The **Time-out after** box is the amount of time to keep the RAS connection open after all the outbound mail has been sent. This should be long enough to give the system to which your server issued the ETRN command enough time to start transmitting queued messages. If you set this value too high, though, it is possible that the connection will never hang up. Somewhere between five and ten minutes should be sufficient.

The **Mail Retrieval** button opens the Mail Retrieval dialog box which is used to configure the connection for ETRN or TURN.

The **Logon Information** button allows you to specify the user account and password information at the ISP.

The **Schedule** radio buttons allow you to determine whether the ISP connection will be made every day (Daily) or only certain days of the week (Weekly). If you choose weekly, you will have additional check boxes for Monday through Friday and the option of disabling the connection on the weekend.

The **Dial** section is used to determine how often to connect to the ISP. Within the Dial section, you have several different options:

Every specifies that the connection is made at specified intervals regardless of whether or not there is outgoing mail. For most installations, I would use this selection and specify a value of two hours.

At specifies the connection will be made only at a certain time of the day. This is useful if you want to connect only once per day.

When mail queued, but at most every selection specifies that a connection will be made every time there is mail waiting to be transferred outbound. However, the outbound connections will not occur more often than the specified number of minutes.

The **All Day** check box, when selected, means those connections will be made 24 hours a day. If you clear the All Day check box, you can specify the times when connections will be made and when they will not be made.

For most installations, once the Internet Mail Service is set to retrieve messages using ETRN and to route all outgoing messages to the ISP, and the dial-up connection is configured, there are usually few additional options you need to set. However, the Mail Retrieval dialog box allows you to further customize mail retrieval. The options found in the Mail Retrieval dialog box have the following functions:

Retrieve mail using ETRN causes the ETRN command to be issued to the host listed in the Forward All Messages To Host box on the Connections tab.

The **Domains** section allows you to specify the domain names that will be requested when the ETRN connection is made. By default, the domain names are found on the Routing tab, but you can specify your own list.

Send ETRN to specified host instead of outbound mail host allows you to override which host the ETRN command is sent to. The IMS assumes that the same host that it sends all outbound mail to is the same one that queues messages for retrieval.

Issue TURN after delivering outbound mail allows you to use the TURN command instead of ETRN.

Custom Command can be used to issue a mail retrieval command for systems that do not support ETRN.

ETRN and Dial-on-Demand Routers

While the easiest way to configure ETRN is using Dial-Up Networking, it is also possible to use a dial-on-demand router. If you have configured a dial-on-demand router, messages will be sent out anytime they need to be delivered to the host designated in the Forward All Messages To Host option on the Connections tab.

However, since Dial-Up Networking is not used, the ETRN command will not be issued when outbound messages are sent. You can configure the IMS to always use the ETRN command when it connects to an SMTP host. This configuration must be made through the Registry.

To do so, locate the \HKLM\System\CurrentControlSet\Services\MSExchangeIMS\ Parameters Registry key and create a new value called AlwaysUseETRN with a data type of REG_DWORD. In the data field, enter **1** to set the IMS to always send the ETRN command or **0** to never send the ETRN command.

NOTE This solution works great as long as messages are being sent outbound, but what happens if no messages are going to the outbound mail relay host? You need to create some type of process that will periodically generate a bogus message and send it out to the Internet. You can do this with the Exchange link monitor functionality, or you can create a scheduled job using the Windows NT schedule service and the mapisend.exe utility from the BackOffice Resource Kit.

Message Interoperability

Users are often going to call you and ask about a particular attachment on a message that originated from the Internet. This is probably because the transmitting system did not properly convert the message into a format that your mail clients can understand. As an act of good Internet etiquette, you don't want to send users messages that contain unknown attachment types or attachment types that are not usable.

Within an Exchange site or organization, messages are transported using a Microsoft encoding format called Messaging Database Encoding Format (MDBEF). The message remains in this format as long as the message is being transported using RPCs, the site connector, the dynamic RAS connector, or the X.400 connector, and it is staying within the Exchange organization. When a message leaves the Exchange organization, it has to be converted to a format that the receiving system can understand.

If a message is to be delivered via SMTP, or if it is being read by an IMAP4, NNTP, or POP3 client, an information store process called IMAIL converts the message to the appropriate format. IMAIL is also responsible for converting messages that have been delivered via SMTP or NNTP before they are stored in the information store. Messages are always stored in the public and private information store database in MDBEF format.

When messages are transported across a non-Microsoft connector, such as the IMS, the messages are converted to another encoding format called Transport Neutral Encapsulation Format (TNEF). Messages transported using TNEF have an extra attachment associated with them that describes all the rich text formatting such as bold, italic, font changes, and so on that may be in the message text. When a message arrives at its destination, the mail client must understand how to reassemble the messages back to its original appearance. If the mail client does not understand this formatting, then an extra attachment will appear on the message. This attachment will often appear as an unknown file type, though its MIME content type is *application/ms-tnef*. If non-Microsoft clients receive messages with unknown or application/ms-tnef attachments, you can bet that someone sent them a message formatted with rich text.

Inbound Internet Messages

Messages that are delivered to the IMS are automatically converted from the standard Internet message formats to an Exchange MDBEF message. The IMS recognizes MIME and uuencode.

If a message arrives that has unknown attachment types, then it is quite possibly the sending system that did not convert the message properly. Alternatively, the problem might be that the sender is sending you a MIME type that your IMS does not recognize and therefore does not associate the correct extension with.

Figure 10.7 shows the MIME Types tab of the Protocols container. From this page, you can create, edit, and delete MIME types.

Connectivity

PART 3

Figure 10.7 The Protocols container's MIME Types tab

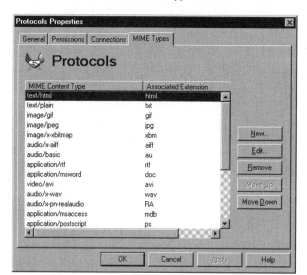

You can configure MIME types for the entire site (*Site Name* ➤ Configuration ➤ Protocols Container properties ➤ MIME Types tab) or for each individual server (*Site Name* ➤ Configuration ➤ Servers ➤ *Server Name* ➤ Protocols Container properties ➤ MIME Types tab).

Resetting the MIME Database   Okay, for some reason you've trashed your Exchange server's MIME settings; this can happen if you accidentally delete or edit an item you did not mean to. It can also happen if you install Internet Explorer 4 *after* you have already installed Exchange Server.

There is a utility on the Exchange Server CD-ROM that resets the MIME database to its defaults. The utility filename is reset.inf, and it is found in the \Server\Support\ MIMEDB directory of the CD. To reset the MIME database, locate the file, right-click it, and choose Install.

Outbound Internet Messages

Unfortunately, the IMS cannot automatically determine the correct format to convert a message to when transferring a message to another host. By default, the Exchange IMS sends all messages out as plain-text, MIME messages. The IMS Internet Mail property page has a section called Message Content that controls what default message type is used when sending out an SMTP message.

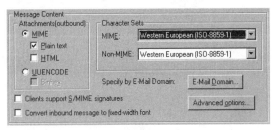

I recommend leaving the default attachment type as MIME; it is now the de facto standard for SMTP messaging, and all modern systems support it. If you need to support MHTML or MIME Encapsulated HMTL, select the HTML check box under the MIME radio button. MHTML allows HTML attachments to be encapsulated in a MIME messages and allows the format of HTML pages to be preserved.

The E-Mail Domain button allows you to override the default attachment, character set, and other message options on a per domain basis.

On the Message Content section of the Internet Mail property page, there is an Advanced Options button. Clicking this button opens the Advanced Options dialog box:

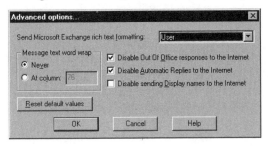

From the Advanced Options dialog box, you can specify whether or not the IMS will send out messages as rich text. The default is user-specified, but you can override this by specifying Always or Never in the Send Microsoft Exchange Rich Text Formatting drop-down list box. I recommend leaving this selection at User. You can override this per domain.

The Advanced Options dialog box also allows you to specify whether or not Automatic Replies and Out Of Office messages are always sent out to the Internet. This feature should probably be left disabled except in special cases; for most people who send me messages, I don't want to advertise the fact that I am on vacation. However, keep this tidbit in the back of your mind, because if automatic responses to the Internet are disabled, then no client or public folder rules will be allowed to automatically send responses back to the Internet.

User-Specified Rich Text Formatting If a user wishes to send an Internet recipient messages using rich text formatting, she can specify this when she addresses the message or in her Outlook Contacts folder. To do the latter, the user locates the SMTP address either in the To field or in the Outlook Contacts folder, right-clicks the SMTP address, and chooses Properties. The SMTP Address property page opens; the user then clicks the check box that says Always Send To This Recipient In Microsoft Outlook Rich-Text Format.

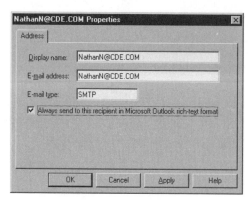

As an administrator, you can also specify to send rich text messages to custom recipients. On the Custom Recipient object's Advanced property page, enable the Allow Rich Text In Messages option.

Exchange@Work: Overriding Message Type by Domain

XYZ Corporation made heavy use of its Internet Mail Service to many customers and vendors. When XYZ Corporation began doing a lot of business with Company CDE, they exchanged a lot of e-mail messages. Company CDE was also using Exchange Server and the Outlook 98 client.

The messages that traveled back and forth between the two companies were highly formatted, but the users at XYZ were forgetting to specify to send rich text formatting to users at CDE. Users complained that they couldn't always remember to select RTF when sending the message or to make the changes in their personal address books. Further, users in both companies wanted to be able to have Out Of Office messages and automatic replies sent between the two companies.

Exchange@Work: Overriding Message Type by Domain *(continued)*

XYZ and CDE administrators to the rescue: They decided to create an exception to the standard user-defined rich text formatting. They did this by using the E-Mail Domain button on the Internet Mail tab of the IMS property page. By clicking Add, they were able to add new domains to this exception list.

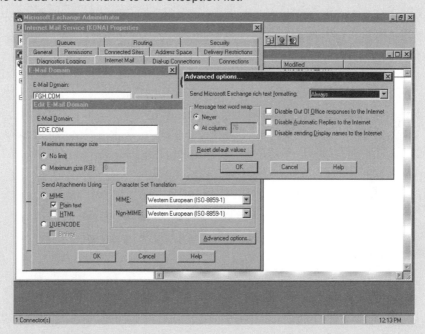

On the Edit E-Mail Domain dialog box, the XYZ administrator specified CDE.COM in the E-Mail domain box, then clicked the Advanced Options button. In the Advanced Options dialog box, the XYZ administrator cleared the Disable Out Of Office Responses To The Internet and the Disable Automatic Replies To The Internet check boxes and set the Send Microsoft Exchange Rich Text Formatting drop-down list box to Always.

Once the Internet Mail Service was stopped and restarted, the users at XYZ no longer had to remember to specify rich text formatting for addresses at CDE.COM. And Out Of Office and Automatic Replies will be sent to addresses at CDE.COM.

Exchange@Work: Overriding Message Type by Domain *(continued)*

XYZ Corp later used the same feature again except this time it was to send all mail to a specific domain using uuencode. Older SMTP gateways and clients do not handle MIME messages; messages were being delivered to a company that had clients that did not support MIME, but they were getting MIME messages. Well, the message was formatted as a MIME message, but the user saw a lot of garbage characters.

So the ability to override message types sent to specified domains can be quite useful in a number of different ways.

Internet Mail Service and Security

Microsoft first introduced basic security features into the Internet Mail Service with Exchange Server 5. With Exchange 5.5, the security capabilities have greatly improved. These new security features include:

- Restricting SMTP relay
- Requiring authentication/encryption from SMTP clients
- Sending authentication/encryption requests to SMTP servers when connecting outbound

Restricting SMTP Relay

The Exchange IMS is capable of acting as a relay server; this means that it will deliver any message that is submitted to it regardless of the message's origin or where it is to be delivered. This capability is required if you have IMAP4 and POP3 clients. The IMAP4 and POP3 protocols are "retrieve only" protocols, meaning that these protocols can only be used to retrieve messages from a message store. IMAP4 and POP3 clients deliver their outbound messages to an SMTP server, which in turn relays the messages to their ultimate Internet destination.

Figure 10.8 shows the IMS Routing tab for Somorita Surfboard's Exchange server. The Reroute Incoming SMTP Mail radio button is selected.

Figure 10.8   The server highlighted here will relay any message submitted to it.

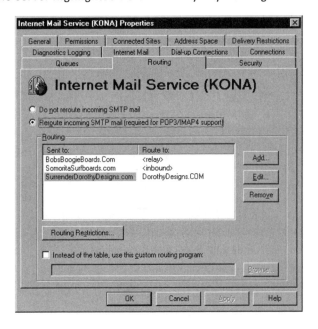

The IMS in Figure 10.8 is wide open as far as mail relay is concerned; anyone can submit a message to this server for delivery, including someone who wants to use your server to send 10 million spam messages. The solution is to turn off mail relay using the Do Not Reroute Incoming SMTP Mail radio button. From that point forward, the IMS will only accept or relay messages for the domains specified in the Routing box. You can add, edit, and delete domains that will be accepted as inbound or relayed.

WARNING   If your IMS permits SMTP relay from anyone, you are inviting unscrupulous spammers to use your server for mail relay.

However, turning off mail relay will break any IMAP4 or POP3 clients that were using this Exchange server to relay mail. A new feature was included in Exchange 5.5 that allows you to restrict which IP addresses your IMS will reroute messages for. If you click the Routing Restrictions button on the IMS Routing tab, the Routing Restrictions dialog box will appear (see Figure 10.9).

- The default timeout period for a message waiting to be delivered to another host is 48 hours. I recommend bumping the time up to 72 hours (three days). If the destination SMTP system is offline because of some hardware, software, or internetwork problem, this gives the destination's manager one more day to get the problem corrected. You set the timeout period on the Connections tab of the IMS property page; click the Time-outs button to set message timeouts for Urgent, Normal, and Non-Urgent messages.

- If you have specified a host to deliver outbound mail to (on the Connections tab of the IMS property page), that hostname *must* be available when the IMS starts. Otherwise the service will not start. If the IMS fails to start and you notice event IDs 4032, 4057, and 4014 in the application event log, this is why.

- You can use the IMS Pickup directory to submit messages that are formatted as RFC-821 messages. This can be useful for automating message delivery of maintenance or system maintenance. This path for this directory is \exchsrvr\ IMCdata\Pickup.

NOTE See Microsoft Knowledge Base article Q201314 for more information on the IMS Pickup directory.

For Further Information...

For more information on topics discussed in this chapter, here are some resources:

- The Coalition Against Unsolicited Commercial E-mail (CAUCE) has a good Web site containing an overview of anti-spam resources: www.cauce.org.

- Mail Abuse Prevention System (MAPS) is a non-profit company dedicated to stopping spam; they have an interesting Web site and links to other anti-spam efforts: maps.vix.com.

- See Microsoft Knowledge Base article Q185216 for a list of common mail abuse phrases and their definitions.

- Exchange gurus Simpler-Webb have put together an Exchange resource Web page that includes some great tips and resources for connecting Exchange to an ISP. This site is especially useful if you don't have a full time connection. Check them out at www.swinc.com.

Maximizing Use of SMTP

Organization RST makes heavy use of SMTP and always has, even before they deployed Exchange Sever and the Internet Mail Service. When they began deploying Exchange Server to their various locations, they had to choose a messaging connector to connect their Exchange sites together. Though they had virtually no security previously using a Unix-based SMTP mail system, one of the strong selling points for Exchange was better security.

The first choice was the X.400 connector, since it handles low bandwidth situations very well and the connector administrator can restrict not only who uses the connector and the maximum message size, but also the times when the connector operators. However, many of RST's offices were connected through the Internet, and the lack of security using X.400 over TCP/IP troubled RST's Information Services team.

RST evaluated the Exchange site connector. Though the site connector was easy to install and configure, RST found that it did not work well on some of their lower speed links, which were quite often saturated during the business day. The site connector did not permit the connector to be scheduled so that it would operate only during specified hours, nor did it allow restriction of large messages or which users could use the connector.

Since neither the X.400 connector nor the site connector completely satisfied RST's requirements, they selected the IMS as their intersite messaging connector.

To ensure the security of data being transferred between RST's Exchange sites over SMTP, each site had a bridgehead server installed that operated the IMS. SASL/SSL was enabled for each of these IMS servers, and the IMS servers were configured to use authentication and encryption. In each domain, a Windows NT account was created for each of the Exchange sites. This account was used by the respective IMS servers for authentication to the other sites; a single account could have been used for all sites, but the company's IS group wanted each site to have it's own user account and password.

The IMS servers were also configured so that SSL was required between all the company's internal IP addresses to further guarantee that SSL was used for all intra-organization message transfer. In order for SSL to be supported on each of the IMS bridgehead servers, Internet Information Server 4 was installed. A CSR (Certificate Signing Request) file was created using the IIS Key Manager application. This CSR file was sent to VeriSign where it was signed and returned. The purpose of sending the certificate to VeriSign is to get the certificate signed by a known and trusted certificate authority. See Chapter 13 for more information about certificates and certificate authorities.

Once the official certificate was signed by the trusted signing authority and returned, the certificate was installed onto the appropriate IIS server. Certificates are created

11

Client Automation

No one wants to visit each and every workstation on a network each time new software has to be installed or a user needs to create a new profile. Yet this is exactly what many administrators do—and these visits are time consuming.

To save time, there are a number of software products on the market that automatically distribute software, such as Microsoft Systems Management Server. However, Microsoft provides some tools (free of charge) for automating the distribution of Outlook, automatically creating messaging profiles, and making changes to the user's environment. In this chapter, I discuss some of the tools that will quite possibly make your life as a network administrator much easier. These include:

- The Office 97 Network Installation Wizard for helping to create automated installations of Outlook 97

- The Outlook 98 Deployment Kit for creating and distributing Outlook 98 and Internet Explorer

- The automated profile generator utility (PROFGEN) which can automatically create a messaging profile

- Enhancements for the Windows NT System Policy Editor to enforce Outlook settings for the entire network or specific groups

---

NOTE   Office 2000 will include tools to help deploy, fix, and administer the productivity tools in the Office suite. At a glance, these tools include the Custom Installation Wizard, the Office Profile Wizard, new System Policy Editor and templates, and language packs supporting over 50 languages.

Automatic Client Software Deployment

If you need to deploy Outlook to many desktops, one option is to send all of your users instructions on how to install the software. Well, okay, maybe that is not an option after all. What you need is a way to automatically install the software without having to answer all those inevitable installation questions.

The software that allows you to do this is free and easily available from Microsoft's Web site (www.microsoft.com). Currently there is software available for Outlook 97 and Outlook 98; by the time you read this, the Office/Outlook 2000 deployment tools should also be available.

TIP   As with anything you have never worked with before, you should install this software on your test network and work with it until you know you can reliably achieve the results you want in the production environment.

Installing Outlook 97

The Office 97 Resource Kit includes an application called the Network Installation Wizard (NIW). This software allows you to create a customized network installation for Office 97 and Outlook 97. When you run the wizard, it goes through numerous installation screens and questions, allowing you to make all the choices seen during a typical installation. The setup files are then saved and can be run in batch mode. After running the NIW, if you launch the Setup program from the logon script and with the right startup parameters, the installation will run automatically and no user intervention will be required.

Using the Network Installation Wizard

I want to quickly review a couple of the steps involved in running the Network Installation Wizard. Download this utility from the Web at www.microsoft.com/office/ork/ and install it on the machine from which you want to create the custom setup files; this does not have to be the file server.

Next, you need an administrative install of Outlook 97. This is all the software installed to a shared drive on the server. From the Outlook 97 CD, run SETUP /A and install Outlook 97 to a shared location on a file server. During the administrative setup of Outlook 97, you will be prompted for your organization name (company name, *not* Exchange organization), Outlook 97 product ID, and the location for the shared files.

TIP If you are using Exchange Server 5.5, use the Outlook CD that ships with Exchange Server 5.5 (version 8.03), not the version that comes with Office 97.

Now you are ready to run the NIW and specify the options for your setup. Here are the basic steps you need to go through to get the wizard working (clicking the Next button after each step):

1. After launching the NIW, you will be required to provide the location of the LST or STF file. If you have just run an administrative installation of Outlook 97 (SETUP /R), specify the setup.1st file in the administrative setup directory and click Next.

2. Provide a location for the Outlook software; the default location is the \Microsoft Office directory under the C:\Program Files directory (or whichever drive the \Program Files directory is located on).

3. Provide a location for the default documents; the default is C:\My Documents.

4. Next you are presented with a choice for the location of the shared files. If you are planning to run this with no user input (which I recommend), choose the Local Hard Drive option.

5. The wizard then asks if you want to create a log file that contains information about the setup. This is useful for debugging when things go wrong. For the file location, I enter something like **C:\Temp\Outlook97.log**.

6. Next you are prompted for the installation type. I always choose Custom so that I can further customize what is installed and which options are used.

Automation

PART 4

16. The next screen allows you to specify the path to a custom Outlook Bar file and custom Outlook 98 toolbars and menus. If you don't specify filenames, the default Outlook Bar will be created, and the default toolbars and menus will be used.

17. The Customize Internet Explorer 4.0 dialog box asks if you wish to customize the IE installation with information such as default Web page, default Search page, and Favorite URLs and folders.

18. The Customize User Settings dialog box allows you to customize dozens of Outlook, Internet Explorer, and NetMeeting configuration items.

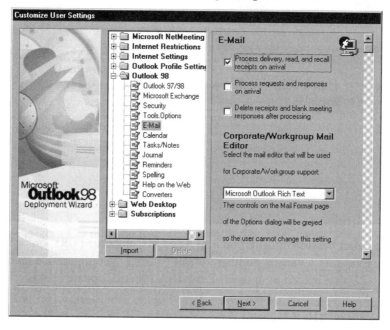

19. Add Registry Entries allows you to specify additional Registry values to be added to the Registry during installation of this package.

20. This is it! When you click Finish, the ODK package will be created. This may take five or ten minutes since files have to be copied and CAB files have to be created.

I have to admit that this list looks pretty intimidating, but after you fire up the ODK Wizard and run it yourself, you will see what a great, easy-to-use program it is.

NOTE   After you create the ODK package, you need to sign all the CAB and EXE files included in the package using the SignCode program included with the ODK.

Automatically Deploying Outlook 98

To deploy a package created by the ODK, you need to run the Setup program either manually or automatically. I placed the package I just created in a shared folder called \\SFOFP001\Outlook.98. To run the Setup program manually, simply click Start ➤ Run and type **\\SFOFP001\Outlook.98\CD\Setup** in the Run box. This is a manual installation, and the user will be prompted for the installation steps.

The Setup program is responsible for running another program, OUTLWZD, that actually does the setup. The OUTLWZD program is compressed and stored in the Setup program. Both Setup and OUTLWZD have a number of command-line options that can be used to create a silent, automated installation.

To deploy the ODK package automatically and without user intervention, add the following lines to the logon script to launch Setup and, subsequently, the OUTLWZD program:

```
If exist c:\temp\outl98.txt goto INSTALLED
net use I: \\sfofp001\outlook.98
I:
cd \cd\en\packages
I:setup /Q /C:"outlwzd.exe /S:""#e"" /Q /R:A"
Echo Outlook 98 installation complete >>c:\temp\outl98.txt
C:
Net use I: /delete
:INSTALLED
```

What does this section of the logon script do? The If exist statement looks to see if there was a file in the \Temp directory called Outl98.txt and, if so, skips the section entirely. Then, the I drive is connected to the shared folder that contains the setup files and switches to the directory containing the package to install. (The Setup program could have been run through the UNC path also.)

The SETUP command launches (in quiet mode, /Q) the OUTLWZD program. The /S option tells OUTLWZD where the source files are located, /Q is for quiet installation, and /R:A tells OUTLWZD to automatically reboot at the end of the installation. Once the

Deployment Kit includes additional Admin templates that you can incorporate into the System Policy Editor to enforce configuration and user settings for Outlook 97/98 and Internet Explorer. Table 11.2 lists these template files.

Table 11.2 Policy Admin Templates Included with the Outlook Deployment Kit

Filename	Function
conf.adm	Configuration and customization for NetMeeting software
inetres.adm	Internet Explorer security-related configuration settings
inetset.adm	Internet Explorer settings related to using IE, such as language, modem usage, default start page, and so on
Outlk98.adm	Outlook 97/98 configuration settings
shell.adm	Active Desktop configuration settings
subs.adm	Active Desktop channel- and subscription-related settings

Copy these files from the \Program Files\ODK\Policies directory to the \WinNT\INF or \Windows\INF directory on Windows NT Workstation or Windows 95/98. Make sure you are using the latest version of the System Policy Editor and the standard policy Admin templates; Windows NT 4 SP 4 contains updates for these files.

When creating policies for Windows 95/98 Workstation, run the System Policy Editor from a Windows 95/98 workstation. When creating policies for Windows NT workstations, run the System Policy Editor from a an NT-based workstation. The format of the Windows 95/98 and Windows NT policy files is different, and the Policy Editor determines which type of file to create based on which operating system the Policy Editor is running.

Launch the System Policy Editor and load the additional Admin templates you wish to use (this must be done prior to creating or loading a policy file). Choose Options ➤ Policy Template to open the Policy Template Options dialog box.

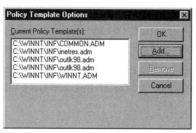

From this dialog box you can see which templates are currently in use and load additional policy template files. If the Add And Remove buttons are grayed out, close the policy you currently have open and try again.

To create a new policy, choose File ➢ New Policy. In the System Policy Editor window, you start with a policy that contains the Default User and Default Computer objects, and you can add to the policy-specific Windows NT global groups, workstations, and individual users. Default User and Default Computer affect all users and computers unless there is a user, workstation, or group policy that overrides that policy. All policies for all groups, users, and workstations are stored in the same policy file.

In Figure 11.1, I included a new policy template when creating this policy; the Outlk98 .adm template file. If you are a veteran Policy Editor user, you should notice the new Outlook 97/98 selection in the list of policies.

Figure 11.1   Outlook 97/98 policies

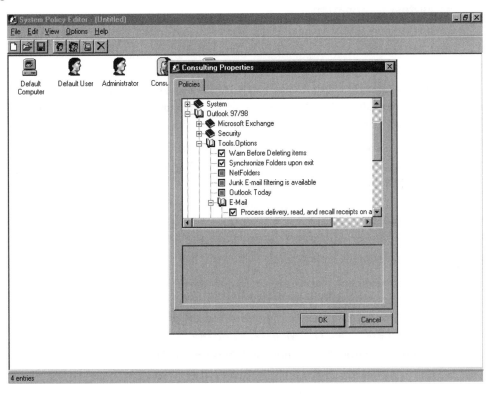

Figure 12.1 Information store maintenance schedule

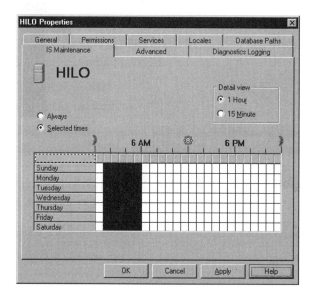

Exchange server responsiveness will be slower during IS maintenance and needs to be scheduled during relatively slow periods of the day. A variety of tasks are scheduled and run during IS maintenance, including:

- Online defragmentation of the database
- Removal of expired messages from public folders
- Cleaning up indexes that have been cached for user views

WARNING Information store maintenance should *never* completely overlap with the time that the tape backup process is running. IS maintenance will not occur as long as an online backup is running.

There are some application event log events that may be of interest to you with respect to IS maintenance:

Event ID	Source	Description
1206	MSExchangeIS Public or MSExchangeIS Private	Indicates that cleanup of items past the retention date for item recovery is starting.
1207	MSExchangeIS Public or MSExchangeIS Private	Indicates that cleanup of items past the retention date for item recovery is complete.

Event ID	Source	Description
179	ESE97	Indicates that online defragmentation is beginning on the specified database.
180	ESE97	Indicates that online defragmentation on the specified database is complete.
1221	MSExchangeIS Public	Indicates how much disk space would be freed up by an offline compaction/defragmentation.
183	ESE97	Indicates that the online defragmentation has not completed, but the IS maintenance window has passed. The defragmentation is suspended until the window comes around again. If you see this event ID often, the IS maintenance window should be lengthened.

WARNING If you set the IS maintenance interval to Always, the information store maintenance processes will run every 15 minutes; this can adversely affect server performance.

Offline Address Book Generation

Each morning at 3:00 A.M., the System Attendant service runs a process to rebuild the offline address book (OAB). The offline address book must be generated for the first time before clients can download it. It must be subsequently regenerated for new changes in the directory to appear in the client's OAB. There is only one offline address book for an entire site (stored in a system public folder), and its regeneration schedule is controlled at the site level. To change the schedule, choose *Site Name* ➢ Configuration, open the DS Site Configuration property page, and view the Offline Address Book Schedule tab (see Figure 12.2).

In Figure 12.2, I have selected that the OAB be regenerated twice per day. This is so that the changes made during the first half of the day will be incorporated into the OAB for those who might want to download the address book that afternoon or evening. I have seen schedules that regenerate the OAB as often as every two hours, but I personally feel that is overkill. If the offline address book takes very long to generate (such as an address book with tens of thousands of users), you should consider running the OAB generation only once per day.

Automation

PART 4

store, private information store, or individual mailboxes). The message, which is not currently customizable, notifies the user of what their storage warning limit is and how much they actually have stored (see Figure 12.4).

Figure 12.4   A storage warning message from the system administrator

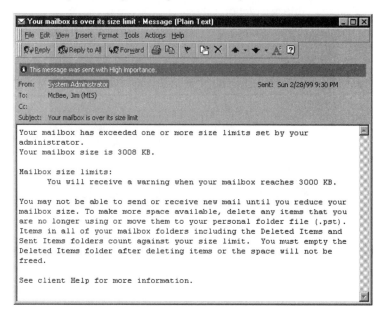

You can change the generation schedule of these warning messages at the site's Information Store Site Configuration object. Choose *Site Name* ➢ Configuration, open the Information Store Site Configuration object property page, and view the Storage Warnings tab (see Figure 12.5).

Note in Figure 12.5 that the storage warnings are only issued on Sunday, Tuesday, and Thursday nights. The way I look at it, this is almost as effective as seven warning messages per week; the user arrives on Monday, Wednesday, and Friday mornings to a notice that they are reaching the limits of their allocated space. If you leave the defaults, they get seven messages per week; many people don't check their e-mail on the weekends anyway, so the weekend messages will be less effective.

Figure 12.5 Storage warnings are set to be issued three times per week.

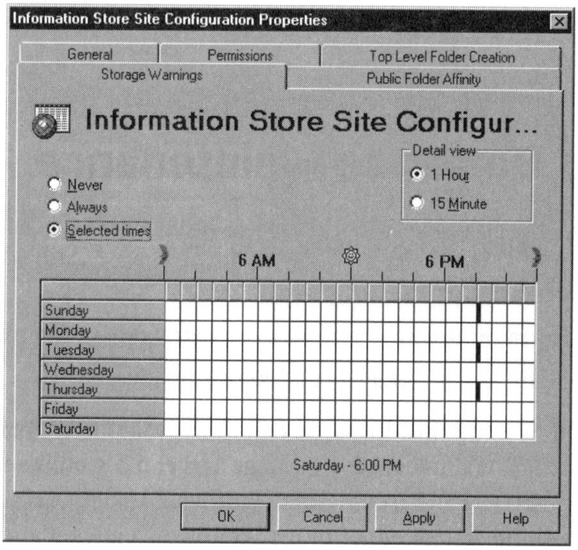

When configuring the time intervals, keep in mind that the storage warning limit messages will be generated every 15 minutes if you have an entire hourly time block selected. If you need to change this, switch to the 15-minute view first. Setting the Never button turns off storage warning limits messages.

> **WARNING** Do not set the storage warning to Always; this will generate a storage warning limit interval to every 15 minutes. While we would all like to do this to some users, this will effectively fill up the disk space even more quickly.

Directory Service Maintenance

Every 12 hours, the directory service performs what is called garbage collection. Essentially, the directory service scans through the directory database and looks for any entries that are eligible for deletion (those whose tombstones are older than 30 days). This is configured at the site level on the DS Site Configuration object; choose *Site Name* ➤ Configuration, open the DS Site Configuration object property page, and view the General tab.

Performing an Integrity Check

You can use the same procedures for offline defragmentation to run a periodic integrity check of the database. Below is a simple batch file for performing an integrity check of the public and private information store databases. In this batch file, I did not stop all services, nor did I make a backup copy, because the integrity check is much less invasive.

```
@echo off
cls
REM Stop the services
net stop msexchangeimc /y
net stop msexchangeis /y
REM Run an offline defragmentation
Eseutil /g /ispriv >c:\temp\integpriv.txt
Eseutil /g /ispub >c:\temp\integpub.txt
REM Restart the Exchange services
net start msexchangeis /y
net start msexchangeimc /y
REM Send a copy of the logs to the administrator
MAPISEND -u JobScheduler -p bogus -r MissyK -s "SFOEX001 -weekly
  offline integrity check report" -m "Attached are report files for
  the offline integrity check of the SFOEX001 server" -f
  c:\temp\integpriv.txt -f c:\temp\integpub.txt
echo\
```

Once you have created the batch file, schedule it as described above.

Other Maintenance Tasks

Most any type of maintenance task can be scheduled if it can be done from a command line. Any job tasks you put to work using the scheduler should be thoroughly tested first.

The information store integrity checker program (ISINTEG) can be scheduled to run as well, however, the –TEST ALLTESTS option cannot be used, because it requires user input.

TIP   You can test your batch file in the scheduler context by running it interactively using the AT command's /K option.

Automating Client and Server Tasks

EKW Corporation runs two Exchange servers that support nearly 1,100 mailboxes. One server is responsible for mailbox storage, and the other server contains a public information store (with no mailboxes). Automation of common tasks is essential for EKW, since there is only one administrator who is primarily responsible for the operation of the Windows NT and Exchange servers. She has automated as many of the common tasks as possible in order to save time, and has divided these tasks into *client-related tasks* and *server-related tasks*.

Client-Related Tasks

When management decided to deploy Outlook 98, EKW's administrator knew she first had to upgrade the company to Internet Explorer 4 (because it is required to run Outlook 98). She also knew she was not going to visit all 1,100 computers on her network. Instead, she chose to use the Outlook Deployment Kit. Since there were several different configurations of Outlook 98 and Internet Explorer that had to be deployed, she created several unique deployment packages representing the different software configurations. A separate Outlook Deployment Kit package was created and burned to CD for users who needed to install Outlook 98 on their home computers.

Using Windows NT logon scripts and the Windows NT Resource Kit MEMBEROF utility (which checks to see if a user is a member of a specified group), the administrator

deployed the package to a group of roughly 100 users per day. Each day, she changed the logon scripts to check the membership of a different group, and if the user, who was logging in was a member of the "group of the day," then the installation package for that group ran. She chose to limit the groups to 100 users so that the installation process would not significantly overburden network resources. The Outlook 98 installations primarily occurred early in the morning, since that is when most users are logging in.

After all the groups of users had been installed, she left a statement in the logon script that would install the correct package for anyone that had not logged on during the period when their group had been selected as the "group of the day."

In order to automatically create user profiles, the EKW administrator used the BackOffice Resource Kit utility PROFGEN to create profiles from the login script. She also gave each user a default.prf preferences file that was stored in that user's home directory. By placing this file in the home directory, she ensured that it would be accessible even if the user moved from one computer to another.

One concern was making sure that users frequently emptied their Deleted Items folder. To enforce this, a system policy was created using the OUTLK98.ADM policy template file included with the Outlook Deployment Kit.

Future updates to Outlook 98 and Internet Explorer 4 are accomplished automatically using Outlook's ability to check the server for updates to the currently installed package. If the server-based package has changed, the software on the client is updated. All the administrator has to do is to update the server-based package.

Server-Related Tasks

Almost all of the maintenance intervals that run on the server did not need to be adjusted. EKW's administrator decided to send storage limit warnings only on Sunday through Thursday, since she figured that warnings that are sent on Friday and Saturday night fall on deaf ears.

The backup process had to be adjusted so that it started earlier. Originally, the backup started at 1:00 A.M., but the administrator noticed that the entire process was taking until very nearly 5:00 A.M., due to the size of the database and the speed of the tape drive. The backup process was completely overlapping the information store maintenance interval, so the administrator changed the backup start time to 9:00 P.M. so that the backup would be finished in time to allow information store maintenance to run early each morning. The backup process was also configured to e-mail the administrator a log file from the previous night; this allowed the administrator to easily check to make sure the backups have run properly.

Prior to upgrading to Exchange Server 5.5, the administrator shut the server down every two months and over the weekend ran an offline compaction of the information store databases. Since upgrading to Exchange 5.5, the only downtime the server experiences is when the server is restarted at the same time that all of EKW Corporation's servers are restarted.

Using a combination of automated server backups and automated client installations, the EKW administrator saves herself (on average) several hours each week.

Part 5

Security

Topics Covered:

- Basics of messaging security, encryption, and digital signatures
- Using Secure Sockets Layer to protect messages on the network
- Protecting message content using Exchange Server Advanced Security and the Key Management Server
- Integrating Microsoft Certificate Server and X.509v3 certificates with Exchange Server 5.5 SP1
- Protecting the Windows NT and Exchange server from outside attack
- Exchange Server and firewalls

13

Messaging Security

DILBERT reprinted by permission of United Features Syndicate, Inc.

The use of electronic messaging has exploded. Five years ago, companies simply used their e-mail system to send phone messages and to ask "Do you want to grab lunch today?" Today that use has broadened to include routing critical company information, expense reports, sales proposals, custom communication, and confidential client information. Not only do companies use e-mail within their own organizations, but they use it to communicate with vendors and customers.

With the advent of e-mail's modern usage come some common, resounding questions from e-mail users. Is the e-mail I send safe? Is my message protected from prying eyes? Is there something that prevents someone from modifying my message after I have sent it? Unless you have specifically done something to protect your messaging system, the answer to all three questions is "No!"

Messaging security is not rocket science, but if you have not worked with encryption before, this chapter will introduce you to some new terms and concepts. The topics in this chapter include:

- The major locations where messages can be intercepted and compromised
- A discussion of public/private key encryption, secret key encryption, and usage of certificates
- The use of Remote Procedure Calls to ensure messages sent by Outlook are secure on the network
- The use of Secure Sockets Layer to ensure data sent via HTTP, IMAP4, LDAP, NNTP, and POP3 are secure on the network
- Some concepts behind Exchange Server Advanced Security

NOTE   Almost daily, someone asks me, "Why did you choose to work in the networking industry?" I have given up trying to explain that a summer job during college accidentally turned into a career. Now I just tell people, "Cool things." Exchange Server definitely qualifies as a cool thing, but message security and encryption are even cooler things.

Message Vulnerability and Security

To know how to go about securing your messaging system, you need to first understand where the message is vulnerable. Where can a message be viewed or changed? What types of risks is your messaging system susceptible to? What are the requirements needed to make sure that you have adequately secured your messaging system?

Messages are vulnerable and can be intercepted in a variety of places; consequently, a clever person can alter a message in transit or after it has been stored.

Message Capture on the Wire

If you read through Chapter 7, you may have noticed a protocol trace that I did with the Microsoft Network Monitor. The Network Monitor is a powerful tool that is included with Windows NT Server and Microsoft Systems Management Server. This tool allows you to capture the network conversation between two computers; further, it can decode and display much of the information contained in that transmission.

Many messaging systems transmit an e-mail message across the network in clear text, or "in-the-clear." Clear text messages can be captured by just about anyone with a network analyzer, and anyone can download simple network analyzer tools for Windows NT or Windows 95/98.

The SMTP protocol is one of many protocols that transfer messages over the wire in clear text. From the time a message leaves the SMTP client until the SMTP server receives it, the message can be read at any point along the way.

> **NOTE** I have several friends who refuse to give their credit card number via a Web site. However, these same friends don't give a second thought to e-mailing their credit card number across the Internet.

Exchange Messaging Connectors

If you are connecting two or more sites using one of the messaging connectors provided with Exchange, you should understand the implications of each.

The Exchange site connector is the most easily securable of all the messaging connectors. It uses Remote Procedure Calls (RPCs) between Exchange servers; RPCs are encrypted with 40-bit RSA RC4 streaming encryption (except if you have the North American edition of Windows NT SP3 or later, in which case Windows NT uses 128-bit encryption).

The X.400 connector provides no native encryption or security beyond basic encoding of the message data. Though the X.400 connector is robust and flexible, it provides no network-level security.

Using the Internet Mail Service (IMS) to connect sites is not secure by default; all messages are exchanged using the standard SMTP format. However, the IMS with Exchange 5.5 provides the ability to use Windows NT authentication and encryption or SSL encryption. Both methods employ 40-bit encryption unless you are using the North American edition of Windows NT 4, in which case Windows NT uses 128-bit encryption.

> **WARNING** Messaging systems that pass messages over the wire in clear text have a much greater risk. These systems (in the case of POP3 and IMAP4) also pass the user ID and password in the clear. For Exchange-based systems, this is the Windows NT user account and password. If that password is compromised, you have a lot more problems on your hands than just messages being read by bad guys.

Security

PART 5

A Common Misconception

A common misconception is that messages are secure as long as they do not leave your organization. People believe that as long as a message remains on their internal LAN or WAN, it is safe. Consequently, they only take steps to protect messages that leave the organization. I have demonstrated to a number of clients (with their permission) how easy it is to place a network analyzer on their network (also known as "internal espionage"). Keep in mind that messages should not only be secure outside of your network, but that there is the possibility messages can be intercepted within your network as well.

One customer told me that there would be no way I could place a network analyzer on his network and leave it there undetected. I smiled and asked him if it would be okay to try; he said sure, but that I would be detected. I gave him a couple of days to batten down the hatches, so to speak, and then I installed the Network Monitor Agent on his own computer. I started it and set the access password. Naturally, I had to be alone for a few minutes with his computer to do this.

I accessed his computer from the Internet using the Systems Management Server Network Monitor and filtered all the network traffic between his computer and his POP3 mail server. After the next batch of mail was retrieved, I called him and asked him about a couple of the messages he had received.

Needless to say, he was blown away. He was so proud of his network's manageable hubs that would detect any authorized computer being plugged in that he had completely overlooked the possibility of a software intrusion.

Finding Messages on a User's Local Hard Drive

Once a mail program has removed the message from the server, it has to be stored somewhere. Usually, the mail messages are stored on the user's local hard disk drive. If a technically adept, curious person can get access to a user's computer, chances are good this person can find the user's e-mail message files.

In the case of Outlook, all local messages are stored in a personal folder (or PST file). Even if the user's primary message storage location is on the server, the user may still have messages stored on their local hard disk in PST files. Users are often asked to make backup copies of important messages, to archive messages they want to keep, and to use the Outlook AutoArchive feature to put all messages on their local hard disk into a PST file.

If you study the PST file, as well as many other messaging systems methods for local storage, you will find that either the files are encrypted or they can be password protected. However, this is not a problem for a tech-savvy person who is intent on reading your mail.

TIP Although the Outlook program can set a password for the PST file, there are PST-cracking utilities easily available on the Web. Try www.lostpassword.com for a sampling of these tools, or search the Internet for words such as "exchange," "pst," "file," "pstupq19," and "crack."

Messages in the Exchange Information Store

Messages that are stored in a user's private mailbox on an Exchange server are also vulnerable. An Exchange server mailbox cannot be opened by just anyone; the person must have a Windows NT user account. Although a mailbox is safe from the majority of people who have mailboxes on an Exchange server, administrators can give themselves the User role to the mailbox.

In order to do this, the administrator must have the Permissions Admin role to the mailbox. They simply display the mailbox properties and choose the Permissions tab. Figure 13.1 shows the Permissions property page for a mailbox.

Figure 13.1   Permissions property page for a mailbox

The mailbox in Figure 13.1 has three inherited permissions: The site services account (Administrator) has the Service Account Admin role, the global group Ex_Mailbox_ Admins has the Admin role, and the global group Ex_Security_Admins has the Permissions Admin role. Notice that Windows NT user SneakyHacker has given herself the User role to this mailbox, which includes Mailbox Owner permissions. Perhaps a member of the Ex_Security_Admins left his computer unlocked and unattended?

TIP Permissions tab for mailboxes not showing up? Make it visible using Exchange Administrator. Choose Tools ➤ Options, select the Permissions tab, and check the Show Permissions Page For All Objects check box. If you also want to see the permissions that a role gives to a user, check the Display rights for roles on Permissions page.

WARNING An Exchange administrator should *never* have the Service Account Admin role to any container; this gives that administrator complete access to all mailboxes.

Catching Improper Mailbox Access

If you are watching your Windows NT application logs, you can scan for an event that will tell you if someone other than the mailbox owner is trying to access the mailbox. The event ID is 1016, and the source is MSExchangeIS Private. If you see this event in the application log, it means that someone other than the user assigned to the primary Windows NT account has accessed the mailbox. The description of the event will tell you which Windows NT user account was used and which mailbox was accessed.

These messages will also appear if a user has been given delegate access and is merely accessing a mailbox that they have been given official permissions to use. Further, certain virus-scanning programs and backup programs that perform brick-level backups also log this event. So before you jump to any conclusions, think about why you might be seeing the message.

Another useful event to watch for is event ID 1175, generated by the MSExchangeDS. This event indicates that the security attributes of an object (primary Windows NT account or permissions) have been modified.

Snagging a Message during Gateway Conversion

Is the message being routed to another system other than its native system? If so, the message is probably going to be converted to a text file before it is migrated into the destination system. In the Exchange world, message connectors extract messages from the

Exchange server database and usually write the messages to disk in some sort of standardized file format.

While these messages are stored on the disk in temporary format, anyone can read them if they have the correct file and directory access to the directory in which the messages are stored. These messages can usually be opened and clearly read with a utility as simple as Notepad.

> **WARNING** Please refer to your connector's architecture information to determine the "conversion" working directory. You should consider securing this directory so only the Exchange site services account can access it. If necessary, you may need to add appropriate foreign mail system accounts so that they can gain access.

Secure Messaging Should Be...

Now that I have scared you with all the places that messages can be intercepted, read, and possibly modified to serve a Dogbert-like agenda, I want to take a look at some goals you need to have for securing your messaging system:

- Messages should be **private**. Only the sender and the intended recipients should be able to examine the content of a message during its journey through the messaging system or after it is stored.

- Message **integrity** should be verifiable so that the receiver can confirm that the message has not been modified since it was transmitted.

- Message **origin** should be verifiable, meaning that the receiver can verify that the person in the From field really did send the message.

- Messages should be subject to **non-repudiation** so that the sender cannot later on come back and say "I did not send that message."

Encryption

To truly secure your messaging system, you should lock all your doors, never send a message to the outside world, and post armed guards at all computers. Well, we have come a long way from the days of the Cracker Jack secret decoder rings, and today the data encryption world is a booming business. Therefore, I suspect you are going to want to use a more flexible security approach—a combination of message encryption (Microsoft calls this *sealing*) and message signing (digital signatures).

NOTE   Don't confuse digital signatures with the text that Outlook and other clients can automatically insert on the bottom of a message to identify things such as your phone number, address, favorite quote, and so on.

Has anyone thrown at you a series of terms such as public/private key pairs, secret keys, hashing, message digests, and certificates? The next few sections discuss what all this means and how it applies to the message world.

The Key to Encryption

A *key* is a set of characters of varying length that is used with the cipher (encryption formula) to generate encrypted data. There are many ways to define a key and many types of keys, but for purposes of this book, I will stick to the two relevant types of keys.

A *secret key* is much like having a secret password. For example, I make up a password, such as Super+=Pass123, and use it to encrypt a Microsoft Word document. When I want to retrieve this document once again, I must enter **Super+=Pass123** in order to gain access to the file. Basically, the same password that is used to encrypt the file is also used to decrypt it. Secret keys are also called *symmetric keys*, because there is only one key for encryption and decryption.

The advantage of a secret key cipher is that it is generally very fast; a computer can encrypt a large amount of data in a very short time using a secret key cipher. However, if I want to send this file to a friend, I must somehow give her that password. I could put it on a Post-It note, I could e-mail it to her, or I could call her and give it to her over the phone. However, even if someone else did not overhear my password, what if my friend gives it to someone else? My password is compromised and I can never use it again.

So how do I get my password (secret key) to her? A *public/private key pair* (sometimes called *asymmetric keys*) is a special type of key relationship. This arrangement consists of two very large keys (512 bits and longer) that are mathematically related to one another, but the mathematical relationship is very difficult (if not impossible) to calculate. In this relationship, I have two keys; I can give one to anyone who wants it (hereafter known as the public key), and I alone have access to the other key (hereafter known as the private key.)

If I wish to send a secret document to a friend, I ask her for her public key. Since the key is public, she doesn't care who has it. She can send it to me over unencrypted e-mail, give it to me over the phone (if I wanted to write down a 512-bit number!), or put it on a Post-It note.

Once I have her public key, I run the encryption program on the data I wish to encrypt using *her* public key, not my own private key. I then transmit the encrypted data to my friend over any type of network. My friend runs the decryption program and uses her private key. Whether the data is sent over the network or stored it in a file, it does not matter if the data is intercepted because it is encrypted. Even if everyone on the network has my friend's public key, the *only* key that can decrypt the data is her private key.

The advantage to public/private key encryption is that the keys are much more secure since you alone control access to the private key. Also, since the key size is so large, the encrypted data is very hard to decrypt. However, since the key size is so large, encryption and decryption is *very* time-consuming and CPU-intensive.

Hashing

Hashing is a mathematical function that you apply to a string of characters of any length, or to an entire file. The hashing function reduces any length of characters to a fixed length. Hashing is also called a *message digest*, because the hashed value uniquely represents the original data. Even if you have the message digest and the formula that was used to produce the message digest, you cannot reverse engineer it back to the original data. If you alter one single bit in the original data and run the hashing function again, the message digest will change.

Hashing functions are commonly used in message signing (digital signatures) to create a unique "signature" of the message in question. There are a number of algorithms that are used to create a message digest, including RSA's MD2, MD4, and MD5, which all create a 128-bit hash.

Common Encryption Terms

The first term that you hear often in the encryption world is *cipher*. A cipher is the algorithm (formula) that is used to encrypt and decrypt a piece of data. The encrypted data is sometimes referred to as *ciphertext* or an *opaque item*, whereas the unencrypted data is sometimes referred to as *plaintext*.

There are two types of ciphers that are commonly used; they define how a block of text is processed as it is being encrypted:

- A *block cipher* takes a block of data (or even an entire file) and processes the data a block at a time. The block cipher produces a ciphertext block for each plaintext block it is given.

- A *stream cipher* (a.k.a. *streaming encryption*) processes elements of a stream of data continuously. It is not uncommon for a stream cipher to encrypt data either one bit or one byte at a time.

Table 13.1 lists common cipher and hashing algorithms that are used with Microsoft products, including Exchange.

Table 13.1   Common Algorithms

Algorithm	Description
CAST	Carlisle Adams and Stafford Tavares developed this 64-bit symmetric block cipher. The symmetric block cipher is similar to DES. It supports keys between 40 bits to 128 bits.
DES	Data Encryption Standard, developed by IBM for the government, is an NIST (National Institute of Standards and Technology) data-encryption standard that uses 56-bit keys with a 64-bit symmetric block cipher. This is probably the best known and mostly widely used encryption in the world.
3DES	Triple DES has several different approaches to encrypting data, but all of them involve three separate encryption passes.
DH	Diffie-Hellman is a method for secret (symmetric) key exchange.
KEA	Key Exchange Algorithm is an improved version of Diffie-Hellman.
MD2	Message Digest is a hashing algorithm that creates a 128-bit hash value; it was developed by Ron Rivest of RSA (Rivest, Shamir, and Adleman).
MD4	An RSA hashing algorithm that creates a 128-bit hash value.
MD5	An improved version of the RSA MD4 that creates a 128-bit hash value.
RC2	A RSA 64-bit symmetric block cipher (RC stands for Rivest's Cipher or Ron's Cipher).
RC4	A RSA stream cipher that can use variable length keys. Microsoft commonly uses either a 40-bit or 128-bit key.
RSA	A very popular public/private key encryption scheme developed at RSA, naturally.

Table 13.1   Common Algorithms *(continued)*

Algorithm	Description
SHA	Developed by NIST, Secure Hash Algorithm produces a 160-bit hash value. It is similar to MD5, but more secure (and slower).
Skipjack	An 80-bit symmetric block cipher used by the Clipper and Capstone chips.

Diffie-Hellman Key Exchange

Public/private key is very secure and provides better key management, but it's slower than the symmetric secret key. What's an encryption dude to do?

Whitfield Diffie and Martin Hellman (hereafter known as Diffie-Hellman) asked the same question. (I think Diffie and Hellman are extraordinarily clever; when I mention their names, you have to stand, bow to the West, and chant thrice.)

Diffie-Hellman developed a method of key exchange suitably known as Diffie-Hellman key exchange. In a nutshell, they took the best of both the secret key and public/private key worlds. Simply, if I (and my friend) have a program that is capable of using Diffie-Hellman key exchange, I run the encryption program and enter my friend's public key. The program randomly creates a secret key and uses some predefined method of encryption (in this case, probably a block cipher of some sort) to encrypt the data. Since the secret key was used to encrypt the data, it was encrypted very quickly. This solves the problem of slow encryption.

The secret key is then encrypted with my friend's public key and attached to the end of the encrypted file. This solves the problem of how to deliver the faster symmetric (secret) key to my friend. When my friend receives the file, she opens the file and uses her private key to begin decrypting the message. What really happens is that the private key is used to decrypt the encrypted symmetric key. The encryption program can now decrypt the entire file because it has the secret key, which was used to encrypt the message body and attachments. Pretty spiffy, eh?

> **NOTE**   The symmetric key is placed into a virtual "lock box" attached to the message. It is considered a lock box because strong encryption of the public/private key is used to secure it.

Key Strength

One of the jobs of the *cryptographer* is to perform *cryptanalysis*, the process of trying to figure out or reverse engineer ciphertext. One approach is to attack the method of encryption itself; if the cipher is weak, adept cryptographers may be able to break the encryption. The well-known ciphers used today are considered strong enough to resist most attempts to compromise them.

Many efforts at decryption focus on using a brute-force attack—that is, trying all possible combinations of the key. Key size is normally measured in bits; the more bits used in the key, the more possible combinations exist in the *key space*. The larger the possible key space, the longer the key—and the more difficult a brute-force attack is.

To really appreciate how difficult this is to do, think about the total number of combinations for a specific key length.

Key Length	Number of Possible Keys in the Key Space
40-bit	1,099,511,627,776
56-bit	72,057,594,037,927,936
64-bit	18,446,744,073,709,551,616
128-bit	340,282,366,920,938,463,463,374,607,430,000,000,000

Actually, my calculator cannot even handle 2 to the 128th power, so I had to do some rounding for the 128-bit value.

With some effort, a very resourceful person and several very fast computers could break 40-bit encryption within a few days. Both DES and 56-bit RSA have been broken by the Distributed Project, a collection of people from all over the world taking a small piece of the key space and processing it. It took them many months to break both of these. I am currently running one of their clients trying to break RSA 64 encryption, and I process about 700,000 keys per second. At this rate, I will break the break 64-bit encryption in about 580 years. Let's not even think about trying to break 128-bit encryption; it is still quite strong. However, if the private key is compromised because the owner of the "private" key is careless, the whole process breaks down, and all secured messages that are sent to that person are compromised.

NOTE If you want to learn more about the Distributed Project, check out
www.distributed.net.

Certificates

Suppose you send me a message and ask for my public key. In a few days you receive a reply from me with my public key. This was pretty simple, wasn't it? You can now use my public key to encrypt messages and data for me; only my private key can decrypt the secret and confidential data you sent me. Further, let's say that I send you a message that I have "signed" to guarantee its authenticity. I give you my public key so that you can verify that the message did indeed come from me and that the message has not been altered.

Do you see a possible hole here? Did I hand my public key over to you personally? Did you check my passport or driver's license? (Not that this is fool-proof—identities are even stolen with forged driver's licenses and fake passports.) Do you know me personally? Do you know someone that can vouch for me? If not, how do you know that it was really my public key and not the work of a hacker intent on getting your secrets?

This is where certificates come into play. A *certificate* is a digital document that attests to the validity of a public key. This digital document establishes your digital credibility. Typically, a certificate contains:

- The name of the person to whom the certificate was issued
- The certificate serial number
- The certificate expiration date
- The certificate holder's public key
- The digital signature of the authority that issued the certificate

Depending on the type of key and the issuer, a certificate may be kept in a central location so that anyone can easily access it. In the case of Exchange, some certificates are stored in the Exchange directory. Note that the certificate does not contain a copy of the private key, only the public key.

A *certificate authority (CA)* issues keys and certificates and is responsible for managing security credentials for keys. The certificate authority will not issue you a certificate until it can verify that you are who you say you are. Remember that the certificate is your digital ID. Would the government issue you a passport just because you asked for one? That is unlikely; you must prove to the authority that you are really you. Just like the government will stand behind you once they have issued you a passport, your CA will verify that your certificate is real and valid.

A certificate authority is part of a *public key infrastructure (PKI)*, which provides the ability for a root CA to allow subordinate CAs to issue keys. If a subordinate CA issues a key, the validity of the subordinate's signature can be confirmed by contacting the root certificate authority.

For example, let's say that I want to issue a digital certificate to all of my users so they can send S/MIME messages. I could pay a root authority to create and issue all my certificates, or I could become a subordinate authority to a well-known root. VeriSign, Inc. is the largest and best known of these root authorities, so I would contact them about becoming a subordinate authority. They would give me a certificate that I would use to authorize my Microsoft Certificate Server. I then would use Certificate Server to generate certificates; the authenticity of my server could be verified using the signature given to me by VeriSign.

S/MIME? What Is All the Fuss About?

MIME (Multi-Purpose Internet Mail Extensions—RFC 1521) describes how to organize an electronic mail message to be transmitted using SMTP (RFC 822). MIME formatting permits e-mail to include attachments such as documents, text, multimedia, and more in a standardized manner via MIME-compliant mail systems. However, MIME alone does not define any security capabilities.

S/MIME (Secure Multi-Purpose Internet Mail Extensions) is an extension of MIME that provides a way to send encrypted messages between two dissimilar clients. It extends the MIME capabilities by describing how to encrypt message data and attach digital certificates to the message. S/MIME follows a syntax described in the Public-Key Cryptography Standard (PKCS) format #7. As of this writing, RSA has submitted S/MIME to the Internet Engineering Task Force for consideration as an Internet standard.

S/MIME has industry support from vendors such as Lotus, Novell, Microsoft, VeriSign, Qualcomm, and of course, RSA. For more detailed information on S/MIME, check out www.rsa.com/smime.

Trusting Other Organizations

If you often send mail to another organization, you need the public keys for anyone in that organization to whom you are going to send mail. The users in the other organization need to send you their own certificates (which you store in your personal address book or in the Outlook Contacts folder).

But how do you know you can trust certificates generated by another organization? Exchange Server 5.5 with SP1 or later supports a feature called *certification trust lists (CTLs)*. The CTL gives an administrator the ability to publish a list of external entities that his organization trusts. Now your users will be able to automatically authenticate any signed messages accepted from a trusted company (a signed message includes a copy of the user's signing certificate). However, users will still need a copy of the remote user's public sealing (encryption) certificate.

What If My Private Key Is Compromised?

Suppose the bad guys get their hands on your private key. Is all lost? Not exactly, but different systems handle this in different ways. In the Exchange world, you could contact your Exchange security administrator as soon as you thought your private key had been compromised. The administrator would revoke your current keys and issue you a new set. Your old certificate number would then be placed on a list called the *certificate revocation list (CRL)*, which contains a list of all certificates that should no longer be considered valid.

Types of Certificates

The ITU has a recommendation that covers the creation of digital certificates; this is the X.509 recommendation. There are two flavors of X.509: X.509v1 and X.509v3.

X.509v3 certificates are the most widely accepted and used; the new S/MIME standard uses X.509v3 certificates. Exchange 5.5 SP1 used in conjunction with the Microsoft Certificate Server can issue X.509v3 certificates. If you use the Exchange 5.5 Key Management Server (KMS), it issues X.509v1 certificates only. If you are given a choice, you should choose to issue X.509v3 certificates. Only Outlook 98 and Outlook 2000 can take advantage of the ability to use X.509v3 certificates and send S/MIME messages.

> **NOTE** The Exchange 4, 5, and 5.5 KMS supports the issuance of X.509v1 certificates; however, the X.509v1 certificates that the KMS issues are only interoperable with other Exchange systems.

Certificate Expiration   Don't be surprised if your certificate has an expiration date. This is normal and important for ensuring that the validity of the certificate is maintained. Some certificates have a lifetime as short as one year, such as Microsoft Exchange's KMS certificates. I have seen certificates that are good for up to five years, but they have been for special situations.

However, not to fear—as the life of your certificate approaches the end, you can renew the certificate, effectively extending its life.

Network Security

If you are worried about the content of your messages being intercepted within your LAN or between two points on a WAN, you can employ some method of security on the network wire. This means that while data is being transmitted across the network, it is encrypted. We break this procedure of securing a network into two separate categories: RPC/MAPI clients and standard Internet clients.

Security

PART 5

You can also set up the Microsoft Certificate Server and generate your own certificates. If you set up your server as a root server, then anyone who communicates with your SSL services must trust your server's certificate. Web browser clients will receive an annoying security alert message like the one seen in Figure 13.3, informing them that the certificate issuer is untrusted.

Figure 13.3   Untrusted certificate issuer message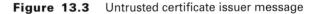

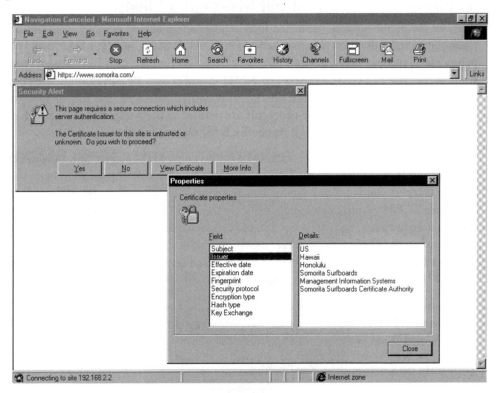

To correct messages such as the one seen in Figure 13.3, the client needs to get a copy of the CA's certificate. If you are using Microsoft's Certificate Server, you can get this through the client's Web browser by connecting to the `certificate_web_server_name`\CertServ\CertEnroll page, selecting Install Certificate Authority Certificates, and selecting the certificate you wish to request. Choose Open, and you will be prompted to install a new certificate for this Web browser.

Enabling Secure Sockets Layer

Before you can enable SSL to secure your Internet messaging protocols, you must first install Internet Information Server (IIS) on *each* Exchange server that you wish to support SSL. Ideally, you should install IIS before installing Exchange Server, but if Exchange is already installed, I have found that re-installing Exchange Server and the service packs after installing IIS does the trick.

NOTE   Before you start, make sure that the Exchange Server site services account is a member of the Domain Admins group. Otherwise, SSL will not work with Exchange services.

I am going to use the POP3 as an example, but each of the standard Internet protocols is enabled similarly for SSL. Also for this example, I am assuming that you are using Exchange Server 5.5 or later, IIS 4, and the Certificate Server that comes with the Windows NT 4 Option Pack.

To start, ensure that the protocol you wish to enable for SSL has been configured to use SSL. Highlight the protocol's properties at either the site configuration level or the server level and choose *Site Name* ➢ Configuration ➢ Protocols container or *Site Name* ➢ Configuration ➢ Servers ➢ *Server Name* ➢ Protocols container. Figure 13.4 shows the Authentication tab of the POP3 object property page. Make sure that SSL is chosen for at least one of the Authentication settings; Basic (Clear Text) and Basic (Clear Text) Using SSL are the most common.

Figure 13.4   Authentication methods available for POP3

From a machine that is running IIS and the Certificate Server, run the `keyring.exe` application in the `\WinNT\System32\INETSRV` directory. This is the Key Manager application. To connect to the server you wish to create certificates for, choose Computers ➤ Connect To Computer. Figure 13.5 shows the Key Manager application with two servers listed, the HNLEX001 server and the Local Computer.

Figure 13.5   The Key Manager application displaying certificates created for POP3 and SMTP

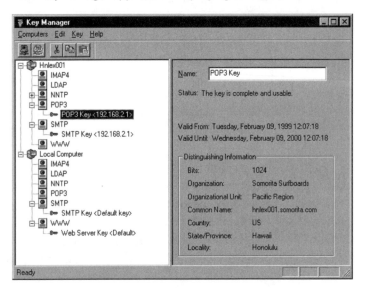

There are already several certificates created in this list. You can highlight the certificate you are interested in learning more about and see the details in the right pane.

Highlight the protocol that you wish to create a certificate for and choose Key ➤ Create New Key. You will be prompted with two choices. The default choice allows you to automatically send the request to an online authority. The online authority would be either your own Microsoft Certificate Server or an authority with whom you have previously established a relationship for key signing. The other choice is to put the key request into a file that you send to a trusted CA to be signed.

Automatically Sending a Key Request to an Online Authority   If you choose to send the key request to an online authority, you will see several dialog boxes. The key must have a name, password, and bit length. The longer the bit length, the stronger the encryption will be, but also the slower the processing will be. You have three choices for bit length: 512 bits, 768 bits, and 1024 bits. A password is required to link public and private passwords together; guard this password and make sure that you remember it.

After entering the key name, password, and bit length information, you will be presented with a dialog box that asks for organizational information. Provide your Organization name, such as the name of your business, and your Organizational Unit name, such as the name of your department. Also, you are prompted for a common name, this name should match the DNS name for the host. This name is important when you are creating certificates for HTTP servers, and it should match the name the client uses to connect to the POP3 server (for example, `HNLEX001.somorita.com`). If you do not enter this correctly, or if the POP3 server name changes, the client may give you a message such as, "The certificate you are viewing does not match the name of the site you are trying to view."

After entering the organizational information, you are prompted for the country name, state, and locality (city). When you click Finish, the certificate request is sent to the CA and signed immediately. When the process is finished, you will be allowed to specify IP addresses with which the certificate can be used.

If I applied all of this to my previous example, the server HNLEX001 would be ready to accept POP3 connections using SSL.

Sending a Key Request File to an Authority   If you choose to manually send your key request to a trusted authority for signing, you are prompted for many of the same options when creating the key request as if you were forwarding it automatically to a certificate authority. You must provide a key name, password, key length, organizational, common name, country, state, and locality information. In addition, you will be prompted for some contact information (name, e-mail address, and phone number) that can be used by the CA if they need to get in touch with you; this information is not placed in the certificate.

When finished, you will have a text file that contains the key request. You can send this file to VeriSign or another Microsoft Certificate Server to be signed. You will notice that the key appears in Key Manager, but it has an icon represented by a key and a red/yellow mark through it. This means that they key certificate has not yet been installed.

The CA will return to you a CER file, which is the signed certificate. You need to install this certificate using the Key Manager application (KEYRING). When you receive the CER file, using the Key Manager, highlight the key that is waiting for the signed certificate and choose Key ➤ Install Key Certificate, then specify the location of the CER file. This certificate is now ready to be used.

Enabling SSL for the Client   After getting your key signed, the one step left is to enable the client to use POP3 and SSL. The procedure varies from client to client. For Outlook

Express, this is set on the Advanced tab of the POP3 account's properties: choose Tools ➤ Accounts, view the E-Mail tab, select the POP3 account's properties, and choose the Advanced tab.

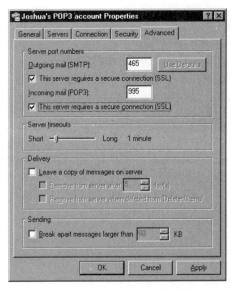

From here, you can select whether the outgoing (SMTP) server or the incoming (POP3) server requires SSL. (The incoming server is the Exchange server that contains your mailbox.)

For clients who are going to use Outlook Web Access, you must change their URL to include HTTPS:\\ rather than HTTP:\\. This instructs the Web server to use SSL. You can also set IIS so that it requires an SSL connection for your OWA Web site. This is done through the IIS on the Web site properties page. Select the Directory Security tab, click the Secure Communications Edit button, and pick the Require Secure Channel When Accessing This Resource check box.

TIP If you are planning to use SSL to protect information between your Internet clients and the Exchange server, it would be a good idea to disable all non-SSL authentication mechanisms. In Figure 13.4, you would need to deselect Basic (Clear Text) and Windows NT Challenge/Response. This would leave only the SSL choices enabled. This must be done for all the Internet protocols in the protocols container: IMAP4, LDAP, NNTP, and POP3. All HTTP protocol settings are set through IIS.

Message-Level Security

Exchange Server includes a feature called the Exchange Advanced Security. This feature allows you to digitally *seal* (encrypt) a message and/or digitally *sign* a message. These functions allow message senders and recipients to ensure that privacy is maintained, that the integrity and the origin of the message can be verified, and that the sender cannot deny later on that he sent it. The Outlook/Exchange client, not the Exchange server, performs the signing and sealing functions.

Sealed messages are not only transferred across the network as encrypted messages, but they are stored in the private information store or PST file as encrypted messages. Signed messages contain a digital signature that is protected by the *sender's* private key so that it cannot be altered.

NOTE In a sealed message, the entire message body and attachments are encrypted, however the To, From, CC, and Subject fields are not.

NOTE You can sign and seal a message; I just chose to illustrate them separately.

Message Sealing

To seal a message, an Outlook user clicks the Options button to display the Message Options dialog box (see Figure 13.6) and chooses the Encrypt Message Contents And Attachments check box in the Security section.

Figure 13.6   A client seals (and signs) a message in the Message Options dialog box.

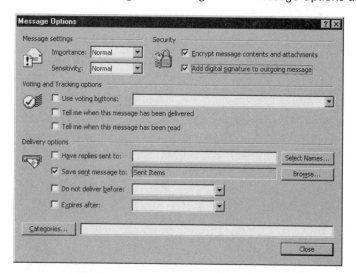

The Outlook client is then responsible for sealing the message when the user clicks the Send button. The process goes something like this:

1. The Outlook client software checks the list of recipients to make sure it has a public sealing certificate for each of the users. The public certificates may be stored in the Exchange directory or in the user's private address book.

2. Outlook randomly generates a secret (symmetric) key between 40-bits and 64-bits in length (depending on your configuration and country) and encrypts the message using the secret key.

3. The secret key is then encrypted once for each message recipient and once for the sender using the recipient's public sealing key and placed in a lock box. These lock boxes are attached to the end of the message.

4. The message is transmitted and stored.

Remember Diffie-Hellman key exchange? Well, this is where it is applied. A large message can be encrypted very efficiently with a secret key, and then the smaller secret key is encrypted and transmitted to the recipient.

When the message arrives at the recipient's mailbox, the recipient opens the message. The messages must be decrypted, so it goes something like this:

1. Outlook accesses the recipient's private sealing key (usually stored on the recipient's local hard disk). The recipient may be prompted for a password so that Outlook can retrieve the private key.

2. Outlook locates the recipient's lock box and decrypts the secret key using the private sealing key.

3. Once Outlook has the secret key, the message content can be quickly and efficiently decrypted.

Message Signing

To sign a message, an Outlook user clicks the Options button and chooses the Add Digital Signature To Outgoing Message check box in the Security section. The Outlook software takes care of creating the signature and attaching it to the message like this:

1. Outlook verifies that the sender has a signing certificate.

2. The Outlook software applies a hashing function to the message and its attachments. This reduces the entire message and attachments down to a 128-bit string called the message digest. If one single bit in the message or any attachment were to change, the original message digest would no longer agree with the new message digest.

3. The Outlook client accesses the sender's *private signing* key; the user may be prompted for a password to allow Outlook to retrieve the private signing key.

4. Outlook then encrypts the message digest (the hash) using the sender's private signing key (not their public key).

5. Outlook attaches a copy of the sender's signing certificate (which contains the public signing key) and the encrypted message digest to the message and transmits it.

NOTE   Note that nowhere in the signing process was the message encrypted. Signing does not encrypt the message content; it merely allows the message to be verified.

When the signed message arrives, the user retrieves the message and notices a new icon on the right-hand side; in Outlook 98, this looks like a little red and yellow certificate. If the user clicks this certificate, she will be given a dialog box that will verify the digital signature:

From this dialog box, the user can tell if the message was altered during transit, if the sender's certificate was revoked or expired, if the CA can be trusted, and if the e-mail address on the certificate matches the sender's address. Further, the user can click the View Certificate button for information about the certificate.

The Outlook client takes care of validating the digital signature in this way:

1. Outlook runs the message and attachments through the hashing formula and comes up with its own message digest.

2. The sender's public signing key is retrieved from the public signing certificate attached to the message. The attached, encrypted message digest, is decrypted using the sender's public signing key obtained from the attached certificate.

3. The calculated message digest and the original message are compared. If they are identical, then the message has not been modified during or after transmission.

Keys and Certificates for Sealing and Signing

Sealing and signing both require public and private keys. In order for the public keys to be distributed and to make sure that the keys are authentic and authorized, certificates have to be generated. That is the responsibility of the CA.

TIP As an Exchange security administrator, you can contact VeriSign and, for a price, they will create public/private key pairs and X.509v3 certificates for your entire user community. For a larger organization, this may not be advisable or affordable.

NOTE Part of Exchange Server Advanced Security is the Exchange Server Key Management Server, which can either work stand-alone or with a Microsoft Certificate Server, to generate keys and certificates for your users. The KMS generates two key pairs, a signing key pair and a sealing key pair. Installing and using this service is the subject of Chapter 14.

Tips for Securing Your Messaging System

The next two chapters look at some specific things that you can do to make your messaging system more secure. Before delving into that, however, here are some general tips:

- Practice good Windows NT security and strong passwords.
- Limit the Exchange administrators who have the Permissions Admin role.
- Neither administrators nor users should *ever* leave their computers unattended and logged in. Password-protected screen savers are critical.
- Implement message-level encryption for the best protection.
- Disable messaging features that you are not using. If you don't need POP3, IMAP4, LDAP, or NNTP, disable them at the site level.

For Further Information...

Did this chapter tell you everything you need to know about cryptography? Well, as a network administrator, I hope it did. But cryptography is a fascinating subject, and you might want to learn more. Here are two books that I frequently refer to:

- *Cryptography and Network Security Principals and Practices*, Second Edition, by Williams Stallings (Prentice Hall, 1998).

- *Applied Cryptography*, Second Edition, by Bruce Schneier (Wiley & Sons, 1996).

Some other resources that you may find enlightening can be found on the Web:

- VeriSign is probably the largest and best known of the certificate authorities. They have a lot of great reference material on their site: www.verisign.com.

- RSA Data Security is the public/private key experts. On their Web site you will find many white papers and other reference materials on cryptography: www.rsa.com.

- Consider visiting the Computer Emergency Response Team Web site: www.cert.org. CERT Computation Center is a division of Carnegie Mellon University, so you will often see it referred to as CMU's CERT/CC.

14

Exchange Server Advanced Security

At the core of Exchange Server Advanced Security is Key Management Server (KMS) and public/private key pairs. Chapter 13 reviewed the basics of messaging security and how the Outlook client can take advantage of certificates to send messages that are not only encrypted, but also digitally signed, so that their authenticity and origin can be traced. This chapter introduces the Exchange Server's Advanced Security features which allow your organization to distribute public/private key pairs to your users.

Exchange Server Advanced Security is not just "casual" intruder protection. Exchange Server does a good job of protecting message content from the casual snooper, like Snuffy from Sales who decides to surf around and see if he can read Sadie's e-mail messages. Advanced Security protects against much higher-level intrusion by using certificates and public/private key pairs.

In order to use public and private keys, something has to create and distribute keys and certificates. That is the job of Key Management Server. This chapter specifically covers:

- Using Exchange 5.5 Key Management Server
- Using Exchange 5.5 Key Management Server with Microsoft Certificate Server
- Enabling the Outlook client to use certificates provided by Key Management Server

Managing KMS is going to add an additional layer of complexity to your network infrastructure and to your (or someone else's) job. The Key Management server must be kept secure, and permissions to operate it should be restricted to a select group of very trusted administrators.

In addition, you need to decide to whom you will issue digital certificates: Will you give them to all of your users, or just to a select few who actually require higher-level message content protection and message signing? Understanding the basics of the Exchange KMS will help you get started with the KMS configuration and management.

Key Management Server Basics

There are two flavors of the Exchange 5.5 Key Management Server. Both are significantly different from the implementation of KMS on Exchange Server 4 and 5. First there is the standard Key Management Server that ships with Exchange Server 5.5. Then there's a new capability provided by Exchange 5.5 with Service Pack 1 or later; this is the ability to use Microsoft Certificate Server to generate certificates.

Exchange Server's native KMS generates X.509v1 certificates that are not interoperable with any other client except for other Outlook clients. However, Certificate Server can generate X.509v3 certificates which are used in standard S/MIME clients including Outlook Express, Outlook 98, and Outlook 2000. X.509v3 certificates are interoperable with the S/MIME standard and can thus be exchanged with customers and vendors who are not using an Exchange/Outlook-based messaging system.

TIP   If you have never set up KMS, then fear not; it is not too difficult. However, like anything else that you may not be vastly experienced at, I recommend setting it up on your test network and getting a feel for it prior to putting it in production.

Before delving into configuring and enabling KMS, I want to first look at its basic features. These are features that are going to be required regardless of whether or not you are integrating with Certificate Server.

Locating the Key Management Server Software

When deciding on a location for the Key Management Server software, here are a few hints:

- The physical location of the server should be secure.
- Key Management Server must run on the same machine as an Exchange Server. Pick an Exchange server that will be in place for a long time; moving KMS to another server is a pain in the neck.

- From the network's perspective, the Exchange server that hosts Key Management Server should be in close proximity to the Exchange security administrator. The administrator must be able to connect to this server using an RPC connection.

- Though Exchange Server 5.5 permits more than one Key Management server per Exchange organization (Exchange 4 and 5 did not), you should keep the number of KMS servers to a minimum. You are still limited to a single KMS per site.

Key Management Server Installation

Unlike the Key Management Server that shipped with Exchange 4 and 5, the Exchange 5.5 KMS is installed using the Exchange 5.5 Setup program. When installing Exchange Server 5.5, do the following to install KMS:

1. During the Exchange Server 5.5 setup, choose the Custom installation option.

2. Highlight the Microsoft Exchange Server option and click the Change Option button.

3. Make sure that the Key Management Server option is selected.

4. Click OK and Continue to begin the installation of the Exchange Server (and KMS software).

NOTE If you neglected to install KMS during the initial Exchange Server installation, you can run Setup again and choose the Add/Remove option. (This will require that you kick off your users.) Don't forget to reapply the service pack and any relevant hot fixes before letting your users back on.

During the Key Management Server installation, you will be prompted for the site services account; if you do not have this password, then make sure that the person who does is nearby when the installation starts.

After you provide the site services account password, the next two dialog boxes relate to the KMS startup password. When the installation is complete, there will be a new service in the Control Panel ➤ Services list; this is the Key Management Server service. Every time KMS starts, it has to be provided with a special password which is used to decrypt the KMS database. This is *different* than the Windows NT user account and password that the service uses to start; that is, the site services account user account and password.

The dialog boxes offer you two choices regarding the KMS password:

- Display the password so that you can write it down. You must manually enter the startup password each time you start KMS.

Certificate Authority Object

Each time you attempt to perform an operation on a CA (or Site Encryption) object, you are prompted for a password. When prompted, notice there is a Remember This Password For Up To 5 Minutes check box. If you click this check box, Exchange Administrator will not prompt you for your KMS administrator password again for five minutes.

Displaying the Certificate Authority object's properties, you will see six tabs, including the Permissions tab. Each of these affects certain configurations of the CA (either the Exchange server or the Certification server).

General

The General tab of the CA object's property page contains the display name and directory name for the object. There is a Certificate Server field that is used to designate which Microsoft Certificate Server is used. This name is set up during the Certificate Server setup process and should not be changed.

Administrators

The CA object's Administrators tab is used to assign additional KMS administrators and to change the KMS password. This password is not the same as your Windows NT password, and the default is *password*. If an administrator is going to be responsible for generating, revoking or recovering keys, he must be in this list.

Passwords

If a company is sending a lot of critical and confidential data via e-mail, the organization is vulnerable to intrusion by a sneaky administrator (with the Permissions Admin role) giving herself the User role to the CEO's mailbox and reading all the confidential messages she wants. That is why encryption is included with Exchange. However, if this same sneaky administrator was also the KMS administrator, she could also initiate a security key recover and get the user's private keys. This is why Microsoft introduced "missile key" technology to Exchange Server 5.5 SP1.

Have you ever been in a missile silo? Probably not; me neither. However, the people who work with nuclear missiles have a safeguard in place: No single person can launch a missile. Launching a missile requires two unique keys (and the key slots are too far away for a single person to turn both keys simultaneously). Figure 14.2 shows the CA object's Passwords tab for enabling missile key–type protection. From this tab, you can set policies to require more than a single password to perform certain KMS administrative tasks.

Figure 14.2   Missile key protection comes to the Desktop!

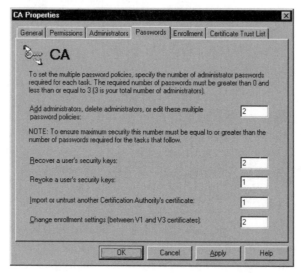

In the page shown in Figure 14.2, you can set between one and three password requirements on any of the tasks. The maximum is the number of KMS administrators that you assign on the Administrator's tab.

There are five categories of password policies:

Add administrators, delete administrators, or edit these multiple password policies should require the most passwords (at least two), because this is the most critical policy. If someone could easily add additional administrators or change the password policies, he could override all of the other policies.

Recover a user's security keys specifies the number of passwords required to recover a user's security key in the event the user loses his keys or forgets the password that his key file is encrypted with. This policy should be at least two passwords.

Revoke a user's security keys specifies the number of passwords required to revoke a user's certificates in case the user's advanced security needs to be revoked or the keys are compromised.

Import or untrust another Certification Authority's certificate specifies the number of passwords required to import or remove a trust to another CA.

Security

PART 5

Change enrollment settings (between V1 and V3 certificates) specifies the number of passwords required to change the types of certificates that are created (on the Enrollment tab).

The default for all password policies is one password. If you are the only KMS administrator in your organization, these default settings will probably be sufficient. These policies are useful in an organization that has multiple KMS administrators and wishes to protect critical functions that not just a single administrator should be changing.

Enrollment

When a mailbox is first configured with Exchange Advanced Security, Key Management Server generates a temporary key that I call an "activation token" or an "enrollment token." The CA object's Enrollment tab sets policies for transmitting these enrollment tokens and the types of certificates that will be generated. In Exchange Server 4 and 5, this token was temporarily displayed on the screen; the administrator then wrote the token on paper and delivered it to the user by phone, hand, or e-mail. Some administrators just took a print screen of the activation token and pasted it into an e-mail message along with instructions for using it.

Exchange Server 5.5 provides the Allow E-Mail To Be Sent To The User check box (shown in Figure 14.3), which gives the administrator the option of generating an e-mail message and sending the token automatically. Further, the Edit Welcome Message button allows the administrator to change the message the user sees when she gets the activation token.

Figure 14.3   The CA object's Enrollment tab

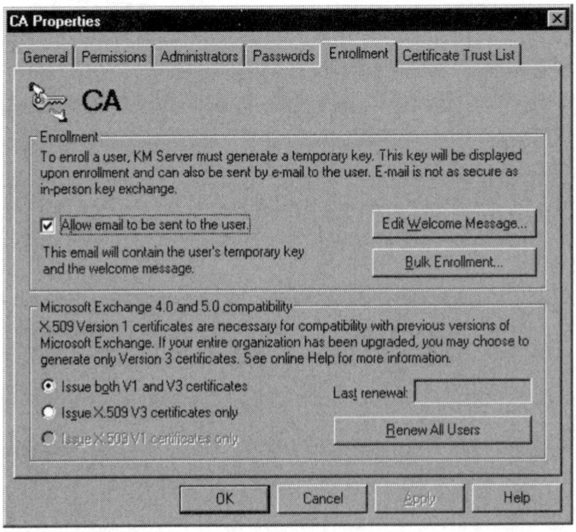

In the Microsoft Exchange 4.0 And 5.0 Compatibility section, the lower half of the Enrollment tab, the type of certificates that will be generated is set. This section offers three options:

Issue both V1 and V3 certificates requires Certificate Server, because it is responsible for generating X.509v3 certificates. You will need to use this option if you have already been using Advanced Security and need to issue certificates for backward compatibility with Outlook 97 and the Exchange client, but you also want to start deploying S/MIME clients.

Issue X.509v3 certificates only must be used in conjunction with a Microsoft Certificate server. In order to use X.509v3 certificates, you must be using clients that are capable of handling S/MIME messages, such as Outlook 98 and Outlook 2000.

Issue X.509v1 certificates only issues only X.509v1 certificates. This works fine with all Outlook and Exchange clients; however, users of Outlook 98 and Outlook 2000 will not be able to use the S/MIME capabilities.

The Renew All Users button sends a message to all users telling them that they should renew their certificates. You can use this option to implement any changes you wish to enforce, such as using a new encryption algorithm or upgrading all users to have an X.509v3 certificate in addition to an X.509v1 certificate.

Certificate Trust List

The CA object's Certificate Trust List tab allows you to import digital certificates from other organizations so that your own users can verify that certificates from that organization are properly authorized. This would be useful if another company wanted to send signed and sealed messages to your company (using an S/MIME client). The other company would have to send you a certificate from their own Certificate server. Once this was done, users could then exchange certificates that can be properly verified.

From the Certificate Trust List tab, you can Import new certificates, Remove certificates you no longer require, Trust or Untrust a certificate, and view a certificate's properties.

Site Encryption Configuration Object

In the site-level configuration container, there is an additional KMS-related object called Site Encryption Configuration. From this object, you control which site the KMS server is located in and the types of encryption that will be used. The object's properties page has three tabs.

Security

PART 5

From the Security tab, you can see the mailbox's current security status. The possible states include:

Undefined   The mailbox has not been enabled.

New   The mailbox has been enabled with the temporary security credentials, but they have not been received back from the client.

Active   Security is enabled and the temporary security credentials have been received back from the client.

Disabled   The mailbox has been disabled.

Key recovery in progress   Either the user has forgotten his password and his keys are being recovered, or the mailbox was disabled and is now in the middle of being re-enabled.

The Security Certificate For This Mailbox area of the Security tab shows when the certificate was issued and when it expires.

Enabling a Mailbox for Advanced Security

To enable a mailbox for Advanced Security, display the mailbox properties and choose the Security tab (as shown in Figure 14.6). You will probably need to enter your KMS password if you have not recently been working with Advanced Security.

Now you must generate temporary security credentials for each mailbox. These credentials are in the form of a 12-character (no numbers) password such as HZUFDJOPQXYY. This is sometimes called an *enabling token*, because it is only used once by the user to finalize their security configuration.

To create the temporary security credentials, click the Enable Advanced Security button. If you have configured the CA object's Enrollment tab to allow a user's temporary security credentials to be sent to the user via e-mail, you will be given the option of sending the key (enrollment messages) via e-mail.

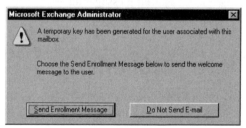

Even if you sent the enrollment message via e-mail, the temporary key will be displayed after the message is sent. The user then uses that temporary token to enable her mailbox.

> *TIP* You can generate temporary security credentials for all users simultaneously using the CA object's Enrollment tab. Click the Bulk Enrollment button, and you will be given the option of sending users an e-mail message with their temporary security credentials or sending them to a text file. If you use the text file option, you will need to distribute the credentials manually.

Key Recovery and Revocation

There may come a time when a user forgets his password that is used to protect his private keys, and you may have to recover his keys. Or a person may leave a company and have critical company information in his mailbox that someone legitimately needs to decrypt. These situations often result in the need for the process of *key recovery*. To recover a user's security keys, simply click the Recover Security Key button (seen in Figure 14.6). Doing so gives you the option of either sending the user new temporary security credentials via e-mail or doing it the old-fashioned way—having them displayed on the screen.

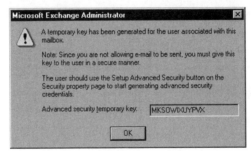

It is also possible to revoke a user's certificates. *Key revocation* may become necessary if the user no longer needs to send signed or encrypted mail; it would also be necessary if the user's keys have been compromised. You can re-enable the user's at a later time if the user needs to be able to send signed and encrypted messages again. To revoke a user's ability to sign and encrypt messages, click the Revoke Advanced Security button.

Setting Up a Secure Client

Once Key Management Server has been installed and a mailbox has been enabled for Advanced Security, the owner of the mailbox needs to use her temporary security credentials (that 12-character password) to activate her mailbox and generate her real certificates and keys. Some administrators prefer to give the mailbox owners their temporary security credentials in person; the administrator would then immediately help users enable their mailboxes. This is much more secure than sending everyone their credentials via e-mail, but if you are enabling hundreds or thousands of mailboxes, the in-person approach is not practical.

Enabling the Outlook Client

If you have sent security credentials to your users via e-mail, they will have an e-mail message in their mailboxes from the System Attendant that will look similar to the one in Figure 14.7. This message can be edited to suit your specific environment on the CA object's Enrollment tab; to do so, click the Edit Welcome Message button.

Figure 14.7 Message containing instructions for enabling Advanced Security

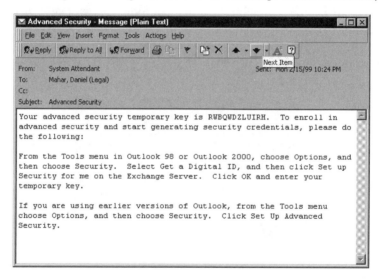

If you have not chosen to send the temporary security tokens to users via e-mail, you will need to find a secure way to distribute the tokens to your users.

Enabling Outlook 97

Outlook 97 stores the certificates and private keys in an EPF file. The private keys stored in this file are password protected. To enable the Outlook 97 client and generate this file, from the Tools menu, choose Options and click the Security tab (see Figure 14.8).

Figure 14.8   Outlook 97 Security tab

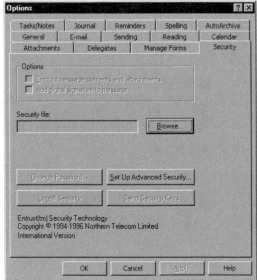

The Security tab has five buttons:

Browse allows you to select a previously created EPF file. You might need to do this if your EPF file is located in your home directory on a server and you frequently have to move between computers.

Set Up Advanced Security is used when you initially set up Advanced Security. When you click this button, it prompts you for the temporary security credentials that you were sent along with a password that will be used to protect the private keys in your EPF file.

Change Password allows you to change the password that protects the private keys in your EPF file.

Send Security Keys allows you to send your public sealing certificates to another Outlook user outside of your organization.

Logoff Security forces Outlook to "forget" the Advanced Security password that you may have previously asked Outlook to remember for this particular login session.

In addition to these buttons, the Security tab has two options that control the default Advanced Security settings. These are the Encrypt Message Contents And Attachments and Add Digital Signature To Message check boxes. Encrypt Message Contents And

Attachments tells Outlook to always encrypt the message contents. Add Digital Signature To Message tells Outlook to always put a digital signature on the message. You can check both if desired.

Click the Set Up Advanced Security button and you will receive the Setup Advanced Security dialog box.

Enter (or cut and paste) the temporary security credentials in the Token box, provide a path and name for the EPF file in the Security File box, and enter a password that will be used to protect the private keys. Click OK. A message will be sent to the Key Management server.

In a few minutes, you will receive a reply back from the System Attendant; open the message and you will be prompted for a password. If you entered the token and password correctly in the previous step, Outlook 97 is now enabled for Advanced Security.

> **NOTE** Once Advanced Security is enabled, the temporary security credentials are no longer usable and can be discarded.

Enabling Outlook 98 and Outlook 2000

Outlook 98 and 2000 certificates and keys are stored in a protected store (a.k.a. the Microsoft Wallet) as part of the user's Windows profile. To enable the Outlook 98 and 2000 clients, from the Tools menu, choose Options and select the Security tab (shown in Figure 14.9).

From the Security tab, you can control the default Advanced Security settings for all messages. There are three choices: Encrypt Contents And Attachments For Outgoing Messages, Add Digital Signature To Outgoing Messages, and Send Clear Text Signed Messages (messages that have been signed, but not encrypted).

Figure 14.9   Outlook 98/2000 Security tab

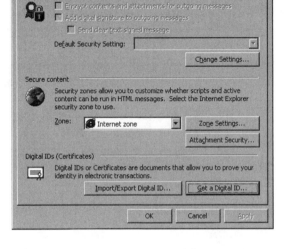

The Security tab further allows you to select your current default settings, so you can have multiple security settings using different encryption and signature types. You can also specify the zones for which content is considered secure and insecure.

The Import/Export Digital ID button allows you to export your X.509v3 certificate to be used on other platforms as well as to import certificates used on other platforms (such as an Outlook 97 EPF file).

To enable Outlook 98/2000 for Advanced Security, click the Get A Digital ID button. If you see a Web browser launch and connect to Microsoft Web site, then your client does not recognize that your Exchange organization has Advanced Security enabled; you should see the following dialog box:

Select the Set Up Security For Me On The Exchange Server option. You will then be prompted for the temporary security credentials (token) and a keyset name, which can be left as the mailbox name. The keyset name is used to identify this key request. When you click the OK button, the key request is sent to the Key Management server.

Usually, in a few minutes, you will receive a message back from the System Attendant that includes your new certificates. When you open this message, you will be prompted as to whether or not you want to add the certificates to the root store.

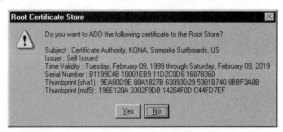

You will also be asked to set the security level of the private keys. You have three security-level options, which apply to any item stored in the protected store:

High means that you are prompted for a password each time you access your private keys (each time you sign or seal a message). If you select High, you must provide a password. If you forget this password, your keys will have to be recovered. This password is not the same as your Windows NT password.

Medium simply displays a message reminding you that you are using your private keys. This is the default.

Low uses the keys, but does not prompt you for a password or notify you that they are being used.

Once you have accepted all the certificates into your protected store, Outlook 98/2000 is ready to use for sending signed and sealed messages.

Importing and Exporting Certificates

Certificates issued by Certificate Server can be imported and exported. This is especially useful if the user works from more than one computer or needs to take the digital certificates home so that they can be used on a home computer as well.

Click the Import/Export Digital IDs button on the Tools ➤ Options ➤ Security tab. From here you can import certificates from EPF files (Outlook 97) as well as standard Internet security files (PFX and P12 files). You can also export the Exchange or S/MIME security information to an EPF, PFX, or P12 file.

> **NOTE** Key Management Server encryption does not work with POP3 or IMAP4 clients unless you are sending messages using S/MIME and have a client that understands S/MIME, like Outlook Express. This means that you must be issuing X.509v3 certificates. HTTP clients through OWA do not support any KMS encryption.

Certificate Renewal

When Key Management Server issues a certificate to a client, the certificate is valid for 12 months (18 months for X.509v1 certificates). At a certain point during the life of a certificate, the user will receive a client-generated message each time she uses the Advanced Security functions reminding her that the certificate will expire soon. The message gives her the option of responding and renewing her keys immediately. If the user ignores the message until the end of the certificate lifetime, she will no longer be able to use the Advanced Security functions, and the administrator will need to renew her certificates manually.

Final Notes about Advanced Security

To close things up in this chapter, I have compiled a few additional thoughts about using Exchange Server and Key Management Server, including potential problems with signed messages and the Internet Mail Service, and possible alternatives to KMS.

The Internet Mail Service and S/MIME Signed Messages

If you are using S/MIME clients (Outlook 98 and Outlook 2000) with Exchange and your users are going to send and receive signed messages from the Internet, you have one additional step you need to take. The Internet Mail Service (IMS) has no problems passing a mail message through that has been sealed (encrypted) or signed *and* sealed. The IMS just sees the sealed data as a blob of binary data, just like a Word document, and passes this blob on through the IMS, unmodified and undisturbed. The encryption and decryption of S/MIME messages is handled by the S/MIME client, *not* the server.

However, if the S/MIME message is signed (but no encryption is used), the signature (the encrypted hash and the sender's public certificate) are attached to the message as a separate file. Since initially Microsoft did not ship an S/MIME client for Exchange, the IMS would strip off the attached signature information. Microsoft did so because the client had no way of knowing how to handle the attachment, and the signature would appear as an unknown file attachment type on the message. The Exchange 5.5 IMS continues to handle messages in this way.

Once you are well on your way to deploying S/MIME clients, and people start sending you S/MIME signed messages from the Internet, you will want to instruct the IMS to leave these signatures intact and undisturbed. To do this, display the properties of the IMS. On the Internet Mail property page, enable the Clients Support S/MIME Signatures check box. Once this is done, if someone on the Internet sends a signed message to one of your Outlook 97 or Exchange client users, they will receive an attachment type that will not be understood, but the rest of the message will be fine.

Alternatives to the Exchange KMS

Key Management Server is not the only option available if you are looking for a product to sign and seal messages. There are a number of third-party vendors that have developed products for e-mail security.

NOTE Though the KMS is an excellent product, many people consider it to be weak due to the fact that only 40-bit encryption can be used outside of the United States; this is due to U.S. export restrictions on encryption formulas.

The best known of these third-party security enhancements is PGP (Pretty Good Privacy) from Network Associates (www.pgp.com). PGP Personal Privacy is a plug-in for Outlook or the Exchange client that enhances those clients with additional security options. This product depends on you managing your own keys; this can get quite sticky if you have more than a few hundred users who require the ability to send secure messages.

Two other products that provide additional security for Exchange are WorldSecure Client for Microsoft Exchange (WorldTalk Corporation at www.worldtalk.com) and Secure Messenger for Microsoft Exchange from Baltimore Technologies (www.baltimore.ie).

For Further Information...

For information relating to recent third-party products to enhance Exchange, check out www.microsoft.com/exchange and www.exchangesoftware.com.

15

Protecting Your Exchange Server

Solid Exchange server security and solid messaging security begins with solid Windows NT platform security. This chapter reviews some of the key areas to consider when protecting your Exchange server and the messages it contains from prying eyes. This chapter reviews:

- Windows NT security basics
- Windows NT vulnerabilities
- Physical security
- Virus protection for the Windows NT server and for Exchange messages
- Message content security

Windows NT and networking security is a huge topic and cannot be covered adequately in a few pages, or even a few dozen pages. This chapter hits on the high points of protecting your Exchange server, but your library should include a thorough Windows NT security book.

> *TIP*   Did you know that some security studies estimate that between 50 and 80 percent of all instances of data theft and system intrusions come from within the organization?! Protecting yourself from the outside world is all well and good, but thorough internal auditing and security procedures are also important.

Solid Windows NT Security

Solid Windows NT security should be on your front line of defense against unauthorized access of your Exchange server and the messages that it contains. Sound security not only includes securing the server against outside access but making sure that users do not accidentally gain access to files or get administrative access permissions that they should not have.

Denial of Service

Windows NT servers (as well as most other software and hardware devices that plug in to a network) are susceptible to hacker attacks called Denial of Service (DoS) attacks. While these attacks may not necessarily gain access to your critical data, their intent is to make a network service or device unavailable.

There are many types of DoS attacks to which Windows NT is vulnerable, though most of these are correctable by applying the latest version of the Windows NT service pack.

> *TIP*   Most well-known DoS bugs are fixed quickly. The latest service packs and hot fixes should contain these cures. Keep up-to-date on the latest security problems and their fixes.

Disabling Services

An excellent approach to Windows NT security is to load and run only those services that are necessary to operate the server. Some services that often get loaded but are unnecessary include the Simple TCP/IP services, TCP/IP print services, Web server, FTP server, gopher server, DNS server, WINS server, and DHCP server.

If you do not need these services, do not load them as part of the Windows NT and Windows NT Option Pack installation.

NOTE   If you are using SNMP agents, make sure that the Public group is either removed or not used. Another option is to limit access to the SNMP service. Public is a well-known group, and much information can be garnered using simple tools like SNMPUTILG from SMS 2.

A Few Thoughts about Passwords

The weakest point in most networks is most of their passwords. There are utilities on the Internet that I can easily download and then quickly crack even passwords of medium difficulty; the most notorious and well known of these is a utility called L0PHT Crack (pronounced "loft crack"). Remember, passwords should be strong and difficult to guess, and the passwords database should be well protected.

WARNING   The Windows NT Administrator user (or whatever you rename this account to) should always have an extremely strong password. Other accounts that should have very strong passwords include any Windows NT user account that has administrative rights, that has operator rights, and that is used as a services account (such as the Exchange site services account).

Strong Passwords

You don't have to send your passwords to the gym to make them strong (maybe just to karate school so they can withstand an attack). My definition of a strong password is one that has at least eight characters and contains a special character (such as one of these: ` ~ ! @ # $ % ^ & * ( ) _ - + = { }] [| \ " ' ; : < > , .). The password should also contain at least two of these:

> Uppercase characters (A–Z)
>
> Lowercase characters (a–z)
>
> Numbers (0–9)

The special character is essential, because most password-checking programs avoid checking the special characters in a password so they can finish more quickly. If the password-checking program includes the special characters in a brute force password attack, the total time to crack a password could extend into the hundreds or thousands of days.

Secure Thoughts

Here are a couple of thoughts on security. These are mostly procedural and user education issues.

- A workstation should *never* be left unattended and logged in. **NEVER**. Not even for a few minutes. In any environment that has security concerns, this should be grounds for termination.

- Users should never share passwords with anyone, and passwords should never been written down. This includes Windows NT logon passwords and passwords to protect advanced security keys.

- Limit the number of users who actually have administrator-level rights on Windows NT and the number of users who have the Permissions Admin role in Exchange. Everyone *thinks* they need this permission, but few really do.

Physical Security

If someone can get physical access to your server, you may as well have handed them a lovely printout of all of your confidential data. Physical security for any type of server is of paramount importance. If a user can get physical access to your system, she can bypass file system security using the NTFSDOS utility, she can change the administrator password while the server is offline, she can copy your databases and critical files to another server—well, you get the idea. Even servers in remote locations should be kept physically secure.

Another issue that people don't often think about is protecting backup tapes and tape drives. I know many companies that have a fireproof tape vault; immediately upon the completion of the tape backup procedure, the tapes are removed from the tape drives and stored in a locked container or safe. This is a smart procedure to follow.

A possible indication that an Exchange server or Exchange data is being tampered with is when you see application event log IDs that indicate that one of the Exchange services have restarted. These events include:

Event Source	Event ID	Description
MSExchangeSA	1000	Microsoft Exchange Server System Attendant is starting.
MSExchangeDS	1000	The directory service has started.
MSExchangeIS Public	1001	The Microsoft Exchange information store has started.

Event Source	Event ID	Description
MSExchangeIS Private	1001	The Microsoft Exchange information store has started.
MSExchangeMTA	9298	Microsoft Exchange Server MTA Service startup is complete.
MSExchangeIMC	1000	The Microsoft Exchange Internet Mail Service, version 5.5.2232.9, has started successfully.

If you see any of these events in the application event log, they should correspond to a scheduled shutdown of your Exchange server or services.

Virus Protection

Virus protection, while not directly related to security, is a critical issue in the operation of any network. One of the largest networks I have worked on was paralyzed for nearly five days because a virus continued to spread unchecked. While the virus did not delete files or damage hard disks, it did make the computer unusable. The virus spread to each computer on the network and rendered it unusable. Can you imagine shutting your servers and workstations down for five days? It was not pretty. Every hour, vice presidents and executives were coming by the computer room to tell us (rather loudly) how much money we were losing an hour.

Today, the average virus is a macro-type virus usually embedded in a Word document. These are much more innocuous than something like Jerusalem-B, but nonetheless, they are an inconvenience that must be removed. The infamous Melissa virus (W97M_Melissa) is a Word macro virus that uses Outlook and Exchange to propigate itself. In the case of Melissa, the virus mailed itself to addresses in the Exchange global address list as well as to user's personal address books. In the process, the additional traffic overwhelmed many Exchange MTAs and Internet Mail Services.

There are two approaches to virus protection when dealing with Windows NT and Exchange servers. First is protection at the Windows NT level, which protects against and scans for virus on the file system. The second is to use virus software that intercepts viruses that are attached to messages.

Exchange-Based Virus Protection

Exchange-based virus-scanning software usually works on the MAPI-level. This means it works by opening each mailbox and scanning for new messages. Some types of software

Security

PART 5

are designed to catch the virus as it enters a connector, such as the Internet Mail Service, and prevent the virus from arriving at the user's mailbox from outside the server.

Exchange Server Virus Protection

I have no specific recommendation for Exchange server virus-scanning software. There are quite a few vendors that provide such features. The only recommendation I make to customers and students is to choose the same vendor for Exchange server virus protection that you use for file and print server virus scanning.

Several companies and products that you may want to check out for information include:

- Norton AntiVirus for Microsoft Exchange from Symantec: www.symantec.com

- McAfee GroupShield for Exchange from Network Associates: www.mcafee.com

- ScanMail for Microsoft Exchange from Trend Micro: www.trendmicro.com

---

Hints for Effective Virus Software Usage

Here are some tips that you should follow when using virus software:

- Keep your virus signatures and scanning software up-to-date. Most virus software companies update their signatures monthly.

- The best protection against viruses is to stop them where they enter the network. Any workstation that has a floppy disk, CD-ROM, or access to the Internet should have memory and disk-level virus scanning installed. Since most workstations usually have a floppy disk drive, a good policy is to install virus-protection software on all desktop computers. The virus-scanning software should be configured to protect the memory of the computer, scan any floppy disks, and make a periodic scan of the computer's local hard disk.

- The hard drives of all file, print, and application servers should be scanned a few times per week for viruses stored in files.

- Check to see if your virus-scanning software offers an option to scan Internet mail as it enters the Exchange server rather than scanning each user's mailbox individually.

Content Security

It seems like everything relating to a messaging system can be considered dangerous these days. Companies can be sued for message content, confidential data can easily be e-mailed directly to a competitor, and it seems that every day I have 10 or 15 new pieces of junk mail (a.k.a. spam).

A relatively new area of messaging security is emerging that is loosely labeled *content security*. Content security programs are set between your messaging system and the Internet and scan the incoming and outgoing messages based on business rules that you have defined.

The company that seems to be pioneering this field is a company called Content Technologies (`www.contenttechnologies.com`) with a product called MIMEsweeper.

> **NOTE** Another interesting product is Praetor from Computer Mail Services (`www.cmsconnect.com`); this product takes a sophisticated approach to detecting and rejecting UCE.

Rather than making this section of the book a press release for the MIMEsweeper product, I will just mention some general requirements that I would require from a content security solution, and then I will let you seek out your own products. Here is what I would like to see a content security product do:

- Automatically stamp a signature/disclaimer at the bottom of all outgoing messages stating that the message may contain confidential or proprietary data; if the receiver has received it in error, please forward it to a specified address.
- Scan outgoing file types to make sure that only allowable file types are being transferred.
- Scan all mail for the presence of a list of words such as confidential, proprietary, and so on. I would also like to scan for terms that could be construed as inappropriate in a business environment such as profanity or something that suggests harassment.
- Scan incoming mail looking for messages that may possibly be spam messages, officially known as unsolicited commercial e-mail (UCE).
- Integrate or provide virus-scanning abilities for all incoming and outgoing e-mail.

Security

PART 5

Exchange and Firewalls

For networks and servers that are connected directly to the Internet, a firewall is your first line of defense. Quite simply, a *firewall* is a device (hardware and software) that sits between you and the outside world; the firewall examines every incoming (and possibly outgoing) data packet to make sure the IP addresses and protocols are permissible. If your networks or servers are connected to the Internet, you should seriously consider a firewall.

There are two common philosophies when installing a firewall: allow everything except restricted services, or restrict everything and allow only certain services. I like the second approach much better.

One of the ways that firewalls block inbound and outbound data flow is by restricting TCP and UDP ports. Think of a TCP (Transmission Control Protocol) or UDP (User Datagram Protocol) port number as the address of the software. A computer is assigned an IP address; individual software programs running on that computer have a unique address (between 0 and 65535) assigned to them. These numbers are normally the same for all platforms and are assigned by the Internet Assigned Numbers Authority (IANA). The common (or well-known) port numbers are between 0 and 1023. Table 15.2 contains a list of common port numbers that are used with Windows NT and Exchange.

Table 15.2   Common TCP and UDP Port Numbers Used with Windows NT and Exchange

TCP/UDP Port Number	Usage
21	Used for FTP file transfers
23	Used by Telnet clients
25	Used by SMTP clients to contact SMTP servers
53	Used by the DNS clients and servers
80	Used by Web browsers to contact Web (HTTP) servers
102	Used by X.400 over TCP/IP
110	Used by POP3 clients to retrieve mail
119	Used by Usenet news clients and servers

Table 15.2   Common TCP and UDP Port Numbers Used with Windows NT
and Exchange *(continued)*

TCP/UDP Port Number	Usage
135	Location service or RPC end-point mapper used by clients to locate the specific port address of other services
137	NetBIOS name service (used by WINS)
138	NetBIOS datagram service (used by the Microsoft Browser service)
139	NetBIOS session service (used for connections such as connecting to shared folders)
143	Used by IMAP4 clients to retrieve mail
161/162	Used by SNMP management consoles and agents
389	Used by LDAP clients to query
443	Used by Web browser clients when using SSL to connect securely to a Web server (HTTPS)
636	LDAP over SSL for querying directories securely
993	Used for retrieving mail securely via IMAP4 using SSL
995	Used for retrieving mail securely via POP3 using SSL

NOTE   Table 15.2 is by no means a complete list of port numbers, but it does contain many of the common ones used by Windows NT and Exchange. For a complete list, see RFC 1700 at www.rfc-editor.org.

Exchange MAPI/RPC Communication through the Firewall

I encounter the following problem with a student or client every few weeks. You have set up a firewall (or packet filter) to protect your network and servers from the evil Internet. Your users want to be able to use Outlook to retrieve their e-mail through the Internet from home and while on the road. You ask the firewall administrator to open up TCP

Stop and restart the Exchange information store and directory services for the change to take effect.

Other Static Port Mappings

You can also statically map the System Attendant and message transfer agent ports to static ports. This might become necessary if you have to manage Exchange servers that are located on the opposite side of a firewall. These values are also configured through the Registry and are case sensitive. The Registry keys discussed in this section are found in \HKLM\System\CurrentControlSet\Services\.

To configure the System Attendant to use a specific port number, add a new value called TCP/IP port with a data type of REG_DWORD in the \MSExchangeSA\Parameters subkey. Enter the port number you wish to assign in the data box.

To configure the message transfer agent to communicate with other X.400 MTAs using a port other than the default (102), in the \MSExchangeMTA\Parameters subkey, create a new value called RFCPortNumber with a data type of REG_DWORD. Enter the port number that you wish to use instead of 102. All X.400 MTAs that this MTA communicates with will have to be modified.

The port that the MTA uses for RPC communication (such as between other Exchange MTAs and with the site connector) can also be configured statically. In the \MSExchangeMTA\ Parameters subkey, create a new value called TCP/IP port for RPC listens with a data type of REG_DWORD. Enter the port number you wish to use.

TIP   If you are working with decimal port numbers, remember that the Registry editor displays REG_DWORD data as hexadecimal. Click the Decimal radio button to display or enter data as decimal.

Firewall Tips

Here are a few hints and thoughts about using firewalls and Exchange:

- If you are using the Exchange site connector, you will need to follow the same procedure that I outlined for connecting the Outlook client through a firewall.
- When using the X.400 connector, make sure that the X.400 port is open.
- Refer back to Table 15.1 for ports that IMAP4, HTTP, LDAP, and POP3 use. Consider using these protocols over SSL for improved transport security.

Exchange and Microsoft Proxy 2

It is possible to locate an Exchange server behind a Microsoft Proxy Server 2 to handle incoming POP3, IMAP4, and NNTP client requests from the Internet and to receive SMTP mail. This process is called *reverse hosting*. The computers on the Internet must be configured to contact the IP address of the proxy server, not the Exchange server. If the Internet Mail Service is used, the Internet A and MX records should point to the proxy server.

After you are confident the proxy server is functioning properly, install the Winsock proxy client software on the Exchange server. You will now need to configure two wspcfg.ini files: one for the store.exe program which hosts POP3, IMAP4, and NNTP, and one for the msexcimc.exe program, which is the Internet Mail Service (if supported).

Configuring the Information Store

You will need to configure a wspcfg.ini file in the \exchsrvr\bin directory (the directory in which the store.exe file is found). This file will tell store.exe which TCP ports it needs to bind to the Proxy server. If you want to support IMAP4, NNTP, and POP3, then the wspcfg.ini file will look like this:

```
[STORE]
ServerBindTcpPorts=110,119,143
Persistent=1
KillOldSession=1
```

The information store service will need to be restarted for this change to take effect.

Configuring the Internet Mail Service

Create a wspcfg.ini file in the \exchsrvr\Connect\msexcimc\bin directory (this is the directory that holds the msexcimc.exe program). The file will look like this:

```
[MSEXCIMC]
ServerBindTcpPorts=25
Persistent=1
KillOldSession=1
```

The Internet Mail Service will need to be restarted in order for the IMS to bind to the Proxy server and accept SMTP mail.

Security

PART 5

For Further Information...

To get more information on some of the topics discussed in this chapter, refer to these sources:

- My favorite reference for Windows NT and network security is *NT 4 Network Security* by Matt Strebe, Charles Perkins, and Michael Moncur (Sybex, 1998).

- A great reference for using TCP/IP with Windows NT is *Mastering TCP/IP for NT Server* by Mark Minasi and Todd Lammle (Sybex, 1997).

- Microsoft has a special series of Web pages for Microsoft-related security information and bulletins: www.microsoft.com/security.

- Microsoft has a number of Knowledge Base articles related to using Exchange Server and firewalls. These include Q155831, Q161931, and Q148732.

Putting Advanced Security to Work

Company CDE was becoming increasingly concerned about the security of the messages their executives sent internally. Once they were connected to the Internet, company managers and executives began communicating with vendors and customers using e-mail, and the company's concerns about the security of their e-mail continued to grow.

During the development of a new ordering system, this all came to a head. The current system for processing purchase orders involved calling and/or faxing purchase orders to the vendors. On more than a few occasions, mistakes were made while ordering, or a vendor accepted an order without a purchase order. Numerous times, orders were placed and delivered without adequate documentation from the accounting system. During the overhaul of the system, the company president inquired about the possibility of submitting purchase orders to vendors using the e-mail system. Of the 100 or so primary vendors, nearly 90 of them were using some type of Windows-based mail system, and they could receive e-mail from the Internet.

The Information Services team was assigned the task of finding a way to automatically deliver purchase orders to any vendor who could receive them via e-mail (the remainder was to be faxed using a third-party fax connector). The vendors were brought in on the discussion and had one major concern: The messages had to be verifiable so that no orders were placed without authorization. The executives also had a concern: They did not want authorized people seeing the electronic purchase orders as they crossed the Internet.

The IS team had been considering an upgrade to Exchange Server 5.5 for nearly six months, so this was the perfect opportunity to implement the new Key Management Server to ease the executives' fears about internal message security. The existing servers were upgraded to Exchange 5.5 with Service Pack 2. Rather than attempting to use proprietary message signing and encryption provided natively with Outlook, they choose to use Outlook 98, X.509v3 certificates, and S/MIME messages. This posed some initial problems for both Company CDE as well as for their vendors; clients had to be deployed to support S/MIME. Company CDE had already decided they wanted to use Secure Sockets Layer (SSL) for a secure Web server and for a secure Outlook Web Access server.

They thus began and deployed two Microsoft Certificate Servers, one designated as the root server and one designated a subordinate to the root server. The root server's certificate was then signed by VeriSign so that certificates that the root generated would be trusted by general Internet users. The root server was used to generate standard X.509v3 certificates and SSL certificates.

16

Diagnosing Client Problems

During the initial rollout and deployment of Exchange and Outlook, a huge chunk of time is taken up diagnosing client-related problems. These fall into a couple of categories, the biggest being problems related to client/server communication, which is followed closely by client lockup problems and client interoperability. In this chapter, I shed some light on and offer solutions to common client-related problems, including:

- Basic Exchange/Outlook client communication problems
- The mystery of the slow client startup times
- Client interoperability issues
- Problems concerning local message storage

Basic Problem Solving

When trying to diagnose any problem, the most important task is isolating the cause. Outlook client problems are like any other network problems, and to solve them, you need to eliminate the extraneous issues and focus on communication with Exchange Server.

When the client issues a DNS lookup request, what name is it going to request from the DNS server? It cannot request the IP address for just HILO; the client has to use FQDNs. Therefore, the client takes its own Internet domain name and uses that. You can find the client's Internet domain name on its TCP/IP property page under the DNS tab (see Figure 16.3). Notice the client's domain name is Somorita.Com (which is different than the Windows NT domain name).

Figure 16.3   TCP/IP properties DNS tab

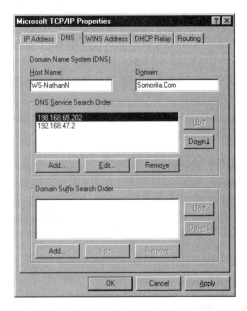

When the client needs to resolve an IP address for a host and only has the host name, it sends a request to the DNS server using the host name with its domain name appended onto the host name. In this case of the HILO server, the actual DNS lookup for the HILO server would be HILO.Somorita.Com.

If there is not a host or CNAME record for the HILO server in the Somorita.Com DNS zone, then the client will timeout and move on to NetBIOS name resolution, but this timeout can take a few minutes.

> **NOTE**   All clients should have a valid TCP/IP domain name, which can be set manually or using DHCP, and the Exchange servers should have an A or CNAME record entered for that domain name. To verify this, check with the person who manages your DNS.

Troubleshooting

PART 6

Exchange@Work: Speeding Up Name Resolution

Company HIJ was experiencing extremely slow client startup times. From the time a user clicked the Outlook icon until the time he could start reading his messages, three minutes had passed!

One resourceful network guru broke out the Windows NT Network Monitor and watched the network when a client connection was initialized. The first thing she saw was a DNS query for EXCHSERV1.PHOENIX.HIJ.COM, then a long timeout before the DNS server returned a message informing the client that it could not resolve that name. (The Exchange server's host name was EXCHSERV1, and the client's TCP/IP domain name was PHOENIX.HIJ.COM.)

There was no host record for a host called EXCHSERV1.PHOENIX.HIJ.COM. The Exchange administrators contacted the DNS administrator for the PHOENIX.HIJ.COM domain and requested that a host record be created for EXCHSERV1. Once the record was created, client startup time was reduced to less than 20 seconds on the test clients.

However, the administrators later found that clients were still having the same delay during startup. Some additional investigation led them to the fact that many clients did not have a TCP/IP domain name configured, and those who did were often inconsistently named. Since IP addresses (and other IP parameters) were issued using DHCP, the domain name was included as one of the DHCP scope options. When this change was implemented, the startup time for all clients was improved.

Though this was a tricky problem, company HIJ managed to find an elegant solution to dramatically speed up their client startup time.

Remote Clients and Host Name Resolution If you have notebook users or remote users whose TCP/IP domain name may have to be different that the one your require for your LAN users, create a HOSTS file that contains the IP addresses of all the Exchange servers. This file would look something like this:

```
192.168.22.202    HILO
192.168.53.144    KONA
```

The only problem with this approach is that if additional servers are installed or the IP addresses change, the HOSTS files have to be updated.

- Messages remaining in the Outbox folder
- Repairing damaged PST and OST files
- Hanging clients

Access to the Mailbox Is Denied

If a user is being denied access to his mailbox, the notifying message is certainly one that has annoyed every Exchange administrator I know:

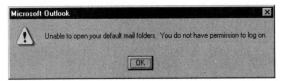

There are several potential reasons for the appearance of this message box.

The Wrong Person Is Logged In

When a user accesses a mailbox, the currently logged in user credentials are passed to the Exchange server by default. If this user account is not the primary Windows NT account assigned to this mailbox or has not been assigned permissions on the Permission tab, the user will be denied access.

NOTE   Often, a message profile for a user is created while another person is logged in to Windows NT or Windows 95/98. When creating the Exchange portion of the messaging profile, make sure that you have the correct mailbox name and Exchange server name configured.

For example, Figure 16.4 shows the Exchange Server service for the message profile. If the person who is currently logged in to the workstation does not have permissions to Giovanni's mailbox, or if the person is not the primary Windows NT account on the mailbox, that person will be denied access.

Let's say the person who is currently logged in to Windows is user DaveyT. Davey has no permissions to Giovanni's mailbox, but the profile was created on Davey's computer, because Giovanni occasionally has to check her mail there. Still, she will be denied access unless she logs Davey out, logs herself in, and switches the Logon Network Security option to None on the Advanced tab of the Exchange Server service property page. After so doing, each time Giovanni chooses her own messaging profile, a username, domain name, and password box will appear requesting her Windows NT credentials.

Figure 16.4   Exchange Server mailbox service properties

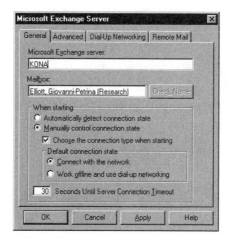

Getting the Mailbox and Server Name Right

A common problem when configuring clients is entering an incorrect mailbox name or server name in the Exchange Server service (see Figure 16.4) when creating the messaging profile. After you enter the mailbox name and the server name, click the Check Name button. If the mailbox and server names are underlined, then you have correctly entered the information. If the mailbox name is incorrect and you don't use the Check Name button to confirm it, you will receive the following dialog box:

When entering the mailbox name, you can enter either the mailbox display name or the alias. I find entering the alias to be easier, but either will work. Once you verify the name by clicking the Check Name button, the display name is shown.

Access Denied? But It Was Just Working!

If a new account is added to the Primary Windows NT Account property on the mailbox and the new user immediately tries to access the account, he will be denied. This is a feature, not a bug. In order to improve performance and reduce the number of times that the information store has to consult with the directory service to get information about a mailbox, the Exchange information store caches directory information about the mailbox (such as what the primary Windows NT account is).

Every 120 minutes, the information store re-reads this information from the directory service. The improves performance, but can result in a user having to wait up to 120 minutes before she can open a mailbox to which you have just given her access.

One solution is to restart the information store, but this is not acceptable since it interrupts all of the currently logged in users. A better solution is to adjust the amount of time that the information store will cache the directory information more frequently. This is done through the Registry:

1. Locate the \HKLM\System\CurrentControlSet\Services\MSExchangeIS\ ParametersSystem\ Registry key.

2. Add a new Registry value called MailboxCacheAgeLimit with a data type of REG_DWORD.

3. In the data field, click the Decimal button, then enter the number of minutes you want the information store to refresh its directory data. (Though some people set this value down in the one- or two-minute range, I think a value of 10 to 15 minutes is more than adequate.)

4. Stop and restart the information store service for these changes to take effect.

Outlook Command-Line Switches

Outlook has some useful command-line switches that you can use when starting Outlook. Some of these switches create new items while others reset or cleanup Outlook settings. Table 16.1 lists some command-line switches that you can use to clean up erroneous information and to optimize Outlook.

Table 16.1   Outlook Command-Line Startup Options

Command-Line Switch	Purpose
/C *item type*	Creates the item type specified. See the Outlook Help file for information about the types of items available.
/select *path name/* folder	Displays the folder name specified on startup.
/folder	Hides the Outlook Bar.
/A *path name/filename*	Creates an item with the specified filename as an attachment.
/CleanFreeBusy	Cleans and regenerates the free/busy information.

Table 16.1   Outlook Command-Line Startup Options *(continued)*

Command-Line Switch	Purpose
/CleanReminders	Cleans and regenerates reminders.
/CleanViews	Restores default views.
/ResetFolders	Restores missing folders for the default delivery location (Calendar, Contacts, Inbox, and so on).
/ResetOutlookBar	Rebuilds the Outlook Bar.
/CleanSchedPlus	Deletes all Schedule+ data.
/Regserver	Rewrites all Outlook-specific Registry keys and reassociates file extensions. This is useful for rebuilding Registry information without reinstallation.
/UnRegServer	Deletes all Registry keys and file associations for Outlook.
/CheckClient	Prompts for the default manager of e-mail, news, and calendar information. Outlook 98/2000 only.
/NoPreview	Turns off the preview pane and removes the option from the View menu. Outlook 98/2000 only.

To use a switch, simply right-click your Outlook icon and add the appropriate switch to the end of the line; for example: C:\Program files\Outlook\outlook.exe **/cleanfreebusy**.

NOTE Remove the switch from the command line of the Outlook icon after you have activated it once. You should not run these switches every time you open Outlook simply because you probably don't need these options each time you start Outlook.

Non-Delivery Reports

A fairly common problem happens when a user sends a message—she receives a non-delivery report (NDR) indicating that the mail did not get to the intended recipient. There are several approaches you can take to resolve this problem.

Figure 16.6   Mail delivery location options

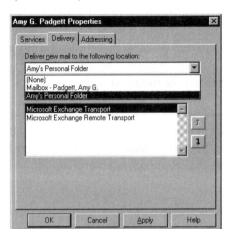

If the PST file is configured locally, and a user has a messaging profile on more than one computer, the PST file should be stored in her home directory on a shared server. If not, the new messages, calendar items, contact items, and so on will only be stored on the copy of the PST file that the user was working on when the message arrived or the item was created.

Mail Stays in the Outbox

If outgoing mail is staying in the Outbox, this is possibly a signal that either the connection to the server has been lost or the Exchange information store service is not running. Try restarting the client to reestablish the connection. Check the server and make sure that the information store service is running. If it is not running, restart it.

Another reason a message might not leave the Outbox is if the user opens the message in the Outbox folder before it was sent. This will change the status of the message, and it will not be sent. You can check a message's status by looking at it's title in the Outbox. If the message title is no longer in *italics*, then the status has been changed . In order to send the message, you must take the following steps to return the message to Send status:

1. Double-click the message to open it in the Outbox.

2. Click the Send button or File ➤ Send. This will return the message to Send status, and it should be sent when it connects with the server.

One final thing to check is to make sure the user is working in online mode. If the user is working in offline mode, she needs to reconnect to the server and synchronize or send their mail.

Problems with PST and OST Files

There is a lot of confusion regarding offline storage folders (OST files) and personal folders (PST files), but their usage and purpose are very different. When a user creates a personal folder, he is creating a PST file somewhere either on his workstation or on a shared network drive. He can then move mail to his personal folder, or even have his mail delivered to it, rather than retaining it in his mailbox on the Exchange server.

The Exchange and Outlook clients can be configured to automatically retrieve mail from the user's mailbox on the Exchange server and place it in a PST file. When you use the archive feature of Outlook, it creates an `archive.pst` file and moves all information to be archived to that file. You can then add that archive file as a personal file in your messaging profile to access archived information, if needed.

An offline storage folder is basically a mirror of the user's mailbox on the Exchange server, which enables the user to download, read, and prepare new mail when she is not connected to the Exchange server. An OST file is not generally an exact mirror, as the user selects the folders in her mailbox to be synchronized and therefore made available to her when she is offline. For example, she may choose to have only the basic folders available and synchronized offline (Calendar, Contacts, Deleted Items, Inbox, Journal, Notes, Outbox, Sent Items and Tasks are the basic default folders). To make offline folder synchronization work, she has to create an offline storage folder and synchronize it while connected to Exchange. The user must connect to the Exchange server and synchronize whenever she wants to send the mail created while offline or to receive new mail when in offline mode.

There can be difficulties with both PST and OST files. Many administrators use PST files as the preferred delivery location for all mail—a practice that I am uncomfortable with. As these files are often located on the user's workstation, they tend not to be backed up. If they are lost, deleted, or corrupted, the information contained within them is simply gone.

Repairing a PST or OST File

Though the PST and OST functions are dramatically different, if the files are damaged, they are repaired with the same utility. The utility is called SCANPST and can be found

> **NOTE** When troubleshooting Exchange Server software problems (especially those related to performance), don't forget the Windows NT Performance Monitor. Performance monitoring and Exchange Server are discussed in detail in Chapter 7.

Troubleshooting Basics

At the first hint of trouble with an Exchange server, there are several basic things to check that will help you isolate the problem. Before you start troubleshooting more complicated scenarios, perform these steps to verify that the basic potential problem areas are not causing the problem(s):

- Check the system and application event logs using the Windows NT Event Viewer for any error (red) or warning (yellow) events that may have been generated recently.

- Check Control Panel ➤ Services to make sure that all Exchange Server services are started. The four core Exchange services (System Attendant, directory service, message transfer agent, and information store) must be started for basic Exchange services to happen.

- Confirm that there is sufficient hard disk space available on all disk drives that Exchange Server is using. I am uncomfortable if any disk drops below 100MB (or 10 percent, whichever is lower) of free disk space.

  - If circular logging is turned off and disk space is low, run a normal or incremental backup as soon as possible. The normal and incremental backup procedures purge the old transaction logs.

  - Check the \exchsrvr\IMCdata\in\archive, \exchsrvr\IMCdata\out\archive, and \exchsrvr\IMCdata\log directories for Internet mail archives and logs that can be purged.

  - When message tracking is enabled, the log files can take up a considerable amount of disk space. Check the \exchsrvr\tracking.log directory to make sure the log files are being purged accordingly.

- Verify network connectivity. Make sure that the server can be pinged and that it can ping others. Also verify that you can connect to the server's shared folders.

- Verify the server can be pinged using the RPC Ping tools. The Exchange servers communicate using the RPC session protocol.

Troubleshooting

PART 6

If you have indeed found that a service is stopped, a database is corrupt, or you are having communications problems, this chapter discusses some solutions to these common problems.

Solving Database Problems

If the Event Viewer's application event log indicates that there is a problem related to the public or private information store databases, the first step you should take is to perform a backup. This will ensure that if things get worse, you can always go back to where you were prior to your troubleshooting. If the server is currently online, attempt an online backup. If the services will not start, perform an offline backup. (These methods are discussed in Chapter 6.)

If the application event log is generating errors that indicate a corrupted database, you are probably going to be better off immediately restoring the database from the last normal tape backup. However, it does not hurt to make sure that the database is actually in good shape before doing so.

TIP   The golden rule of disaster recovery is: "Do no further harm." Prior to beginning any sort of database maintenance or operations, perform a full backup.

Checking the Database

If the database is experiencing problems, the two main ways to check for problems are to run a consistency check and to verify the database integrity.

WARNING   All ESEUTIL and ISINTEG options must be performed with the information store service stopped.

Database Consistency Check

A consistency check lets you know if the database service was shut down properly and if all outstanding transactions have been committed to the database. To check and make sure the database is consistent, use the ESEUTIL command with the /MH option, which dumps the header of the specified database. You must explicitly refer to the filename using the /MH option.

To check the consistency of the private information store database that is on the E drive, type **ESEUTIL /MH E:\exchsrvr\MDBdata\priv.edb >priv.txt**. This redirects the results of the /MH option to the priv.txt file. Examine this file for a line that contains "State:".

If all is well, this line should say "State: Consistent". If it says "State: Inconsistent", then the database is in an inconsistent state.

Restarting the information store service should correct consistency problems. However, sometimes when the services restart, the consistency problems don't always get fixed automatically. It may be possible to fix these problems using ESEUTIL /R /ispriv or ESEUTIL /R.

Running ESEUTIL /P /ispriv or ESEUTIL /P /ispub can also adjust consistency problems, but you should resort to this utility only as a last resort.

Database Integrity Check

The database integrity check examines the low-level database structure and pages. This ensures that the database file is actually in good shape.

To perform an integrity check on the private information store database, at the command prompt, type **ESEUTIL /G /ispriv >priv.txt**. Examine the content of the priv.txt file for errors with the database. If you find errors, Microsoft recommends that you contact their PSS folks for assistance in fixing the problem. The first question they'll ask you is whether or not you have a recent backup, and then they'll ask you to check if circular logging is disabled. Chapter 18 covers database recovery from tape and some of the options you have available.

The problem with attempting to recover a database that has damaged pages is that you don't know the extent of the damage or the number of pages that are unrecoverable. It is likely that you will waste many hours attempting to recover a database file that is unrecoverable, or that you will lose most of the data in it, anyway. It is important to remember this data or these pages equate to "e-mail and attachments." You may not notice the missing e-mail for some time. My point is that sometimes it is better just to revert back to the most recent normal tape backup.

If you do not have a recent backup, then ESEUTIL offers a few options that may help return the database to a usable state. For example, if the private information store database will not start, run the ESEUTIL /P /ispriv >priv.txt command. Examine the priv.txt file for reports of problems that may have been fixed, and then start the information store service.

If this is unsuccessful, then try the ESEUTIL recover option; run the ESEUTIL /R /ispriv >priv.txt command. If this option fails to recover the database, then there is very little that can be done if you do not have a good tape backup. Consult with Microsoft PSS for more information.

Troubleshooting

PART 6

> ***TIP*** Anytime you have to run the ESEUTIL /P or ESEUTIL /R options, you should run the ISINTEG program with the –fix option. Refer to Chapter 6 for usage information.

Table 17.1 lists information store–related event IDs and a recommended course of action for each. I am assuming that the source of the event ID is the MSExchangeIS Private source. If you have one of these events generated from the MSExchangeIS Public source, use the –pub option rather than the –pri option specified in the table.

Table 17.1   Event IDs and Recommended ISINTEG Commands

Event ID	Recommended Command
1025	Isinteg –fix –test search
1087	Isinteg –patch
1089	Isinteg –patch
1131	Isinteg –patch
1186	Isinteg –fix –test acllistref or Isinteg –fix –test aclitemref
1198	Isinteg –fix –test folder
2083	Isinteg –path
7200	Isinteg –fix –test mailbox or Isinteg –fix –test folder
7201	Isinteg –fix –test folder,artidx or Isinteg –fix –test rowcounts,dumpsterref
7202	Isinteg –patch
8500 or 8501 or 8502	Isinteg –fix –test message
8503	Isinteg –fix –test message*
8504 or 8505	Isinteg –fix –test folder*

4. A list of messages that meet the search criteria are displayed. Select the message that you are interested in tracking and click OK.

5. The Message Tracking Center dialog box appears. Click the Track button.

6. The Message Tracking Center will display the route that the message took to get to its destination or wherever it is currently stopped (see Figure 17.1).

Behind the scenes, Exchange Administrator follows the course of this message through all the Exchange servers and connectors that it progressed through. Notice in Figure 17.1 that Jill submitted the message, then the HILO server's MTA delivered it to the KONA server. (There are two entries for MTA transfers, one from the HILO server's perspective and one from the KONA server's perspective.)

Figure 17.1   Message Tracking Center for a message that originated on the HILO server

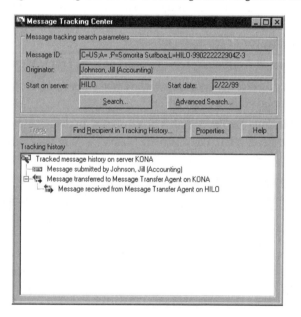

Now, the strange part about the message tracking information seen in Figure 17.1 is that there seems to be no trace of where the message went after it arrived at the KONA MTA. A little investigation reveals that Les Iczkovitz's mailbox is on the KONA server. That MTA routed the message to the correct server, but there should be an entry saying that the message was delivered to Les's mailbox. Checking the KONA server's MTA discloses that Jill's message is still waiting in the private information store queue. Upon further investigation, checking the Exchange services shows that the information store service is stopped.

Most of message tracking you are doing will probably not uncover such a dramatic problem, but it will provide a revealing look at message flow though the Exchange organization.

Exchange@Work: Other Uses for Message Tracking

Company NEM uses the Exchange message tracking feature for a completely different use than finding stalled messages. NEM's Exchange messaging infrastructure includes a number of redundant routes between sites. They use the Exchange server monitor and link monitors to ensure that servers are available and that messages are being delivered in a timely fashion.

One administrator periodically sends messages to administrators located in other sites to confirm that messages are taking their expected path through the Exchange messaging connectors. In at least once instance, this pointed out that a WAN connection had failed and the messages destined for the site connected by the WAN connection were taking an alternate path.

Troubleshooting the MTA and Queues

In a multi-server or multi-site environment, or in a system with connectors, the MTA is a critical component. I like to tell people that "nothing leaves the server without the MTA touching it." When the MTA stops working, the problems may not be noticeable immediately, but the severity of the problem will grow as more and more messages fail to be delivered.

A good approach to solving MTA problems is to be proactive about MTA management. The first step in this process is checking the queues daily to make sure that messages are not stacking up.

However, an even better approach is to implement Exchange server and link monitors. For administrators who want an up-to-the-minute status of each queue, you can create a Windows NT Performance Monitor chart that plots the number of messages queued (Queue Length) for each connection.

NOTE See Chapter 7 for a detailed discussion of monitoring and optimization tools that will help you be proactive when working with the MTA.

As Exchange has matured over the last few years, the MTA software has become more and more robust. Still, regardless of how proactively you manage your MTA, an occasional flaw is going to slip through and trip up your server. I have seen MTA problems caused by large numbers of messages, corrupt messages, and corrupt queue databases.

TIP Remember that the MTA can usually keep up with most WAN links. So if an MTA queue to another site is backing up, check to make sure that the bandwidth to that site is not saturated.

NOTE A known MTA bug in Exchange 5 and 5.5 produces a memory leak that causes a very busy MTA to become unable to create additional connections. This will manifest itself by generating event ID 9156, and the message queues will start backing up. Exchange 5.5 SP2 fixes this problem. You can also stop and start the MTA service to clean things up temporarily.

The Message Transfer Agent Databases

The MTA stores all queued messages in a series of database files in the \exchsrvr\ MTAdata directory. In this directory, you will find a series of message queue database files starting with DB000001.DAT, DB000002.DAT, and incrementing upwards in hexadecimal. These files are used as temporary storage for messages being routed through this MTA, internal indexes, and other MTA message queue items. Collectively, these files are referred to as the *MTA database*. You will see a minimum of about 40 files in this directory, but it is perfectly normal for it to have dozens or even upwards of a hundred .dat files. Some of these files may be only one byte in size; this is a feature, not a bug. After a message that is contained in a DAT file is delivered, the data is cleared out, but the DAT file remains and can thus be reused quickly for future messages. This is a performance enhancement and does not affect day to day operations.

In addition, you will see a series of additional files in the MTA database that end with the extension .TPL and .XV2. These files are templates that represent the different types of encoding information that the MTA may need to generate messages. These files should *not* be deleted.

WARNING   On servers responsible for moving a lot of message traffic (hundreds or thousands of messages an hour), the number of files can grow to be very large. I have seen \MTAdata directories on Exchange bridgehead servers with over 3,000 files. This server was very backlogged due to WAN problems, and this was not a normal occurrence, but the drive that holds the MTA working directory *must* be located on an NTFS partition. MTA performance will suffer dramatically if the \MTAdata directory is on a FAT partition.

The MTACHECK Utility

Microsoft provides a utility with Exchange called MTAcheck.exe, which is located in the \exchsrvr\bin directory. This utility is designed to fix corrupt MTA database files, remove orphaned files no longer need by the MTA, delete any objects it believes are corrupt, and remove system messages from the MTA queues.

If the MTA software detects problems with any of the queues, the MTACHECK utility is run automatically. You can run the MTACHECK utility manually, but the MTA service must be stopped. Table 17.2 lists some command-line options that can be used with the MTACHECK program.

Table 17.2   MTACHECK Command-Line Options

Option	Meaning
/V	Report errors verbosely (in as much detail as possible)
/T logfile.txt	Create a log file called logfile.txt
/RL	Remove any link monitor messages from the queues
/RP	Remove any public folder replication messages from the queues
/RD	Remove directory replication messages from the queues

If a WAN link or MTA has been offline for more than several hours, it is possible that many hundreds of messages could queue up for a particular connection. This includes system messages such as link monitor messages, public folder replication messages, and directory replication messages.

You can clear up the queue so those user-generated messages are processed and the system messages are deleted. To do this, stop the MTA service and type **MTAcheck /RL /RP /RD /V /F logfile.txt**.

NOTE   If there are large number of files (500 or more), the MTACHECK process could take an hour or more.

I use the /RD option sparingly because I don't want to have to remember to force directory replication manually. If you use the /RD option, once you are certain that the MTA has caught up with transferring mail messages, force an update on your directory replication connectors to other sites and ask the administrators in the adjoining sites to do the same.

If the MTACHECK program detects any corrupt message queue data files, it will move them to the \exchsrvr\MTAdata\MTAcheck.out directory. Each file moved into this directory represents a message that was queued. The BackOffice Resource Kit includes a utility called MTAview.exe that allows you to view these files, but the information that it displays is in a pretty raw format.

TIP   The first thing I do when I start experiencing problems with messages backing up in the MTA queues is stop and restart the MTA service. You can safely do this while users are logged in and working.

Fixing a Corrupt MTA Database

I have seen a few instances where the MTACHECK program could not fix a corrupted MTA database. In this case, here is what I recommend you do to solve the problem yourself:

1. Copy all the DAT files in the \exchsrvr\MTAdata directory into a backup directory.
2. Delete all the DAT files from the \exchsrvr\MTAdata directory.
3. Copy all the files from the Exchange Server CD-ROM \Server\Setup\Platform\ bootenv directory to the \exchsrvr\MTAdata directory. This replaces the current MTA database with the original MTA database.
4. Start the MTA.

There is a procedure for making sure that all the files you removed from the MTAdata directory are delivered, but it is very time consuming. Get Microsoft PSS involved if you decide to rescue any messages that have not been delivered.

MTA Communications Problems

The Exchange MTA has to be able to communicate with other servers in order to transfer messages. If you notice that an MTA queue is starting to grow, suspect the possibility of a network communications problem. Chapter 16 discusses a series of procedures for testing client-to-server communications. These procedures also apply to server-to-server communications.

One of the most misunderstood features in Exchange is how Exchange resolves IP addresses based on the host's name. (This is also discussed at length in Chapter 16.) Though not the most elegant solution, I will often put a HOSTS file on each Exchange server with the IP addresses and names of all the other Exchange servers. This guarantees that the Exchange server will be able to quickly resolve the IP addresses of the other Exchange servers.

Directory Service Problems

Directory replication within Exchange is a powerful and complicated feature. It does a great job of keeping all the servers and objects synchronized properly, yet every once in a while there may be a need to perform troubleshooting tasks on your directory database. Some of the more common ones include:

- Running the DS/IS consistency adjuster
- Removing orphaned objects
- Re-homing public folders

> **TIP** Keep in mind that directory replication between sites depends on your messaging connectors delivering updates to the directory. If directory updates are not going through, check your messaging connectors to make sure that messages from the directory service are not queuing up.

The DS/IS Consistency Adjuster

Information about mailboxes such as users' telephone numbers, addresses, e-mail addresses, and permissions are stored in the directory. The same is true for public folder information such as ownership, home site, and permissions. However, the information store must also have this information, such as which users have permissions to access a folder or mailbox. So to share this information, each object in the information store has a corresponding object in the directory database.

In rare situations, this information can become out of synchronization. This problem can be reconciled using the DS/IS (directory service/information store) consistency adjuster. For example, you would run the adjuster after:

- *Permanently* removing a server or site from your organization

- Recovering a server from tape

- Moving a database to a new Exchange server

- Accidentally performing a raw delete on a mailbox object or an object that also exists in the information store

---

NOTE   You do not need to run the DS/IS consistency adjuster on any scheduled (weekly, monthly, yearly) interval.

The DS/IS consistency adjuster process can be started from any Exchange server using Exchange Administrator. To do so, choose *Site Name* ➤ Configuration ➤ Servers, view the server's properties, select the Advanced tab, and click the Consistency Adjuster button. The DS/IS Consistency Adjustment dialog box appears (see Figure 17.2).

Figure 17.2   The DS/IS Consistency Adjustment dialog box

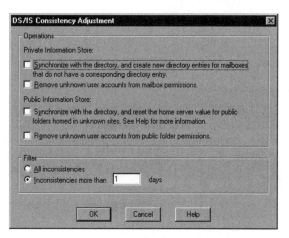

As you can see in Figure 17.2, the DS/IS consistency adjuster corrects four types of inconsistencies:

- It scans the private information store database for mailboxes that do not have a corresponding directory database entry. If a mailbox is found that is not in the directory, a directory entry is created for it. Even though this mailbox is created, it does not have a primary Windows NT account associated with it.

- It reviews mailbox permissions lists for any user accounts that do not exist. If it finds any, it removes them from the list.
- It scans the public folders looking for any that are homed in an unknown site. If it finds any of these public folders, it changes the home server value of these folders to the server that is running the DS/IS consistency adjuster.
- It looks at public folder permissions and removes any mailboxes from the permissions list if the mailbox no longer exists.

Also in the DS/IS adjuster dialog box, you choose to have the tool adjust inconsistencies that are older than a certain number of days or to adjust all inconsistencies immediately.

Danger, Will Robinson, Danger!

The DS/IS consistency adjuster should be run only when deemed *absolutely* necessary. "Why? What is so dangerous about it?" Well, three of the options are not all that problematic (inspecting the private information store, the private information store permissions, and the public information store permissions). The adjustment that causes the problems is synchronizing the public folders with the directory and resetting the public folder home server value.

Though you would not think this need to synchronize is very common, it happens quite frequently. When public folders are re-homed by accident, they have to be put back the way they were manually. I have heard numerous horror stories of how hundreds of public folders had to be re-homed manually (one at a time) after an accidental and unintentional DS/IS consistency adjustment.

Exchange@Work: Avoid Re-Homing Public Folders

JWM Corporation has six regional Exchange sites spread throughout the U.S. Their directory replication architecture consists of their two primary sites, Boston and San Francisco, replicating to one another. Two additional sites in the western part of the U.S. connect to San Francisco for directory replication data, and two additional sites in the eastern U.S. connect to the Boston site. This creates a dual-hub and spoke directory-replication architecture.

Exchange@Work: Avoid Re-Homing Public Folders *(continued)*

During a major leased-line upgrade, JWM's Exchange administrator decided to switch from the X.400 connector to the Exchange site connector, because the site connector is faster and more efficient as long as the bandwidth is sufficient. He also decided to redirect the local directory replication bridgehead servers in the Boston and San Francisco sites.

Then one day, the X.400 and directory replication connectors deleted. Due to a problem in the San Francisco office, the site connector could not be reconfigured. Everyone agreed that messaging could wait until the next morning to resume, so they decided to fix the problem the next morning.

The administrator in Boston arrived early the next morning and mistakenly decided that since the directory replication connector had been deleted, that it would be a good time to run the DS/IS consistency adjuster. Though he did not fully understand the implications of this selection, he configured the DS/IS consistency adjuster to re-home any public folders that were located in an unknown site. Unfortunately, all the public folders in the directory that were located in the three western U.S. sites were then re-homed to the server in Boston!

Once directory replication was re-established later that day, the damage became evident. The western U.S. public folders were no longer homed in their respective sites and could not be administered anywhere but from the Boston site.

Though the folders were organized by site, the western sites had nearly 80 folders. Each of these folders had to be re-homed back to its original server using the PFADMIN utility. The home folders for many of the servers was not known, so a recovery server had to be built in order to determine this.

The entire process took nearly two days to complete. This entire problem could have been avoided if the administrators all had a better understanding of the DS/IS consistency adjustment process.

Re-homing Public Folders

Chapter 4 outlined a procedure to assign a new home to a public folder. This procedure, of course, requires that you assign the new home in the correct order.

If a public folder inadvertently becomes homed in a site that it does not belong in (such as an accidental DS/IS consistency adjustment), you can re-home it. This procedure is not as simple as pointing and clicking to assign the home server back the way it was before someone accidentally ran the DS/IS consistency adjuster. You are going to need some information, some software, and some preparation, including:

- The original home server name for any public folder that you wish to re-home. If you don't have this information, you will have to restore the public information store from a backup. This should be a copy of the original server prior to the accidental DS/IS consistency adjustment on a recovery server, not in the production system. (Chapter 18 reviews restoring the information store databases to a recovery server.) Once the database is restored, you can create a report of the original public folder hierarchy. I recommend you use the PFINFO utility from the BackOffice Resource Kit to generate a report on all the public folder configurations.

- The PFADMIN utility from the BackOffice Resource Kit. One of the many things this utility does is re-home public folders. (Make sure you have the latest version of this software.)

- A user account that has the Service Account Admin role on both the source server (the server that the folder is now homed on) and the destination server (the server to which you want to re-home the folder, or the original server).

- Create a mailbox whose primary Windows NT account is the one that has service account role on the two servers in this home/re-homing project.

- Create a messaging profile (avoid spaces in the profile name) for the mailbox you just created. This profile should be created on the server on which you are going to run the PFADMIN tool. (Yes, this tool should be run from the Exchange server.)

- Ensure that directory replication is working between all sites in the organization before attempting to fix this problem (remember, that was partly what broke it in the first place).

NOTE If the source server and the destination server are not available on the same intranetwork (i.e. the remote site is accessible only through Dynamic RAS), PFADMIN will not work for re-homing folders. You must move all the public folder data into a PST file, delete the public folder, allow time for the data to replicate back to the original site, re-create the public folder, and copy the data back into the folder.

Once you are set up to re-home these public folders, here is the procedure you need to follow:

1. On the source server (the current home of the public folders that need to be re-homed), display the instances of public folders listed on that server. To do so, choose *Site Name* ➤ Configuration ➤ Servers ➤ *Server Name*, view the public information store properties, and select the Instances tab.

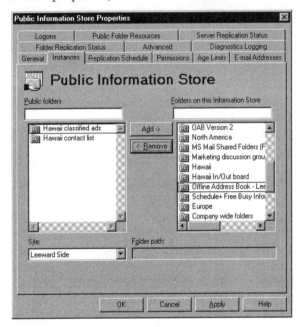

2. Make sure that the folders you are about to move are listed in the Folders On This Information Store list. If they're not, locate the folder name in the Public Folders list on the left-hand side of the screen and click Add.

3. For each public folder you want to re-home, type **pfadmin /e5** *Profile_Name* **rehome** *Folder_Name Site_Name\Server_Name* **/NO** at the command prompt.

4. When all public folders have been re-homed, run the DS/IS consistency adjustment on each server that has had a public folder re-homed to it. Select the Synchronize With Directory And Reset The Home Server Value For Public Folders Homed In Unknown Sites check box.

Run the DS/IS consistency adjuster only when you are sure that all directory replication connectors are working properly and that the replicated data is up-to-date.

Here is an example using PFADMIN to re-home public folders. The folders are called Hawaii Folders, and they are being re-homed to server HNLEX001 in the PACIFIC site.

```
pfadmin /e5 ServiceProfile rehome "Hawaii Folders" PACIFIC\HNLEX001 /YES
```

In this command, the /YES option tells PFADMIN to re-home the Hawaii Folders folder and *all* subfolders. The /e5 option tells PFADMIN to send the results to a log file, but instead you can specify a /e3 option, which will send the results to the application event log.

Orphaned Objects in the Directory

Each copy of the Exchange directory database has copies of all objects found in all sites in the organization. However, only objects created in a site can be edited or deleted by an administrator of that site. An object that originated in one site is set to read-only when it is replicated to other sites. This is normally not a major issue; if you need to edit an object, you must connect to a server in that object's home site.

However, this becomes a major issue when an object is deleted in its home site, but the replication message instructing the other sites to delete the object is not received (possibly because MTACHECK /RD was run). The result is an *orphaned object* in the other sites; this object cannot be deleted, because the home site had the only read-write copy.

Cleaning up orphaned objects is a major pain in the neck. There are several methods for doing so (see KB articles Q183739 and Q179573), but the easiest and most reliable way is to display the raw properties of the object and locate the Obj-Dist-Name using Exchange Administrator's raw mode feature (admin /R), as shown in Figure 17.3. The Obj-Version number below Obj-Dist-Name needs to be noted as well.

The object in Figure 17.3 is an orphaned mailbox object, and its Obj-Dist-Name attribute is /o=Somorita Surfboards/ou=Leeward Side/cn=Recipients/cn=REsmond. To delete this orphaned object, the administrator in the Leeward Side site needs to recreate this mailbox (in the Leeward Side site) so that its Obj-Dist-Name is exactly the same. Then, she needs to modify the object several times so that its Obj-Version number will be higher than that of the orphaned object. She then needs to give the newly created object time to replicate to all sites.

Figure 17.3   The Obj-Dist-Name as seen from Exchange Administrator's raw mode

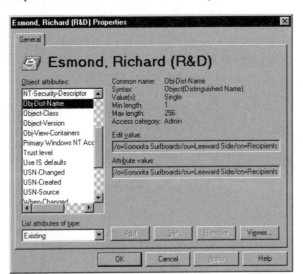

Once the object replicated to all sites, the Leeward Side site administrator can delete the object. As long as directory replication is working properly, the message to delete the mailbox object will be replicated to all sites.

Avoiding Orphaned Objects

Well, I fibbed a little bit when I said that a message would be replicated to all sites instructing them to *delete* the object. The object is not really deleted immediately, but that is a simple way to think about it. Rather than risk a visit by Phil, Prince of Insufficient Light, I will give you the real scoop.

Each object in the directory has a property commonly called a *tombstone* (the raw mode attribute name is Is-Deleted). If you delete an object, the tombstone is set, and that change is replicated to all copies of the directory. An item with a set tombstone is kept in the directory (you just can't see it anymore) for 30 days by default. This is configured at the site level on the General tab of the DS Site Configuration object (see Figure 17.4).

Every 12 hours, a process runs on each server's directory service that is called *garbage collection* (also configured on the DS Site Configuration object). Any objects whose tombstones are older than 30 days are removed from that copy of the directory database.

Figure 17.4   DS Site Configuration object's General tab.

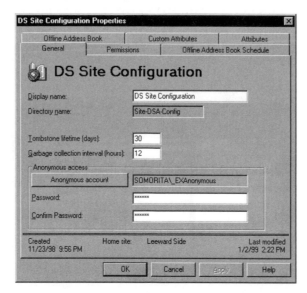

So how do you avoid those little orphaned objects? Here are two suggestions to keep you orphaned-object free:

- Don't use the MTACHECK /RD to remove directory replication messages.
- Do not adjust the tombstone lifetime value seen in Figure 17.4; 30 days is more than sufficient.

Common IMS Problems

Though I generally experience very little trouble with the Internet Mail Service on a regular basis, I do have some troubleshooting tips that prove useful when the IMS is causing problems. These include:

- Monitoring for errors
- Confirming that name resolution is working properly
- Cleaning up corrupt files

Monitoring for Errors

Your first line of defense against IMS errors is the Windows NT Event Viewer. To monitor errors generated by the IMS, you first need to turn on diagnostic logging. To do so,

DWORD. In the data field, enter a value of 100 and make sure that the Hex radio button is selected. When you enter the data, it should appear as 0x100.

In the same Registry key, locate the `ConsoleStatFrequency` value. This controls how often data is updated to the console screen. The default is 20 (decimal) seconds (0x14, in hexadecimal), but you can adjust this to suit your own needs.

Stop the IMS and open a command prompt. Change to the IMS software directory, usually located in `\exchsrvr\connect\msexcimc\bin`. From the command prompt, type **msexcimc –console** and press Enter. The IMS is now in console mode, and you will see a screen similar to this.

Close this window and start the IMS normally.

Confirming Name Resolution

In order to deliver SMTP messages to the correct host, the IMS depends on being able to resolve mail exchange records and host names. The Exchange server first does a special type of DNS query looking for a mail exchanger (MX) record for the domain to which it is about to send mail. There is a utility on the Exchange Server CD-ROM called RESTEST that will show you the results of a MX query. (This utility is in the CD's `\Server\Support\Utils` directory.) If there is no MX record, the Exchange server then resorts to standard host name resolution and assumes that the name it is querying is a host name instead.

For example, assume the IMS is attempting to deliver a message to `JonasG@microsoft .com`. The IMS will do a MX query to the DNS for all MX records at `microsoft.com`; if there is more than one host, the hosts will be listed in their order of preference. If the SMTP host with the lowest preference value is not available, the IMS will attempt to deliver to the SMTP server with the next highest preference value. You can use the RESTEST utility to see this list of MX records. Here is a sample querying microsoft.com:

```
D:\Temp>restest microsoft.com.
Microsoft (R) Name Resolution Test Utility (5.5.1960.3)
Copyright (C) Microsoft Corp 1986-1997. All rights reserved
host[0] = '131.107.3.124'
host[1] = '131.107.3.122'
host[2] = '131.107.3.125'
host[3] = '131.107.3.123'
host[4] = '131.107.3.121'
D:\Temp>
```

Similar results could be obtained by typing **NSLOOKUP –Q=MX MICROSOFT.COM.**

But suppose there is not a MX record. For example, the IMS is attempting to deliver a message to Mike@mail.backman.com. The IMS will first assume that mail.backman.com is a domain name and will generate a query for any hosts that will accept messages for mail.backman.com. If that query fails, the IMS will resort to standard host name resolution and see if there is an address record or alias (CNAME) for Mail.Backman.com. When creating MX records, don't use an IP address in the MX record; use an A or CNAME record for the Exchange IMS.

Cleaning Up Corrupt Files

Chapter 10 has some information on cleaning up corrupt files once they are stored in the IMS mailbox on the information store. However, corrupt files can also be stored in the IMS working directories, and these files can cause the IMS to fail or to not start.

If this occurs and the IMS generates an event ID 4037, it is possible that there is a corrupt message in either the \exchsrvr\IMCdata\in or the \exchsrvr\IMCdata\out directory. To correct this problem, follow these steps:

1. Move all the files in the exchsrvr\IMCdata\in directory to a backup directory.
2. Delete the exchsrvr\IMCdata\queue.dat file.
3. Start the IMS and test it. If it stays on, it is working normally. If the IMS stops again, repeat the process for the exchsrvr\IMCdata\out directory.

NOTE If the IMS does not work after cleaning out both the IN and OUT directories, the corrupt message is probably in the IMS mailbox in the information store. There is a procedure in Chapter 10 that covers how to open the IMS mailbox and remove bad messages from it.

If the above procedure works and you were able to reliably restart the IMS, you can still deliver the messages that you moved to the backup directory. Here is how to recover those messages:

1. Stop the IMS and delete the `exchsrvr\IMCdata\queue.dat` file.

2. Copy about half of the messages you moved to the backup directory back in to the \in (or the \out directory).

3. Start the IMS and see if the messages are delivered. If the IMS stops again, you know that the bad message is in the list of messages that are currently waiting in the queue. Though slightly time consuming, you can use the process of elimination to figure out which message is causing the problem.

TIP   If the IMS is locked up, you may be able to find out which message caused the lockup. Before killing the IMS service, attempt to copy all the messages out of the \in or \out directories. If you get a "file in use" message, chances are good that it's the message file that caused the problem.

Other Internet Mail Service Problems

Here are some problems that I commonly see when working with the IMS, as well as some tips for troubleshooting them.

- If the TCP/IP host name and domain name are missing, the IMS will not start. You must make sure these fields have valid values. To do so, go to Control Panel ➢ Network, select the Protocols tab, click TCP/IP Properties, and select the DNS tab. Confirm that the Host Name and Domain Name fields are correct.

- When the IMS starts, it checks to make sure that it can resolve IP addresses for hosts specified as relay hosts. If any of these hosts are not resolvable , the IMS will not start. This can be checked on the IMS Connections tab and the Specify E-Mail By Domain selection under the Forward All Messages To Host box. You may need to add the relay host to the hosts file or use and IP address. It is important to make sure the that relay hosts are specified properly.

- The IMS will shut down if disk space becomes too low (less than 15MB available). Check the \log, \in, and \out\archive directories for files that can be deleted.

- If the IMS becomes seriously backlogged with hundreds or thousands of messages to deliver, you can set the Transfer Mode on the IMS Connections tab to None (Flush Queues). The IMS will not accept any new inbound or outbound messages; this will allow time for it to deliver all the messages that have stacked up in the queues.

- You can use the IMCSAVE utility from the BackOffice Resource Kit to save the configuration of the IMS or to restore it to another machine.

NOTE   See Chapter 10 for more information about advanced features of the Internet Mail Service.

Troubleshooting Internet Protocols

If you have IMAP4, NNTP, POP3, or LDAP, here are some troubleshooting tips and techniques that may prove helpful. While basic troubleshooting for these protocols is the same as for the Outlook client (see Chapter 16), there are some additional elements that come into play.

When troubleshooting an Internet protocol, first make sure the protocol is enabled. It can be enabled at the site level, at the server level, or per mailbox. If the protocol is enabled at the site level but disabled either at the server or at the mailbox, then the user will not be able to use it. Also, if the protocol is disabled at the server level but enabled at the site and at the mailbox, the protocol is still disabled.

Telnet Troubleshooting

Many people don't realize that if you need to check and make sure that a protocol is working, you can use the Telnet utility to converse with the respective information store. To do so, you must specify the correct port number for the Internet application you are using. Do this either on the command line after the server name or in the Port field in the Connect box of the Windows Telnet program.

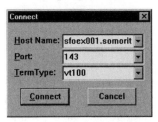

To check IMAP4, type **Telnet** *Server_Name* **143** and press Enter. If the IMAP4 is enabled and responding, you should receive a message similar to this:

```
* OK Microsoft Exchange IMAP4rev1 server version 5.5.2448.8
(sfoex001.somorita.com) ready
```

To check NNTP, type **Telnet** *Server_Name* 119 and press Enter. You should see a response that looks similar to this:

```
200 Microsoft Exchange Internet News Service Version 5.5.2448.8
(posting allowed)
```

To check POP3, type **Telnet** *Server_Name* 110 and press Enter. You should see a response similar to:

```
+OK Microsoft Exchange POP3 server version 5.5.2448.8 ready
```

If you know the actual protocol commands, you can read messages and post news articles. The protocol commands are documented in the RFC for each Internet protocol; see Appendix B for information on where to find this information.

NOTE You cannot Telnet to the LDAP port (389) and discern any useful information.

Internet Protocol Logging

The IMAP4, NNTP, and POP3 Internet protocol logs can enhance the information you get through diagnostics by logging anywhere from basic information as the connection records, to protocol command conversations, and possibly including actual message data. They give you the ability to log detailed information and to create protocol logs similar to the SMTP protocol logging option. You can enable diagnostics logging for the IMAP4, NNTP, and POP3 protocols at the server level; choose *Site Name* ➤ Configuration ➤ Servers, view the server's properties, and select the Diagnostics Logging tab (see Figure 17.5). Under the Services list, open MSExchangeIS and Internet Protocols to reveal the IMAP4, NNTP, and POP3 categories.

Diagnostic logging for LDAP is enabled on the same screen as that in Figure 17.5, but under the MSExchangeDS service. Enable the category called LDAP Interface for LDAP diagnostics logging.

NOTE The protocol logs are created through the Registry; all the Registry keys discussed in the protocol logging section are found in the \HKLM\System\ CurrentControlSet\Services Registry key.

Figure 17.5   IP logging categories for IMAP4

Further, I recommend creating a directory to hold all the log files. This way the log files are not created in the default directory.

> **NOTE**   The protocol logs are continuously locked open. To delete them, set the logging level to 0. The next time the information store restarts, the file will no longer be locked, and you can delete it.

IMAP4 Protocol Logging

To enable IMAP4 protocol logging, locate the \MSExchangeIS\ParametersSystem Registry subkey. Then locate the IMAP4 Protocol Logging Level Registry value and set the data to 0 for no logging, 1 for minimum logging, or 5 for maximum logging (including message data). Next, locate the Registry value IMAP4 Protocol Log Path and change the data to C:\Logs. Stop and restart the information store service for these changes to take effect.

NNTP Protocol Logging

To enable NNTP protocol logging, locate the \MSExchangeIS\ParametersSystem Registry subkey. Then locate the NNTP Protocol Logging Level Registry value and set the data to 0 for no logging, 1 for minimum logging, or 5 for maximum logging (including message data). Next, locate the Registry value NNTP Protocol Log Path and change the

• If the user is being prompted for a user ID and password by his Web browser, make sure that he enters his user account name as *Domain\Username*, such as SOMORITA\GiovanniR.

NOTE If you have access to the OWA server (with Exchange 5.5 SP1 or later), Microsoft has included a Web page with common problems and their solutions. You can get to this Web page by entering this URL: *OWA_Server_Name*\Exchange\ `tshoot.asp`.

For Further Information...

To find out more information about some of the topics discussed in this chapter, check out the following resources:

• Knowledge Base article Q153188 has detailed information about the MTA diagnostics logging options.

• *The MTA Troubleshooting Guide* by Paul Bonrud is available on Microsoft TechNet. This guide contains a lot of detail on troubleshooting MTA-related problems.

• Microsoft has published *The Troubleshooting Guide: Microsoft Exchange Internet Protocols* by Peter Baggiolini, which can be found on TechNet and in the online Knowledge Base.

• When working with Outlook Web Access, an excellent resource for troubleshooting is the *Troubleshooting Guide for Outlook Web Access*, which is available on TechNet and the Knowledge Base.

18

Disaster Recovery

"Anything that can go wrong will go wrong." —*Murphy's Law*

"Any event you are completely prepared for will probably never happen."
—*McBee's Axiom to Murphy's Law*

The day that you have been dreading has finally come. The information store is reporting database errors and will not start. Windows NT generates a blue screen upon startup. Little smoke spirals are coming out of your server, a disk drive has failed and there is no redundant disk, you have just accidentally deleted the CEO's mailbox…

Some of you reading this book will never experience a disk failure or any other sort of catastrophic event that will cause your Exchange server to be unavailable. However, I'm betting that an equal number of you will have a few war stories over the next couple of years that you'll share when you gather around the water cooler with the other Exchange administrators.

It seems the more prepared I become for some catastrophe, the less likely it is that the catastrophe will occur. Thus Chapters 6 and 7 review some of the important operational and maintenance items that you should perform and list some tips from other Exchange administrators on how best to prevent disaster and keep your system running. Additionally,

As your software versions are upgraded and service packs are applied, make sure that you update your disaster recovery kit.

TIP Once you have created the disaster recovery kit, don't "loan out" pieces of it such as CD-ROMs and floppy disks. Loaned items tend to disappear—and you won't realize that an item's gone until you need it.

Practice Makes Perfect

Throughout this book I have been referring to your cold standby server; this is the extra piece of hardware that is configured identically to your other Exchange servers with respect to disk space, disk controllers, and RAM. I am also a strong advocate of performing periodic Exchange Server restores to your standby server.

Every few months, randomly pick one of your servers and pretend that it has had a catastrophic failure and conduct a fire drill.

Start your stopwatch.

Separate the standby server onto an isolated network and begin the restoration process. You will probably have to build the Windows NT server and apply all the necessary service packs. Reinstall the Exchange Server software, service packs, and restore the Exchange databases. Reconfigure the Exchange connectors that this server supported (you probably won't be able to confirm that the connectors are working since this server is on an isolated segment). Do anything else necessary to prepare the server to allow users to log back in.

Stop your stopwatch.

How long did it take? Granted a lot of the time was probably spent watching software installation screens or tape restore progress indicators. Yet the time that it took is important, because it can be used in Service Level Agreements and, in the case of a real emergency, it can be used to inform your users of approximately how long it will take to restore the system to a usable state. (I usually give myself an additional 30 to 50 percent on my test restoration times, just for some slack.)

Evaluate your own performance during the test restoration. Was there anything that you could have done to make the restoration go faster? (Yes, we would all like faster hardware and tape drives.) Did you have all the software and documentation you needed nearby?

NOTE   Restoration of an Exchange server is a complex process. It is not something that you want to try for the first time while 500 users are waiting. It is absolutely critical that you become familiar with the backup and restore procedures *before* you need to know them. I cannot emphasize enough the importance of thoroughly understanding the restoration process.

Exchange@Work: Practicing Disaster Recovery and Verifying Database Integrity

The management at GHI Corporation expects the messaging system to be available 24 hours per day. The GHI Exchange administrator is responsible for two Exchange servers that support almost 850 mailboxes. She has one maintenance window of six hours per month that she uses to restart the servers, apply service packs, and perform a bimonthly offline backup. Her Exchange servers have circular logging disabled, and she performs a normal backup at 11:00 P.M. each night followed by two differential backups, one at 10:30 A.M. and one at 3:00 P.M. Each server's normal backup takes approximately three hours, and the differential backups take an average of about 10 minutes.

During the design phase of her Exchange organization, the administrator was able to convince her superiors to purchase a third server identical to her two production servers. She uses this server as a cold standby and for practicing disaster recovery. Every three months, she picks one of the two servers and builds a recovery server on an isolated network. She then restores the server with the normal backup tape from the evening before and the most recent differential tape. Her time to restore the larger of her two servers (approximately 500 mailboxes and about 20GB of data) is just under four hours.

When the restoration process is finished and she is comfortable with the fact that the users could go back to work if necessary, she takes this recovery a step further. The only way to completely verify that a database is free of corruption is to perform an offline defragmentation. So on the *recovery* server, the administrator stops the directory and information store services and runs ESEUTIL /D with the /ispriv, /ispub, and /DS options to make sure that each of the three databases are truly free of corruption. This is merely done for the sake of testing and quality assurance; these compacted databases are never put back into production.

Exchange@Work: Practicing Disaster Recovery and Verifying Database Integrity *(continued)*

Though this process is time consuming, GHI Corp's administrator is assured that the Exchange databases are corruption free, and she has an excellent understanding of the recovery process.

Disaster Recovery Tips

No amount of tips and hints is going to make your disaster recovery a positive and enlightening experience. Each time you have to recover from some type of system failure, you are going to learn a lot more. However, some things that may prove helpful in making the disaster recovery go a little smoother include:

- Keep your user community informed of how long you expect to be offline. You will be surprised how cooperative they can be if you just give them a straightforward, honest answer.

- Keep your boss and the help desk appraised of your progress. Your boss is your first line of defense against management pressures, and the help desk is your first line of defense against angry end users. If there are major problems, your boss and the help desk are going to find out anyway; it is best if you let them know rather than waiting until they ask. If you *are* the help desk, change your outgoing message on your voicemail to give your users an update to the current situation.

- If you are trying to solve a database corruption problem, know when to quit and do a restore from tape. Restoring from tape is the preferred way to recover from database failures. The database repair tools (ESEUTIL and ISINTEG) should be considered viable options only if you have no recent backup.

- Ask for at least two separate phones in your computer room. One of these should have a hands-free headset, which should either be cordless or have enough cord so that you can access the consoles of all your servers.

- Prior to starting a disaster recovery, re-read the relevant parts of the MS Disaster Recovery document.

Disaster Recovery Scenarios

This section reviews some common disaster recovery scenarios that may cause you to lose some sleep. Some of these scenarios are easier to recover from than others, and the amount of data that you will lose will vary from situation to situation.

> **NOTE** For these scenarios, there are many types of Exchange-aware tape backup and restore software packages you can use. Further, the actual screens and restore options may be significantly different for your software. Consult your software documentation.

Building a Recovery Server

Many sites I work on have an identical cold standby server sitting beside their production systems. If the problem is hardware-related, the Exchange administrator can simply move the disk drives from the failed system to the cold standby system and restart. However, if you do not have an identical system, the first step toward restoring an Exchange server is getting the recovery server built.

> **TIP** If you have an identically configured standby server and a production server fails (memory, CPU, power supply, disk controllers), the first thing the IS team does is move the drive arrays over to the cold standby system and attempt to bring the disks back up on new hardware.

Most of the skills required are going to be drawn from the Windows NT side of your brain rather than the Exchange side. There are two types of rebuilds, and you should base your choice on the result you want to achieve. Are you attempting to recover a mailbox or test your disaster recovery procedures? Or are you attempting to restore your Windows NT system after a complete Windows NT server failure?

Building an NT System for Mailbox Recovery and Disaster Recovery Testing

When you restore Exchange Server databases to new server hardware, the Exchange server will need access to the original site services account. If the server you are restoring to is used only for recovering messages from the public and private information stores, or if it is used just for test restores (fire drills), the server name does not need to be the same as the original Exchange server. (This is not true if you are trying to restoring the server.)

However, this server does need access to the original Windows NT domain database. I know a few administrators who use a Windows NT member server that is a member of the original Windows NT domain as their recovery server, but I am uncomfortable doing disaster recovery near the production system.

For this reason, when I install the recovery Windows NT system, I make it a Backup Domain Controller (BDC) as part of the original domain first. Then, once the server is fully installed and the domain database has synchronized, I move the server to an isolated network and promote it to be a Primary Domain Controller (PDC).

An alternative to this approach is to run the RDISK /S utility on the original PDC and store a backup of the SAM database on the Emergency Repair Disk (that is what the /S option of RDISK does). You then can install your recovery server in an isolated environment. Once installed and the appropriate service packs are installed, you can use the Windows NT Setup boot disks to perform an repair option on the recovery server. Insert the Emergency Repair Disk and instruct the repair process to inspect the Registry and restore only the SAM from the ERD. This will make this machine a PDC in the original domain (don't put the recovery server on the production network).

Building an NT System to Restore the Original Server

Some circumstances, such as a meltdown of the entire Windows NT system, may require that you completely rebuild the original Windows NT server. For example, the system disk fails, Windows NT has to be completely rebuilt as it once was. The server name must be the same, and it must be a member of the same domain. (See Chapter 4 for additional information about rebuilding or reinstalling a server.)

This type of situation emphasizes the need for complete and total documentation of not only Exchange Server, but also the underlying Windows NT platform.

Failure of an Exchange Database Disk Drive or Database File

Chapters 2 and 6 discussed the importance of placing the Exchange transaction logs on a physical disk separate from the disk that contains the Exchange database. Though server's performance will be improved quite a bit, the main reason for this is for disaster recovery (provided you have disabled the server's circular logging feature). If you have not disabled the circular logging feature, then you will not have the old transaction log files necessary to rebuild a database from the last full backup.

If circular logging is disabled, the transaction log files are retained until after a normal (full) or incremental online backup is performed. For example, if it is Wednesday and you have not performed a normal or incremental backup since Sunday night, the log file disk will still have all the transactions since Sunday night. Though these transactions have all been committed to the database, they are kept until the next backup.

Recovery with Circular Logging Disabled

Retaining the log files will help with recovery in two situations: if the disk that contains the Exchange database files fails, or if an Exchange database becomes corrupt. Recovery from the latter situation is quite simple. (If the disk has failed, of course, you will have to replace the failed disk drive.) In this example, I am assuming that the Exchange software and transaction log files are on disks that did not fail. In addition, the logs on the disk have been accumulating since the last normal backup, hence circular logging is turned off.

1. The first law of data recovery is to do no further harm. Since the Exchange Server services are probably going to be offline, you should make a full offline backup, which will include the Exchange Server software and the Exchange server transaction log files. While you may not need this, mistakes can be made during restoration that could cause the recent log files to be purged and replaced with the older log files from the tape.

2. Once the full offline backup is performed, start the Exchange Server System Attendant service. This is required for the backup software to be able to contact and restore data to the Exchange server.

3. Restore the databases from the last normal backup tape, but make sure that you tell the restore software *NOT* to erase existing files. If it does, there go your recent log files.

4. Start the directory service and information store services.

5. Watch the Windows NT Event Viewer's application log for event ID 71 from the source ESE97. This event indicates that a transaction log has been committed to the database. This process can take between three and five minutes per transaction log, and it is not uncommon for a busy server to have several hundred transaction logs.

6. Connect to the Exchange server as a user and verify that the mail data has been restored. (At this point, you might want to use the Logon Only As Registry key to prevent your users from logging in until you have completed your testing. This will keep your users from logging back in before you are ready. See Appendix C or Chapter 4 for additional information about this key.)

7. Confirm that the connectors that were previously installed on the server are still installed and configured. Send at least one message that will use each connector on the server, and have someone on the other side of the connector send a message back to you.

8. Let the users log back on to the system. (If you added the Logon Only As Registry key, don't forget to delete it and restart the information store service.)

The data that the users see should be very close to the most recent data that was saved before the disk or database failure.

What If Circular Logging Is Enabled?

If circular logging is still enabled for the server that has lost its databases, the log files that are on the system will be of no use, because they will not contain all the transactions that

9. The log file numbering will have changed, so immediately run a normal backup. The old backups will not be usable with the current transaction logs.

10. The server is now ready to use again. (If you added the Logon Only As Registry key, don't forget to delete it and restart the information store service.)

What If the Information Store Does Not Restart After a Restore?

When the information store restore operation starts, a new Registry key is created called \HKLM\System\CurrentControlSet\Services\MSExchangeIS\RestoreInProgress. When the restore is finished, this key should be deleted. However, I have seen instances where this was not the case. After the restore is complete and you attempt to restart the information store, you may see errors such as these two:

```
5000 Unable to initialize the Microsoft Exchange Information Store
service. Error 0xc8000713
```

```
1081 Unable to recover the database because error 0xc8000713 occurred
after a restore operation.
```

If you see either of these two errors, it is possible that that the above Registry key has not been automatically deleted. Start the Registry Editor and delete the RestoreInProgress key, and then try to restart the information store service.

Catastrophic Server Failure

At some point, you may experience a complete systems failure. This is usually a result of the system disk failing, which renders the Windows NT operating system unable to start. In this case, you will have to completely rebuild Windows NT as described earlier.

Once you have reinstalled Windows NT, you need to install Exchange Server, and any service packs and hot fixes that you were previously running. Don't upgrade the recovery server to a later version of a service pack until the recovery is completed.

If you are restoring the server, here is a quick (but by no means exhaustive) list of items to make sure have been completed prior to continuing with the Exchange portion of the installation:

- Windows NT Server, any service packs, the option pack (if necessary), and hot fixes have all been installed as they were prior to the failure.
- The Windows NT server has the same server name, protocols, IP addresses, and network services installed.
- The disk configuration is sufficient to reinstall the Exchange data.
- If the tape backup software is locally installed on the Exchange server, reinstall the tape backup software and re-catalog the most recent Exchange server backup tapes.

Once you are sure that the Windows NT server is ready, the next step is to get the Exchange software installed and ready for the database restoration.

1. Set up the Exchange Server with the SETUP /R command. This will install the Exchange software, but it neither creates the information store databases nor starts the services. When prompted, choose to create a new site. Do not join an existing site. Enter the exact organization name, site name, site services account, and site services account password that was used with the original server. Remember to use the exact same upper- and lowercase letters when creating the organization and site names.

2. If the original server had a service pack installed on it, install the service pack with the UPDATE /R command.

3. Run the Exchange Performance Optimizer program and make sure the parameters, working directories, database and log file location files are set correctly. Also make sure you document the location of the working directory, database, and log files locations (and make sure the locations have sufficient disk space to accommodate the data that is about to be restored).

4. If circular logging was disabled on the original server, it must be disabled on the recovery server. Make sure that this is set correctly.

The Exchange server is now ready to have the databases restored. The exact procedures will vary for different tape backup systems. Depending on how you perform Exchange server backups, there are two possible restoration options: online restores and offline restores.

> **NOTE** If you receive software through the Microsoft Select program, the Exchange Server 5.5 Standard Edition Setup program is srvmin.exe, and the Enterprise Edition Setup program is srvmax.exe instead of setup.exe.

Online Exchange Restoration

If the original Exchange server was backed up using an online backup, you'll perform an online Exchange restoration. Online backups are performed while the Exchange server is in production using Exchange Server–aware backup software. To restore Exchange data using the online Exchange agents for your backup software:

1. Make sure that the Exchange System Attendant service is started.

2. Locate the most recent normal backup and insert it into the tape drive.

3. Direct the tape backup software to restore the directory and information store databases to the Exchange server that you are rebuilding.

Look Closely and Keep an Open Mind!

24seven CASE STUDY

BAM Corporation supports nearly 5,500 users across five Exchange servers running Exchange 5 SP1. During a daily scan of the Windows NT event logs, the Exchange operator noticed event IDs 2197 and 2191 appearing in the application event log of one of the servers. The MTA was also stopped on that server. The operator could not get the MTA to restart, so the incident was immediately escalated to the Exchange administrator.

The Exchange administrator's first action was to attempt to restart the MTA herself. Upon confirming the messages in the event log, she checked the Microsoft Knowledge Base and found that these errors were known issues with Exchange 5 SP1, and that SP2 fixes the problem. She applied SP2, and everyone thought that the problem had been resolved.

However, the following morning, the event logs indicated an −1811 error stating that the backup had failed. At the end of the day, the server was shut down, an offline backup was performed, the log files were moved to a backup directory, and the PAT file was deleted (that was left over from the backup that failed). The Exchange services were restarted, and everything looked like it was going to work properly. An online backup was started but failed with the same error message.

The Exchange server was shut down again, and another offline backup was run. The logs were removed, and the administrator tried to run the EDBUTIL /MH priv.edb command (remember, this is Exchange 5

which uses EDBUTIL rather than ESEUTIL) to verify that the database was in a consistent state. EDBUTIL refused to run. The Microsoft Knowledge Base indicated that the problem was related to insufficient permissions. However, the Exchange administrator and the site services account had full control over the directories with the database files in them. In addition, the administrator knew that EDBUTIL /MH priv.edb worked, because she had used it in the past.

The administrator decided that there may be a problem with the information store database, so she ran an ISINTEG −fix −pri −verbose to attempt to repair the private information store. This program ran, but it would not finish. The first pass through, ISINTEG indicates that it fixed problems, but it failed after test number eight. A second pass using ISINTEG also failed at test number eight.

At this point, the administrator had just about decided that the database would have to be restored from tape. The major problem was that the most recent backup had failed, which meant that the users would lose all their messages for the past 24 hours. The curious thing was that everything with the users' mailboxes seemed to be fine—or at least no one had complained.

The Exchange administrator decided at this point to move as many of the important mailboxes as possible to other servers. BAM Corp had a dedicated bridgehead server that functioned as a connector server to other sites as well as running the IMS. Since this server had adequate storage, the administrator decided to move all the mailboxes from the server that was having problems to the bridgehead server. All the mailboxes moved without incident. Later, all public folders that had replicas located on this server were moved to other servers.

Backups continued to fail on the problem server (even though there were now no mailboxes or public folders on it). Since all the data was now safe and sound on another server, the Exchange administrator had the luxury of a little additional time on her side. She placed an incident with Microsoft Product Support Services (PSS). The PSS engineer surprised the Exchange administrator with his diagnosis: –1811 errors are almost always related to hardware problems, specifically SCSI-related problems.

The Exchange administrator then opened up an incident with the hardware manufacturer and learned fairly quickly that there was a known bug with certain versions of their SCSI device drivers which could generate such errors. The SCSI device driver was upgraded, and the Exchange server was reinstalled. Once the server was reinstalled, the mailboxes and public folder data were slowly moved back to the original server, and the problem did not recur.

The BAM Exchange administrator learned an important lesson during this saga—one that most of us often forget. Don't be so quick to blame Exchange for your problem, for Exchange Server may merely be exhibiting symptoms of a larger one.

24seven CASE STUDY

Appendices

Additional Reading and Resources

There are numerous resources available that you can use to learn more about Exchange Server or to solve your Exchange Server problems. Exchange is an incredible product and has tremendous depth and functionality. I never stop learning about Exchange, and I am continually looking for sources of Exchange information. This appendix lists some of these resources. Not all of the items in this appendix are directly related to Exchange, but some are helpful when managing Windows NT networks that include Exchange Server.

Books

If I had the time and if Sybex could print a 5,000-page book, I assure you, this book would be a *lot* bigger. Since you can't easily carry a single 5,000-page book, here is a list of more manageable books that I have in my own library.

Mastering Exchange Server 5.5 by Barry Gerber (Sybex, 1998). Barry's book is the de facto standard for Exchange books. Barry gives you a great start on designing an Exchange organization, installing Exchange, and getting it up and running.

Microsoft Exchange Connectivity Guide by Rodney Bliss and Rebecca Wynne (Microsoft Press, 1997). Rodney and Rebecca have put together the Exchange connectivity bible. Though written for Exchange 4, the information provided about connectivity (especially X.400 and site connectors) is clear, concise, and incredibly detailed.

The Microsoft Outlook E-mail and Fax Guide by Sue Mosher (29th Street Press, 1998). This book is a must for Outlook users and administrators. Sue explains in clear terms how to set-up, configure, and tweak Outlook.

E-Policy: How to Develop Computer, E-mail, and Internet Guidelines to Protect Your Company and Its Assets by Michael R. Overly (AMACON, 1998). The title says it all; this guide helps administrators and managers develop an electronic messaging policy that will help keep you out of court. You can order this book through the Electronic Messaging Association at `www.ema.org`.

Windows NT Server 4 by Mark Minasi (Sybex, 1998). A thorough understanding of Windows NT is essential when implementing any Microsoft BackOffice program, and Exchange is no exception. Mark's book is so good that I own two different editions. It is straightforward and friendly to read with a ton of "inside scoop" and tips I have seen nowhere else.

NT 4 Network Security by Matthew Strebe, Charles Perkins, and Michael Moncur (Sybex, 1998). Can a book on network security be fun? I did not think so until I picked up this book. It is entertaining, engaging, and most importantly, an essential resource for Windows NT administrators.

Cryptography and Network Security Principal and Practice by William Stallings (Prentice Hall, 1995). This is my favorite cryptography book. (Is it time to worry about myself if I have a favorite cryptography book?) The basic theories are explained quite well in this book and the author goes into enough detail to keep the mathematicians happy.

The Cuckoo's Egg: Tracking a Spy through a Maze of Computer Espionage by Clifford Stoll (Pocket Books, July 1995). This is a classic computer hacker tale; I picked it up in an airport one morning when flying east and finished it the next morning at 3:00 A.M.— I could not put it down. It is that good. While not Exchange-related, this is a great book for anyone even minimally working around computers.

Microsoft Press publishes a series of resource kits that contain lots of additional documentation, nifty utilities, and other things not released in the product that the resource kit supports. No Windows NT administrator should be without the *Windows NT Workstation Resource Kit* and the *Windows NT Server Resource Kit*. If you are managing Exchange Server, SNA Server, Systems Management Server, or SQL Server, you should definitely check out the *BackOffice Resource Kit (Second Edition)*. Once you have the resource kits in hand, load the software they include on your test system and go to town. You will find a number of utilities that will make your life easier and may even make something possible you did not think you could do.

Publications

I receive an impressive stack of periodicals every month. Naturally, I don't have time to read all of these cover-to-cover, but there are two that I make sure I read every time they arrive.

Exchange Administrator is a monthly newsletter filled with articles by industry experts on Exchange features, Outlook features, troubleshooting questions and answers, and suggestions submitted by readers. You can find out more about Exchange Administrator at `www.winntmag.com/Newsletter/Exchange/Main.cfm`. Although this newsletter is a little on the pricey side, it is one of only two periodicals I pay for—for good reason.

Windows NT Magazine is the other periodical that I actually pay for. In addition to great articles and tips about Windows NT, each month the magazine contains articles about other BackOffice products such as Exchange. You can find information about subscriptions at `www.winntmag.com`.

Internet Resources

The Internet has more resources than most of us can keep up with. I spend too much of my time reading new material that I have found through the Internet or through a mailing list. Here is a list of Web sites you will find in my Favorites folder.

Sybex has a terrific Web site that contains information about all 24seven books. This book will also have a Web page there, which I will use to post updates to the book as well as any sample programs and documents that will supplement this book. Check this book's Web page often for updates and announcements related to the content of the book and Exchange in general. The Sybex 24seven Web site can be found at `www.24sevenbooks.com`.

Slipstick Systems, `www.slipstick.com`, is a site designed, written, and managed by Sue Mosher. This site is *the* location on the Web for learning more about the Outlook product family—lots of utilities and links, too.

One of the most complete Exchange sites on the Internet is Exchangestuff (`www.exchangestuff.com`). Here you'll find information about Exchange enhancements, utilities, FAQs, links, and more—there's even a glossary. A tremendous amount of work has gone into creating and maintaining this site—it's worth a visit.

The Microsoft Exchange Forum Mailing List is an Exchange discussion group graciously run by volunteer Peter Bowyer. Subscription information is available on the forum's Web site at www.msexchange.org. There is an archive of past messages available on the Web site, and I highly recommend that you search this archive before posting a new question. Many common questions are answered about once a week.

Microsoft's own Web site has some excellent resources for Exchange administrators. Your first line of defense when debugging problems should be the Microsoft Support Online site at support.microsoft.com/support. I cannot emphasize enough how useful this site is. I regularly check the Exchange Server home page at www.microsoft.com/exchange. I also visit the download and trial center for Microsoft BackOffice located at backoffice.microsoft.com/downtrial.

The Electronic Messaging Association (EMA) is dedicated to the promotion and understanding of messaging, directory, security, Web services, and other related technology. They have a great Web site with a lot of links and messaging documents. You can find them on the Web at www.ema.org.

The European Electronic Messaging Association (EEMA) is the sister organization to the EMA. If you are involved with messaging issues in Europe, this site will be of assistance. You can find them on the Web at www.eema.org.

Although www.whatis.com has little to do with messaging, security, or Windows networking in general, I use it frequently. If you ever want to know a definition for a technical term, check it out—it's a lot of fun.

Don Adams' Web page has Exchange and Outlook resources as well as demonstrations, links to other Web sites, and the Exchange Administrators Guide in PDF format. Check it out at www.donadams.com.

Beverly Hills Software has an excellent Web site with shareware, technical information, and links; it is well worth a visit. You can find them at www.bhs.com.

If you work for the U.S. Department of Defense and would like to know more about the Defense Messaging System, visit Lockheed Martin's DMS home page at www.lmdms.com. Here you will find links to all the branches of the Department of Defense. The Army Core of Engineers' Electronic Mail Center of Expertise also has good information on DMS. It is found on the Web at em101.usace.army.mil.

The Internet Mail Consortium is the only international organization focused on cooperatively managing and promoting the rapidly expanding world of electronic mail on the Internet. IMC's home page is www.imc.org.

If you are not a user of the Usenet newsgroups, you should be. There is a lot of information that is shared on the Usenet newsgroups, and there are several Exchange specific newsgroups. Contact your Internet Service Provider for the name of a news server that you can use to access these news groups, or you can search for them at www.dejanews.com. Here is a list of newsgroups:

Public.microsoft.exchange.admin

Public.microsoft.exchange.applications

Public.microsoft.exchange.applications.conversion

Public.microsoft.exchange.clients

Public.microsoft.exchange.misc

Public.microsoft.exchange.setup

Appendices

B

Messaging Standards and Definitions

When I first started working with LAN-based messaging systems in 1987, they were anything but interoperable. And interoperability is the key to exchanging messages between organizations. Over the past fifteen years, a number of efforts to standardize messaging and message interoperability have come and gone.

The most successful of these efforts are the International Telecommunications Union's X.400 recommendations and SMTP. This appendix lists some of the common terms that you will come in contact with when working with these two types of messaging systems.

X.400

The International Telecommunications Union (ITU), formerly known as the CCITT (Consultative Committee International Telephone and Telegraph), is a branch of the United Nations. Starting in 1984, the ITU published a series of recommendations for building an e-mail system that would be interoperable with e-mail systems worldwide. While X.400 is often referred to as a "standard," it is officially considered a recommendation. More specifically, it's a series of recommendations, each numbered in the X.400 number range.

The ITU has released a number of X.400 recommendations, each improving upon the previous. The 1984 and 1988 recommendations are the most common; few vendors fully support the 1992 recommendations, though many support some of the 1992 recommended features. The Exchange Server message transfer agent conforms to the 1984 and 1988 recommendations.

X.400 addresses are not pretty, but they are versatile because they can help an X.400 system identify what country, company, and division a person is in. Here is a sample X.400 address:

```
c=us;a=telemail;p=somorita;o=pacific;g=Jim;s=McBee
```

Not very pretty, and there are a number of other fields that can be in an X.400 address. Here is what the fields in this address mean:

C is the country code; this address is in the U.S.

A is the administrative management domain (ADMD). I like to think of the ADMD as the organization that routes your mail out to the world and to other ADMDs. You can also think of the ADMD as being like your phone company; you can call anyone else in your office using your internal phone system, but when you want to dial another office, you have to use the phone company's lines.

P is the private management domain (PRMD). The PRMD is your company's internal e-mail system. Within Exchange, this defaults to the Exchange organization name.

O is the X.400 organization name, which in Exchange is your Exchange site name.

G is the given name or the first name of the mailbox user.

S is the surname or the last name of the mailbox user.

X.400 Terminology

Here are some terms that you will encounter when working with X.400-based messaging systems:

MTAs (message transfer agents) are the software components that move messages between user agents (UAs) and other MTAs.

UA (user agent) is the client software; Outlook is considered a UA. In a pure X.400 model, the UA submits messages directly to the MTA.

AU (access unit) is a gateway or link to a system outside of the X.400 messaging system, such as an SMTP gateway.

MS (message store) is the storage location for messages until the UA reads the messages.

MTS (message transfer system) is the combination of the local MTA and the remote MTAs.

MHS (message handling service) combines the user agent software and the MTS.

IPMS (interpersonal messaging system) is an X.400 messaging system designed to support the exchange of messages among people. X.400 was designed to move many types of messages, including transactional and terminal data.

IPM (interpersonal message) is an X.400 message that moves actual message data such as text and attachments though the IPMS.

IPN (interpersonal notification) is a special type of X.400 message that is used for notification of delivery of an IPM.

P1 protocol is the X.400 protocol that defines how to encapsulate a mail message to be delivered through the X.400 MTS. The envelope of the message is formatted using the P1 protocol. All message content is contained inside the envelope.

P2 protocol is the X.400 protocol that defines how to format message content, including the message header and body parts. The P2 protocol is defined by the ITU 1984 X.400 recommendations.

P22 protocol is similar to the P2 protocol, except that it is defined by the ITU 1988 X.400 recommendations and contains a few improvements over the P2 protocol.

P42/P772 protocols are used by the U.S. Department of Defense in the Defense Messaging System (DMS). P772 is very similar to the P22 protocol except that it defines a few additional properties sometimes referred to as "military message properties." P42 is a P772 message that includes a digital signature and encryption.

NOTE Unfortunately, the X.400 recommendations are not published online. However, you can find links to related information and purchase the X.400 recommendation documents from the ITU Web page at www.itu.org. Another interesting X.400 resource is www.alvestrand.no/domen/x400/.

X.500

Though not directly related to messaging, the X.500 recommendations are important to messaging systems nonetheless. After all, what good is a worldwide messaging system if you can't find someone's e-mail address? The ITU's X.500 directory service recommendations are an effort at standardizing development of interoperable, global directories. An X.500 directory is hierarchical in nature and is organized in a tree fashion; the root of the tree is usually the country, which contains organizations, which in turn contains organizational units, which contain common names (CNs). A sample X.500 directory name might look like:

```
/c=US/o=Somorita/ou=Pacific/cn=recipients/cn=JmcBee
```

The Exchange Server directory is based on the X.500 recommendations, but does not exactly match the X.500 recommendations.

X.500 Terminology

If you work with an X.500 directory service, here are some terms that you may come in contact with:

DAP (directory access protocol) is a protocol specified as part of the original X.500 recommendation for accessing directory data. Partially due to the way DAP is designed around in the OSI model, there is a lot of overhead involved in using it, and it can be quite slow.

DIB (directory information base) is made up of the actual information stored in a directory such as directory entries and the attributes of those directories.

DIT (directory information tree) defines the directory tree structure and the relationship between parent and child objects.

DMD (directory management domain) is a set of one or more DSA's and zero or more DUA's managed by a single organization.

DMO (domain management organization) manages the DMD and the associated DIT domain.

DSA (directory system agent) is the software on the server that provides clients with access to the directory database. The DSA may also refer to other DSAs to lookup information.

DSP (directory system protocol) is the communications protocol used to link directory clients (DUAs) and directory servers (DSAs). These include DAP, LDAP, MAPI, and XDS.

DUA (directory user agent) is the software that is used by a user to browse or search an X.500 directory database. The DUA software contacts the DSA. The address book in Outlook is a DUA.

LDAP (lightweight directory access protocol) was developed at the University of Michigan as an answer to the heavyweight (my own term) problems associated with DAP. LDAP runs directly over TCP/IP rather than through OSI and provides a more limited set of functions than DAP. There is significantly less overhead associated with using LDAP, and it is becoming widely accepted as a standard protocol of accessing directory databases.

Schema is the rules that define the directory structure, objects, and object attributes.

NOTE To learn more about X.500, check out the ITU's Web page at `www.itu.org`. Another interesting document can be found at `www.infosys.tuwien.ac.at/Standards/X/X.500-88/x500_1.asc`.

Internet Messaging Standards

Though many people see a veil of mystique around the Internet, there is nothing mysterious or proprietary about it. It is one big TCP/IP network. Any data that crosses the Internet and needs to be understood by dissimilar hosts must follow predefined standards. For example, in 1982, a standard was introduced called SMTP (Simple Mail Transfer Protocol) that standardized the way messages were sent and received on the Internet. Many subsequent standards and additional software have been developed around the SMTP document.

Standards on the Internet are managed and controlled mainly by groups of volunteers. The governing organization is called the *Internet Society (ISOC)*. ISOC is a global organization that was created in 1992 to be responsible for internetworking technologies and applications on the Internet. Its principal purpose is to encourage the development and availability of the Internet.

Part of ISOC is the *Internet Activities Board (IAB)*, a technical advisory group. The Internet Activities Board is responsible for setting Internet standards, publishing RFCs, and overseeing the Internet standards process. The IAB oversees three taskforces:

- The Internet Engineering Task Force (IETF) is responsible for developing technical solutions to problems and new challenges as they arise on the Internet, as well as developing Internet standards and protocols.

- The Internet Assigned Numbers Authority (IANA) oversees the assignment of unique protocol identities that are used on the Internet, such as TCP and UDP port numbers, which I will explain shortly.

- The Internet Research Task Force (IRTF) is the research and development arm of the ISOC and is responsible for TCP/IP-related research projects.

TCP/IP and all Internet functions are standardized in a series of documents called RFCs (Request for Comments), which describe how a specific function is supposed to work on a TCP/IP network. However, not all RFCs actually become standards. For example,

Except in the case of Registry values that you may need when documenting your system, I have left out the values that you can set through the Exchange Administrator user interface or the Exchange Server Performance Optimizer.

> **NOTE** Registry Editor displays the data type REG_DWORD in hexadecimal. Make sure that you are entering the correct value type. If you see a value displayed as 0x720, the 0x means that the number is in hexadecimal. The REG_DWORD Editor dialog box has radix buttons for Binary, Decimal, and Hex data. You can convert this value to decimal using the scientific view of the Windows NT Calculator program.

Unless otherwise noted, all Registry values and subkeys included in this appendix are found under the HKEY_LOCAL_MACHINE\System\CurrentControlSet\Services Registry key. Often, throughout this book, I have abbreviated HKEY_LOCAL_MACHINE to HKLM.

> **TIP** I have not included most of the Registry performance tuning values. I recommend you view and set these values with the Performance Optimizer using the verbose option (\exchsvrv\bin\perfopt /V).

Directory Service Registry Values

These values are located in the \MSExchangeDS\Parameters key and affect the Exchange directory service.

Value Name	Data Type	Explanation
Database Log Files Path	SZ	The path for the directory service transaction log files.
DSA Database File	SZ	The path and filename of the directory service database. Do not change the filename.
DSA Hierarchy Table File	SZ	The path and filename for the directory service hierarchy table file.
DSA Temporary File	SZ	The path and filename for the directory service temporary database name.
DSA Working Directory	SZ	The path for the directory service working directory.

Value Name	Data Type	Explanation
Replicator Notify Pause After Modify (secs)	SZ	The period between notifications that the local directory service waits before it sends notifications to servers in the local site for changes made to the local directory. Default is 0x12c (300 seconds or 5 minutes). Increasing this value to as much as 1200 to 1800 seconds is generally not harmful for most Exchange sites.
Replicator Notify Pause Between DSAs (secs)	DWORD	The period specifies the time to wait between notifying servers in the local site informing them that a change has taken place. This ensures that this server is not overloaded with requests all at once. Default is 0x1e (30 seconds).
Replicator Intersite Sync At Startup	DWORD	Specifies whether the directory service will perform a full intersite replication each time the directory service starts. The default is to perform the replication; set to 0 for automatic replication at startup or 1 (default) so that replication occurs at each startup.
Hierarchy Table Recalculation Interval (minutes)	DWORD	The time between automatic recalculation of address book views. Default is 720 minutes (12 hours). You can force this by using Exchange Administrator; highlight the address book view and press the F5 key.
Replicator Intersite Packet Size	DWORD	Maximum number of directory objects that will be replicated to another site in a single update. Default is 0x200 (512). Don't change this unless you know exactly what you're doing!
Replicator Intrasite Packet Size	DWORD	Maximum number of directory objects that will be replicated to other servers in the same site. Default is 0x64 (100). Don't change this unless you know exactly what you are doing!

General Information Store Registry Values

These values, located in the \MSExchangeIS\ParametersSystem key, affect the entire Exchange information store service for both the public and private information store databases.

Value Name	Data Type	Explanation
Circular Logging	DWORD	1 indicates on; 0 indicates off. Use Exchange Administrator to change this value.
DB Log Path	SZ	The location for the information store transaction logs. Change this value through the Performance Optimizer.
Working Directory	SZ	The working directory name for the information store.
DSA Computer	SZ	The name of the computer that runs the directory service for this information store. For Exchange 5.5 and prior versions, this should be the Exchange server name.
MTA Computer	SZ	The name of the computer that runs the message transfer agent for this information store.
This Server	SZ	The name of this computer.
Logon Only As	MULTI_SZ	Distinguished Names (DNs) that are listed in this list are the only ones that can access the information store. This key should not exist during normal operations. (See KB Q146764.)
Mailbox Cache Age Limit	DWORD	The amount of time that the information store will cache data that it obtains from the directory service. The default is 120 minutes.
Mailbox Idle Limit	DWORD	The amount of time that must pass before the mailbox (if idle) is removed from the mailbox cache. Default is 15 minutes.

Value Name	Data Type	Explanation
No Local Delivery	DWORD	If set to 1, all messages are routed to the MTA for delivery, regardless of server destination. If set to 0, local delivery can take place. This is used with message journaling.
Max Recipients On Submit	DWORD	The maximum number of recipients that can be in a single mail message. (See KB Q126497.)
TCP/IP Port	DWORD	The TCP port assigned to the information store. This is not a default value.
IMAP4 Protocol Log Path	SZ	Drive and directory in which IMAP4 protocol logs will be created.
NNTP Protocol Log Path	SZ	Drive and directory in which NNTP protocol logs will be created.
POP3 Protocol Log Path	SZ	Drive and directory in which POP3 protocol logs will be created.
IMAP4 Protocol Logging Level	DWORD	0 disables logging, 1 provides minimal logging, and 5 provides maximum logging.
NNTP Protocol Logging Level	DWORD	0 disables logging, 1 provides minimal logging, and 5 provides maximum logging.
POP3 Protocol Logging Level	DWORD	0 disables logging, 1 provides minimal logging, and 5 provides maximum logging.

Public Information Store Registry Values

These values are located in the \MSExchangeIS\ParametersPublic key and affect the Exchange public information store database.

Value Name	Data Type	Explanation
DB Path	SZ	Path to the pub.edb file.
Background Cleanup	DWORD	The time in milliseconds between which the information store reclaims space used by deleted folders, messages, and attachments.

Value Name	Data Type	Explanation
Disable Replication Messages At Startup	DWORD	Disables public folder hierarchy replication message when information store is restarted. A value of 1 disables the message; a value of 0 enables it.
Log Downloads	DWORD	Logs to the application event log every time a user downloads a certain type of message from the public information store. The values are: 1 = attachments only, 2 = messages only, 3 = attachments and messages, 4 = folders only, 5 = attachments and folders, 6 = messages and folders, 7 = everything.

Private Information Store Registry Values

These values are located in the \MSExchangeIS\ParametersPrivate key and affect the Exchange private information store database.

Value Name	Data Type	Explanation
DB Path	SZ	Path to the priv.edb file.
Background Cleanup	DWORD	The time in milliseconds between which the information store reclaims space used by deleted folders, messages, and attachments.
Log Downloads	DWORD	Logs to the application event log every time a user downloads a certain type of message from the public information store. The values are: 1 = attachments only, 2 = messages only, 3 = attachments and messages, 4 = folders only, 5 = attachments and folders, 6 = messages and folders, 7 = everything.

Message Transfer Agent Registry Values

The MTA has a *lot* of Registry values found in the \MSExchangeMTA\Parameters key. Many of these deal with thread counts and should only be changed through the Exchange

Performance Optimizer or on the recommendation of Microsoft PSS. Here are some Registry keys that might prove useful when troubleshooting or making MTA adjustments:

Value Name	Data Type	Explanation
MTA Database Path	SZ	Path to the MTA database files.
MTA Run Directory	SZ	Path to the MTA run directory.
DSA Address	SZ	The name of the Exchange server that handles directory services for this MTA. This should be the same as the server name.
RFC1006 Port Number	DWORD	TCP/IP port used by the MTA when communicating with other X.400 MTAs.
Text Event Log	DWORD	Setting this value to 1 tells the MTA to create text events in ev*.log files. Setting it to 0 (the default) turns this feature off.
Dispatch Remote MTA Messages	DWORD	If set to 1, this MTA will replay message database files that were created on another MTA. If set to 0, it does not.
Journal Recipient Name	SZ	The DN of the mailbox that is to be used for the message journaling feature.
Per-Site Journal Required	DWORD	If set to 0, journaling is done organization-wide. If set to 1, journaling is done per site.

System Attendant Registry Values

The System Attendant service's Registry keys can be found in \MSExchangeSA\Parameters.

Value Name	Data Type	Explanation
LogDirectory	SZ	The path in which the System Attendant will keep message tracking logs.
TCP/IP Port	DWORD	Allows assignment of a TCP port to the System Attendant service.

Appendices

Value Name	Data Type	Explanation
SiteDomain	REG_SZ	Specifies the domain to be used in the originator address for reports generated by the IMS. This overrides the site address.
SMTPRecvTimeout	DWORD	SMTP protocol timeout waiting for packet transmission. Default is 396 seconds.
SMTPWaitForAck	DWORD	SMTP protocol timeout waiting for acknowledgement so next command can be sent. Default is 396 seconds.
SMTPWaitFor-Banner	DWORD	SMTP protocol timeout waiting for the HELO banner from SMTP server. Default is 396 seconds.
SMTPWaitForMailFrom	DWORD	SMTP protocol timeout waiting for response to the MAIL FROM command. Default is 396 seconds.
SMTPWaitForRcpt	DWORD	SMTP protocol timeout waiting for response to the RCPT TO command. Default is 396 seconds.
SMTPWaitForDataInitiation	DWORD	SMTP protocol timeout waiting for the initiation of the data block. Default is 120 seconds.
SMTPWaitForDataBlock	DWORD	SMTP protocol timeout waiting for the other host to send the .CRLF termination to the data block. Default is 600 seconds.

Documentation Administrators Should Keep

Are you currently having a problem that you know that you have read the solution to, but you just can't remember where you read it? Have you ever had the pleasure of taking over a system that someone else installed? Has something failed? Do you know what has changed recently?

System documentation takes time and preparation to correctly prepare. There is always the temptation to skimp on the documentation portion of your installation. Further, when I install a system, I think to myself, "I don't need to document this system. I just installed it, and I won't forget the parameters that I used during the installation." Much to my surprise, only a few days later, I had forgotten the details of the installation.

I cannot emphasize enough the importance of good documentation—tracking changes and building yourself a repository of information. This appendix covers the following techniques:

- Building your own knowledge base
- Keeping good system documentation
- Tracking system changes and incidents

Your Encyclopedia of Knowledge

If you were able to stare past the pages of this book and into my office, you would see shelves of books, magazines, file folders, and three-ring binders. (Okay, okay, it's a mess; if I had known I was going to have company, I would have tidied up a bit more.) For each product that I support, I create what I used to call a Book of Knowledge. I used to call it a "book" when it was a single binder for Exchange and a single binder for Windows NT. Now I have combined all of my binders and created my own Encyclopedia of Knowledge.

This encyclopedia consists of ten binders, each containing white papers, useful Knowledge Base articles, notes I have typed up, performance data from various servers, client documentation, magazine articles, conference presentation printouts, newsgroup discussions, and e-mail messages people have sent me, all relating to Exchange. So much for the paperless office at my house! Now I have the information—I just can't remember which binder it is in! And believe it or not, I use this information on a fairly frequent basis.

To get your own Encyclopedia of Knowledge started, run out and buy a three-ring binder. Then compile the following items to put in it:

- The first thing you should put in your encyclopedia is the standards and design document that you and your co-workers have worked so hard to develop and that everyone agrees upon.

- Next, add useful Microsoft Knowledge Base articles, white papers, vendor documents, the current readme file from Exchange, and more.

- Finally, stick in a copy of the system documentation for each Exchange server you are supporting.

NOTE Throughout this book, I have given you other things to add to your encyclopedia, including maintenance procedures (Chapter 6) and a disaster recovery plan (Chapter 18).

System Documentation

Documentation on how your system is configured and the information you will need to rebuild it is essential. You can keep this information handwritten or in some type of computer-based filing system, but you should always have a recent printout.

TIP   Your system documentation should be dynamic. Set up a process whereby it can be updated easily and quickly.

The system documentation needs to be broken up into two categories: the information needed to rebuild the Windows NT server and the information necessary to rebuild the Exchange server.

Windows NT Server Documentation

The information needed to rebuild the Windows NT server should include:

- Server hardware configuration
  - Boot configuration information
  - SCSI, CD-ROM, RAID 5, tape drive configuration information
  - Configuration for additional adapters installed (network, serial adapter, video)
- Windows NT server role (PDC, BDC, member server)
- Windows NT domain name
- Windows NT server NetBIOS name
- Network adapter drivers installed
- Protocols installed
- IPX/SPX network numbers and frame types
- TCP/IP information (IP address, subnet mask, default gateway, DNS address, WINS address, and DNS domain name)
- Network services installed (DNS, WINS, DHCP, Internet Information Server, Certificate Server, and so on)
- Customized network-binding information, if any
- Video driver installed and display resolution used
- Page file size and location information
- Hard disk configuration, partition sizes, drive letters, and formats in use
- Operating system version, service packs installed, hot fixes installed, and the recommended order of installation

HOSTS file
  in moving mailboxes, 113
  in name resolution, 514–515, 517–518
hot fixes
  applying, 231
  for Certificate Server, 470
  in upgrading, 96, 98
hot keys, 169
hot swapping controllers, 42–43
HTTP protocol, 563
hub and spoke architecture, 349
hyperlinks, **519**
hyphens (-) in server names, 23

I

-I option in PROFGEN, 410
%i substitution in SMTP addresses, 361
IAB (Internet Activities Board), 603
IANA (Internet Assigned Numbers Authority),
    494, 603
IEFT (Internet Engineering Task Force), 7, 603
IIS (Internet Information Server)
  for SSL, 449
  troubleshooting, **563–564**
IMAIL process, 377
IMAP4 protocol
  checking, *559*
  logging, 561
  in moving mailboxes, 113
  recovering messages in, 175
  RFCs for, 604
IMAP4 Protocol Log Path value, 561, 611
IMAP4 Protocol Logging Level value, 561, 611
IMC (Internet Mail Connector), 364
Import/Export Digital ID button, 479–480
Import From A Personal Folder option, 120
Import Items Into The Current Folder button, 120
Import Items Into The Same Folder In button, 110
Import Or Untrust Another Certification
    Authority's Certificate setting, 465

importing
  certificates, **480–481**
  directory database, **169–172**, *170*
IMS. *See* Internet Mail Service (IMS)
IMS Connections property page, 373
IMS Dial-Up Connections property page,
    374–375, *374*
IMS Queues chart, 260
IMS Statistics chart, 260
IMS Traffic chart, 260
in-house training staffs, **68**
Inbound Bytes Total counter, 248
Inbound Messages Total counter, 247–248
inbound sites in directory replication, 349
Inbox folder, AutoArchive actions for, 182
Inbox rules, Mailbox Migration with, 112
incremental backups
  characteristics of, 217–218
  in disaster recovery, 576
inetres.adm template, 412
inetset.adm template, 412
information store (IS) databases
  consistency with DS, **545–548**, *546*
  failures in, **577–578**
  location of, 200–201
  monitoring, 262
  in moving mailboxes, 108
  Registry for, **610–612**
  server automation for, **415–417**, *416*
  transaction log location, 201
  working path location, 201
Information Store Site Configuration property
    page, 420, *421*
infrastructure reviews, **16–17**
Initialization/Termination logging category, *554*
installing
  Certificate Server, 470
  Key Management Server, **461–462**
  Outlook 97, **398–401**
  Outlook Deployment Kit, 402
Instance option in Performance Monitor, 251

Index

Index

How to...